HITCHCOCK

Hitc

ROBERT E. KAPSIS

hcock

REPUTATION

HITCHCOCK IN HIS STUDY, 1962
Courtesy Gary Crowdus

THE UNIVERSITY OF CHICAGO PRESS   CHICAGO & LONDON

The University of Chicago Press, Chicago 60637
The University of Chicago Press, Ltd., London
© 1992 by The University of Chicago
All rights reserved. Published 1992
Printed in the United States of America

01 00 99 98 97 96 95   5 4 3

ISBN 0-226-42489-8 (ppbk.)

Library of Congress Cataloging-in-Publication Data

Kapsis, Robert E.
      Hitchcock : the making of a reputation / Robert E. Kapsis.
            p.   cm.
      Includes bibliographical references and index.
         1. Hitchcock, Alfred, 1899–   —Criticism and interpretation.
      2. Hitchcock, Alfred, 1899–   —Appreciation.   3. Detective and
      mystery films—History and criticism.   I. Title.
      PN1998.3.H58K36   1992
      791.43'0233'092—dc20   92-7028

FOR MY FAMILY

CONTENTS

PLATES

Frontispiece. Hitchcock in his study (1962).

ACKNOWLEDGMENTS

I am indebted to Susan Marsden Kapsis, Steve Ostrowski, Baylis Thomas, Robert Stam, Janet Staiger, John Belton, Peter Brunette, Ernest Callenbach, Muriel Cantor, Gary Crowdus, Robert Fisher, Maurice Greenbaum, George J. McCall, Mindy Pomper, Howard Prouty, Jonathan Rieder, Thomas Schatz, Michael Selig, and Buddy Timberg for editorial suggestions, encouragement, or other assistance at various stages of this project. It is with great pleasure that I thank Sam Gill, Linda Mehr, Barbara Hall, Valentin Almendarez, and the staff of the Margaret Herrick Library of the Academy of Motion Picture Arts and Sciences for their professionalism and hospitality during the many months I spent there researching the book. I am especially grateful to Sam Gill for guiding me to key documents from the Hitchcock Collec tion. I would also like to thank Charles Silver, Ron Magliozzi, Terry Geeskin, and Mary Corliss of the Film Department of the Museum of Modern Art, Ann Schlosser, formerly of the American Film Institute, Los Angeles, Leith Adams and Ned Comstock of the Department of Special Collections, University of Southern California, and the staff of the British Film Institute. The staff of the Billy Rose Theatre Collection of the Lincoln Center Library for the Performing Arts provided ample assistance throughout the duration of the project.

Among the many other individuals and institutions I wish to acknowledge are Leland Faust, Patricia Hitchcock O'Connell, Yvonne Halsman, the Academy of Motion Picture Arts and Sciences, the Museum of Modern Art Film Stills Archive, the Bettmann Archive, MCA Publishing Rights, a division of MCA, Warner Bros., Wesleyan University Film Archives, Orion Pictures Corporation, Janus Films Company, Turner Entertainment Company, Debra Hill Productions, and *Cineaste* for allowing me to reproduce movie stills and other related materials for use in the book.

My research was supported by two grants from the National Endowment for the Humanities and five grants from the Professional Staff Congress—Board of Higher Education Program of the City University of New York, and a scholarship incentive award from Queens College, where I teach sociology and film. I am grateful to my department (sociology) for easing my burden while working on the book and to the Film Studies Program which provided a congenial environment for testing my ideas. I am indebted to a number of colleagues and administrators at the City University of New York and would especially like to thank Andy Beveridge, Royal Brown, Jonathan Buchsbaum, Helen Cairns, Stuart Ewen, Nick Jordan, Miriam Korman, Manfried Kuechler, Stuart Liebman, Brenda Newman, Mike Prasad, Lauren Seiler, and Gaye Tuchman.

A faculty development award from the City University of New York enabled me to participate in a writing seminar under the direction of Mason Cooley which advanced considerably the progress of the manuscript. I am grateful to all members of the seminar—Evelyn Barish, Abby Kleinbaum, Marvin Koenigsberg, John Babcock, Marjorie Da Pena, and Herb Liebman—for their help and support. I am especially indebted to Evelyn Barish for her incisive comments and editorial suggestions. The ongoing guidance and wisdom of Mason Cooley have been crucial to the completion of this project.

Finally, I would like to express my appreciation to the staff of the University of Chicago Press, especially my editor, Douglas Mitchell, whose early and unflagging committment to *Hitchcock* helped to keep the project on track.

NOTE ON SOURCES

I have used various sources of information for this work. The cornerstone of chapters 2 and 3, on the transformation of Hitchcock's reputation from popular entertainer to serious artist, is the collection of Hitchcock's personal files, which his daughter donated to the Academy of Motion Picture Arts and Sciences in 1984. The Hitchcock Collection includes scripts, papers, production notes, publicity files, correspondence, and memorabilia spanning Hitchcock's entire career. The collection is most detailed about the 1960s and 1970s—the period in which Hitchcock's reputation as a "serious artist" was established. Materials most relevant to my study include: fifty-two hours of taped interviews with François Truffaut and correspondence with Truffaut spanning nearly twenty years; correspondence between Hitchcock and various arts organizations and institutions, such as the Museum of Modern Art, the American Film Institute, and the Cinémathèque Française; speeches that Hitchcock delivered between 1960 and 1975; fan mail; correspondence with film scholars (e.g., Donald Spoto); production information and correspondence relating to Hitchcock's TV series (1955–65); and, finally, more or less detailed production records, correspondence, and script, publicity, and exhibition files on all of Hitchcock's realized projects after 1959. These include *Psycho* (1960), *The Birds* (1963), *Marnie* (1964), *Torn Curtain* (1966), *Topaz* (1969), *Frenzy* (1972), and *Family Plot* (1976).

Journalistic reviews of Hitchcock's films are drawn mainly from Hitchcock's personal collection as well as from the files of newspaper and magazine clippings of motion picture criticism at the Lincoln Center Library for the Performing Arts, New York City (hereafter, Lincoln Center Library), and the Margaret Herrick Library, the Academy of Motion Picture Arts and Sciences, Beverly Hills (hereafter, Academy Library). The British Film Institute is the primary source for British reviews of Hitchcock's films. By comparing American with English reviews, I can better clarify what is distinctive about the development of Hitchcock criticism in the United States.

Augmenting the archival materials are personal interviews with Hitchcock's associates, collaborators, and staff.

My sources for the scholarly critiques, assessments, and reassessments of specific Hitchcock films that are the subject of chapter 4 range from specialized books and anthologies on Hitchcock (see, e.g., Wood [1965], 1977; La Valley 1972; Rothman 1982; Deutelbaum and Poague 1986) to articles which have appeared in the leading academic film journals.

A major source of information for chapters 5 and 6 on the Hitchcock legacy are the files of newspaper and magazine clippings of motion picture criticism at the Lincoln Center Library, and the Academy Library. From the latter, I also obtained studio publicity files—an invaluable source of historical data on which generic labels are "live" and which are "dead" from the perspective of the film companies. Such publicity materials reveal, especially, how the studios attempt to shape or manipulate critical opinion about their films. Biographical information on Brian De Palma and other thriller directors was gleaned from the Academy Library's collection of newspaper and magazine clippings as well as from the "official" studio biographies on file there. By examining De Palma's "official biography" at different points in time, I could gauge how his public reputation was changing over the years.

The section on the Hitchcock legacy also draws upon detailed information I collected on the pre-production, filming, post-production, and marketing of several low-budget horror films. For one of the films examined, *Halloween II* (1981), members of my West Coast research staff were on the set gathering detailed field notes every day during the film's six-week shooting schedule. During post-production, we interviewed members of the cast and crew (including the on-line producer, director, and cinematographer) in order to gain an understanding of the routine factors which influence the content of genre films (e.g., changes in the way the potential audience is perceived). I also interviewed executives from Universal Studios involved in the marketing and advertising of the film. Subsequently, I interviewed artistic and financial decision-makers involved in other recent horror films. For additional valuable information about the horror cycle of the early 1980s I relied upon the newspaper and magazine clipping service at the Academy Library and from the major trade papers of the film industry (*Variety* and the *Hollywood Reporter* in particular).

The Art World of Film

At whatever level, reputations develop through a process of consensus building in the relevant art world. Like all forms of consensus, the consensus on reputations . . . changes from time to time. Base media become noble media . . . genres fall out of favor, and artists thought second-rate rise in favor as stars fall.
(Becker 1982, 359–60)

The reputation of an artist is frequently tied to the genre or medium in which he or she works, reflecting the consensus of the art world as to whether serious work can be done in that mode. Alfred Hitchcock is a case in point. Prior to the 1960s, most American film critics and scholars did not rank Hitchcock's films as "serious art," in large measure because in their view significant work could not be achieved in the "thriller" genre. While American critics recognized Hitchcock as a master craftsman as early as the 1930s, it was not until after 1965 that they began to take him seriously as an artist. When this did occur in response to encouragement from European artists and Hitchcock's own efforts, many of his earlier films were reappraised. For instance, *Vertigo*, which was dismissed as a flawed thriller by the more "serious" reviewers when first released in 1958, came to be regarded by many prominent American critics as the crowning achievement of a great film director. Indeed, the most recent *Sight and Sound* international critics' poll, in 1992, selected *Vertigo* as one of the "top ten" films of all time. Concurrently, major film critics such as Andrew Sarris (1962a, 1968a, 1968b) and Pauline Kael (1970) turned their attention to the once disreputable genre films (including the thriller), renouncing the earnest "social problem" film previously endorsed by such influential critics as Bosley Crowther (see Beaver 1974) of the *New York Times*. Indeed, the story of how Hitchcock's reputation and that of the thriller genre have improved over the past twenty years is also the story of how film aesthetics have changed.

My subject in this book is the creation of reputation in the art world of film, and I use Alfred Hitchcock's career and legacy as a genre director and film auteur as a case study. I analyze the impact of self-promotion, sponsorship by prominent members of the film community, and changing aesthetic standards on the critical acceptance of Hitchcock as a significant film artist and how this acceptance, in turn, affected the reputation of the thriller genre. The transformation of Hitchcock's reputation is an intriguing case study of how the figure of an "artist" or "auteur" is socially constructed and of the forces which influence reassessments of reputation and cultural meaning. By showing how critics have varied over time in their evaluation of Hitchcock thrillers, the study also illuminates the conditions that are crucial in shaping the historical reception of films and other artifacts of culture. The book, therefore, has relevance for both the sociology of aesthetics and for film studies. In tracing the transformation of Hitchcock's reputation among widely diverse groups of critics (e.g., "feminists" [Modleski 1988] versus "auteurists" [Wood 1966]), the study also contributes to the issue of canon formation in the arts.

First, I chronicle the change over the last three decades in Hitchcock's reputation, from popular entertainer to distinguished auteur. I begin by tracing the active role that Hitchcock and his publicity machine played in the 1950s in establishing his reputation as the master of the suspense thriller. Next I examine both the role of sponsors and Hitchcock's own efforts throughout the sixties and seventies to elevate his reputation. While their campaign finally did succeed, it took over ten years for a significant number of American journalistic film critics to embrace the notion of Hitchcock as a serious artist, for reasons I will develop. In chapter 4, I show how academic criticism, particularly during the 1970s when the auteur theory dominated film studies, has strengthened Hitchcock's reputation as a great "film artist." In addition, I demonstrate how the rise of feminist film theory in the late seventies (see, e.g., Mulvey 1975) has profoundly influenced Hitchcock's reputation in academia.

In the second half of the book, I concentrate on the Hitchcock legacy, especially Hitchcock's impact on contemporary trends in the thriller genre. I discuss the youth-oriented horror thrillers of the 1980s, the recent revival of the adult thriller, and the controversial film career of director Brian De Palma, the most renowned of the thriller directors working in the post–Hitchcock era. My major concern is to show how the canonization of Hitchcock is reflected in recent developments and evaluations of the thriller genre.

THEORETICAL UNDERPINNINGS

The dominant theoretical orientation of most sociological and historical studies of film genres and cycles is the reflection-of-society perspective. According to this viewpoint, shifts in film content reflect changes in audience taste preferences which are, in turn, linked to major shifts in the structure of society. The underlying assumption of many studies in this tradition is that popular films are a more or less accurate mirror of social structure because, by choosing the films it attends, the audience reveals its preferences to film studios and distributors which, in turn, produce and finance films reflecting audience desires. Siegfried Kracauer's *From Caligari to Hitler* (1947) was a pioneering effort at viewing film content as a reflection of the psychological tendencies of a nation as a collectivity.

The reflection approach has also been applied to American cinema. Three important studies are *The Six-Gun Mystique* (1970) by John Cawelti, *Sixguns and Society* (1975) by Will Wright, and *Hollywood Genres* (1981) by Thomas Schatz. All three studies are preoccupied with the mythmaking qualities of Hollywood genres. Consider the following passage from Schatz, which is typical of this approach:

> Throughout this study we have discussed Hollywood film genres as formal strategies for renegotiating and reinforcing American ideology. Thus genre can be seen as a form of social ritual. Implicit in this viewpoint is the notion that these ritual forms contribute to what might be called a contemporary American mythology. In a genuine "national cinema" like that developed in Hollywood, with its mass appeal and distribution, with its efforts to project an idealized cultural self-image, and with its reworking of popular stories, it seems not only reasonable but necessary that we seriously consider the status of commercial filmmaking as a form of contemporary mythmaking. (1981, 261)

In addition, each book treats genre films primarily as symbolic reflections of the society and historical period in which they are created. Wright (1975), for example, describes changes in the content of popular Hollywood westerns between 1930 and 1970, from a concern for solitary heroes fighting it out with villains for the sake of the weak but growing community (which Wright calls the "Classical Plot" western) to a preoccupation with elite bands of heroes, who fight not for the community, which they have rejected, but to affirm themselves as professionals (which Wright calls the "Professional Plot" western). According to Wright, this structural progression in the western is the result of a profound change in American economic institutions occurring at roughly the same time, from a free market (the gunfighter as *homo economicus*) to a corporate economy (the gunfighter as technocrat).

Theoretically more ambitious than Wright or Cawelti, Schatz's approach to genre promises to deliver more—to show how the content of genres reflects not only the wider society but also the way the film industry routinely conducts business. Consider the following passage from Schatz's introduction which asserts the importance of generic or filmic conventions within the context of the studio system:

> The filmmaker's inventive impulse is tempered by his or her practical recognition of certain conventions and audience expectations; the audience demands creativity or variation but only within the context of a familiar narrative experience. As with any such experience it is difficult for either artist or audience to specify precisely what elements of an artistic event they are responding to. Consequently, filmic conventions have been refined through considerable variation and repetition. In this context, it is important to remember that roughly 400 to 700 movies were released *per year* during Hollywood's classic era, and that the studio depended increasingly upon established story formulas and techniques. Thus any theory of Hollywood filmmaking must take into account the essential process of production, feedback, and conventionalization. (1981, 6)

Unfortunately, in the individual chapters devoted to specific genres such as the western, screwball comedy, and hard-boiled detective story, Schatz falls back to a societal-reflection orientation or simply to describing individual films in relation to the generic form, largely ignoring the role of the Hollywood studio system. The industrial model with its emphasis on the importance of the contract between the genre filmmaker and his audience is merely invoked as an untested interpretation of why genres exist and change (cf. Schatz 1988).

In contrast to the reflection viewpoint, there is what has been termed the art world (or production of culture) perspective. Developed by sociologists, this orientation is less polemical than either the more general critique of the mass media developed by the Frankfurt school (see, e.g., Horkheimer and Adorno 1972) or recent neo-Marxist criticisms of classical Hollywood films (e.g., *Cahiers du Cinéma's* [1970] collective text on John Ford's *Young Mr. Lincoln*). The art-world viewpoint begins with the observation that the nature and content of all cultural products (including film) are influenced by or imbedded in the immediate organizational, legal, and economic environments in which they are produced (Cantor 1971, 1980; Peterson 1982; Becker 1974, 1982; Tuchman 1984). The various milieus of symbolic production examined from this perspective have included book publishing, television, popular music, painting, and more recently film.

Howard Becker's (1982) "art world" framework is the most comprehensive sociological picture to date of how works of art are produced. At the core of Becker's perspective is the view of art as collective action. Artists create their work, Becker says, "at least in part, by anticipating how other people will respond, emotionally and cognitively to what they do. That gives them the means with which to shape it further, by catering to already existing dispositions in the audience, or by trying to train the audience to something new" (1982, 200). According to Becker, artists take into account not only the existing dispositions of the primary audience (readers, viewers, listeners) but also how other members of the art world (e.g., critics or distributors) will respond "to what they decide" (1982, 202).

Becker has also applied his art-world viewpoint to how artistic reputations emerge and change in the art world. As he puts it: "At whatever level, reputations develop through a process of consensus building in the relevant art world. Like all forms of consensus, the consensus on reputations, at every level, changes from time to time. Base media become noble media, the greatest work of the twentieth century is superseded by a new discovery (as are the greatest works of earlier centuries), genres fall out of favor, and artists thought second-rate rise in favor as stars fall" (1982, 359–60). One of Becker's important insights is that the consensus about the appropriate standards by which works, genres, and artists are judged important is inherently fragile, since no art world can insulate itself entirely from the impulses for change.

A sizeable body of literature in the art-world tradition has also focused its attention on mass media organizations, showing how the complex interorganizational network of production companies, distributors, mass-media gatekeepers, and retailers influences the production and dissemination of a wide range of cultural commodities (Hirsch 1972, 1978). A recurring theme in the literature on movies and television is that, because of uncertainty over the future tastes of the audience, the production process characteristically involves interpersonal conflict between producers, directors, script writers, and distribution executives over what the audience will like or accept. Not surprisingly, as Hirsch (1972) has pointed out, the role of mass-media gatekeepers is especially important in cultural industries such as the movie business where both demand uncertainty is high and formal vertical integration has been made formally illegal. "Cultural products provide 'copy' and 'programming' for newspapers, magazines, radio stations, and television programs; in exchange, they receive 'free' publicity. The presence or absence of coverage, rather than its favorable or unfavorable interpretation, is the important variable here" (Hirsch 1972, 647).

A number of writers influenced by the art-world perspective (e.g., Gitlin 1983; Kapsis 1986b, 1991) have also observed that the very existence of genre films and cycles is, to a large extent, a product of the entertainment industry's attempt to overcome the problem of uncertainty, that is, of not knowing the future tastes of the mass audience.[1] To reduce this uncertainty, the movie studios, like other mass entertainment industries, fall back on notions about "live or dead genres, doomed formats, cycles that come and go" (Gitlin 1983, 23). Which genres finally get made depends on how organizational gatekeepers at various stages of the film production process assess the potential product in relation to their perception of the audience's future tastes. For example, film production companies often make films from which marketing executives then determine which generic label is most appropriate for promoting the film. While the audience and, by extension, society has some indirect influence on film content through ticket sales, that influence is filtered through the in-house conflicts and interorganizational decisions that determine what films are made and get released. According to the art-world perspective, then, the impact of the audience (or wider society) on the production of genre films is ultimately quite modest compared to the inputs from other more active members of the film art-world such as directors, marketing executives, and even film journalists who cooperate to bring such films and their categorizations into existence.

In conjunction with a reception approach (see below), the present study applies the art-world perspective (or production-of-culture approach) to illuminate Alfred Hitchcock's reputation history and legacy as a thriller director and film auteur. There are four major reasons why I believe this approach is a useful tool for examining Hitchcock and the thriller film.

First, unlike the once standard art-history argument that artistic reputations are based on works (e.g., Read 1937; Zilsel 1926), the art-world orientation expects change in an artist's reputation also to reflect changes in the aesthetic judgments and standards of critics, aestheticians, and other key art-world members rather than simply changes emanating from the works themselves. According to the earlier view of how reputations change in the art world, a major reason for an artist's stature improving during his or her lifetime is that the artist's work became better, that is, more in line with the prevailing aesthetic standards of the art world. This explanation cannot account for the improvement in Hitchcock's overall reputation in the United States among newspaper, magazine, and academic critics during the late 1960s and early 1970s since most film critics regarded Hitchcock's post-1960 films to be inferior to his earlier output. Moreover, the standard art-history viewpoint cannot explain changes in critical evaluation of a given film over time. Today, many critics consider Hitchcock's *Vertigo* (1958) and *Rear Window* (1954) to be great works of cinematic art. However, when these films were first released in the 1950s, they were judged for their entertainment value. Practically nobody took them seriously. By contrast, an important research strategy of the art-world orientation is to show how aesthetic standards are linked to particular art products "through the collective action of specific actors seeking to maintain, undermine, or establish the artistic merit of their own or of others' work" (Mulkay and Chaplin 1982, 118; see also Becker 1974, 1982; Lang and Lang 1988; Zolberg 1990).[2] During the 1960s Hitchcock and his publicity machine played an active if covert role in attempting to redefine his aesthetic status among influential members of the American and international film world. While the impetus to improve his stature came from Hitchcock's earlier enthusiasts, especially the maverick French critics and directors writing for *Cahiers du Cinéma*, Hitchcock fully exploited these opportunities, illustrating more generally that not only does it take two to tango, but that in the highly charged world of Hollywood filmmaking, both partners may take turns leading.

Second, this perspective is sensitive to the fundamental role that mass-media gatekeepers such as newspaper and magazine editors, reporters, and critics play in informing audiences about the availability and desirability of certain cultural products such as films. An important source of audience expectations about the Hitchcock thriller during the 1950s came from media hype in the form of advance notices, press releases, staged interviews, and newspaper and magazine articles reportedly authored by Hitchcock.

Third, the art-world perspective is a useful framework for exploring the extent to which the transformation of Hitchcock's reputation from popular entertainer to serious auteur has affected subsequent developments in the suspense-thriller genre. Becker's approach suggests that the upgrading of an artist's reputation could in time also improve the stature of the genre and medium in which the artist worked. "Schools develop reputations, made up in part of the reputations of the individual artists who belong to them and the works those members create. . . . Genres develop reputations, just as schools do, which reflect the consensus of the relevant art world about the degree to which important works can be done in them" (Becker 1982, 358).

Fourth, while acknowledging the obviously primary input from artists, the art-world orientation is also sensitive to how critics and audiences contribute to the "making" of an art work. As Becker has put it, "any work has only those characteristics its observers notice and respond to on any particular occasion" (Becker 1982, 214). Becker's orientation is compatible with the "reception" or "reader-oriented" approach (see, e.g., Jauss 1982; Bennett 1982; Tompkins 1985; Griswold 1986, 1987; Bennett and Woollacott 1987; Kapsis 1988; Rodden 1989) which I shall implement in order to illuminate how changes in Hitchcock's reputation and in film aesthetics generally shaped the critical assessment and re-assessment of a number of Hitchcock films, especially *Rear Window* (1954), *The Man Who Knew Too Much* (both the 1934 and 1956 versions), *Vertigo* (1958), *Psycho* (1960), *The Birds* (1963), *Marnie* (1964), *Frenzy* (1972), and *Family Plot* (1976). I will also apply this orientation to more recent thrillers such as those associated with director Brian De Palma.[3]

A major tenet of reception theory and other reader-oriented criticism is that "meaning" is produced or "fabricated" by the interaction between reader and text.[4] The term "fabricated" I have borrowed from cultural sociologist Wendy Griswold's (1987) excellent reformulation of reader-oriented criticism.

According to Griswold, the meaning of a cultural object is "fabricated" in the sense that the realization of its meaning results from the interaction between "the symbolic capacities of the object itself" and "the perceptual apparatus of those who experience the object" (1987, 1079). Griswold's orientation assumes that cultural meaning is "humanly made and remade . . . rather than simply residing in the cultural work itself" (1987, 1080). On the other hand, "cultural works vary in their coherence and their multivocality, but this variation can be ascertained only through interaction, since a cultural object has no meaning independent of its being experienced" (1987, 1082; cf. Denzin 1990; DeVault 1990).

The reception approach has influenced recent scholarly work on film. Rather than present an aesthetic history of "films," advocates of the reception approach (e.g., Allen and Gomery 1985) recommend tracing the history of a film's "realization" by audiences and critics, whose "readings" are themselves shaped by history.[5] As Robin Bates (1987) puts it, this orientation assumes that a film text has a multifaceted nature that is part of its complexity: "a text engages with a particular set of audience needs and expectations and changes as these needs and expectations change" (4).

Although film scholars have often justified the reception perspective on the grounds that a film text reveals "different faces to different historical periods," reception studies of film have been essentially case studies of the historical reception of a single film at one point in time (e.g., Budd 1981; Staiger 1986; Allen and Gomery 1985, 91–104). An important exception is Charles J. Maland's (1989) recent book on the dynamic relationship between Charles Chaplin and American culture, which bears similarities with my own orientation. Like my study, Maland's is sensitive to how the interpretation of a film can change over time. While Maland's primary concern is with tracing "the complex evolution" of Chaplin's star image, showing how and why it fluctuated from 1913 to the 1980s, a related theme "is how a culture's response to an artist's work is cumulative, shifting, and multifaceted" (1989, xvi).

One of his most provocative illustrations of this subsidiary theme is his examination of the historical reception of Chaplin's 1947 film, *Monsieur Verdoux* at two different points in time, 1947 and 1964. During its initial domestic release in 1947, *Monsieur Verdoux* was poorly received by both audiences and critics. One reason for its failure, says Maland, "relates to the social structure of stardom" (1989, 250). Guided by a framework first developed by Richard Dyer (1979), Maland shows that all four media sources out of which a star's image is created and maintained—films, promotion, publicity, and criticism/commentary—failed in the case of *Monsieur Verdoux* to sustain for Chaplin a positive star image. Advance promotion and publicity for the film were virtually nonexistent and failed to prepare the audience for the unaccustomed portrayal of Chaplin as a systematic murderer. "The film itself," says Maland, "by breaking Chaplin's aesthetic contract with his audience in a number of ways (especially by presenting a new central persona different in class and interests from the familiar Charlie), also undercut Chaplin's star image." And, as Maland demonstrates, the reviews and commentaries rejected the film on similar grounds.

Another important reason why *Monsieur Verdoux* failed in the United States, says Maland, relates to cultural values. This seems plausible in light of the fact that the film was much more successful in London and Paris than in the United States, which had "embraced the assumptions of the Cold War more quickly and fully than most West European countries." Whereas many Americans who saw the film "understood Chaplin's social critique as a leftist denunciation of his host country," many European viewers were apparently more in approval of the film's political stance. By contrast, when *Monsieur Verdoux* was released in New York in 1964 as part of the Chaplin revival, it was enthusiastically received. According to Maland, this new and more favorable response provides a good test of Hans Jauss's theory of reception, especially his assumption that a literary work (and by extension all art works) is not a kind of "monument" revealing a "timeless essence" but rather "like an orchestration that strikes new resonances" among recipients over time (Jauss 1982, 21). This occurs because what audiences expect from a work, or what Jauss has called their "horizon of expectations," will vary over time.[6] One important difference between 1947 and 1964 which undoubtedly made the film seem less controversial to American audiences in the 1960s was the "shifting political climate." While few "remembered Chaplin's political activism from the 1940s," many more "recalled the circumstances that drove him from the country in 1952 as a victim of the McCarthy era." Thus, audiences in 1964, says Maland, "were more inclined to understand and sympathize with the social criticism in the film" (1989, 331–32).

In contrast to studies which are temporally invariant, a project such as Maland's that explores how receivers of culture vary over time has the potential to evaluate the effects of different historical variables (such as the changing political climate or reputation of a filmmaker) on the reception of a film. Unfortunately, Maland's investigation lacks the requisite rigor for such an undertaking. So many factors are introduced that it becomes next to impossible to discern which are crucial. Only through a more systematic comparative analysis where conditions are analytically manipulated to approximate the logic of experimental design can film historians and cultural sociologists begin to converse intelligently about which factors are the most critical (cf. Smelser 1976). In the final chapter, I introduce material on the reputation history of other film directors (mainly contemporaries of Hitchcock) in order to check further on the validity of my interpretation of the historical reception of Hitchcock's films. Below I identify several factors which in the course of the book I will show are basic to such an understanding.

One factor important in the historical reception of films is the biographical legend or *public reputation* of the artist. As literary critic Boris Tomasevskij (1978) has suggested, "The biography that is useful to the literary historian is not the author's curriculum vitae or the investigator's account of his life" but rather "the biographical legend created by the author himself. Only such a legend is a *literary fact*" (47–55; see Bordwell 1981, 5–10). Film historians have applied Tomasevskij's concept of the biographical legend to film directors "who are known not only as credit lines on their films, but also as public figures" (Allen and Gomery 1985, 88; see also Bordwell 1981; Ryall 1986). One reason the biographical legend or public reputation of a filmmaker such as Hitchcock or De Palma is important to the film historian is that it can influence how viewers derive meaning from a given film. Moreover, a change in a filmmaker's reputation or persona may also affect how the same film is evaluated years later by changing the "horizon of expectations" (Jauss 1982) against which the filmmaker's work is interpreted by critics and audiences.

For instance, I show how Hitchcock's firmly entrenched persona as popular entertainer and master of suspense adversely affected how journalistic critics responded to his boldly experimental film *Marnie* when it was first released in 1964. In addition, I show how Hitchcock's campaign (in conjunction with Truffaut and other champions of his work) during the early sixties to manufacture for himself a new persona—that of film auteur—also hurt the film's reception. On the other hand, during the second phase of *Marnie* criticism, from roughly 1965 to 1976, most critics who came to *Marnie*'s defense were from academia and were strong advocates of the auteur view that Hitchcock was an important and serious artist (see e.g., Wood [1965] 1977).

In a later chapter devoted to thriller director Brian De Palma, I show how De Palma's early reputation as an "underground" filmmaker with roots in the independent film movement of the 1960s shaped how many journalistic critics reacted to his later films such as *Sisters* (1974), *Obsession* (1976), *Carrie* (1976) and *Dressed to Kill* (1980), which he allowed to be identified as homages to Hitchcock. In his discussion of *Obsession,* the *New York Post* critic Frank Rich (1976c) put it this way, "While De Palma has obvious affection for traditional Hollywood filmmaking forms and frequently pays homage to those forms in his films, his heart belongs to his roots—and his roots are in the independent filmmaking movements of the 1960s. De Palma's movies refuse to be a part of any cultural system except the one that's in his head." Although *Obsession* "is an undisguised homage to Hitchcock's magnificent 'Vertigo,'" continues Rich, "it's not a true thriller and it's less a remake of 'Vertigo' than it is a meditation on that 1958 film's themes." Moreover, the film's "hot-headed style is the esthetic antithesis of the Master's ironic cinematic reserve."[7]

A second important factor, *conventions of critical discourse about genre,* refers to the ways of talking about a genre, including the critical vocabulary and frames of reference that critics apply to appropriate projects. When Stanley Kubrick's horror film, *The Shining,* was first released in 1979, many critics were turned off because the film deviated too much from the conventions of the contemporary horror film. (For example, most critics didn't find the film scary enough.) By contrast, Hitchcock's films (especially since the 1940s) have for the most part been evaluated according to the standards Hitchcock himself established in his earlier spy films.[8] That is, the Hitchcock canon provided critics with their major frame of reference. Thrillers made since Hitchcock's death in 1980 have precipitated similar responses from critics who continue to invoke Hitchcock's work as the measure against which to evaluate new works in the thriller genre.

A third important factor in the historical reception of films is the *critical discourse on the cinema,* which refers to more general criteria (usually of an aesthetic nature) affecting how reviewers from a particular time period evaluate current or past films. From the 1930s to the late 1960s, many of America's best known and most influential film critics and historians (e.g., James Agee, Bosley Crowther, Arthur Knight, and Richard Griffith) had asserted the value of "realism."[9] The best films, it was argued, were those "quality" productions which dealt with serious social issues. At the same time, these writers in general dismissed the vast number of popular entertainment films, especially genre films, which Hollywood had produced; their blatant commercialism was considered incompatible with artistry and seriousness. Hitchcock and the thriller genre were casualties of this type of aesthetic discourse. By contrast, subsequent efforts by French and American auteur critics to call attention to Hitchcock's artistry were tied to the broader agenda of removing the barrier between art cinema and commercial cinema by revealing the presence of artists (typically directors were the ones proclaimed as such) in the seemingly monolithic commodity production of Hollywood. The acceptance of the auteur theory among journalistic and academic critics during the late 1960s and early 1970s heightened the reputations of both Hitchcock as artist and the suspense thriller as genre. It also elevated the reputations of other Hollywood directors (e.g., Howard Hawks and Vincent Minelli) and popular genres (e.g., the musical and family melodrama). The rise of feminist film theory in the seventies is another major development in critical discourse on film and has had an important impact on Hitchcock criticism as well as on recent developments in the thriller genre.

A final key influence on the historical reception of films is the various marketing and publicity strategies developed by film companies and filmmakers to promote their films. The mechanism for creating publicity for his latest film became the vehicle for disseminating to journalists and critics the proposition that Hitchcock was a serious artist (cf. Bennett 1982; Bennett and Woollacott 1987; Klinger 1989).

THE PLAN OF THE STUDY

This book examines how Hitchcock became an "auteur" and how his stature as an auteur affected the reputation of the thriller genre. In chapter 2 I examine the relationship between Hitchcock and his audience during the fifties and early sixties. It is during this period, especially after the 1955 premier of his successful television series, that Hitchcock solidified his reputation as a popular entertainer and master of the suspense thriller. After providing some background on his career prior to 1950, I show how with increasing frequency during the fifties, Hitchcock used advance notices, press releases, staged interviews, and newspaper and magazine articles allegedly written by himself to instruct audiences on what to expect in a typical Hitchcock film or TV program (Hitchcock 1950, 1957; Martin 1957). Next I explore how these expectations affected both the popular and critical reception of several Hitchcock feature films (e.g., *Vertigo*, 1958; *North by Northwest*, 1959; *Psycho*, 1960; and *The Birds*, 1963), which were released during the period in which Hitchcock's television series flourished.

In chapter 3, I trace the reevaluation of Hitchcock's work and reputation among American journalistic film critics during the sixties and early seventies, emphasizing both the successes and failures of Hitchcock's own efforts and those of others to reshape his reputation. Since the campaign to establish Hitchcock's standing as a significant artist typically unfolded against the backdrop of the films Hitchcock was working on at the time, I use reactions of newspaper and magazine critics to Hitchcock films released during the 1960s and 1970s to gauge the progress of the campaign. Among the films discussed are *The Birds* (1963), *Marnie* (1964), *Torn Curtain* (1966), *Topaz* (1969), *Frenzy* (1972), and *Family Plot* (1976). The very success of Hitchcock's promotional efforts during the fifties to establish himself as the "master of suspense" made critics suspicious of his subsequent efforts to be taken seriously as an artist. Highlighted in this chapter is the crucial role that changing aesthetic codes play in the reputation-building process. Other findings reported here also show how changing conventions of genre can affect a filmmaker's reputation.

Chapter 4 focuses on how academic criticism solidified Hitchcock's reputation as a serious "film artist," showing, for example, how films such as *Marnie* (1964)—poorly received by critics during their initial release—were rediscovered as forgotten masterpieces by academic critics under the sway of the auteur theory (see, e.g., Wood [1965] 1977; LaValley 1972). In addition, the chapter reveals how, despite the recent shift away from auteurism, academic critics have continued to discuss Hitchcock's films (see, e.g., Mulvey 1975; Bellour 1977, 1979; Wexman 1986; and Greig 1987), especially feminist-oriented scholars, who have invoked Hitchcock's work to illustrate how women function as objects of spectacle for the pleasure of the male viewer in classical Hollywood cinema (see Mulvey 1975). The chapter concludes with an assessment of how "Hitchcock scholarship" has affected journalistic reviewers in both the United States and England.

Exploring the thesis that the transformation of Hitchcock's reputation from popular entertainer to serious artist *caused* American critics to increasingly view the thriller as an effective vehicle for art, chapter 5 examines critical reactions to two recent cycles of thriller films. Focusing first on the horror cycle that followed the enormous commercial and critical success of *Halloween* (1978), the chapter shows how reviewers often invoked Hitchcock's work as *the* standard against which to evaluate such films. In addition, it reveals how filmmakers who worked in horror during the early 1980s also used Hitchcock's name to give an aura of respectability to their own works, thereby facilitating the effective marketing of them. The second half of chapter 5 focuses on the adult thrillers released between 1985 and 1988 such as *Jagged Edge* (1985), *Black Widow* (1987), and *The Stepfather* (1987), which precipitated similar responses from intellectual critics who continued to invoke Hitchcock's work as the standard for evaluating other works in the thriller genre (see, e.g., Corliss 1987). Overall, the evidence suggests that critics increasingly came to view the thriller (especially the adult thriller) as an effective vehicle for art not simply because of the change in attitude toward Hitchcock but mainly because of the adoption of auteurism, which resulted in a general upgrading of many other popular Hollywood genres as well. I also explore how more recent developments in film aesthetics, such as the rise of feminist film theory, have influenced how certain types of contemporary thriller films are perceived.

Chapter 6 focuses on Brian De Palma who many critics regard as heir to Hitchcock's throne. Applying a reputational approach to De Palma's career, I show how both his early reputation as an underground filmmaker and his admiration for Hitchcock (as reflected in his films as well as in published interviews) have shaped critical response to his thriller films, especially *Sisters* (1973), *Obsession* (1976), *Carrie* (1976), *Dressed to Kill* (1980), and *Body Double* (1984). I also examine how broad changes in film aesthetics (what I have called "the critical discourse on cinema") as well as more genre-specific changes in the way of talking about the thriller (what I have called "conventions of critical discourse about genre") have affected assessments of De Palma's work. To a considerable extent, then, the chapter on De Palma provides another testing ground for hypotheses about the historical reception of films first introduced in earlier chapters of the book.

In the final chapter I assess the theoretical significance of the reputational patterns reported in the book, using the technique of controlled comparison. Here I extend the discussion beyond Hitchcock and De Palma to include other film directors, such as Howard Hawks, Frank Capra, Fritz Lang, and Clint Eastwood, whose reputations have also fluctuated dramatically over the years. In addition, I speculate about the applicability of my perspective to other art worlds.

The Making of a Thriller Director

If I filmed "Cinderella," people would be expecting a corpse to fall out of the coach.

(Hitchcock, ca. 1961)

. . . because what we believe a genre to be sets up expectations that condition our responses to a genre film from the very first shot, . . . an analysis of the generic contract in operation . . . becomes crucial.

(Grant 1986, 115)

From the beginning of his directorial career in England in the mid-1920s, Hitchcock used publicity to promote himself, his films, and the idea of directorial preeminence and authority (Yacowar 1977; Spoto 1983; Ryall 1986; Deutelbaum and Poague 1986; Leff 1987). In 1925, several months before he would direct his first film, Hitchcock met with a group gathered at the British Film Society to discuss who made a film succeed—publicists, stars, exhibitors, producers, critics, directors, and others. Hitchcock told the group that it was the director who made the difference. Therefore, it was important that the public learn to associate the name of the director with a quality product. "Actors come and actors go," insisted Hitchcock, "but the name of the director should stay clearly in the mind of audiences" (Spoto 1983, 80).

In the European film culture of the twenties, it was quite common for a director's name to be used in selling a film. The artistic image of European directors such as Fritz Lang, F. W. Murnau, Abel Gance, and Sergei Eisenstein figured prominently in the marketing of their films (see Edwards 1985; King 1984). Even in the United States there were a few directors, most notably Cecile B. DeMille and D. W. Griffith, whose names were used to promote their movies (see Schapiro and Chierichetti 1979). Four years before Hitchcock's appearance at the British Film Society, D. W. Griffith had expressed a similar sentiment on behalf of directorial preeminence when he told a reporter, shortly before the world premier of *Orphans of the Storm*, that "there are two classes of picture fans; the unthinking class who worship the star, and the thinking class interested only in pictures that reach an artistic standard and known not for the actors, despite their valuable contribution, but for the director" (Schickel 1984, 465; see also 290–91 and 467). In spite of the growing box-office clout of star performers, Griffith continued during the early 1920s to use his name, not that of his players, in marketing his films. According to a biographer of Griffith, he was "entirely unable to acknowledge and act upon the obvious, which was that his name and fame were no longer able to compete effectively against the rapidly growing box office power of star performers" (Schickel 1984, 465). Hitchcock's early efforts at self-promotion, then, were not unusual, as they were part of standard European and American industrial and advertising practices. What was novel about Hitchcock is that he became successful at self-promotion while so many others who also tried this tactic failed.

Before cultivating a popular persona, Hitchcock developed an artistic reputation at odds with the expectations of business people in the industry. Undoubtedly, his association with the British artistic mavericks who met at the British Film Society contributed to his growing reputation as a director with an "artistic" agenda. Founded in 1925, the Film Society was set up to advance the course of British film by exposing its members to alternative forms of cinema. One of the founders, Ivor Montagu (who would later work with Hitchcock), expressed the society's mission in the following manner in an early 1970s interview:

> We thought there are such a lot of films that we are interested in that are being made abroad that we would like to fertilise British film ideas by seeing some of them. . . . In this way we could draw into film artists, sculptors, writers, who up to then disdained films. . . . Also, we would be drawing new people into the cinema, new talent. (Ryall 1986, 11)

British film historian Tom Ryall maintains that one of the key factors responsible for Hitchcock acquiring a formidable artistic reputation before any of his films were tested at the box office was the influence of opinion-makers like critic Cedric Belfrage, "who occupied the ground between the 'artistic' wing of the film culture and the entertainment sector" (Ryall 1985, 91).[1] In March 1926, the film magazine *Picturegoer* had featured an article by Belfrage titled "Alfred the Great," which praised Hitchcock as a young director who possessed "such a complete grasp of all the different branches of film technique that he is able to take far more control of his production than the average director of four times his experience." Having just seen Hitchcock's first completed film, *The Pleasure Garden* (prod. 1925), Belfrage, described by British film historian Rachael Low as "one of the better educated and more serious entrants in the film industry" (Low 1971), was genuinely surprised when the film's distributor had refused to release it. W. Woolf, who headed the distribution company, had felt that the film's artistic flourishes, such as Hitchcock's use of odd angles and shadows, would confuse and upset audiences. In part, Belfrage's tribute to Hitchcock was a response to Woolf's decision to shelve the picture (see plates 1 and 2).

While Belfrage's opinion of Hitchcock may have carried some weight in the world of art cinema in Britain during the mid-twenties, the fact remains that his review had little impact on Hitchcock's distributor, since Woolf also refused to release Hitchcock's next two films, *The Mountain Eagle* (prod. 1925) and *The Lodger* (prod. 1926), rejecting the latter on the grounds that it was "too 'highbrow', too involved with 'art'" (Montagu 1972, 76–77; see also Ryall 1986, 88).[2] *The Lodger* received a second life, however, when Hitchcock's producer, Michael Balcon, who in the 1930s would establish himself as one of England's leading film producers, brought in Ivor Montagu, a founding member of the Film Society, to assist Hitchcock in improving the film. One significant change Montagu introduced was to reduce considerably the number of title cards in the silent film, enhancing the importance of the images in telling the story.[3]

In mid-September 1926, a special screening of the revised version of *The Lodger* was held exclusively for the press and theater exhibitors. This time the response was affirmative. Ecstatic about the film, the trade reviews proclaimed *The Lodger* as possibly "the finest British production ever made" (*Bioscope,* 16 September 1926) and "one of the first real landmarks in the coming advance of British pictures" (*Kinematograph,* 23 September 1926). "As an essay in film technique," wrote the reviewer for *The Evening News,* "it ranks with the best films ever made" (20 September 1926). Much of *The Lodger*'s critical appeal, as Ryall has pointed out, can be attributed to what was then perceived as its uniqueness—its attempt, in a manner reminiscent of the best German art films of the period, such as *The Cabinet of Doctor Caligari* and *Nosferatu,* "to differentiate itself from American films" (Ryall 1986, 24). The reviewer for *Kine Weekly,* for example, declared that "*The Lodger,* and other new productions, give promise of a genuine reaction against the deeply-rooted Wardour Street superstition that America will only buy pictures similar to her own" (7 October 1926).[4]

While acknowledging the many stylistic similarities between *The Lodger* and the German expressionistic films, the critics predicted that Hitchcock's film would be more successful in reaching a wide audience. "Whatever the earlier German pictures lacked in popularity," said the *Kinematograph* review, "they certainly exhibited a freedom from American screen conventionality, and also a better understanding of the fact that they were attempting to present drama pictorially and not in subtitles. . . . Alfred Hitchcock has absorbed a good deal of what was best in those productions into his own, and has . . . excelled it in that he has made something which will be appreciated by more than those whose interest in the screen is rather deeper than the average 'fan's'" (*Kinematograph*, 23 September 1926). In fact, most reviewers agreed that *The Lodger* was extremely entertaining. "The experienced audience which viewed the film were gripped from the start," wrote the *Daily Express* critic, "and hardly dared to breathe until the conclusion" (15 September 1926). With a successful trade show behind him, the distributor decided to schedule release dates for all three of Hitchcock's completed films. Since theaters were usually booked several months in advance, the public would still have to wait until after the first of the year to finally sample Hitchcock's art.

By the end of 1926, Hitchcock was "the most sought-after" British director. Earlier that year, he had been approached by a rival studio, British International Pictures (BIP), which offered him a multipicture deal and a salary nearly three times what he was getting at Gainsborough. Hitchcock accepted. Still, not one of the three films he had already made (*The Pleasure Garden*, prod. 1925, *The Mountain Eagle*, prod. 1925, and *The Lodger*, prod. 1926) had been tested at the box office.

The first Hitchcock film to be shown publicly was *The Pleasure Garden*, which opened in London on January 24, 1927. However, it was *The Lodger*, premiering just three weeks later, on February 14, that audiences, aroused by the early rave reviews and commentaries, really wanted to see. Attracting huge crowds during its initial run, *The Lodger* marked "the first time in British film history," says Hitchcock biographer Donald Spoto, "that the director received an even greater press than his stars" (1983, 105). The film featured England's leading matinee idol, Ivor Novello (see plate 3). While it is true that Hitchcock received more coverage in the London papers than did Novello, many reviews and commentaries appearing in newspapers from more provincial areas tended to characterize *The Lodger* as an Ivor Novello film, failing to mention Hitchcock's name at all.[5] On the other hand, it would not be long before Hitchcock became better known outside of London, reflecting his cultivation of new strategies for self-publicity. It was in *The Lodger* that Hitchcock made his first cameo appearance, a role that would become a trademark of his films for the next fifty years.

In November 1927, Hitchcock continued his campaign for self-publicity, writing an open letter to the *London Evening News* in answer to questions purportedly put to him by a reporter. He seized the opportunity to stress his views of the director as the primary force in filmmaking. The letter strongly suggests that at this early stage in his career, Hitchcock already took himself quite seriously as an artist and recognized the potential of motion pictures as a significant art form:

> Perhaps the immediate opportunity lies in more careful and more intelligent treatment of film stories. The American film directors under their commercially minded employers have learnt a good deal about studio lighting, action photographs, and telling a story plainly and smoothly in moving pictures. They have learnt, as it were, to put the nouns, verbs, and adjectives of the film language together.
>
> But even if we conceive the film going no further as an art, it is obvious that what we must strive for at once is the way to use these film nouns and verbs as cunningly as do the great novelist and the great dramatist, to achieve certain moods and effects on an audience. . . . Film directors live with their pictures while they are being made. They are their babies just as much as an author's novel is the offspring of his imagination. And that seems to make it all the more certain that when moving pictures are really artistic they will be created entirely by one man. (Spoto 1983, 114)

Hitchcock pursued self-promotion on other fronts as well. By December 1927, he had developed the original sketch of his now widely recognized profile. He introduced it by sending it to friends and colleagues as a Christmas present—a small linen bag containing wooden puzzle pieces which, when assembled, produced his eight-stroke profile caricature. The founding of Hitchcock-Baker Productions in 1930 signaled another effort at self-publicity. The company's sole purpose was to keep Hitchcock's name before the public.

Hitchcock's promotional activities during this phase of his career suggest that his actual relationship with the British public during the 1930s was considerably less personal and direct than the strong bond he would so diligently cultivate with American audiences during the 1950s. In fact, Ivor Montagu was of the opinion that film critics, rather than the public, were really Hitchcock's primary audience. Montagu recalled that Hitchcock would frequently include unusual or arty shots in his films to help generate good press coverage. Reviewers were "the reason for 'the Hitchcock touches'—novel shots that the critics would pick out and comment upon—as well as the trademark he later made his own (picked up admittedly from Chaplin's [cameo appearance as a] porter shouldering the trunk in *A Woman of Paris*) of a momentary flash appearance in every film he directed" (Montagu 1980, 190; see Leff 1987, 190).[6] By the late 1920s, Hitchcock had also established his practice of sensitizing critics to key sequences from his films, often discussing them with critics well before the film's release (see, for example, the scrapbook of press releases, commentaries, and reviews for his 1927 film, *The Ring*, Hitchcock Collection). Hitchcock feared that without strong critical support for his work he would have difficulty finding a distributor for his films. Recalled Montagu, "You take, for example, when we made *The Man Who Knew Too Much* (1934); Hitch said 'you're not making it for the public because by the time the public sees it it doesn't really matter what happens to it. The main thing is the public will never see it if the distributor doesn't like it. Are you making it for the Press?' He decided that you were making it for the Press, and the trade was quite right in smelling this out and feeling that he was trying to get good notices" (Montagu 1972, 80). Thus, Hitchcock had the intelligence to realize that in England during the 1930s a good critical response to his films was essential for a successful career in the film business.

Hitchcock's reputation as a thriller director evolved more slowly than his reputation as England's finest director. During his first decade of filmmaking in England, he worked in a variety of genres, including middle-brow theatrical adaptations (*Easy Virtue*, 1927; *Juno and the Paycock*, 1930; *The Skin Game*, 1931), romances (*Rich and Strange*, 1932), a musical (*Waltzes From Vienna*, 1933) and, of course, thrillers (*The Lodger*, 1926; *Blackmail*, 1929; *Murder*, 1930; *Number Seventeen*, 1931). While two thrillers—*The Lodger* and *Blackmail*—were among his most critically acclaimed films from this period, so too were a number of his nonthrillers, including *The Ring*, a boxing melodrama from an original idea of Hitchcock's, and *Juno and the Paycock,* a surprisingly faithful and uncinematic adaptation of the Sean O'Casey play. It was not, however, until 1934 when he filmed *The Man Who Knew Too Much* that Hitchcock started making thrillers on a regular basis. In fact, that film marked the first in a series of six consecutive thrillers made between 1934 and 1938 which in time would become known as Hitchcock's "classic thriller sextet" (see plate 4).

One of his biographers has maintained that the consistency which characterized Hitchcock's filmic output between 1934 and 1938 reflected his growing realization that the thriller genre best suited his temperament (Taylor 1978). In addition, I would argue, following Ryall's (1986) line of reasoning, that the high degree of continuity and consistency among the films of Hitchcock's thriller sextet was also a function of the "consistencies in the production context from which they emerged" (Ryall 1986, 118). All six were made for the same company, Gaumont British Picture Corporation. Moreover, a high degree of continuity was maintained among the creative and technical personnel on the six films. For instance, Ivor Montagu was brought in as the associate producer on the first four films of the thriller sextet. In addition, Charles Bennett worked on four of the scripts and was the inspiration behind a fifth, *The Man Who Knew Too Much.* As Ryall has observed, these consistencies in personnel relate to "the stable period of production that characterized the British film industry during the years from 1934 to 1937." Hitchcock's films had become "one of the production categories for the Gaumont British output during the 1930s" with Hitchcock himself firmly "lodged on the studio production schedules as a kind of genre in himself" (118).[7] The subsequent variety of his output in Hollywood in the 1940s adds credibility to the view that personal choice was not the only factor affecting his filmmaking assignments at this time.

Hitchcock accelerated his promotional activities during the mid-to-late 1930s. The personal idiosyncracy which he seemed most anxious to exploit at this time was his obesity. In fact, when meeting with journalists, he would frequently wear clothing that accentuated his girth. As Leff describes it, Hitchcock's portly figure became a key element in the interaction ritual that he cultivated at this time:

> A reporter who climbed the four flights to Hitchcock's flat probably expected to see the director in his business clothes, a plain blue serge suit, bagged at the knees. Instead, the five-foot-eight Hitchcock wore a dressing gown over a pair of deep-dyed Chinese silk pajamas, no doubt exaggerating his weight yet also lending an

air of informality, perhaps even conspiracy and intimacy, to the meeting of writer and subject. He seduced journalists not only with his pithy opinions on cinematic style but his manner—the snapping black eyes, drawling voice, and expressive hands, surprisingly gentle and soft. By the mid-1930s in Great Britain's trade and fan publications, the Hitchcock film and the Hitchcock persona had begun to reinforce and promote each other. (Leff 1987, 13)

When he began seriously to consider moving to Hollywood during the late 1930s, Hitchcock used publicity about his Falstaffian girth to attract the American press. While American reporters knew of his formidable reputation as a director, they had no knowledge of his appearance. It is during this period that articles first appeared describing Hitchcock's various dieting bouts. Press clippings and reports about the director eventually reached Hollywood, and it wasn't long until a number of Hollywood film studios, especially Selznick International, became interested in "Alfred the Great" (see plate 5).[8]

By the late 1930s, the New York critics had also joined the Hitchcock bandwagon. Applauding his "mastery of the melodramatic film" in such recent thrillers as *The 39 Steps* (1935) and *The Lady Vanishes* (1938), they concluded that his reputation as "England's greatest director" and "one of the greatest directors in motion pictures" was richly deserved (*The Lady Vanishes* scrapbook, Hitchcock Collection). Impressed with his consummate craftsmanship in the comedy-thriller *The Lady Vanishes*, the New York film critics voted Hitchcock the best director of 1938.

After moving to the United States in 1939, Hitchcock resumed his efforts to remain in the public eye. One effective way of doing this involved lecturing audiences about the art of suspense. In 1940, as part of the promotion for his first American film, *Rebecca,* Hitchcock had told a radio interviewer that he was interested in directing any kind of film, so long as it "lends itself to suspense." "I know *that* sounds pretty far-reaching," he continued, "most stories lend themselves to suspense, but I relish a story that is so full of suspense that the audience is clutching at chair arms. In fact, I might say my slogan is 'keep them awake at the movies'."

During the interview, Hitchcock articulated (for one of the first times on record) the distinction between suspense and surprise—a distinction he would repeat many times over the next thirty years, especially in the late fifties. In response to the radio announcer's query, "just what do you mean by suspense?" Hitchcock, without using the term, replied, "I mean the quality that lasts throughout a picture and leaves the spectators limp as dish rags at the end. None of this quick, smashing excitement that lasts about 10 seconds—a good six or seven reels of worry is what I aim for." Moreover, asserted Hitchcock, suspense is an important ingredient not only in detective and mystery films but in other types of stories as well. "There is suspense," he added, "when you wonder if the boy will get the girl in a romance." After providing illustrations of Hitchcock's principles of suspense with a few previews of scenes from *Rebecca,* the radio program ended with the interviewer thanking Hitchcock "for giving us this highly interesting lesson in the art of keeping an audience on edge" ("On Your Hollywood Parade," undated transcription of radio broadcast [ca. 1940], Hitchcock Collection). While Hitchcock gave relatively few such lessons on the art of suspense during the decade of the 1940s, by the mid-1950s his lectures on suspense would become commonplace in America.

In his dealings with the press, Hitchcock continued to promote himself as the complete filmmaker in full control of all phases of the production process. The specifics of his long-term contract signed in 1939 with Selznick International suggested otherwise. The contract granted Selznick's company Hitchcock's nonexclusive services as director for two pictures the first year. While the contract had its attractive features from Hitchcock's standpoint (he could veto loanout offers), it also put serious limits on his autonomy as a filmmaker. For example, he did not have the right to prepare the final cut for his films. At Selznick's studio, Selznick was the one in charge of post-production. It was he who supervised final shot selection and thus determined the final shape of the film (for more on the Hitchcock-Selznick collaboration, see Leff 1987; Schatz 1988).[9]

Yet one would never know this from the interviews and press releases of the period. Even Selznick's own publicity machine stressed Hitchcock's authorship. Before his first American film, *Rebecca* (1940), went into production, Hitchcock told a *Newsweek* reporter that the film would "reflect no personality other than his own" (Leff 1987; see also "On Your Hollywood Parade," Hitchcock Collection). As Leff has succinctly put it:

> No less than Clark Gable's love of sport or Joan Crawford's supposedly warm home life, Hitchcock's assertion of independence helped to define a persona that Selznick's publicity department

and later Hitchcock himself could use in selling pictures. As long as Hitchcock played his act on the road and not in the executive offices of Culver City, no one strenuously objected; his contract, after all, negated his claims of authorship. (Leff 1987, 56)

Throughout the 1940s Hitchcock continued his practice of including unusual shots or sequences in his films for their calculated effect on the more serious critics (see Leff 1987, 137–40). In 1944 he commissioned the surrealist painter Salvador Dali to design a dream sequence for the film *Spellbound,* which generated more publicity than any other sequence in the film (see *Spellbound* Production File, Academy Library). At that time, Dali was extremely popular among high-culture critics. Undoubtedly Hitchcock expected that Dali's reputation would lure the serious critics to this film. As Leff has pointed out, there is also good reason to believe that Hitchcock wanted Dali's name even more than Dali's images. Hitchcock compromised Dali's original conception for the sequence by making it both less metaphoric and more humorous. "By diluting Dali with wit and popular psychology," says Leff, Hitchcock "raised the entertainment value of the film but compromised the dream sequence" (1987, 159). As Hitchcock remarked to a reporter a few months after the release of his next film, the enormously successful *Notorious* (1946), "There's the constant pressure. . . . You know: people asking, 'Do you want to reach only the audiences at the Little Carnegie or to have your pictures play the Music Hall?' So you compromise" (Nugent 1946; quoted in Leff 1987, 159).

The Paradine Case (1947) was the last of Hitchcock's films made under Selznick. By that time, Hitchcock and a former business associate and friend, Sidney Bernstein, had set up an independent production company, Transatlantic Pictures. The company produced two films, *Rope* (1948) and *Under Capricorn* (1949), both directed by Hitchcock. Both films exploited technical means at the expense of narrative flow and neither one generated much business. It would seem that Hitchcock had temporarily lost touch with his audience. During the fifties, however, the two would rediscover each other, effecting a bond much stronger than ever before.[10]

HITCHCOCK IN THE FIFTIES

After his success with the spy thriller *Notorious* in 1946, Hitchcock's career had floundered. His venture into independent film production had been disappointing, with both films his company had produced faring poorly at the box office and with the critics. While enjoying somewhat more success during his four-year stint at Warner Bros. (1949–53), especially with the release of *Strangers On A Train* (1951), his filmmaking activities during that time were often punctuated by long stretches of relative inactivity. Between the completion of *Stage Fright* in September 1949 and the beginning of pre-production work on *Strangers On A Train* in spring 1950, over seven months had passed. Indeed, almost two years lapsed between the completion of *Strangers On A Train* in December 1950 and the start of his next project, *I Confess,* in late winter of 1952.

Beginning in 1952 Hitchcock became professionally more active. Indeed, he was entering the most productive period of his career. Between 1952 and 1960, he completed three feature films for Warners, six for Paramount, and one for MGM. And with the successful launching of his TV series in 1955, he became the first Hollywood director to become a bonafide TV star.[11]

Hitchcock's first major box office hit in the early fifties was *Rear Window* (1954), which also proved to be popular with the critics. Starring James Stewart and Grace Kelly, this film, his first for Paramount, focuses on a temporarily disabled photo-journalist who passes the time using binoculars to peer unobtrusively out of the rear window of his Greenwich Village apartment, observing the lives of his neighbors. On the day that we observe with him, he sees what he thinks is a murder taking place in one of the apartments within his view (see plate 6).

Most American reviewers evaluated *Rear Window* almost exclusively in terms of the standards Hitchcock himself established in his early British thrillers. From that vantage point, the film was a success—with a large majority of reviewers agreeing that it was Hitchcock's best—most entertaining—film in a long time (see, e.g., *New York Herald Tribune,* 15 August 1954; *Los Angeles Times,* 5 August 1954; *Time,* 2 August 1954). Even the critic for the *New Yorker,* who disliked the film because of its technical conceits—confining all the action "to an implausible backyard" (as just *Rope* and *Dial M For Murder* used confined spaces improbably)—judged the film in terms of the Hitchcock canon, hoping that some day Hitchcock would "burst out the way he used to, and then we'll have satisfactory films" (7 August 1954; for a similar critique, see Knight, *Saturday Review,* 21 August 1954).[12] What the vast majority of reviewers found especially engaging about *Rear Window* was its wonderful blending of suspense, droll comedy, and romance—qualities that critics were quick to point out had made Hitchcock's early works such as *The 39 Steps* and *The Lady Vanishes* so successful. While acknowledging the film's generous supply of suspense and thrills, a number of critics cited *Rear Window* as Hitchcock's "most amusing film in a long time": the real news about the film was that Hitchcock had rediscovered his sense of humor. As *New York Herald Tribune* critic Otis L. Guernsey put it, "the Hitchcock touch has acquired its old-time quality of humor in *Rear Window,* in which there are actually more laughs than chills" (15 August 1954). Virtually all reviewers praised the film for its entertainment values—"exhilarating," "full bodied," "the most roundly enjoyable" Hitchcock film in years. At the same time, practically no one saw it as a significant film or as a deeply personal statement.

New York Times critic Bosley Crowther's carefully worked out response to *Rear Window* made clear that the film, as with Hitchcock's previous works, should be judged in terms of its value as entertainment, not as art (5 August 1954). Crowther's preeminence during the forties and fifties as acknowledged dean of the New York reviewers makes his views on Hitchcock of special interest. In addition to helping shape opinion about Hitchcock's work among American journalist reviewers, Crowther's reviews also influenced Hitchcock's reputation among Hollywood professionals. From 1941 to 1961, for a movie to win the best-picture Oscar, it had to appear on Crowther's list of ten best films of the year. During this twenty-one-year period, only three Hitchcock films— *Spellbound* (1945), *Notorious* (1946), and *Psycho* (1960)—made Crowther's annual list.

Since 1940 Crowther had been serving as a daily film reviewer for the *New York Times,* America's most powerful newspaper, a post he would hold until his retirement in 1967. From the beginning, Crowther had believed that the critic should be a catalyst in developing the public's taste in films (*New York Times,* 25 February 1945, sec. 2, p. 1). Throughout his career, Crowther campaigned for a socially conscious and responsible cinema. His social concerns established him "as a social critic of the motion picture rather than a literary stylist or aesthetician" (Beaver 1974, 3–4).

Crowther maintained that the essential requirement of any film was to entertain in the sense of holding and stimulating the audience. But, in addition, he believed that a film should have something "significant" to say:

> The last thing that any movie-goer in a reasonable state of mind would neglect to require of a movie is that it fascinate and absorb. What's the point in looking at a picture which fails to stimulate?

But as well as being entertaining, it is also possible that a film contain some truth or some rigor of expression which renders it "significant." (*New York Times,* 3 February 1946, sec. 2, p. 1; see also Beaver 1974, 20)

The motion picture, he maintained, was uniquely equipped to render significant communication because of its intrinsic affinity with realism, enabling the filmmaker to explore the actualities of daily life. For Crowther, plausibility and realism were the key to significant social and artistic achievement on the screen. Therefore, Hollywood formula pictures such as westerns, gangster stories, romances, and Hitchcockian thrillers, since they lacked sufficient doses of plausibility and realism, were not significant forms of expression. More to his liking were the Italian neorealist films of Roberto Rossellini and Vittorio de Sica, first released in the United States after 1945. Crowther's enthusiasm for neorealism is exemplified in the following passage from his 1946 review of Rossellini's *Open City* (1945):

To us who have been accustomed to the slickly manufactured sentiments of Hollywood's studio-made pictures, the hard simplicity and genuine passion of the film lend to its not unfamiliar story the smashing impact of a shocking expose. And its sharp estimation of realities gives it a rare intellectual authority. (*New York Times,* 3 March 1946, sec. 2, p. 1)

Overall, Crowther liked *Rear Window.* Despite his criticisms (e.g., that the wide-screen VistaVision process caused "some of Hitchcock's fast cutting and panoramas to blur"), he concluded that the "important thing" about the film for the average moviegoer is that "Hitchcock has found the old timing and sense of humor."[13] The film, in his view, succeeded as entertainment. On the other hand, unlike most other mainstream reviewers, who never raised the issue, Crowther expressed quite explicitly his sentiment that the film should not be confused with art. "Mr. Hitchcock's film," wrote Crowther, "is not 'significant.' What it has to say about people and human nature is superficial and glib." While the film "does expose many facets of the loneliness of city life," continued Crowther, the film's purpose is "sensation, and that it generally provides in the colorfulness of its detail and in the flood of menace toward the end" (5 August 1954; see also Crowther 1954b).[14]

During its initial run, then, journalistic reviewers were not inclined to characterize *Rear Window* as a significant work of art. Rather, the film and the critical response to it helped to revive and strengthen the view of Hitchcock as a master entertainer—a view which his next film for Paramount, *To Catch A Thief* (1955), also reinforced.[15]

Hitchcock's rise to television stardom would further underscore his image as master entertainer. In 1955 Lew Wasserman, president of MCA (Music Corporation of America), and Hitchcock's exclusive agent, took the step which eventually elevated Hitchcock to TV stardom by persuading him to host a weekly TV series.[16]

Wasserman had been responsible for involving many of MCA's clients in television during the early 1950s, well before the major studios became actively engaged in television production. Until the 1940s, the major film companies controlled not only the production of their films but their distribution and exhibition as well. "With stars, producers, directors, writers all under contract, and studio-owned theater chains providing a captive distribution system," says Gitlin, "the studios were the companies who ran the company town" (1983, 145). This all changed during the late 1940s when the Justice Department forced the movie studios to sell their theater holdings. Meanwhile, television was cutting into the movie market.

Not that the studios had been uninterested in exploiting television. Paramount and Warner Bros. had developed elaborate plans to purchase TV stations in major markets and to experiment with video projection in their theaters as a way of reducing distribution costs (Schatz 1988, 472). But the Supreme Court's 1948 Paramount decree put an end to such schemes. In addition to ordering the studios to divest themselves of their theater holdings, the decree forbid them to purchase TV stations. Of course, the majors could have become suppliers of television programs, but at first they resisted.

According to film historian Thomas Schatz, 1955 was "a watershed year in filmmaking history, [marking] the end of the majors' resistance to active television production and thus the beginning of a full-scale transformation and recolonization of Hollywood" (Schatz 1988, 476). In fall 1955, three studio-produced series, "Warner Bros. Presents," "The 20th Century-Fox Hour," and "MGM Parade" premiered on network television. All three reworked or repackaged previous studio hits and promoted upcoming releases. None of these programs proved successful. Apparently, the self-promotional format turned off audiences and sponsors alike. A fourth program with a Hollywood aura to premiere that same year was "Alfred Hitchcock Presents." Unlike the others, it succeeded, lasting in various formats for over a decade.

Weekly anthology series devoted exclusively to suspense melodramas had been around since the late 1940s—shows with titles such as "Suspense," "Danger," "The Web," "The Unexpected," "The Whistler," and so on. Even such prestigious series as "Kraft Television Theater" and "Studio One" occasionally featured thrillers.[17] Moreover, the idea of Hitchcock himself hosting a series was hardly a revolutionary concept. Most dramatic anthology series on television featured a host or hostess, from Ronald Reagan to Loretta Young. Even movie mogul Walt Disney had recently gotten into the act. What was new and refreshing about Hitchcock's suspense series was how his personality became so integral to the series.

Initially, Hitchcock had not found the television idea especially appealing. Satisfied with his production schedule at Paramount, he was, as we have seen, in the midst of the most productive period of his filmmaking career.[18] But Wasserman persevered, explaining the advantages of the television series. It could be filmed at MCA's telefilm company, Revue Productions.[19] Moreover, like a number of lucrative publishing deals Wasserman had recently negotiated for Hitchcock, the series would require very little input. For the use of his name and image on various publications such as short-story anthologies and a mystery magazine, Hitchcock received both a licensing fee and a percentage of the royalties on each venture. Commenting on his contract with Richard E. Decker, publisher of *Alfred Hitchcock's Mystery Magazine,* Hitchcock said, "I simply sold him the right to use my name," adding that, like Fred Astaire with his dance studios, he had nothing to do with day-to-day operations (Spoto 1983, 386).

Upon learning that CBS and Bristol-Myers were willing to pay him $129,000 per episode and that he would become the sole owner of each episode once it aired, Hitchcock finally agreed to try his hand at television. Although it would not be apparent to his fans, Hitchcock's involvement in the new venture was from the outset only peripheral. His contract stipulated that he would serve as executive producer and script supervisor in name only, and that he would introduce each program. Two long-time Hitchcock associates, Joan Harrison and (from 1957) Norman Lloyd, were brought in to handle the actual production duties. Together, they shared the major responsibilities for the TV series: story selection, hiring of writers and directors, casting, and supervision of each production. "Hitchcock contributes nothing except script supervision," Harrison is reported to have said, adding that it was her responsibility to hire writers and directors for the individual episodes.

Hitchcock did not conceal his limited involvement in this venture: "Miss Harrison does the casting, yes, and Norman Lloyd. I try to put out fatherly words of advice without trying to usurp their position" (Spoto 1983, 398–99).

"Alfred Hitchcock Presents" premiered on 2 October 1955 and lasted in various formats until 1965. Of the 372 teleplays produced by Hitchcock's Shamley Productions during this ten-year period, Hitchcock actually directed only twenty of them. His importance to the series, however, must not be underestimated. Not the least of his contributions to the program were his personality and physical presence. At the opening of each show, audiences would see Hitchcock metamorphosed from an abstraction (his profile drawing), to a shadow magically replacing the silhouette, to finally Hitchcock himself addressing the audience. The succession of images (along with the show's theme music), as Howard Prouty (1984) has persuasively argued, "was certainly inspired—it established almost subliminally, the *idea* of 'Alfred Hitchcock'" (xiv); it evoked, in addition, I would suggest, the idea of Hitchcock as the creative and almost supernatural force behind the program.

A close analysis of the opening sequence of each program vividly conveys the probable impact that the opening had on audiences and suggests the force of Hitchcock's image on the viewer. The show begins with the first sustained note of the program's musical theme, Gounod's "Funeral March of a Marionette," followed by the sudden appearance of Hitchcock's silhouette. The title, "Alfred Hitchcock Presents," appears, superimposed on the silhouette and remains on the screen for approximately three seconds until it finally disappears. For the following six seconds all that is visible on the screen is the silhouette. We then see Hitchcock's shadow appear. It moves from the right side of the screen until it virtually covers the silhouette, which is center screen. The still visible portions of the outline then disappear as if by magic. Next the shadow seems to move left until it leaves the screen altogether; meanwhile, the camera moves to the right until the real Hitchcock is in the frame. The camera stops. The movement from shadow to Hitchcock's physical appearance appears as a single unedited camera movement which of course is impossible if indeed the shadow belongs to Hitchcock. Upon closer inspection of the shot, we see that there is a cut as the camera swoops to the right, but the cut is barely perceptible. The impression given by this sequence, I would argue, is of Hitchcock the creator, Hitchcock the dominant force behind the show, Hitchcock the magician and master of illusion. Hitchcock's fan mail for the TV series indirectly supports this interpretation, documenting that many viewers came to believe not only that Hitchcock had directed all the teleplays but that he also wrote all of them as well. As one of Hitchcock's writers put it, "it was apparent from the Shamley mailbox that there were hundreds and maybe thousands of viewers out there who believed that Alfred Hitchcock was the author of the tales he told. So much for credits" (Slesar 1985, 4).

As host of the series, Hitchcock established further the tone of the show. On the occasion of his TV debut, Hitchcock's introductory remarks effectively set the mood for the entire series:

> Good evening. I am Alfred Hitchcock, and tonight I am presenting the first in a series of stories of suspense and mystery, called, oddly enough, "Alfred Hitchcock Presents." I shall not act in these stories, but will only make appearances—something in the nature of an accessory before and after the fact, to give the title to those of you who can't read, and to tidy up afterwards for those who don't understand the endings. Tonight's playlet is really a sweet little story. It is called "Revenge." (October 2, 1955)

For many of his fans, Hitchcock's witty introductions and epilogues became almost inseparable from the teleplays themselves, which were often about criminals who got away with their crimes, at least until the epilogue when Hitchcock would return to explain, typically in a humorous vein, that justice had eventually triumphed. In "Lamb to the Slaughter" (1958), for example, a pregnant housewife, learning that her husband, a policeman, plans to leave her for another woman, fatally batters him over the head with a frozen leg of lamb. The teleplay ends with her serving up the evidence to the hungry policemen investigating the case. At the end of the show, Hitchcock returned to report that the woman was finally apprehended when she tried the same thing on her second husband, only that this time around the roast had defrosted.[20] As Hitchcock remarked during an often quoted 1957 interview, "in selecting the stories for my television shows, I try to make them as meaty as the sponsor and the network will stand for" (Martin 1957). In contrast to the teleplays, then, were the programs' epilogues, through which Hitchcock hoped to "offset any tendency toward the macabre with humor." Thus, Hitchcock's appearances at the beginning and end of each program were more than just amusing. They became integral to the style of the series (see plate 7).

In addition to introducing the show, his prologue provided Hitchcock with the opportunity to poke fun at sponsors, the network, and, of course, himself, which he did on a regular basis. For example, in one of his early shows, we find Hitchcock in Puritan costume, his hands and feet in stocks. "Good evening," he says. "Methinks I should never have come to the colonies. Here I am: the producer's dream—a captive audience. Unfortunately, being the producer, I have already seen tonight's story ["One For The Road"] several times." Hitchcock next explains to viewers why he has been imprisoned. "If you think we have freedom of speech here, just try speaking your mind about television commercials." We see Hitchcock wriggling his hands, trying to free them. He next tells us that he has learned his lesson. "Ladies and gentle-men, may I present my esteemed sponsor, who will give, as a public ser-vice, a short and candid appraisal of his superb product."

Following the teleplay, Hitchcock returns. He is free, standing next to the stocks. After rubbing his wrists, he says, "It's good to be free again. Which is more than Beryl Abbott is, for she was arrested and paid for her crime. Now, before I return, we shall have the last commercial—one for the road. And no doubt it will be just as deadly as the drink in our story." After the commercial break, we find Hitchcock in the stocks again. Unperturbed, Hitchcock utters, "My, the sponsor's a sensitive fellow," adding that the viewer should "tune in next week and see if he [the sponsor] has relented. I suspect I shall be here and we shall have a story as well. Good night" (Script, TV Files, Hitchcock Collection).

The tongue-in-cheek tone of Hitchcock's weekly appearances had a cumulative effect and established his persona as an entertainer. His reg-ular presence on the show also established Hitchcock as a TV star.

As many media experts have noted, the TV business "presumes, with reason, that characters—and therefore stars—are central to a show's success" (Gitlin 1983, 146). On the surface, "Alfred Hitchcock Presents" fit the anthology format—"a series of dramas, each with its own cast and plot, often introduced by the same host" (Swidler et al. 1986, 326). But Hitchcock's weekly presence on the show transcended that of a mere host, meaning that he also provided the series with the continuity of an episodic series. Through his intervention at the end of each program, Hitchcock saw to it that law and order were restored.

Hitchcock acknowledged that it was during the period of his TV series that he became known the world over. Even during a trip to Japan, people recognized him (Hitchcock Clipping File, Lincoln Center). Hitchcock also reported receiving many more fan letters than he had before becoming a TV personality. Eight months after the premiere of his television show, Hitchcock told a journalist, "Before TV, I'd get about a dozen letters a week. Now it's several hundred. . . . Thirty years I've been directing pictures on the set. Just the other day I overheard a lady guest say . . . 'There's Alfred Hitchcock of television' " (*New York Herald Tribune*, 6 June 1956). Not only was Hitchcock one of the best known film directors in the world, he had also become a star, a celebrity. And like most movie and TV stars, Hitchcock's persona on the screen became in the minds of his fans almost indistinguishable from Hitchcock the man. As Richard Dyer (1979) has pointed out in his study of stars and star images, audiences come to see "performances of a star in a film" as a reflection of the actual personality of the star. Says Dyer, "What was only sometimes glimpsed and seldom brought out by Hollywood or the stars was that that personality was itself a construction known and expressed only through films, stories, publicity, etc." (1979, 23).

In 1972 Hitchcock told film critic Richard Schickel that many people he had wanted to get to know, especially women, were reluctant to reciprocate because they believed that he must be like the sinister and murderous characters that peopled his films (Schickel 1972b).[21] This was probably a minority view of him, however. Most viewers of Hitchcock's TV series, I suspect, must have come to view him as a dignified but hammy Englishman with a macabre wit. Promotional materials issued from the studios where Hitchcock worked during the fifties—Warner Bros. and Paramount—reinforced this image. So did feature stories which appeared throughout the fifties, especially in national weeklies and monthlies like *Time, Look, Life*, and *Newsweek*.

The macabre side of Hitchcock's persona is captured in a 1957 *Look* photo essay about him entitled "Hitchcock's World." The article's premise is that "all he has to do is look and act natural for you to imagine that the world is filled with evil." To illustrate this premise, the essay presents photographs showing Hitchcock strolling around the studio where his TV series was filmed. Each photograph elucidates how Hitchcock's presence in an otherwise ordinary setting transforms it into a situation which is both sinister and life-threatening. One photograph features Hitchcock outdoors looking at a workman digging a hole. The caption reads "His presence near two gaping coffin-sized holes is enough to transform an honest workman's dull labor into actions that suggest a situation both grave and frightening." Another photograph shows Hitchcock seated on a stool, his face reflected in a puddle of water.

The caption reads, "Inscrutable mien of suspense master Hitchcock, eerily reflected on the floor in front of him, gives no clue as to whether the liquid is a harmless puddle of water or a sinister pool of blood" (*Look*, 1957).

The humorous side of Hitchcock's persona often surfaced in odd places. Consider, for instance, an article which appeared on 4 August 1957 in *This Week Magazine*. The piece is in the form of a photo thriller purportedly written by Hitchcock in response to a query from a reader of the magazine who wrote, "On his TV show, 'Alfred Hitchcock Presents,' Hitchcock does stories by others." "Has he ever written a story himself?" Hitchcock agreed to write a photo thriller for *This Week Magazine*. The written text, however, is overshadowed by the accompanying photographs of Hitchcock masquerading not only in all the male roles but in all but one of the female parts as well. "An accident of age and profile makes it impossible for me," writes Hitchcock, "to counterfeit the charming young lady." Be that as it may. But it doesn't preclude Hitchcock from posing as Lady Agatha (the Countess of Windblown) and Withers, her personal maid (see plate 8). Clearly, the article is a triumph for Hitchcock the ham actor at the expense of Hitchcock the mystery writer (Hitchcock 1957a).

Other feature stories from this period attempted to dispel the impression that there was something sinister, unsavory, and heartless about Hitchcock the man. In numerous articles Hitchcock confessed to being a very fearful person, especially with respect to the police. The extent of his fear is captured in his classic remark that the reason he didn't drive a car was because of his fear of getting a traffic ticket. Other journalistic pieces characterized Hitchcock as very much a family man leading an ordinary, even dull, bourgeois existence (see plate 9). In one article, we learn that Hitchcock enjoys helping his wife prepare meals and washing the dishes. In another article, we see him entertaining one of his two granddaughters in a photograph captioned: "Energetic Grandfather busses Terry, 3, as his wife holds Mary Alma, 4. The children's mother, Pat Hitchcock, beams" (Bender 1958).

In sum, by intensifying media interest in him, the enormous success of "Alfred Hitchcock Presents" solidified Hitchcock's reputation as a popular entertainer and media personality.

It was also at this time that Hitchcock attempted to communicate more directly with audiences about his films. With increasing frequency during the fifties, he used advanced notices, press releases, staged interviews, and newspaper and magazine articles reportedly authored by himself to instruct audiences on what to expect in a typical Hitchcock feature film. Specifically, he accomplished this through identifying his work with the thriller genre and by enumerating to his fans the special rules governing that form (for a sample of such articles see Hitchcock 1950, 1959; Martin 1957). Articles of this type appeared on a regular basis in *Life,* the *Saturday Evening Post, Newsweek, Time, TV Guide,* and the *New York Times Magazine,* especially after the launching of his successful television series. Local newspapers were similarly inundated with Hitchcock self-promotion. His instructions to his fans typically included a clarification of the distinction between the Hitchcock suspense thriller and related film genres such as detective story. "The detective story's great flaw," says Hitchcock, "is that it does not contain much real suspense because it must withhold too much information from the reader or viewer" (Hitchcock 1959). To illustrate this distinction, Hitchcock more often than not would cite the story about the ticking bomb:

> Let us suppose that three men are sitting in a room in which a ticking bomb has been planted. It is going to go off in 10 minutes. The audience does not know it is there, and the men do not know it is there either. So they go on talking inanely of the weather or yesterday's baseball game. After 10 minutes of desultory conversation the bomb goes off. What is the result? The unsuspecting audience gets a surprise. *One* surprise. That's all.
>
> Suppose the story were told differently. This time, while the men still do not know the bomb is there, the audience *does* know. The men still talk inanities, but now the most banal thing they say is charged with excitement. The audience wants them to get out of the room but they talk on, and when one finally says, "Let's leave," the entire audience is praying for them to do so. But another man says, "No, wait a minute. I want to finish my coffee," and the audience groans inwardly and *yearns* for them to leave. This is suspense. (Hitchcock 1959)[22]

In addition to the building of suspense. Hitchcock attempted to convey to his fans that a second key ingredient of the Hitchcockian thriller is comic relief. "After a certain amount of suspense," says Hitchcock, "the audience must find relief in laughter." Suspense and laughter he saw as part of a "basic pattern—mounting suspense and then final catharsis in laughter" (Hitchcock 1959).

Finally, Hitchcock hoped through these articles to convey the idea that suspense stories were effective treatment for relieving tension:

> Of course the world of the suspense story is a world of make-believe. Of course it is what the critics call "escape." But is that bad? These are entertainments, designed to take you out of yourself, to make you believe while you read, or look at a screen, in the reality of what is there. When it is over, when the criminal is properly trapped and you are returned to your private worries, you find that your little excursion has made your mind clearer, your nerves calmer, your problems somehow easier to attack. (Hitchcock 1957b)

Hitchcock also sensitized his public to certain questionable practices in the thriller film such as employing shock tactics which, he claimed, could undermine the bond between the filmmaker and his audience. For one thing, the bomb or bomb-equivalent in a suspense sequence should never actually go off, killing innocent victims such as children in its wake. In his 1937 film *Sabotage* a bomb had gone off, killing not only the child carrying it but other innocent victims as well. The film did poorly at the box office. Hitchcock claimed that he received a number of letters from fans upset about the sequence. (British critic C. J. Lejeune also complained about it.) Thus, it was Hitchcock's experience with *Sabotage* that had taught him the valuable lesson to be respectful of audience expectations which he now wanted to pass on to his fans and fellow filmmakers.

In addition to disseminating through newspaper and magazine articles the recurring elements of his movies, Hitchcock also identified the generic features of his TV series—reliance on the short-story formula of a simple tale which "builds to a surprise turn or twist at the end," characters who are average people but find themselves placed in strange and bizarre situations, and, of course, the employment of suspense followed by relief from its symptoms through humor.[23] Hitchcock often highlighted the differences between the TV series and his movies, thereby further solidifying, in my view, the differences in audience expectations concerning his work in motion pictures and television. Articles juxtaposed descriptions of the increasing lavishness of Hitchcock's Hollywood films, particularly those made since 1950, with judgments that Hitchcock had found television a suitable outlet for his earlier, less flamboyant style. Indeed, the authors of a special *Newsweek* article on Hitchcock appearing in 1956 hoped he would take more advantage of his connection with television:

> As for Hitchcock's older and less lavish style, the solution is obvious. It is ideally suited to the strictly confined, claustrophobic world of TV drama. If he would just pitch in himself, he could, thanks to television's vast coverage, curdle half America's blood, give their spines a salutary tingle and raise their hair, right in their own parlors once a week. The medium could use this help. (*Newsweek*, 1956)

Several articles also reinforced audience expectations that, unlike his teleplays, Hitchcock's feature films always ended affirmatively. A number of commentators had complained about Hitchcock selling out to Hollywood with the mandatory happy ending, pointing to recent films such as *Rear Window* (1954), *To Catch A Thief* (1955), and *The Man Who Knew Too Much* (1956) as evidence (see, e.g., *New Yorker*, 26 May 1956). Defending himself, Hitchcock blamed the Hollywood studios and, indirectly, the moviegoing public for forcing him to make such upbeat escapist fare. To make a film with "an unhappy ending," he said, was "to commit the unforgiveable Hollywood sin called 'being downbeat.'" Much to his surprise, Hitchcock had found television more receptive to experimentation than the movies. Although he met some resistance from the network and sponsors, Hitchcock told journalists that he was allowed to end his TV films "on a downbeat note as often as not." This was allowed, he implied, because TV audiences were more sophisticated and tolerant. In one article, Hitchcock offered the following sociological insight to explain why TV audiences were more flexible than film audiences:

> I believe we too often underestimate the intelligence of the grown-up audience. They are grown-up, you see, when they are getting something for free in their own homes. They become children again when they have to pay. The drive to the theater, the parking lot, the ticket at the box office, they expect something cheerful. They like the happy ending. After all, why should they pay their good money just to be made miserable? (*TV Guide*, 1957)

The TV show's consistently high Nielsen ratings during the fifties suggest that Hitchcock was more successful in meeting audience expectations with his TV series than with his feature films. While his two most lavish and upbeat films from this period, *The Man Who Knew Too Much* (1956) and *North by Northwest* (1959), were popular with audiences, two of his other films from the late 1950s, *The Wrong Man* (1956) and *Vertigo* (1958), performed sluggishly at the box office, the latter films failing commercially, as I shall argue, partly because they lacked some of the key ingredients which audiences had come to associate with Hitchcock's films from the fifties—wit, charm, and, of course, the mandatory happy ending.

In addition to his audience, Hitchcock's inner circle of co-workers on the TV series also judged his work against the formulas and impressions that he himself had created and exploited through the media. Their devotion to maintaining "the spirit of Hitchcock" in the teleplays was probably a major reason why the program lasted as long as it did. Moreover, the input from Hitchcock's co-workers on the series also reinforced the popular view of Hitchcock and his work that evolved in the fifties. With little coaxing from the Master, his TV associates succeeded in reducing his work to a formula that was so powerful yet sufficiently unsubtle that it could easily be copied. Both Joan Harrison and Norman Lloyd, who co-produced the series, judged potential properties according to a rather narrow set of guidelines. With few exceptions, they adhered religiously to these guidelines throughout Hitchcock's ten-year stint on prime-time television. By always trying to please him, Hitchcock's associates became, in some sense, more Hitchcockian than Hitchcock himself. Thus, an important source of the TV show's consistency was that Hitchcock's co-producers were strongly committed to maintaining that consistency. In a sense, they too helped popularize the fifties view of Hitchcock as entertainer, showman, and master of the thriller form. Some background on the actual workings of Hitchcock's TV series will illustrate this point.

As mentioned earlier, "Alfred Hitchcock Presents," premiered in the fall of 1955. Early that year Hitchcock had developed specific guidelines for the series. In a letter dated February 24, 1955, he instructed a researcher based in England to start doing some special research and reading of short stories by well-known authors. "The type of short story," Hitchcock wrote, "should definitely be of the suspense, or thriller type. It can be, for example, a ghost story, if necessary, but there is one important factor that should be common to all of them, and that is that the ending should have a 'twist' almost to a point of a shock in either the last line or the last situation." Hitchcock requested that the researcher assemble around one hundred such properties, indicating that eventually the list would "be whittled down to possibly forty for a final choice" (TV Production Files, Hitchcock Collection).

The shock or surprise ending became an important part of the Hitchcock gospel according to Harrison and Lloyd. The only stories they seriously considered for the series were those which contained these twists or surprises at the end. After reviewing such stories, Harrison and Lloyd would have them summarized and then send them on to Hitchcock for his approval. Typically, all he would do is say "Yes, I like it," or "I don't like it," or "I don't know, why don't you put it on a reserve list?" (Lloyd 1977).

In that rare instance when Hitchcock did comment on a summary, his concern usually revolved around what he referred to as the "key shot" of a film, that is, the one that would deliver the payoff or revelation. The synopsis for the teleplay of "An Unlocked Window" (1965), for example, caused some concern. The story focuses on a female nurse who, we learn, has murdered some of her patients. Not until the final shot is it revealed that the murderer is actually a female impersonator. According to Lloyd, who directed this particular show, Hitchcock asked him who was going to play the nurse. Lloyd was considering hiring a real-life female impersonator, T. C. Jones, for the role. Hitchcock thought that a good idea. However, Hitchcock wanted to know how it would be revealed to the audience that the nurse was really a male in drag. Lloyd informed Hitchcock that T. C. Jones would wear a wig which would accidentally come off. Hitchcock did not believe this scenario would work because T. C. Jones was rather feminine-looking to begin with. If only the wig were removed, one might think that it was a woman whose hair was shaven. According to Hitchcock, the fact that it was not a woman but a man could only be strictly established by a revelation of the chest of the actor. "That is why," recalls Lloyd, [the show ends with] that shot of the hairy chest of T. C. Jones. That became the key shot. Now you know it was a man. I thought that was really thinking ahead. Because you could have been left thinking, 'Was it a man or woman?' Then your whole picture would be defeated" (Lloyd 1977).

Once Hitchcock approved a story, Lloyd and Harrison would hire a writer and together develop a script. While Hitchcock never actually looked at a preliminary script, he would look at the rough-cut version of the picture after it was shot. Then, according to Lloyd, Hitchcock would usually say, "Well, maybe you need a close-up or an insert or something." "That," says Lloyd, "was the extent he played in the actual making of it. He never got down to drawing it" (Lloyd 1977). So, except for final script approval, Hitchcock's direct input on the vast majority of shows was minimal.

Yet, although Hitchcock directed only 20 of the 372 shows aired during the series' ten-year history, many of the shows not directed by Hitchcock *seem* to have been directed by him; the so-called "Hitchcock touch" is still much in evidence. As mentioned earlier, Hitchcock's psychological presence during the production of his TV series was very strong. "The whole style of the series," recalls Lloyd, "was totally influenced by his style. The suspense with humor, with irony, with twist; it is totally Hitchcock. So our whole point of view . . . is sort of, well, it was his point of view that we were looking for . . . in stories" (Lloyd 1977).

Hitchcock's psychological presence was also evident during the actual filming of the teleplays. This is reflected in one of the most memorable teleplays from the series, "Man From the South" (1960), which Lloyd himself directed. Two men meet in a Las Vegas barroom. The younger man (Steve McQueen) makes a bet with the older man (Peter Lorre). If McQueen can get his cigarette lighter to work ten times in succession, Lorre will give him his brand-new convertible. On the other hand, if McQueen loses he must give up the little finger on his left hand; that is, if McQueen loses, Lorre chops off the finger. In preparation for the contest, Lorre ties McQueen's left hand to a table so that only the little finger can freely move. Each time McQueen prepares to use the lighter, Lorre lifts a butcher's chopping knife as if to get ready to chop off the finger should McQueen's lighter fail to light. McQueen is able to get the lighter to work seven times in succession. The filming of each lighting sequence is reminiscent of Hitchcock at his best. Each sequence is shot from a different angle. Moreover, two supporting characters in the story, McQueen's girlfriend and a middle-aged man who is refereeing the contest, function as surrogates for the audience as the tension mounts. However, it is in the teleplay's final moments that the "Hitchcock touch" is most evident. Before McQueen attempts to ignite the lighter for the eighth time, Lorre's wife arrives to bring a halt to the contest. We learn from the wife that Lorre has been engaging in such contests for years. During a recent binge, he severed no less than forty-seven fingers and lost eleven cars. At the close of her speech, we learn that Lorre's wife is at least as deranged as her husband. After informing McQueen that the car belongs to her and not her husband, she continues, "No. He had nothing to bet with, I assure you. Nothing in this world. I managed to win it all. It took a long time and it was very hard work. But I won it all in the end." While Lorre's wife is delivering the above speech, the camera moves in to reveal that the middle three fingers of her left hand are missing—a shot which Hitchcockians are quick to point out is reminiscent of the camera movement in Hitchcock's 1935 classic, *The 39 Steps*, which reveals Professor Jordan's missing finger, thus exposing his complicity in the foreign plot against England. In discussing this teleplay with students at the American Film Institute, Lloyd suggested that Hitchcock had no direct input in the making of it. Yet, ending it with the shot of the wife's missing fingers may have seemed to Lloyd the only way to go in light of how the Master had shot that functionally similar sequence in his 1935 classic. Though effective, the ending of "Man From the South" seems highly derivative of *The 39 Steps*, illustrating how matter-of-factly such copies were made.

In sum, during the fifties Hitchcock coaxed his fans into evaluating his feature films and TV work according to the guidelines he himself developed and disseminated to them. Similar rules of thumb also shaped the production of his TV series. Hitchcock's co-producers, as a matter of course, filmed the teleplays as they imagined Hitchcock would have done them. As a result, Hitchcock's collaborators on the series reinforced the view of Hitchcock as entertainer, showman, and master of suspense that so dominated the way both audiences and critics viewed him during much of the fifties and sixties.

AUDIENCE AND CRITICAL REACTIONS TO HITCHCOCK'S FEATURE FILMS BETWEEN 1955 AND 1960

In order to maximize a film's performance in the marketplace, a filmmaker with a well-established reputation must manage or take into account that reputation each time he or she is about to release a new film, especially if the film deviates in significant ways from the type of film audiences expect routinely from the director. With his TV shows, Hitchcock had been able to establish a generic contract with his TV audience. By routinely referring to a body of conventional understandings—a framework of clearly defined form and content—Hitchcock and his colleagues achieved some measure of control over the audience's reception of his TV shows.[24] With his feature films, on the other hand, he had to renegotiate the aesthetic contract with his audience and with the critics each time a new film came out. His successes and failures at both luring audiences to his feature films and shaping the critical response to them are the subject of the present section.

Consider first the promotional strategies for *The Man Who Knew*

Too Much (1956), released seven months after Hitchcock's TV series premiered. Unlike the press materials for other feature films made during the period of his TV shows, promotional and publicity materials for this film were relatively straightforward. In addition to identifying *The Man Who Knew Too Much* as a remake of Hitchcock's 1934 spy thriller which inaugurated the "classical" Hitchcock period, the press releases emphasized the film's entertainment values. The press kit accentuated the film's lavish production values—a Technicolor and widescreen thriller extravaganza shot on location in northern Africa and London and featuring two top-drawing stars, Jimmy Stewart and Doris Day (see plate 10). Another selling point was the film's humor. In an article appearing close to the film's release date, *Newsweek* featured an in-depth report on Hitchcock (referred to earlier) which examined, among other things, the famous "Hitchcock touch," especially his habit of introducing humor as a way of relieving "the tension that he builds before it becomes ridiculous or downright unbearable." As evidence that Hitchcock had not lost his touch, the article referred to a running gag. When the suspense gets too unbearable, Hitchcock shifts to a "party of silly Britishers" who are waiting through much of the film for their host, the character played by Jimmy Stewart, to return from his errands to join them for tea. They are left completely in the dark about the fact that Stewart's son has been kidnapped, making their banter seem doubly ridiculous but also chillingly ironic. Whenever possible, Hitchcock used promotional opportunities for *The Man Who Knew Too Much* to stress the similarities between his work in television and motion pictures. For example, Hitchcock told a *Los Angeles Times* reporter that there was nothing fundamentally different between filling a small TV screen and one 90 feet wide by 64 feet high. "Yet in this movie," says Hitchcock, "I still fill that vast screen at one point with Jimmy's [James Stewart] mouth whispering into the ear of another man. And I would do that no matter what the size of the screen. I have a purpose in it. I must isolate that whisper. I must focus on it away from the rest of the scene. That use of isolation, of focus, that is the art of telling stories on the screen, whatever the size" (*Los Angeles Times,* 1955). Hitchcock, then, chose to sell *The Man Who Knew Too Much* as a typical Hitchcock film in much the same spirit of his recent Paramount hits and current TV show but on a considerably grander scale.

The Man Who Knew Too Much performed solidly at the box office and received generally favorable reviews, especially in newspapers and periodicals directed to the more general public.[25] Again, it was characteristic of reviewers to discuss the film in relation to Hitchcock's previous works. (Indeed, I found not a single reference to a non-Hitchcock film.) Many reviews stressed that Hitchcock, after making several detours, had returned to his specialty, the international spy thriller. As the reviewer for the *Los Angeles Mirror-News* succinctly put it, "After experimenting with whimsy, romantic jewel thievery and pictures filmed entirely on one set, Director Alfred Hitchcock returns to a more familiar forte. . . . His subject is international intrigue" (*Los Angeles Mirror-News*, 23 May 1956). Reviewers also praised the film's suspense, humor, and scale, echoing the slants of the film's publicity campaign.

Many reviewers also discussed the 1956 *The Man Who Knew Too Much* in relation to Hitchcock's 1934 version. Like the majority of the New York critics, Bosley Crowther (1956) compared the remake quite favorably to the original. According to Crowther, Hitchcock had "cleverly combined his old style and modern screen processes of Vista-Vision and color" to make a thriller which still had "punch" (see also the *New York Herald Tribune*, 1956). In his opinion, the film worked because Hitchcock had been faithful to his earlier published pronouncements about what constituted an effective thriller. In fact, Crowther believed that the current *The Man Who Knew Too Much* even surpassed *Rear Window*. One of his reservations about the earlier film was that Hitchcock had waited too long to place his characters "in a high state of peril and suspense" (15 August 1954). By contrast, Hitchcock, from the beginning of his "lean" and "fluid" remake of *The Man Who Knew Too Much,* compels his characters to be on the move, as he always did, according to Crowther, in his best films, where the "chase" was the main source of the film's excitement (cf. Crowther 1954b to Crowther 1956). As Crowther pointed out to his readers, Hitchcock had "virtually educated critics in the techniques and refinements of the 'chase'" (Crowther 1956). Six years earlier, for example, Hitchcock had discussed the role of "the chase" in an interview published in the *New York Times Sunday Magazine* (Hitchcock 1950).

Overall, the critics for prestigious or elitist publications such as the *New Yorker* and *Saturday Review* were more likely to discuss the film in relation to the 1934 version than were those journalistic reviewers catering to more mainstream moviegoers. Among those who compared the two versions, the highbrow critics were considerably more inclined than other reviewers to regard the current version as inferior to the original. These critics who believed that Hitchcock's recent Hollywood films did not measure up to his British thrillers from the 1930s used the release of the American version of *The Man Who Knew Too Much* as another opportunity to complain about the Hollywood Hitchcock (see, e.g., *New Yorker,* 26 May 1956, and *Nation,* 9 June 1956).[26] For example, critics of the 1956 version attacked Hitchcock's use of box-office stars like James Stewart and Doris Day, the picture-post-card settings in exotic French Morocco, the "gimmicky" VistaVision wide-screen process, and the film's glossy Technicolor look. The length of the film also annoyed them. The film ran for 120 minutes, while the original took only 74 (see, e.g., *New Yorker,* 26 May 1956; *Saturday Review,* 26 May 1956; *Nation,* 9 June 1956). As a result of its gargantuan length, according to these highbrow critics, the remake's fundamental weakness—its implausibility—was all too apparent. "This weakness," wrote *Nation* critic Robert Hatch, "was probably in the original but if the action swirled fast enough, no one would have objected. Now you have what seem like hours to poke holes in the unbalanced equations." (For virtually identical views, see the *New Yorker* 1956, and the *Saturday Review* 1956.) For the more intellectual critics, then, the restraint and understatement of the "British Hitchcock" were clearly superior to the high-gloss excesses of the "Paramount Hitchcock." (Most British reviewers, incidentally, agreed with this assessment.)[27]

Still, the overall critical response to the remake of *The Man Who Knew Too Much* was favorable. Indeed, the film's solid box-office performance seemed to mirror the overall positive critical response among more mainstream reviewers. It was the Hitchcock who had brought to the screen this film and, earlier, *Rear Window,* that would shape how mainstream critics and (I would argue) audiences alike would respond to his subsequent works during the fifties.

Hitchcock's next film, *The Wrong Man* (released in late December 1956), for Warner Bros., was so different in subject and scale from *The Man Who Knew Too Much* and his other Paramount releases that Hitchcock decided to prepare his public for it. Based on a real incident, this bleak and depressing film tells the story of an ordinary man, Christopher (Manny) Balestrero of Queens, New York, a Stork Club bass player, who is arrested for a crime he did not commit. Much of the film was shot on location, in Queens and Manhattan. "I've seen many stories about the arrest of an innocent man from the point of view of his champion—a lawyer or reporter, and so on," explained Hitchcock to a reporter who interviewed him during the shooting, "but it is never told from the point of view of the person who underwent the ordeal" (Esterow 1956). And what an ordeal it is, for Manny and his family, especially his wife, who as a result of his pending conviction suffers a nervous breakdown and is committed.

Much of the publicity for *The Wrong Man* honestly conveyed that the film represented a significant and serious departure for Hitchcock. Promotional materials earmarked for the press stressed the serious nature of the project and its uniqueness for Hitchcock. The production notes are particularly revealing. They report that, for the first time, Hitchcock has transferred to the screen "a great drama from real life"— events which many New Yorkers read about in local newspapers only a few short years ago (1953). The production notes also mention that Hitchcock assembled an unusually distinguished ensemble of collaborators, including Pulitzer-Prize-winning playwright Maxwell Anderson and the prolific British screenwriter Angus MacPhail, who worked with Hitchcock on the development of the screenplay. Most of the production story, however, is organized around the numerous things Hitchcock did to add to the realism of the film. He shot the film in black and white. In addition, he included in his cast many "talented performers drawn from the stage" with whom motion picture audiences were not familiar. He also took great care to be as historically accurate as possible. "He not only visited, measured and inspected every real-life locale for the story, but also had his staff record with stop-watch accuracy the way the subway ran at the time of the events depicted in *The Wrong Man,* the block-by-block itinerary of the hero and the experiences of all the principal characters in the drama." Moreover, scenes were shot on location—at the Stork Club, the Queens subway, the city's police stations and court rooms—which meant that a good deal of the filming had to take place at night, when these public places were relatively free of people. Finally, Hitchcock even insisted that Henry Fonda, who played Manny, take bass lessons "until he could play a repertoire of dance tunes with professional ease" (Production Notes, *The Wrong Man,* Warner Bros. Archives).

Hitchcock also spoke directly to his audience about the seriousness of his latest film. Consider the trailer for *The Wrong Man,* in which Hitchcock makes a personal appearance, announcing to his fans that the hero of his latest film would be nothing at all like the criminal types that dominated his television show:

> This is Alfred Hitchcock speaking. In the past I have introduced you to many kinds of people; murderers, thieves, swindlers. Many of them geniuses of the business of crime. Now I'd like you to meet an entirely different person . . . an average sort of fellow who

leads a very normal life. . . . The big difference is that his story is true. (Transcript, Warner Bros. Archives)

After describing the straight and narrow routine of Manny's life, from "tucked away at the rear of the bandstand of the Stork Club in New York," and then to "the same subway, the newspaper, home to Rose and the kids," Hitchcock shows the horror of his arrest and imprisonment. "What twist of fate could take the quiet soul of a simple man," asks Hitchcock, "and wring it into a shape like this" (see plate 11).

In the prologue to the actual film, Hitchcock makes a brief appearance, reiterating how atypical *The Wrong Man* is compared to his other thrillers:

> This is Alfred Hitchcock speaking. In the past I have given you many kinds of suspense pictures, but this time I would like you to see a different one. The difference lies in the fact that this is a true story, every word of it. And yet it contains elements that are stranger than the fiction that has gone into many of the thrillers that I have made before.[28]

Overall, critical response to *The Wrong Man* was positive.[29] Typical were the New York newspaper reviewers, a majority of whom gave the film rave notices. What mainstream reviewers most admired about the film was that Hitchcock had attempted something bold and out of character. Except for a minority of mostly highbrow critics, the consensus was that Hitchcock had met the challenge with great aplomb. It is interesting how closely the mainstream reviews reflected the spirit of the official studio interpretation of the film as represented in studio promotional materials. Despite the generally favorable critical assessment, the film did not have a successful commercial run in 1957, earning less than one million dollars in domestic rentals.

Of course, not having detailed survey data about the moviegoing public's tastes around the release date of *The Wrong Man,* one cannot know with any degree of certainty why audiences rejected the film. However, by examining some of the variation in the critical response to the film, we may discover some important clues as to why it did not perform better than it did.

While the vast majority of critics admired Hitchcock's effort at trying something different, reviewers for mass-circulation newspapers such as the *New York Daily News* and the *Los Angeles Examiner* were more likely to unequivocally praise the film than were reviewers for more prestigious and influential publications such as the *New York Times* and the *Los Angeles Times*. The pattern of reviews suggests that the most favorable reviews were directed to readers least likely to be interested in viewing a film that apparently deviated so dramatically from Hitchcock's more entertaining thrillers. By characterizing *The Wrong Man* as a film that departed significantly from the Paramount Hitchcock, reviewers may have unintentionally turned off the more mainstream movie patron who preferred a conventional Hitchcock film to one apparently inspired by Italian neorealism. Consider, for example, the *New York Daily News* review of the film. While praising it (*"The Wrong Man* is very fine drama, a thought-provoking film based on an actual miscarriage of justice . . ."), the reviewer also pointed out how dramatically different it was from the more standard Hitchcock fare (*"The Wrong Man* is an Alfred Hitchcock picture, not a typical Hitchcock picture, so don't expect excitement, humor and suspense . . . " — 24 December 1956). What I would like to suggest here is that while Hitchcock's promotional efforts may have succeeded in convincing mainstream reviewers of the film's merits, the reviews probably alienated the filmgoers who routinely attended a Hitchcock film to be entertained, not to be stimulated intellectually.

The likely market for *The Wrong Man* should have been the more educated filmgoer who after the war had discovered the European art film. Before the fifties, the American film industry had viewed its potential market as a more or less undifferentiated mass. All films—the artistic and commercial—were directed to the same homogeneous mass audience. As Richard Schickel observed, "There was no great temptation to appeal to a small group of *cognoscenti*" (Schickel 1964, 162). However, by the early 1950s, that mass audience had become fragmented. Not only was it smaller (partly a result of competition from television), the movie audience was also, according to film historian Robert Ray, "sharply divided between what Pauline Kael came to call 'the art-house crowd' and old-fashioned, entertainment-seeking moviegoers. To an extent, one could have accounted for the rise of the art-house audience by certain practical facts: in the postwar period, there were more foreign films being imported into the United States than ever before and more theaters to show them in. Cut loose from the studios by antitrust decrees, small movie houses previously content to play fourth-runs now converted to foreign features in order to survive" (Ray 1985, 138). Among the most successful of the foreign imports were the Italian neorealistic films. "With their harsh frankness about postwar realities, movies like *Open City, Shoeshine, Paisan,* and *The Bicycle Thief,*" con-

1. Hitchcock on location at Lake Como in Italy directing
his first film, *The Pleasure Garden* (prod. 1925/rel. 1927).
Hitchcock Collection, Academy of Motion Picture Arts and Sciences.

2. A scene from Hitchcock's first film, *The Pleasure Garden*.
Hitchcock Collection, Academy of Motion Picture Arts and Sciences.

3. Ivor Novello in *The Lodger*, Hitchcock's first commercial
and critical success (prod. 1926/rel. 1927).

Hitchcock Collection, Academy of Motion Picture Arts and Sciences.

4. Peter Lorre (center) in the 1934 British
version of *The Man Who Knew Too Much*.
Museum of Modern Art Film Stills Archive.

5. Hitchcock had to smuggle himself fat and
thin into one of his early American films,
Lifeboat (1943), by means of a newspaper.
Museum of Modern Art Film Stills Archive.

6. James Stewart and Grace Kelly
in *Rear Window* (1954).
Museum of Modern Art Film Stills Archive.

7. Hitchcock hosting his television series
that was launched in 1955.

8. Hitchcock masquerading
as Lady Agatha, *This Week
Magazine* (1957).
Hitchcock Collection, Academy of
Motion Picture Arts and Sciences.

9. Hitchcock and his wife, Alma, at home (ca. 1955).
Hitchcock Collection, Academy of Motion Picture Arts and Sciences.

10. Advertisment for the 1956 Hollywood version of *The Man Who Knew Too Much*.

Paramount Collection, Academy of Motion Picture Arts and Sciences.

"THE WRONG MAN"
(TRAILER)
(DIALOGUE TRANSCRIPT)

HITCHCOCK: This is Alfred Hitchcock speaking. In the past I have introduced you to many kinds of people; murderers, thieves, swindlers. Many of them geniuses of the business of crime. Now I'd like you to meet an entirely different person, --

HITCHCOCK'S VOICE: --an average sort of fellow who leads a very normal life.
INSERTS:
STORK CLUB CROWD: (signs along street) FORD'S CUT RATE DRUGS
(on and off)
(chatter not distinct continues beh'nd following speech)

HITCHCOCK'S VOICE: The big difference is that his story is true. This is Manny Balestrero, tucked away at the rear o' the bandstand of the Stork Club in New York. He lived in a simple routine world. When the lights went out the fiddle was put away. Then the same subway, the newspaper, home to Rose and the kids. Yes, Manny's life was straight and narrow until the night of January the fourteenth, Nineteen fifty-three, when ---

BOWERS: Is your name Christopher Emanuel Balestrero?

MANNY: Yes, it is.

BOWERS: We wanta speak to you. We're police officers.

MANNY: What about?

BOWERS: .....How do you explain it?

MANNY: I made a mistake.

BOWERS: And so did the holdup man! And it happens to be the same mistake.

TOMASINI: .....Do you see the man who was in your office on July the ninth in this courtroom

MRS. JAMES: Yes.

TOMASINI: Will you step down an' point 'im out to us?

MRS. JAMES: (off)
Right there.

HITCHCOCK'S VOICE: What twist of fate could take the quiet soul of a simple man and wring it into a shape like this.

INSERT: (over cell door)   222

DISSOLVE IN
TITLE:
              EVERY STEP
           A JOURNEY IN
              DARKNESS

DISSOLVE IN
TITLE:
              EVERY MOMENT
           AN ETERNITY OF
              SUSPENSE

11. Dialogue transcript of the trailer for
The Wrong Man (1956).
Warner Brothers Archives, University of Southern
California.

12. The Saul Bass-inspired "art" ad for
Vertigo dropped by the studio (1958).
Paramount Collection, Academy of Motion Picture
Arts and Sciences.

13. Hitchcock as part of Mount Rushmore in an ad for
North By Northwest (1959).
MGM Collection, Academy of Motion Picture Arts and Sciences.

14. Cary Grant in the "classic" crop duster
sequence from *North by Northwest* (1959).
Museum of Modern Art Film Stills Archive

15. The ad for *Psycho* featuring Janet Leigh, a bold image for its time (1960).

tinues Ray, "had no possibility of widespread acceptance. But the discovery that there was an audience sizable enough to make even these bleak movies profitable unsettled the American film industry" (Ray 1985, 138). For the sophisticated art-house patron who had become "Europeanized" by recent events—World War II, the atom bomb, and the Cold War, the European art film was becoming the new aesthetic model for assessing whether a film was important or significant.[30] Hitchcock's *The Wrong Man* should have appealed to that group. However, the art-house patrons were more likely to read reviews appearing in more prestigious newspapers and periodicals such as the *New York Times,* the *Los Angeles Times,* the *New Yorker,* the *Saturday Review,* and the *New Republic.* Unfortunately for Hitchcock the reviews appearing in more sophisticated publications tended to pan the film. That is, the more prestigious or elitist a publication, the more likely it gave *The Wrong Man* a negative review (see the reviews in the *New York Times,* 1956;[31] the *Los Angeles Times,* 1957; the *New Yorker,* 1957; and the *Saturday Review,* 1957; cf. the more positive but guarded review in the *Nation,* 1957). The *Saturday Review*'s assessment was typical. While conceding that *The Wrong Man* was better than Hitchcock's more recent films, the reviewer still did not believe that it was a very good film: "the movie might have emerged as a very good one, indeed, if it were not for the fact that he has shown more interest in the details of justice than in the emotions of his characters" (*Saturday Review,* 1957). Other periodicals catering to a more highbrow audience, such as the *New Republic,* didn't even bother to review it.[32]

After the bleakness and harshness of *The Wrong Man,* many of his fans must have hoped that with his next film, *Vertigo,* Hitchcock would return to the type of romantic suspense thriller that audiences (and critics) had come to expect from him. *Vertigo* proved not to be that type of film. Before describing the promotional campaign for the film, I would like to convey by way of a brief synopsis the extent to which the film represented a significant departure for Hitchcock.

Scottie, a former cop who experiences dizzy spells when looking down from great heights, is hired to tail his client's wife, Madeleine, who, according to her husband, has been engaging in bizarre behavior. Scottie, after rescuing her from one suicide attempt, is unsuccessful in preventing her the next time, when she ascends a tower only to fall to her death. After suffering a nervous breakdown following his failure to protect Madeleine, with whom he had fallen in love, Scottie is hospitalized for roughly a year before returning to his regular haunts. Still obsessed with the memory of Madeleine, he finds a woman (Judy) who reminds him of Madeleine. He attempts to transform her into a Madeleine look-alike. By this point in the film, the audience has already learned that Judy had been hired by Scottie's client to masquerade as his wife, as part of a plot to murder his real wife while making it appear that her death was a suicide. Eventually, Scottie figures out that Judy and Madeleine are one and the same. Returning to the scene of the crime, Scottie forces Judy to ascend the tower with him. Although there is the promise for no more than a split second that all will be forgiven and that their mutually felt love for one another will be consummated, the film ends in tragedy as Scottie helplessly watches Judy/Madeleine fall to her death. The power of this final scene is beautifully conveyed in the following excerpt from a recent commentary on the film:

> An astonishing burst of applause greeted the penultimate mo-
> ments of Alfred Hitchcock's 1958 *Vertigo* at the performance I at-
> tended last week—astonishing because, only seconds later, the
> film's real ending left the audience gasping in disbelief. Those who
> had cheered the happy-looking near-finale must not have seen *Ver-*
> *tigo* before. They must have been caught off-guard by this film's
> stubborn, single-minded intensity, and by its uncharacteristic (for
> Hitchcock) reluctance to please. (Maslin 1984)

The early information that was made available to the public did not adequately prepare audiences for such a downbeat film. Rather, the early publicity seemed more compatible with the type of romantic thriller associated with the Paramount Hitchcock. The new film would star James Stewart and Kim Novak, would be shot in color and VistaVision, and would take place in San Francisco. On the surface, then, *Vertigo* seemed to have all the trappings of the Paramount Hitchcock. It had big-name stars—James Stewart, who judging from fan polls conducted at that time, was the most popular Hollywood actor during most of the fifties. The dual role of Madeleine/Judy would be played by Kim Novak, on loan from Columbia where she was being both groomed and pro-moted as Hollywood's next sex goddess. Like many other films of the fifties, *Vertigo* also seemed to have an eye on the tourist trade or, more precisely, on those who liked to be vicariously transported to glamorous and scenic spots like the French Riviera, French Morocco, and San Francisco. Wide-screen processes such as Cinerama, Todd AO, Cinema-Scope, and Paramount's own VistaVision were technical means implemented by Hollywood during the fifties to enhance this illusion of transport to exotic places. The movie as travelogue had become one of Hollywood's strategies, along with biblical films, for coping with the onslaught of television by offering something—spectacle—that television itself plainly could not deliver. Interestingly, Hitchcock had decided on his stars and the San Francisco locale early in the production process, well before Samuel Taylor's script for the film was completed. Indeed, Hitchcock's production designer, Henry Bumstead, had already made several trips to San Francisco to scout locations. "These circumstances," writes film scholar Virginia Wright Wexman, "suggest that the stars and locations were primary considerations in the director's mind, and that the actual script and story were a secondary and contingent concern" (1986, 34). In other words, it would seem that the more commercial aspects of the film, "its stars and its status as travelogue," had been on Hitchcock's mind from the start. Much of the advance publicity for the film would underscore these elements as well. Moreover, there was no indication that with *Vertigo* Hitchcock would be presenting a different side of his persona. The biographical profile of Hitchcock which Paramount prepared for the press prior to the film's release simply rehashed the familiar ingredients of Hitchcock's persona that he had worked so hard to plant in the public's imagination—his obesity, his macabre sense of humor, and his talents as both producer and director of entertaining suspense thrillers. (Between 1954 and 1958, Paramount's official biography on Hitchcock hardly changed at all.)

In the early promotional materials for the film, there were no hints that *Vertigo* would be qualitatively different from many of Hitchcock's recent Paramount hits. The radio spots and promotional articles appearing in Paramount's press book for *Vertigo* also reinforced the impression that the film would be more in the spirit of Hitchcock's other recent successes at Paramount—*Rear Window, To Catch A Thief,* and *The Man Who Knew Too Much*—than the bold departure it really was. Consider, for example, the well-chosen elements making up the twenty-word radio spot for the film, which, except for the teaser about not revealing the ending, in no way distinguishes *Vertigo* from Hitchcock's other lavish Paramount productions: "See Alfred Hitchcock's greatest . . . 'Vertigo', Paramount's Technicolor, VistaVision, thriller, starring James Stewart, Kim Novak . . . and don't tell the ending."

The vast majority of publicity articles included in the press book characterized *Vertigo* as simply another film in the grand Hitchcockian tradition of "suspense-without-horror": "A new motion picture produced by the master of suspense-without-horror, Alfred Hitchcock, comes under the heading of big entertainment news for show-wise fans who rightly have come to expect from the famed producer-director exciting, edge-of-seat thrills." The only real news about the film was that it featured two big stars—James Stewart and Kim Novak: "When, as is the case with Hitchcock's new Paramount production, *Vertigo*, the names of stars James Stewart and Kim Novak head the cast, then the news is big indeed."[33]

On the other hand, a number of the original newspaper ads for *Vertigo*, which contain swirling lines adapted from Saul Bass's opening graphics for the film, suggest a more poetic and less mainstream film, which in fact it was (see plate 12). The idea for this ad design was Hitchcock's, and Paramount reluctantly went along with it. However, a few days after the film's release, when it became clear that audiences were not flocking to see it, Paramount blamed the Bass-inspired ads, and Paramount's East Coast marketing office hurriedly put together a new design. The new ads for the film conveyed the impression that *Vertigo* was simply another great thriller in the tradition of Hitchcock's other recent Paramount triumphs. Typical of this approach was a newspaper ad featuring more representational renderings of key events and settings from the film—the Golden Gate Bridge, Novak in bed with Stewart by her side, a female body falling from a tower with a tiny male figure discernible at the top looking down, and a realistic representation of the Stewart and Novak characters engaged in physical combat. The size and positioning of the lettering for the ad also gave more prominence to the film's stars than did the earlier Hitchcock-inspired ads such as the one displayed in the *New York Times,* which characterized *Vertigo* as "Hitchcock's masterpiece."

The impact of Paramount's new ad campaign for *Vertigo* appears to have been negligible.[34] After its first year of release, *Vertigo* had earned significantly less than did *Rear Window, To Catch A Thief,* and *The Man Who Knew Too Much* during comparable periods. What the marketing campaign for *Vertigo* had failed to accomplish was to convey to audiences that *Vertigo* was a very different type of film from what audiences had come to expect from the Hitchcock-Paramount collaboration.[35] Hitchcock's decision to reveal the solution to the mystery two-thirds of the way through the film not only annoyed some critics (see, e.g., Knight 1958; cf. Lejeune 1958) but probably many members of the general public as well. The film's tragic ending, in addition, must have upset viewers expecting a more conventional Hollywood finish. At no time during *Vertigo*'s publicity campaign, as we have seen, did Hitchcock really prepare audiences for these significant deviations from the standard Hitchcock thriller. Nor did the reviewers of the film alert moviegoers that the film was a dramatic departure from what they had come to expect from Hitchcock. Indeed, many reviewers for daily newspapers characterized *Vertigo* as vintage Hitchcock (Crowther, *New York Times* 1958a; *New York Daily News* 1958; and *Los Angeles Examiner* 1958; cf. Griffith 1958b). None divulged the film's surprise ending or commented on any other unusual twists and turns of its plot. The real surprise for filmgoers came, I suggest, when they discovered how different the film was from the usual Hitchcock work. The problem with *Vertigo*, then, was not that Hitchcock's advertising campaign or the initial reviews kept audiences away. Rather it was that the early filmgoers who saw it were disappointed because of its deviations from the more conventional Hitchcock thriller and, thus, complained about the film to family, friends, and acquaintances.

Vertigo generated a wide spectrum of critical response, making it difficult to accept any simple causal hypothesis concerning the relationship between *Vertigo*'s advertising campaign and the critical response to the film. Contrary to recent commentary that the first generation of reviewers and critics responded unsympathetically to *Vertigo*, we find, at least among the daily newspaper reviewers, that the response was generally very positive. Bosley Crowther's reaction was fairly typical. Like other New York reviewers, Crowther chose not to jeopardize audience enjoyment by divulging any of Hitchcock's surprises, except to mention that *Vertigo* was based on a story by the same authors of "that excellent French mystery, 'Diabolique.' That film, if you remember, told of a terribly devious plot to simulate a murder that didn't happen" (29 May 1958). In a follow-up piece, Crowther suggests that Hitchcock had recently become worried that Henri-Georges Clouzot, the director of the critically acclaimed *Wages of Fear* (1952) and *Diabolique* (1955), might overtake him as the international "Master of movie suspense." (Press releases for recent Clouzot films had characterized him as "the French Hitchcock.") According to Crowther, with *Vertigo* Hitchcock had successfully met the challenge by making a romantic thriller that compared favorably with some of Hitchcock's greatest triumphs, including *Notorious* (1946)—a film Crowther had included on his "top ten" list for 1946. "[M]aking characters grow important and sympathetic in the midst of peril," says Crowther, "is one that is obviously mastered by Mr. Hitchcock and M. Clouzot. Let us hope that each will go right on trying to do it better than the other has done it in successive films." A majority of daily newspaper reviewers would probably have agreed that with *Vertigo* Hitchcock had successfully met the Clouzot challenge (for an important exception see Scheuer, *Los Angeles Times,* 1958).

Critics for the more prestigious and intellectual weekly magazines and monthly journals, however, were of a different view. Judging from their earlier glowing reviews of *The Wages Of Fear* and *Diabolique,* these critics clearly preferred the French Clouzot to the Hollywood Hitchcock.[36] To these critics, who were partly responsible for the film's early bad reputation, *Vertigo* was even more defective than Hitchcock's other recent Hollywood productions. As long-time Hitchcock nemesis John McCarten of the *New Yorker* put it, "Alfred Hitchcock, who produced and directed the thing, has never before indulged in such far-fetched nonsense" (McCarten, *New Yorker,* 1958; see also Knight, *Saturday Review,* 1958; Hatch, *Nation,* 1958). Reviews of *Vertigo* in more middlebrow magazines, such as *Time* (1958) and *Newsweek* (1958), were also highly critical of the film. Like McCarten, *Newsweek*'s critic complained that Hitchcock had "overdone his deviousness, overreached the limits of credibility" (*Newsweek,* 1958).[37]

While mainstream and highbrow reviewers may have disagreed in their assessment of *Vertigo,* they shared the view that Hitchcock's work belonged in the realm of popular entertainment, not art. By contrast, a few trade-paper reviews—precursors of the later auteurist analyses of the film—pointed to *Vertigo* as "an artistic and entertainment triumph" (*Film Daily,* 1958) and proof of Hitchcock's "absolute genius" (*Hollywood Reporter,* 1958). Hitchcock exhibited "absolute genius," according to the *Hollywood Reporter* review, because he was able to inspire each of his collaborators "to rise above their usual competence." Moreover, the review expressed the belief that Hitchcock had demonstrated that the thriller genre could be a vehicle for "the greatest form of emotional drama." Interestingly, the review concluded that *Vertigo* was "one of the most fascinating love stories ever filmed"—an opinion that would become widespread among American critics during the seventies, when the auteur theory dominated film criticism.

According to cultural sociologist Wendy Griswold (1987), a cultural product is a significant work of art if it elicits among critics some consensus as to its content but a diversity of responses as to its deeper meaning. By contrast, a more formulaic or univocal work elicits more standardized or predictable responses. Judging from how critics initially critical responded to it, Hitchcock's next film, *North by Northwest* (1959), would seem to be a formulaic film par excellence. Perceived as the quintessential Hitchcock film when first released in 1959, *North by Northwest* elicited a more strikingly uniform and favorable response from critics than did *The Man Who Knew Too Much* three years earlier. Not only did the vast majority of reviewers agree that *North by Northwest* was an excellent film, they concurred in their assessment of why it was so good. Yet future generations of critics would find deeper meanings, subtleties, and ironies in the film (see Wood 1977, 96–105; Rothman 1983; Cavell 1986; Brill 1989, 3–21), suggesting that critical expectations at the time of the film's initial release, independent of the film's content, may also have influenced how critics responded to it.

For critics who reviewed the film when it first came out, *North by Northwest* seemed a perfect illustration of Hitchcock's highly publicized theories about how to make an effective thriller—views he had repeatedly articulated to audiences through the media during the fifties. Well before the film's release, Hitchcock had told reporters that *North by Northwest* would meet viewer expectations about what constituted the quintessential Hitchcock film. In that context, Hitchcock often invoked the film's classic crop-duster sequence to illustrate his theories about suspense. At the beginning of this sequence, the audience knows the hero is in danger but the hero does not. This produces mounting suspense. The mounting suspense, in turn, must be relieved by humor. Here is Hitchcock's description of the final minutes of the crop-dusting sequence:

> The plane flies over and starts buzzing and strafing him with a machine gun. He runs, dodges, throws himself in ditches. Suddenly the wide, sunny countryside is not a peaceful haven but a deadly open place in which the slightest shelter means life or death. Grant dives into a cornfield; the plane promptly flies over it, billowing deadly fumes that drive him back into the open. He tries to hail cars, but none will stop. Finally he stands before an oncoming oil-tank truck and forces it to stop for him. The plane makes one more pass at him, dips too low and crashes into the truck, bursting into flame. Motorists stop to see the fire. Grant is safe, but he must get back to Chicago. He steals a truck driven by one of the people who stopped and drives off in it. The scene ends rather humorously with the owner running after him, shaking his fist and yelling futilely—a brief chuckle for the audience. (Hitchcock 1959)

To a considerable degree, the initial reviews of *North by Northwest* mirror those aspects of the film emphasized in Hitchcock's exchanges with the press just prior to the release of the film. Many reviewers saw the film as exemplary of Hitchcock's talent of blending the macabre with humor and romance. As a reviewer for the *New York Times* put it, "Although they are involved in lightning-fast romance and some loose intrigue, it is all done in brisk, genuinely witty and sophisticated style. With Mr. Hitchcock at the helm, *North by Northwest* is a colorful and exciting route for spies, counterspies and lovers" (*New York Times,* 1959). Several reviewers cited the highly publicized crop-duster scene as one of the film's most memorable sequences (see, e.g., *New York Herald Tribune,* 1959).

Critics also singled out *North by Northwest* as one of Hitchcock's most successful works in years. According to the mainstream critics, a successful Hitchcock film was above all else a "wonderful roller-coaster, merry-go-round of pure entertainment" (*New York Post, 1959*). The *New York Post* reviewer characterized it as "the liveliest Hitchcock film since *Rear Window*" and "the most entertaining generally." Many of the more highbrow reviewers also concurred with this assessment (see, e.g., Alpert, *Saturday Review,* 1959), although the *New Yorker* review denounced the film as an unintentional parody of Hitchcock's own work (*New Yorker,* 1959). For the remainder of Hitchcock's career, critics would frequently allude to *North by Northwest* as the quintessential Hitchcock film (see plates 13 and 14).

Hitchcock's next film, *Psycho,* is an interesting case, with significant parallels to *Vertigo.* Both films are essentially anti-romances, violating many of the conventions and rules that were associated with the Hitchcock thriller during the late fifties. As Lesley Brill (1988) has correctly pointed out, "The great majority of Hitchcock's films have elements of both romance and irony, with outcomes that usually favor romance. *Vertigo* and *Psycho,* however, constitute practically homogeneous ironic exercises. They doggedly frustrate and reverse any romantic impulses toward clarity and fulfillment" (Brill 1988, 200). Given the expectations of Hitchcock's audience, accustomed to "outcomes [in his films] that . . . favor romance," one would have expected both films to disappoint them. While *Vertigo*'s box-office performance was lackluster, *Psycho* became Hitchcock's biggest commercial hit.

Hitchcock was drawn to *Psycho* precisely because it was so different from anything he had done previously. He had never made a pure horror film before. Aware that cheaply made horror films from Hammer and American International were currently popular with younger audiences, Hitchcock wondered whether a quality horror film might do even better. By mid-May 1959, he had obtained the movie rights to Robert Bloch's recently published horror novel, *Psycho,* at a cost of only $9,000. When Hitchcock first proposed the idea of making a terror film based on Bloch's pulp shocker to Paramount, the studio was not interested. In time, Hitchcock and Paramount agreed to the following deal, reflecting Paramount's unwillingness to provide Hitchcock with a big budget for what the studio perceived as a risky project. Hitchcock would put up the money himself, with Paramount serving only as the film's distributor. Instead of receiving a salary for making *Psycho,* which would be shot in black and white, he would receive 60 percent ownership of the film negative.

Under these economic constraints, Hitchcock soon made a virtue out of necessity. In a *New York Times* article, which appeared in the summer, where he for the first time publicly discussed his new project, Hitchcock characterized it as a low-budget horror film in the *Diabolique* tradition where nothing would "distract from the telling of the tale." "It takes place near Sacramento, California, at a dark and gloomy motel. Some very ordinary people meet other ordinary people and horror and death ensue in a manner that can't be unraveled unless you have the book as a guide" (Rebello 1986, 51; see also Rebello 1990). According to Hilton Green, who worked on Hitchcock's television crew and who served as assistant director on the film, Hitchcock was already viewing *Psycho* as a good opportunity for "proving to his Hollywood peers that he could make a quality film without spending a lot of money." "That's why he went with his television crew, not his feature crew," said Green. "We were more accustomed to shorter schedules" (Hilton Green, personal interview, April 1986).

Hitchcock also viewed *Psycho* as an ideal vehicle for working over his audience. In that respect, his treatment of the Marion Crane character would be critical. While Bloch began his novel with Norman Bates, Hitchcock's screenwriter, Joseph Stefano, had suggested to Hitchcock that they start the film with the girl instead of Norman. "We'll find out what the girl is all about, see her steal the money and head for Sam [her boyfriend]—on the way, this horrendous thing happens to her" (Rebello 1986, 52).[38] It was Hitchcock's inspiration that they get a "big-name actress" to play the role of Marion, his rationale being that nobody would expect a star to die one-third of the way into the story.

(Janet Leigh was subsequently selected for the role.) As for the significance of the famous shower scene in which Marion is murdered, journalist Stephen Rebello put it this way, "Not only was it a technical tour de force," says Rebello, "but it also sledge-hammered five decades of movie convention which had it that the star never died (if at all) until the last reel" (Rebello 1986, 70).

How did Hitchcock prepare audiences for this most unconventional of films? *Vertigo* had also been unconventional, but Hitchcock had failed to take into account how his reputation as an entertainer and showman might shape both the popular and critical response to that film. He would not repeat this mistake with *Psycho*.

Judging from a number of newspaper and magazine stories about Hitchcock that appeared around the time of the release of the film, Hitchcock expected that *Psycho* would appeal primarily to younger audiences. Several articles announced *Psycho* as Hitchcock's first exercise in "pure horror," containing more violence and shock than any of his previous films. In addition, many of these articles emphasized that the film would also be more explicit in its depiction of sexuality. As Hitchcock told Hollywood gossip columnist Sheila Graham, "You can't put scenes on the screen today where lovers just peek at each other— young people would laugh" (Graham 1960). "Our big problem today," he related to Graham, "is trying to make the censors understand that the young people are much more sophisticated than they used to be. I'm aware of one or two scenes in *Psycho* that you might call strong. We got a B rating with the Legion of Decency—yet in Australia where censorship is very tough, we only had to cut 7 feet of the film." The greater sexual frankness of *Psycho* was also evident in ads and posters for the film which featured Janet Leigh in bra and half-slip and John Gavin stripped to the waist (see plate 15).

Another aspect of *Psycho* promotion that youthful audiences must have found especially provocative was the unusual admission policy enforced during the time of its release. Virtually all newspaper ads, posters, and radio and TV spots featured Hitchcock himself proclaiming that "No one . . . *but no one* . . . will be admitted to the theatre after the start of each performance of . . . *Psycho*" (Paramount press book for *Psycho*). Undoubtedly, the gimmick of hiring Pinkerton guards to enforce this policy was designed to heighten the whole experience of attending a showing of *Psycho*. Such gimmicks were nothing new to young people familiar with the promotional strategies accompanying the release of other low-budget horror films of the period.

At the same time, many of Hitchcock's additional remarks to reporters and columnists about *Psycho* also seemed to reflect a concern for his older fans. Shortly before *Psycho*'s opening in New York City, Hitchcock informed reporters about the shower scene, in which the girl, played by Janet Leigh, is stabbed while nude. In describing what is now regarded as a classic sequence, Hitchcock emphasized that the challenge of shooting it was to suggest rather than to show nudity so as to placate the censors, "The scene occupies only forty-five seconds in the film, but it took me six days to shoot it so as to avoid censorship and yet create the illusion of nudity" (Ross 1960). Clearly, Hitchcock had his older fans in mind when he added that the film did not contain sex and violence for their own sake. Rather, his interest was to "excite and shock audiences only within the bounds of good taste."[39] His older fans also must have found Hitchcock's high visibility in the promotional campaign for the film reassuring. In effect, the promotional articles were proclaiming *Psycho* as a significant departure for Hitchcock but well within the Hitchcock tradition.

Still, Hitchcock worried about the commercial prospects of the film, fearing that once the initial audience saw *Psycho*, they would divulge the ending, thereby diminishing interest in the picture. To minimize the chances of this happening, Hitchcock decided not to hold advance screenings for critics and other opinion makers. Agreeing with Hitchcock that word of mouth could hurt the film, Lew Wasserman reportedly advised him to open *Psycho* nationally in thousands of theaters after the film's prerelease engagement in two New York City theaters. At the very least, Hitchcock's name would lure people into the theater for two weeks or so, long enough for *Psycho* to break even.

For all of Hitchcock's worry concerning the box-office potential of *Psycho*, the film was an unqualified financial success. On 16 June 1960, *Psycho* opened at two showcase theaters in Manhattan, where it played regularly to near-capacity audiences for nine weeks before opening at neighborhood theaters. An unusual feature about the New York City run of the film was that *Psycho* remained at the first-run Manhattan theaters while opening at neighborhood theaters. A major factor behind this unusual booking pattern was that, although the film was playing for many weeks in the two first-run houses, there had been very little fluctuation in the box-office performance since opening day, as compared to the usual experience of a 10 to 20 percent drop in box office after the first week. *Psycho* also performed impressively in all other major U.S. film markets. In addition, it was enormously successful in foreign countries.[40]

A major reason for *Psycho*'s commercial success was that it did attract many young people. According to several eye-witness reports, a high proportion of *Psycho*'s audience consisted of teenagers and young adults. As one New York resident reported in the *New York Times* (1960), "any number of teenagers have gone to see this movie several times over and the word is apparently out around the suburbs that 'the blood in the bathtub scene' is hot stuff." Apparently, for the young horror-film fan, *Psycho* was a film that really delivered (see also Delaplane 1960).

But Hitchcock's prominence in the promotional campaign for the film also meant that many of his older fans, familiar with his feature films as well as his TV program, would also see the film during its initial run. Many of these viewers, especially those who had seen the film's macabre six-minute preview trailer featuring Hitchcock as a guide leading a tour of the Bates Motel, must have expected that *Psycho* would be in the tradition of Hitchcock's macabre little teleplays. As James Naremore (1973) has pointed out, Hitchcock's TV audience must have found many aspects of *Psycho* pleasurable in the Barthian sense of finding elements compatible with the "repertoire of expectations" they brought with them to the film. These included the black-and-white photography, the moments of suspense, the sardonic wit and macabre humor, the ordinariness of its characters and the drabness of its setting, the revelation at the end that Norman masquerading as his dead mother murdered Marion Crane, and the psychiatrist's explanation of why Norman behaved the way he did (Naremore 1973).

On the other hand, as William Rothman (1982) has convincingly argued, devoid of a teleplay's frame, *Psycho*'s world becomes the world in which we dwell. "Part of *Psycho*'s myth," says Rothman, "is that there is no world outside its own, that we are fated to be born, live our alienated lives, and die in the very world in which Norman Bates also dwells" (1982, 255). Perhaps even more unsettling to audiences is that they were forced to identify with a psychopathic murderer. Hitchcock's fans who had been exposed to the publicity and promotional materials for *Psycho* were somewhat prepared for the film's iconoclasm and boldness and, therefore, may have found the film less disorienting than those unaware that *Psycho* was no ordinary Hitchcock thriller film. On the other hand, the fan mail for *Psycho* suggests that Hitchcock's older audience, especially married women, did find the film unacceptable, so much so that they discouraged friends from seeing it. The disorientation resulting from the film's seemingly "realistic" onslaught on audience sensibilities is reflected in a number of letters, mostly from women, received by Hitchcock's office shortly after the release of *Psycho,* such as the following:

> I am not writing this letter as a crank. I am very sincere in what I am going to say. My husband and I recently saw your movie "Psycho," and I would like to say that it was the most gruesome, morbid, REALISTIC movie I have ever seen. I would further like to state that it was a very unnerving experience, and I was visibly upset for hours after viewing it. To be perfectly frank—it made me sick to my stomach and weak in the knees! (*Psycho* fan mail, Hitchcock Collection)

In the second and final paragraph of the letter, the author vows to never expose herself to another Hitchcock product:

> I have always been a television fan of yours and I thought you were the master of suspense. But I have changed my opinion of you considerably after seeing "Psycho." I will never see another movie of yours—nor do I intend to watch your television programs.

The letter ends with the parenthetical remark "everyone I discussed this with feels the same way I do," implying that the letter is not an isolated case. Indeed, many other letters received by Hitchcock following the release of *Psycho* expressed similar sentiments, including the claim of representativeness.

Moreover, many fans felt that Hitchcock was actually condoning the behavior depicted in *Psycho,* as the following passage from another letter clearly illustrates:

> Acclaim is yours for presenting to humanity the lessons in crime so clearly depicted in *Psycho:*
> You have made love without marriage in a cheap hotel room acceptable.
> You have made respectability, responsibility, and alimony, dirty words.
> You have made robbery forgiveable.
> You have made murder explainable.
> You have made matricide agreeable.
> You have made grave-robbing plausible.
> You have made corpse-taxidermy a national hobby.
> You have given your fellow man complete vindication for any or all such crimes.

Psycho also annoyed audiences familiar with Hitchcock's feature films, who felt that the director had violated their trust. As one viewer complained, "Of course we should expect murders, madness, etc. in a Hitchcock movie with such a name, so there can be no reasonable objection to the murder and the madness, or to the sex, or to being thoroughly frightened. But in the past, we have expected Hitchcock to treat these subjects with a reasonably light touch, and the whole objection to the movie lies in the excruciating scene of Janet Leigh being murdered. . . . The point is that all this is not particularly frightening, but rather sickening. It is not the light-hearted thrill of the usual Hitchcock chase, as in, say, *North by Northwest,* and not what one goes to see."

Viewers who regularly tuned to Hitchcock's TV series during the fifties had come to expect the restoration of a moral balance by the time Hitchcock's epilogue for each show was completed. Yet, with a number of his recent feature films (e.g., *The Wrong Man,* 1956, and *Vertigo,* 1958), Hitchcock had become increasingly "successful" in undercutting such expectations. The responses to *Psycho* reported above reflect audience unease resulting from that kind of manipulation.

The many mixed and negative reviews that *Psycho* received may have also persuaded a sizeable number of Hitchcock's older fans to avoid the film altogether. By contrast, for the teenagers and young adults who, I argue, were the key to *Psycho*'s enormous success, movie ads and trailers were far more important as a source of information about the film than what the critics said about it (cf. Austin 1989, 68–71). For the younger moviegoer, in particular, attending *Psycho* came to be perceived as a major social event not to be missed.

Psycho received mostly mixed reviews from U.S. reviewers and critics when it was first released, reviews that reflected the critics' ambivalence about the film. While admiring the sureness of his techniques, many newspaper and magazine reviewers, especially those catering to the more educated and sophisticated filmgoer, agreed that this time around Hitchcock had simply gone too far. *Time* magazine's reviewer characterized the shower murder as "one of the messiest, most nauseating murders ever filmed. At close range, the camera watches every twitch, gurgle, convulsion and hemorrhage in the process by which a living human becomes a corpse." Because Hitchcock was too heavy-handed here, the reviewer concluded that "the delicate illusion of reality necessary for a creak-and-shriek movie becomes, instead, a spectacle of stomach-churning horror" (*Time,* 1960). A similar view was echoed by *Los Angeles Times* reviewer Philip K. Scheuer. While acknowledging that *Psycho* was one of Hitchcock's "most brilliantly directed shockers," he stressed that it was also his "most disagreeable." "In *Psycho*," says Scheuer, "when the blood is supposed to spurt it really spurts, and on two occasions it forces sickened gasps from the spectator" (Scheuer 1960; see also the *New Yorker*, 1960).

By the end of the year, however, a number of reviewers had revised their assessment of the film. *New York Times* critic Bosley Crowther, who early in its release expressed serious reservations about *Psycho*, became a champion of the film, including it among the ten best films of 1960. In his first review, Crowther had characterized *Psycho*'s "slow buildups to sudden shocks" as "old melodramatics" (Crowther 1960a). By the time of his end-of-the-year reassessment, where he listed and discussed his top choices for 1960, Crowther had acknowledged *Psycho* as both an innovative and sophisticated picture: "Old-fashioned horror melodrama was given a new and frightening look in this bold psychological mystery picture. Sensual and sadistic though it was, it represented expert and sophisticated command of emotional development with cinematic techniques" (Crowther 1960b). Crowther's conversion was not an isolated case. Others also reassessed *Psycho* within a few months of the film's release (see Rebello 1990, 165).

Initially, *Psycho* probably offended reviewers for two principal reasons. Many critics had been angered by Hitchcock's policy that they not be allowed to see the film in advance.[41] This meant that newspaper reviews of the film could not appear on the day it opened. Another problem for several critics was that the film radically departed from Hitchcock's "aesthetic contract" with the popular press. Newspaper and magazine critics, both in the United States and in England, had expected a new Hitchcock film to contain a predictable blend of suspense, romance, and humor. But with *Psycho* Hitchcock had made a film devoid of romance—"a sheer out-and-out shocker" (*Los Angeles Mirror*, 1960), "far above the average film of its type," said the reviewer for the *Hollywood Citizen-News* (11 August 1960), but "hardly up to his last masterpiece, 'North by Northwest'" (*Hollywood Citizen News*, 1960). In her review of *Psycho*, British critic C. A. Lejeune commented that a new Hitchcock film was "usually a keen enjoyment" that made audiences care for its characters. By contrast, Lejeune describes how while viewing *Psycho* she "grew so sick and tired of the whole beastly business" that she walked out before it was over (Lejeune 1960). For critics like Lejeune, *Psycho* was a major disappointment.

Hitchcock always insisted that he had not intended *Psycho* to be a serious film. As he explained to François Truffaut in 1962, "I didn't start out to make an important movie. I thought I could have fun with this subject. . . ." He was satisfied with the extraordinary box-office success of the film, he claimed, because with the film he "achieved something of a mass emotion." "My film caused audiences all over the world to react and become emotional. . . ." (Truffaut 1967). Furthermore, he complained to Truffaut that most serious critics had missed the point, thereby failing to appreciate the true significance of *Psycho*—its use of film art to precipitate "something of a mass emotion." Rather, as Hitchcock lamented to Truffaut, critics were more inclined to say, "What a terrible thing to make. The subject was horrible. The people were small. There were no characters in it."

Yet not long after *Psycho*'s release, a few critics, both in America and Europe, insisted that it was more than merely an expertly made terror film. In his first film review for the *Village Voice*, dated August 1960, Andrew Sarris urged the discerning filmgoer to see *Psycho* at least three times, "the first time for the sheer terror of the experience; . . . the second time for the macabre comedy inherent in the conception of the film; and the third for all the hidden meanings and symbols lurking beneath the surface of the first American movie since *Touch of Evil* to stand in the same creative rank as the great European films." *Cahiers du Cinéma*'s film reviewer also praised *Psycho*'s artistry (see Rebello 1990, 167). It is conceivable that these few glowing reviews helped to rekindle Hitchcock's desire, held somewhat in abeyance since coming to the United States, to be better appreciated as an artist, especially by those so-called serious or highbrow journalistic reviewers who, in his opinion, had missed the whole point of *Psycho*.

THE BIRDS AND THE DETERIORATION OF HITCHCOCK'S RELATIONSHIP WITH HIS AUDIENCE

Throughout his career Hitchcock was upset with critics who failed to see the serious intent behind his films, but it was only after his experience with *Psycho* that he began to speak out about criticism of his work. In chapter 3, I will show how Hitchcock himself campaigned to reshape his reputation among serious critics. This desire to appeal to more discerning or sophisticated filmgoers yet not lose the Hitchcock fans became a powerful influence in the making and marketing of *The Birds* (1963). In the next chapter I describe how journalistic critics responded to *The Birds* when it first came out; here my purpose is to examine the reaction of Hitchcock's fans to that film as a way of calling attention to the deterioration of the director's relationship with those fans during the sixties.

Hitchcock wanted the script for *The Birds* to be the type of suspense thriller that his loyal fans had come to expect—a thriller that is suspenseful from beginning to end. Accordingly, he insisted that all the film's major sequences be punctuated with ideas that would intimate the ominous nature of the birds. Hitchcock believed that, with the inclusion of such sequences, the film would not disappoint his loyal fans. On the other hand, the gloom, the tentativeness, and lack of resolution of the film's final scene are indications that Hitchcock also wanted the film to appeal to a more high-culture audience. In the film's last scene, the birds are in control, with the besieged family escaping by car. After showing the car take off, the camera returns to the family house and looks outward over the porch. We soon realize that we are now alone with the birds. The sound of birds replaces the sound of the car's engine. Instead of ending the picture with the words "The End," Hitchcock dissolves into the words "A Universal Release," imitating the style of European art films.

Among the materials in the Hitchcock Collection is a file of fan mail relating to *The Birds*. This fan correspondence is invaluable for a study exploring the relationship between the genre filmmaker and his audience since, in addition to including letters from his public, the file contains many of Hitchcock's replies to fan inquiries. Moreover, the file includes not only correspondence concerning the initial release of *The Birds* in 1963 but also covers two showings in 1968 and 1969 of *The Birds* on American television. By that time Hitchcock's TV series had been cancelled.

The fan mail reveals that many of Hitchcock's most devoted fans were shocked, confused, and even outraged by *The Birds,* especially the ending. Below is a sample of responses to the film drawn from letters received by Hitchcock's office:

> Sir, I'm quite unhappy to inform you of my disappointment with your latest production, "The Birds." I had counted on your usual excellent direction and I was not let down, but your finish can only be described as useless.

> When friends ask us how we enjoyed "The Birds" we are hesitant to answer. We really did enjoy the picture but feel as if we missed something.

I have just recently seen your newest picture "The Birds." I found it a tremendously exciting picture; however, I found that the ending was a letdown and much too obscure.

I *know* that your movie "The Birds" was the best horror movie I ever saw, but you'll ruin the whole movie unless you finish it.

I enjoyed the opening twenty-five minute "commercial" very much. . . . From that point on, it was a fantastic, arresting story. All the way up to the ending: But please tell me, Why-y-y-y did the birds attack? Even Dizzy Gillespie and Stravinsky resolve their discords. You have violated one of your fundamental rules. Therefore, I'll seriously consider accepting a refund of the price of admission when you mail me a $.95 check (Either that or answer Why? It's still buggin me. Or is that the sequel?)

In a number of letters, Hitchcock's fans even offered speculations of their own to explain the tremendous fury of the birds, hoping that a Hitchcock reply would confirm the fan's favorite thesis. In one letter, dated 19 April 1963, a fan proposed the following explanation for the bird attacks:

In my mind I believe it to be the love birds brought to the bay by Miss Daniels. It seemed that on two or three separate occasions when the birds attacked they were summoned by the whistling of these two love birds. If this is the case, Mr. Hitchcock, I sure would appreciate hearing from you.

The reply from Hitchcock's office, dated 16 May 1963, seems unsatisfactory, suggesting that Hitchcock had not yet worked out many of the film's broader implications:

We have documented proof in the office of birds invading a home in La Jolla, a city near San Diego. Hundreds of birds came down the chimney into the home. Since the picture has been released we have received clippings from all over the United States of this same thing happening currently.

However, by the end of summer 1963, Hitchcock had come up with a more thought-provoking interpretation of *The Birds* for his fans. In one reply, dated 13 September 1963, Sue Gautier, Hitchcock's secretary wrote:

Mr. Hitchcock has asked me to explain that the bird attack was just as any catastrophe. Anything such as this is very bad for a while, and, then, hopefully, things will start to get better.

By 7 November 1963, Hitchcock's office had adopted a more elegant rationalization for the film:

> In the picture, *The Birds,* it was the fact that a catastrophe occurred that affected all these people. As you saw in the film, and as happens each day, some people are more affected than others. In this case it was played up as a bird attack on these people—it could have been a storm or any catastrophe.

These "official" interpretations of the film functioned similarly to the way the epilogues served Hitchcock's TV series—to help clarify the story and restore a moral balance. Moreover, Hitchcock's "personal" communications with his fans about the "meaning" of *The Birds* also reflect his continued interest (at least until the early 1960s) in maintaining a good relationship with his public.

During the 1960s, Hitchcock's contract with his audience progressively weakened. After *The Birds* he made the boldly experimental film *Marnie* (1964), which failed miserably at the box office (see Kapsis 1988a). Furthermore, his TV series was dropped after the 1964–65 season because of low ratings. Rather than focusing attention on his regular viewers, Hitchcock worked hard during this period to further his goal of elevating his artistic reputation (see chapter 3). A trade-paper review of Hitchcock's 1969 film *Topaz* even suggested that Hitchcock's recent highbrow and "intellectual" converts might find his latest film more to their liking than his "older, more demanding viewers":

> It used to be, in years gone by, that when an Alfred Hitchcock thriller was released, the same audiences that relished a Humphrey Bogart vehicle or a John Wayne shoot-'em-up would wait breathlessly for the film to play in their neighborhood theatre, while the "intellectual" film critics would grind out diatribes against the vulgarity and superficiality of the "master of suspense's" stylistics. Times have certainly changed. Now a Hitchcock film is considered a work of art (which, of course, it was all along) on the rarified plane of a Stravinsky symphony or a Picasso painting. (*Motion Picture Exhibitor,* 17 December 1969)

This shift in Hitchcock's allegiance from the general public to a more elitist or intellectual audience is dramatically revealed in his replies to fan mail following the premiere showing of *The Birds* on network television in January 1968 and a later airing in February 1969. Most of the fan mail again focused on the "meaning" or significance of the film. In particular, viewers wanted to know what happened after the car left the Brenner home. This time around, however, Hitchcock had worked out a new way of handling queries about the film's ending:

> Mr. Hitchcock has asked me to thank you for your letter regarding *The Birds*. His reply is:
>
>> "Daphne du Maurier's original story ended with the birds taking over the world. I preferred to leave this question to the imagination of the audience. After all, in life any situation is not necessarily neatly tied up and packaged to completion. You know, perhaps the birds gave up after the family had departed into safety."

Responding a few weeks later to a similar inquiry regarding the film's ambiguous ending, Hitchcock appended to his now standard explanation a remark that his fans might have understandably viewed as testy, "I don't know. Why should I? I'm not omnipotent in these matters."

More letters would pour in following the February 1969 telecast of *The Birds*. Hitchcock's "official" reply to this round of mail, coupled with his cantankerous response of the previous year, makes clear that Hitchcock's honeymoon with his fans was indeed over:

> As to why the birds attacked: you may recall the scene in which Kathy, the young sister, asks Mitch why the birds are attacking and he answers, "I wish I could say. But if I could answer that, I could also tell you why *people* are trying to kill people."
> Perhaps this will clarify it for you.

Reshaping a Legend

Sociological studies of reputation-building tend to emphasize the active role of self-interested others in advancing or establishing the preeminence of a particular artist or other public figure. Mulkay and Chaplin (1982) show that the initial success of the American painter Jackson Pollock was largely the result of a promotional campaign by influential members of the New York art world, who in turn used Pollock to advance their own careers (see also Rodden 1989, on George Orwell; Tuchman 1989, on Victorian novelists; and Posner 1990, on Benjamin Cardozo). Also, Hitchcock's reputation is thought to have improved during the late 1960s and 1970s primarily because maverick French critics writing for *Cahiers du Cinéma*, especially François Truffaut, initiated a sincere but hardly disinterested campaign culminating in Truffaut's book *Hitchcock* (1967). This book, says a biographer of Hitchcock, Donald Spoto, "established Hitchcock's status as a quintessential auteur, or movie 'author,' a director who exerted unprecedented creative control over each of his films" (1983, 524–25). According to this view, Truffaut and his colleagues succeeded in persuading many film critics, scholars, and other members of the international film art-world that Hitchcock was a great artist.

Early in my research on the post-1960 transformation of Hitchcock's reputation I assumed that Hitchcock's own efforts in elevating his stature would be, at the very least, as important as the activities of others, that the completed study would provide strong additional support for one of social science's best supported maxims, namely, that fame begets fame. According to sociologist Gaye Tuchman, "a good reputation is, to use Pierre Bourdieu's phrase (1984), a kind of 'symbolic capital.' That is, the more fame one has, the more one might be expected to accumulate more fame, much as economic capital helps one to amass more economic capital" (Tuchman 1989, 126). Robert Merton (1968) has labeled this tendency the Matthew effect, from the gospel principle "Unto every one that hath shall be given, and he shall have abundance; but from him that hath not shall be taken away even that which he hath." Hitchcock's preeminence as a filmmaker and celebrity plus his skills as a self-promoter led me to believe that he possessed the requisite symbolic capital and influence to guarantee the auteurists' campaign to reshape his reputation a relatively quick realization. Indeed, my preliminary findings seemed compatible with the Matthew effect (see Kapsis 1986a, and Tuchman 1989, 126). However, as the present chapter unequivocally reveals, I was mistaken. Hitchcock's campaign during the sixties to reshape his reputation was largely ineffectual. Not until the early 1970s, when the auteur theory became the dominant aesthetic discourse among journalistic and academic film critics, did his reputation improve. More important than either individual sponsorship or self-promotion, this broad shift in film aesthetics proved to be the deciding factor in reshaping Hitchcock's reputation.

The campaign to establish Hitchcock's reputation as a significant artist was largely dependent on the films he was working on at the time rather than on his earlier films. Therefore, I have used the reactions of newspaper and magazine critics to his films released during the 1960s and 1970s to gauge the success or failure of the campaign. Among the films examined are *The Birds* (1963), *Marnie* (1964), *Torn Curtain* (1966), *Topaz* (1969), Frenzy (1972), and *Family Plot* (1976).[1]

First, I describe some of the efforts of opinion-makers such as Truffaut and Sarris and arts organizations such as the Museum of Modern Art and the Cannes Film Festival to advance Hitchcock's stature in the art world of film. Next, I examine Hitchcock's own agenda with respect to reshaping his reputation. Of special interest is his own complicity in many of these efforts from others to elevate his reputation. Then I document the early setbacks of his campaign by examining the critical reception of two films from this period, *The Birds* (1963) and *Marnie* (1964). Next I show that only when auteurism became the dominant aesthetic discourse among journalistic critics did Hitchcock's reputation significantly improve.[2] Once having achieved the status of "serious artist," Hitchcock and his heirs faced the relentless challenge of maintaining that status.

SPONSORSHIP

During the fifties, several brilliant contributors to France's influential *Cahiers du Cinéma* who would eventually become film directors of international status, most notably François Truffaut but also Claude Chabrol and Eric Rohmer, launched a campaign to advance Hitchcock's preeminence as the classic auteur (see Truffaut [1954] 1964; Rohmer and Chabrol, 1957). In their view, Hitchcock was a genius of cinematic form who created a distinctive moral vision of the human condition which deepened during his years in America.[3] While effective in France, these early efforts to advance Hitchcock's reputation as a serious artist were of little consequence in America.[4]

By the early sixties, Truffaut had come up with the idea of putting together a book of conversations with Hitchcock as a vehicle for up-grading his reputation in America, especially among New York film critics. Truffaut's intent is revealed in a letter to Hitchcock, dated 2 June 1962, where he first proposed the idea for a book:

> And now, to get to the point of this letter: During my conversa-tions with the foreign press, and particularly in New York, I have noted that on the whole, there is too often a superficial approach to your achievements. On the other hand, the propaganda we initi-ated in the *Cahiers du Cinéma,* while effective in France, carried no weight in America, because the arguments were over-intellec-tual. . . . Morcover, now that I am a filmmaker, my admiration was, if anything, increased—strengthened by additional bases for appreciation. . . . I am asking, therefore, whether you would grant me an interview, to be tape-recorded over a span of a week. . . . The material is not intended for articles, but will make up a book to be published in New York and Paris simultaneously. . . . It can eventually be reproduced in other parts of the world (letter, Truffaut to Hitchcock, Hitchcock Collection)*

On 12 August 1962, Truffaut arrived in Los Angeles to interview Hitchcock. The book resulting from the interview was eventually pub-lished in the United States in late 1967 (see plate 16).

As mentioned earlier, many film critics and historians believed that Truffaut's book almost singlehandedly converted many "Hitchknockians" to "Hitchcockians." Anticipating the book's likely impact soon after it appeared, American film critic Andrew Sarris wrote: "Truffaut's *Hitch-cock* may leave the impression that there is no sympathetic criticism of Hitchcock in the English language. Robin Wood, Peter Bogdanovich and

---

* Unless otherwise noted, all correspondence, meetings, scripts, publicity, and production materials referred to in this chapter are from the Hitchcock Col-lection.

Ian Cameron have covered much of Truffaut's terrain . . . but no mere critic is likely to match the influence of the director of *Jules and Jim*" (Sarris 1968c).

Sarris had been one of the first to champion Hitchcock's cause in the United States. In the late 1950s and early 1960s, he introduced the ideas of the French auteur critics to American audiences (see Sarris 1962a). Part of his argument repeated the polemic for the recognition of artistic achievement within popular Hollywood cinema. Like his French counterparts, Sarris pointed to Hitchcock's work as compelling proof that artistic achievement was possible in Hollywood. In 1962, he wrote: "After years of tortured revaluation, I am now prepared to stake my critical reputation, such as it is, on the proposition that Alfred Hitchcock is artistically superior to Robert Bresson by every criterion of excellence, and, further that, film for film, director for director, the American cinema has been consistently superior to that of the rest of the world from 1915 through 1962" (Sarris 1962a, 130).

During the early 1960s, The Museum of Modern Art also honored Hitchcock. On 27 March 1963, the day before *The Birds* opened in Manhattan, a *New York Times* article announced: "Alfred Hitchcock's movies will be the subject of the longest retrospective show ever held at the museum. . . ." "The film selection," continued the article, "was arranged by Richard Griffith, film curator at MOMA and one of the leading historians of the movie industry." The message of this article is clear: the Museum has initiated a film retrospective to honor Hitchcock, and this is the Museum's way of sanctioning Hitchcock as a serious artist.

In March of 1963 it was also announced that Hitchcock's *The Birds* would open the 1963 Cannes Film Festival. The official press release quoted from a cable sent to Hitchcock from the festival's director Favre le Bret, saying, "I am happy and honored to present *The Birds* at the festival inauguration. I consider it a masterpiece in every sense of the word."

When asked at various times during the sixties to comment about recent tributes to his "art," Hitchcock typically chose to do so in a humorous vein, implying that his "highbrow" sponsors were really taking him far too seriously. When Truffaut described Hitchcock as "the doyen of the Nouvelle Vague," for example, this elicited the typical Hitchcock rejoinder: "Oh, dear, I hate to be the doyen of anything; it makes me sound so much older than I feel" (*Marnie* Press Kit, 1964). If Hitchcock saw himself as an important artist, he still refused to acknowledge his status as a serious creator to his mass audience.

Despite his efforts to underplay his status as an artist to the general public, Hitchcock was repeatedly upset with critics who failed to see the serious intent behind his films. It is only after 1960, however, that he began to speak out about criticism of his work. Between 1960 and 1964, Hitchcock himself made a concerted effort to reshape his reputation among the serious journalistic critics.

Hitchcock reveals his frustration with most American critics (and many American writers as well) for not regarding him as a serious artist in a private conversation with speech-writer James Allardice[5] in spring 1963 regarding a talk they were preparing for Hitchcock to deliver at the University of California at Los Angeles for a screenwriters' award ceremony sponsored by the university's theater department. During this taped work session, Hitchcock expressed anger over the cold critical reception to his latest film, *The Birds* (1963), particularly from the so-called highbrow critics who, according to him, had never really understood his films:

> I don't care what the story is about. What I'm concerned with is designing a picture, scriptwise, in such a manner as to excite an audience's interest and their fears and their reactions to certain phases of the structure rather than the content itself. That's where I get away from the average [thriller]. . . . That's why you'll probably read, you know, so-called highbrow reviews where they'll tell you that the story in *The Birds* is either corny or something like that. Well, I don't give a damn about that, you know. What I care about is what I do to that audience through the use of film. And that has to go down on paper. It's no guesswork. You cannot do it in the cutting room. It's got to be laid out. Now, as you know, in *The Birds* the whole first part is very slow and I've had reviews saying, "Well, it's very exciting once it gets going, but it's a very slow build-up." Why, this is as deliberate as anything. I calculate every move I make because I know very well that an audience does not sit down unprepared. They've read the ads, they've heard the word-of-mouth. An audience arrives and sits in the seat and looks at the screen and says, well—you know, *The Birds* is coming, we're told! Now, I take that into account, you see, because I'm a believer in audience, you see. (Hitchcock-Allardice conference, 2 April 1963).

After confiding to his speech-writer why he had limited his work to the thriller format—"I can only do the things that are indigenous and spontaneous to me"—Hitchcock compared his own output to that of a great painter whose works share a distinctive style, "If you take a painter, you know he's a stylist. . . . If you take Paul Klee, well, Klee does a certain type of work." Referring again to his own work, Hitchcock remarked, "They may be all corpse-thriller and suspense pictures, but there's a vast difference between—we'll say, *Rebecca* and *Psycho* and *The Trouble with Harry* . . . and *North by Northwest* or *The Birds*. Look at the difference in all these pictures. Not one of them resembles another in any form except suspense."

Hitchcock's desire to appeal to more discerning or sophisticated filmgoers while, at the same time, not losing his regular customers because a powerful influence in the making and marketing of two films of this period, *The Birds* (1963) and *Marnie* (1964). With *The Birds*, Hitchcock launched the campaign to reshape his reputation among serious critics. While all of Hitchcock's later films, especially *Marnie*, *Topaz* (1969), and *Frenzy* (1972), were also driven by Hitchcock's ambition to be taken seriously as an artist, *The Birds* represents the first, the most ambitious, and certainly the most expensive project the filmmaker undertook for the purpose of reshaping his reputation among serious critics.

At the same time, Hitchcock wanted the script for *The Birds* to be the type of suspense thriller that his loyal fans had come to expect. By early November 1961, Evan Hunter, Hitchcock's screenwriter, had completed his first draft of the script. In a letter to Hunter, dated 30 November 1961, Hitchcock expressed many reservations about the script. It was too long, especially the first half, and the major characters, Melanie Daniels and Mitch Brenner, were insufficiently developed: "There is nothing particular about the young man at present," wrote Hitchcock, "to warrant the girl chasing out to get his car number. . . ." The young man's self-consciousness about wanting to purchase the love birds, Hitchcock feared, would turn audiences off. "People might say, 'What's difficult about buying a pair of love birds?' After all, they are not contraceptives."

After making these points, Hitchcock turned to a more basic problem with the script, namely, how to transform a rather plodding screenplay into one consistent with the principles of the Hitchcock suspense thriller, two of which are implied in the letter of 30 November 1961.

Principle 1: A Hitchcock picture should not contain what Hitchcock called "no scene" scenes, that is, sequences that might have narrative value (move the story along) but are, in themselves, undramatic. Maintaining that the preliminary script contained many such scenes, Hitchcock advised Hunter to eliminate them. "At Bodega Bay," observed Hitchcock, "I can clearly see that we do have one or two scenes with no particular shape. There are the scenes of Melanie buying temporary garments and going to the hotel for a room." "I feel sure," he continued, that "these could be eliminated so that the scene when she presents herself at the schoolteacher's house with only a paper bag can be dramatically capitalized. That is to say that she explains her purchase and wish for a room after the fact."

Principle 2: A Hitchcock thriller is suspenseful from beginning to end. With respect to *The Birds,* Hitchcock thought that all the major sequences should be punctuated with ideas that would "keep the audience a little on edge in the matter of birds." Indeed, audiences should be made to feel uneasy about the birds from the very beginning of the film. While acknowledging that Evan Hunter's original screenplay did open with Melanie walking down the street while a flock of pigeons are fluttering away, Hitchcock wondered if audiences would draw any significance from such a relatively low-keyed and undramatic beginning. Hitchcock thought not, and suggested to Hunter how one might transform the opening scene into a truly suspenseful and memorable moment. "How would it be," asked Hitchcock, "to open the picture on a San Francisco street with a series of cuts of upturned faces, some stationary, others moving slowly along, and what they are looking at is an unusual number of sea gulls flying above the buildings of the city? We could continue the upturned faces until at last we come to Melanie also looking up and pan her right into the bird shop where she could make some comment to the woman inside who dismisses her with a remark to the effect that when the weather is bad at sea, they often get driven inland." Hitchcock also referred Hunter to other spots in the screenplay where material intimating the ominous nature of the birds might be inserted. (For example, at the end of the night scene between Annie and Melanie, Hitchcock suggested adding the business about the women hearing a thump on the front door and then opening the door to discover a dead bird lying there.)

Nine months after the letters were written, when *The Birds* was in post-production, Hitchcock explained to François Truffaut why he inserted these early hints of the potential terror of the birds: "I had to do it that way because the public's curiosity was bound to be aroused by the articles in the press and the reviews as well as by the word-of-mouth talk about the picture. . . . Those references at the end of each scene were my way of saying, 'Just be patient. They're coming soon'" (Truffaut 1984).[6]

One should keep in mind that Hitchcock was articulating these concerns about how advance publicity for the film might shape audience expectations a good six months before the release of *The Birds* and four months before the ads and other publicity relating to the film began appearing with any frequency in the media. This suggests that some of Hitchcock's early comments to Evan Hunter about how to improve the script for *The Birds* were influenced by Hitchcock's calculations about the probable impact of future advertising and publicity (which Hitchcock would help develop) on the film's audience.

Hunter revised the script according to Hitchcock's suggestions, and in his next letter to Hunter, dated 21 December 1961, Hitchcock expressed his overall satisfaction. There was now little reason for Hitchcock to worry about his loyal fans. The film would not disappoint them. But what about the serious critics? What would their reactions be? Wouldn't it bother them, thought Hitchcock, if we failed to relate "the whole of the bird invasion to our central characters? Maybe it's not necessary to do so, but you know we are going to run into all kinds of critiques from the highbrows. Not that they sell us any tickets, but they do write their stuff in certain journals that may affect ticket buyers in metropolitan areas. I am not too serious about this little point, but I think it would be really nice if we could relate the two things."

After spending a month or so revising the script, Hunter informed Hitchcock, "I have carefully gone over each of the bird attacks in the play and the reactions of our principal characters following these attacks." Not only do the characters change throughout the story, he told Hitchcock, but "each change is a logical one following the change before it" (letter, Hunter to Hitchcock, 17 January 1962).

Consider, for example, the scene following the bird attack at the school when Melanie, inside the car, pounds on the horn in an attempt to drive off the crows. In the earlier version, Melanie hits the horn but the crows don't leave until a group of men starts running up the hill. As the men approach the car, the crows suddenly zoom into flight. Inside the car, Melanie continues hitting the horn, even though the crows have left (early screenplay for *The Birds*, November 1961). In the revised script, a new scene replaces the one describing the men approaching the car. In the new version, Melanie is still pounding the horn, but now it "has the effect of driving off the crows and, finally, the windshield and windows are clear of them. They have flown away. Melanie sinks over the wheel in exhausted relief" (script revisions, 19 January 1962).

Hitchcock's worries about the script might have largely evaporated following Hunter's latest revisions had Hitchcock not also asked other writers to comment candidly about the screenplay. One of the people Hitchcock contacted was writer-actor Hume Cronyn, whose wife, Jessica Tandy, portrays Lydia Brenner (Mitch's mother) in *The Birds*. Cronyn's comments about the script arrived a week or so before Hunter's revisions. While Cronyn said he liked the screenplay as a whole, he agreed with Hitchcock that there was still "room for improvement in the development and relationship of the principal characters," especially "in view of the extreme and macabre nature of the events." Cronyn felt that all three of the central characters could be improved upon. Cronyn found Mitch to be a trifle smug and suggested giving him more humor, while Melanie's growth, announced in description, should be more fully dramatized. "The implied arrogance, silliness, and selfishness of the early Melanie," wrote Cronyn, "may need heightening, so that the change to consideration, responsibility, and maturity are more marked—and more enduring."

Not surprisingly, Cronyn's most detailed comments were about Lydia, the role his wife would play. Lydia's extreme vulnerability but basic goodness, he believed, should be emphasized. Her character traits were too ill-defined in the present screenplay and needed to be refined. "Of all the characters," Cronyn wrote, "Lydia seems the most likely to be affected by the birds. Because of that, I hope the audience will like her, identify with her, and tremble for her. The preparation in her character will be important, and if achieved I think her hysterics can be hair-raising because they are understandable, even predictable" (letter, Cronyn to Hitchcock, 13 January 1962).

Soon after incorporating many of Hunter's and Cronyn's suggestions into the script, Hitchcock sent the new version to writer friend V. S. Pritchett for his opinion. (Pritchett, an acclaimed short story writer, for many years had been the *New Statesman's* book review editor.) It was now March, and Hitchcock was already on location at Bodega Bay, California, shooting the picture. Pritchett's critique of the script paralleled Cronyn's earlier comments and what Hitchcock must surely have suspected all along: that the link between the characters' love story and the bird attacks was not very strong. The major flaw of the script, according to Pritchett, was that "the people are under-characterized" and, therefore, audiences would "get the impression that they are in two different stories—in this case a light comedy and a terror tale—that do not weld together" (letter, Pritchett to Hitchcock, 16 March 1962).

Thus, on the eve of shooting *The Birds,* many script problems remained. By this time, the suspense sequences were the least of Hitchcock's worries and would be shot almost exactly as indicated in the current version of the script. But more would have to be done about the development of and relationship between the central characters. And to really win over the serious critics and aestheticians, Hitchcock would have to incorporate into his film some of the conventions of the European "art-house" film—conventions seemingly at odds with those of the typical Hitchcock thriller. (Hitchcock's appointment book reveals that in early summer of 1961, just a couple of months before deciding to make *The Birds,* he viewed a number of European art films in his private screening room. They included *The Virgin Spring, The Magician, L'Avventura,* and *Breathless*—all films that in different degrees reject the Hollywood conventions of resolution, closure, and an upbeat ending.)[7]

The script went through several more revisions during the actual shooting of the film. One radically altered scene was the ending. No other changes in the script would have as profound an impact on audiences' and critics' reactions to the completed film. In mid-March 1962, Hitchcock requested that Hunter rework the ending and make it more poetic and meaningful. Hunter wrote back, and admitted to having difficulty being "poetic when the roof of an automobile is slowly being shredded to bits by attacking birds." Still, he reassured Hitchcock that the new ending would have "a deeper meaning now, and a stronger purpose" (letter, Hunter to Hitchcock, 30 March 1962).

Not entirely pleased with Hunter's handling of the ending, Hitchcock sent the revised script to Pritchett with these instructions: first, the information that Melanie's mother had gone off with another man when Melanie was twelve should be added to an earlier scene of the film; second, after the convertible roof has been destroyed, Melanie should struggle out of Lydia's arms and utter something like, "Let me out. Let me go back! Mother, I want you . . . . I want you. Come back to me, please—please, come back to me." Immediately following this speech, continued Hitchcock, Lydia should pull Melanie down, hold her in her arms, and comfort her. Following this scene would come the final shot of the film, "the long shot with the car speeding away down the straight road to safety."

Perhaps reflecting his own confusion and indecision about how to end *The Birds,* Hitchcock placed a question mark in parentheses at the end of the sentence describing this relatively up-beat ending (letter, Hitchcock to Pritchett, 9 April 1962). Pritchett picked up on Hitchcock's indecision about how to end the film. In the next letter, he urged Hitchcock to end the film on a gloomier note, with the people in the car "looking backwards at the village with fear, rather than forward to the hope of escape" (letter, Pritchett to Hitchcock, 12 April 1962). Although different from Pritchett's version, the ending Hitchcock finally shot captures the spirit of Pritchett's ending.

In late April 1962, the final version of the last scene was entered into the script book. It describes the car leaving the Brenner house, the camera then returning to the house and looking outward over the porch:

> As it looks out, it sees first, on the rail in the foreground, the two rows of crows. Beyond it, the car is pulling away and heading for the road. There are birds everywhere—on the barn, on the wires, on the fences, over the bay; some even skimming the water in the distance. As the car reaches the road, it increases speed and the ROAR of its engine INCREASES: it gains distance and then its sports engine SOUND begins to fade. It is lost to sight round the bend but we can still HEAR the SOUND of the engine ROARING FAINTLY AWAY. Presently we can hear it no more. And now we are alone with the birds. There is an odd CROAK or two from the birds, now and again, a WILD GULL CRY. After a short while, the following small words—The End—appear, almost unobtrusively, at the bottom right-hand corner of the screen. (final script book)

Several months later, during post-production work on the film, Hitchcock decided not to end the picture with the words "The End" but instead to dissolve to a card with the words "A Universal Release," imitating the style of European art films (Memo to National Screen Service Corporation, 28 November 1962).[8]

Thus, the gloom, the tentativeness, and lack of resolution of the film's final scene are further indications that Hitchcock wanted to attract a more elite audience to *The Birds.* As I have suggested, one reason for wanting to appeal to a more highbrow audience is that Hitchcock wanted to be taken seriously as an artist. Another reason may have been purely economic. The size of the moviegoing public had dwindled in the age of television. "With fewer and fewer people going to the movies less and less frequently," says film-audience research expert Bruce Austin,

"Hollywood sought ways to hold onto its audience. Marketing research, with its aura of 'science,' was thought to be one way of achieving this goal" (Austin 1989, 5; see Handel 1950). As this research began to reveal "that only certain age- and income-levels consistently attended certain theatres" (Staiger 1983, 76), the film industry slowly retreated from viewing the audience as an undifferentiated mass. Therefore, it is not surprising that Hitchcock, similarly, revised his strategies. In addition to appealing to the more conventional filmgoer, he also tried to attract the more sophisticated ticket-buyers residing in large metropolitan areas who, he believed, turned to so-called "highbrow reviewers" for advice on which films to see. Hitchcock also tried to see to it that his next film, *Marnie,* would appeal to this more intellectual clientele.

From the beginning, Hitchcock had conceived *Marnie* as primarily a character study (not simply a suspense thriller) that would satisfy the serious or intellectual critics who, he claimed, often had condemned his films for their mechanical plots and underdeveloped characters. *The Birds* was still in post-production when in late August 1962 Hitchcock told Truffaut that in his next film project, *Marnie,* he would experiment with a looser form of narrative rather than cling to what he called "the rising curve or shape of a story." Paying greater attention to "the characters themselves," he hoped, would impress the serious critics (Hitchcock-Truffaut tapes, Hitchcock Collection). Hitchcock described to Truffaut the many facets of the Marnie character:

> You have to photograph the mind that steals—a calculating mind. Then you have the front character who, for example, takes a job as an usherette in a movie house with an eye to taking all the money from the safe. Then there is a part when the husband, trying to fight this frigidity, sends her to a psychiatrist and, of course, the questions of the psychiatrist bring out the gamut in her. . . . And there are very amusing scenes in the way she resists the psychiatrist. But his probings bring out something of the child background. So here you have another area for the character to play and that is the area of the childhood pain which will transfer itself from a comedy scene into moments of fear because the psychiatrist touches sore spots and of course the childhood experiences— when her mother had a man in with her and the man made an approach at her at four years of age. So there are a lot of angles to this character which will be quite a challenge for Tippi Hedren but more for me.[9]

Hitchcock was well aware of the price he might be paying for shifting the emphasis from building suspense to building character. For instance, during a pre-production conference, Hitchcock told Tippi Hedren that in the honeymoon sequence, forward plot progression would be sacrificed for revelations about the film's central characters—Marnie and Mark. In this sequence, we learn (along with Mark) that Marnie is frigid and also that Mark is torn between respecting her wish of not having any physical contact with him and satisfying his own sexual urges. But by failing to provide any forward story progression, as Hitchcock pointed out to Hedren, the sequence slowed down the narrative pulse of the film. On the other hand, Hitchcock reassured Hedren that after the honeymoon sequence things would "start moving pretty fast again" (Transcript of pre-production conference between Hitchcock and Hedren, October 1963).

As mentioned above, Hitchcock was upset with the intellectual critics, particularly the American ones, who, he claimed, had often attacked his films for lacking psychologically motivated characterizations and a plausible narrative structure. He was particularly upset with the *New Yorker* reviewers (unpublished portions of the Hitchcock-Truffaut tapes) who virtually dismissed his entire fifties output.[10] During his August 1962 conversation with Truffaut, Hitchcock had expressed ambivalence about such criticism of his work. On the one hand, he expressed contempt for those critics he derogatively referred to as the "plausibles." "We should have total freedom to do as we like," said Hitchcock, "just so long as it's not dull. A critic who talks to me about plausibility is a dull fellow." On the other hand, he confessed that he really wanted to please the plausibles, logicians, and psychologists. This confession surfaced during a discussion of *Shadow of a Doubt*, a film which Hitchcock had repeatedly told interviewers was his personal favorite.

HITCHCOCK: It's probably my conscience towards the plausibles or the logicians that I feel here is something they cannot complain about.

TRUFFAUT: And the psychologists?

HITCHCOCK: Yes and the psychologists. Probably that is the true reason for my saying it's my favorite film.

Hitchcock admits that his contradictory stance toward the plausibles reveals a personal weakness: "On the one hand, I claim to dismiss the plausibles, and on the other I'm worried about them. After all, I'm only human" (Truffaut 1984, 151).

Hitchcock believed that with *Marnie* he would be showcasing a female character whose behavior would appear entirely plausible to the intellectual critics once the details of her childhood trauma became known. "The husband follows her to her mother's house. It's all worked out plausibly. And her background comes out" (Hitchcock-Truffaut tapes).

By the time of the Truffaut interview, Evan Hunter, who wrote *The Birds* screenplay, had already completed the first draft of the *Marnie* script. Five months earlier, in March 1962, Hunter had started work on the script, completing a preliminary version of it by early June of that year. Details about how the preliminary screenplay evolved strongly suggest that Hitchcock believed that adapting Winston Graham's 1961 novel to the screen would provide an excellent vehicle for displaying the most complex, yet fully "intelligible" and believable character to appear in one of his films (*Marnie* Production Files).

In a letter to Hitchcock, dated 23 March 1962, Hunter informed him that he had scheduled a meeting with a psychologist friend to discuss, among other things, Marnie's frame of mind at various times, for example, when committing a robbery. After conferring with the psychologist, Hunter reported back to Hitchcock that many of the things happening in Graham's book made more sense to him now. The conversation had convinced Hunter that Graham must have either based the Marnie character on an actual case study "or else was simply intuitively correct." Moreover, the psychologist found the new ending that Hitchcock and Hunter had worked out concerning Marnie's childhood trauma to be "more valid" than the book's. Thus, *Marnie's* production files indicate how important the film's psychoanalytic framework was to Hitchcock's campaign to improve his artistic reputation among the serious critics.[11] On the other hand, because *Marnie* would have a conventional ending, he was convinced that the needs of his fans would also be met (unpublished portions of the Hitchcock-Truffaut Tapes). Notwithstanding his pre-production thoughts about the ending, the production information for *Marnie* reveals that, unlike in *The Birds* project, Hitchcock rarely commented to co-workers about the needs of his fans during the making of *Marnie*.

Hitchcock's desire to be accepted by both mass and elite audiences is also reflected in the marketing and publicity campaign he helped develop for both *The Birds* and *Marnie*. Consider first *The Birds*. The numerous tongue-in-cheek interviews with Hitchcock appearing in popular magazines (such as *Life* and *TV Guide*), the coast-to-coast pigeon race, the carefully orchestrated plugs for *The Birds* on popular television programs (the Perry Como, Gary Moore, and Art Linkletter shows, for example), the hilarious radio and lobby spots, and, not least, Hitchcock's ingenious ad campaign for the film featuring the very ungrammatical-sounding but highly effective slogan, "*The Birds* is Coming," all seemed directed to the general public. Indeed, much of the advertising and publicity emphasized the terrifying and horrific aspects of *The Birds* and Hitchcock as the acknowledged master of that popular genre of film (*The Birds,* Publicity Files).

The idea of promoting Hitchcock as the real star of *The Birds* was spelled out in an early memo to Hitchcock (drafted a good year before the film's release and before Hitchcock himself became really involved in the marketing campaign) from William Blowitz, head of the public relations firm handling the film's publicity:

> The star of this picture, as with *Psycho,* is Alfred Hitchcock. Therefore, a pivotal element in publicity and advertising will be Hitchcock. In the notes on the magazine campaign, the trailer and ads, all of this is emphasized. The point of the campaign is to sell tickets to *The Birds;* Hitchcock will be a principal element. (Memo, Blowitz to Hitchcock, 19 March 1962) (see plate 19).

The centrality of Hitchcock in publicity and marketing for *The Birds* is evident in the following lobby spot recorded by Hitchcock to warn patrons that they would not be seated until after the conclusion of each performance of the film:

> Dear Friends, Alfred Hitchcock here with a message of vital importance for you. *The Birds* is coming! Yes, *The Birds* is coming to this theatrical sanctuary very soon. While there is nothing unusual in the appearance of these birds, there is something quite unusual and even terrifying in their manners. I cannot say more at this time; to do so would be tampering with your enjoyment. That is precisely why I am going to ask you not to see *The Birds* until each performance has concluded. Since it is a well-known fact that birds of a feather shock together, I would like all of you to start your enjoyment at the same time; that is, at the very beginning of *The Birds.* Thank you again for your kind indulgence . . . and remember, *The Birds* is coming. (Typed copy of a lobby spot, 11 February 1963)

The lobby spot is also noteworthy for pigeonholing *The Birds* as a terror film—a slant repeated in most of the radio spots aired around the time of the film's release, as, for example, in the following:

> Dear Friends, *The Birds* are here! They are out there . . . massing, millions of them swarming into an army of feathered terror. To understand why they have united and who their target is, you will have to see this unusual motion picture from the very beginning; and remember in the darkness of the theatre, should someone clutch your arm in terror . . . it may be me. . . . Alfred Hitchcock. (Typed copy of a radio spot, 11 February 1963)

In the case of *Marnie*, Hitchcock's interest in attracting his fans is evident in his casting of Sean Connery (Agent 007) for the male lead. On 3 October 1963, a press release distributed to five thousand overseas newspapers announced the choice, making sure to highlight the connection between Connery and James Bond:

> The master of suspense, Alfred Hitchcock, announced he's getting together with the master of counterspies, James Bond—or at least with the man who plays Bond on the screen, Scotland's Sean Connery. . . . It will be Connery's first Hollywood part since he leaped into prominence as Bond in film versions of Ian Fleming novels.

Hitchcock and his publicity machine effectively exploited Connery's association with the Ian Fleming thrillers to generate favorable advance publicity for *Marnie*. For example, a photo journalistic piece, "Sean Connery: The Reluctant James Bond," appeared in *Look* magazine at the time of *Marnie's* release. Four of the eight photos in the story are directly linked to *Marnie*. In the first photo of the piece Connery points an accusatory finger at Marnie (Tippi Hedren) who is out of the frame. The caption reads, "On holiday from his lethal life as Bond, Connery plays a wealthy Philadelphia publisher who marries a beautiful thief in Alfred Hitchcock's *Marnie*" (*Look*, 8 September 1964).

Other marketing and publicity strategies Hitchcock helped develop for both *The Birds* and *Marnie* also reflect his desire to be accepted by more elite audiences. During the period of these two films, Hitchcock dealt behind-the-scenes with cultural institutions (e.g., The Museum of Modern Art), film figures (e.g., François Truffaut), and newspaper and magazine critics in order to promote his image as a serious film artist.

By the time Hitchcock was ready to devote his full energies to marketing *The Birds,* he had become convinced that this was no ordinary Hitchcock thriller. At a meeting (12 December 1962) with his ad men, Hitchcock made it known that he did not want the advertising and publicity for the film to create the impression that *The Birds* was just another film dealing exclusively with the killing of human beings. As Universal executive Ed Greenberg, who attended the meeting, described it, Hitchcock "felt that this was a more elevating film than *Psycho,*" and, therefore, "we should avoid creating a repetition of the *Psycho* ad style approach. This is a bigger and broader picture" (notes of meeting, *The Birds* Publicity File).

Within a month of this meeting, Hitchcock issued a press release directed to connoisseurs of film, announcing that he was in Germany supervising initial recording of a revolutionary electronic sound-effects system to be used in *The Birds,* and that the score for the film would use no music but rather would combine natural and electronic sounds to produce both "musical" and shock effects.

Hitchcock's major promotional coup within elite art circles was realized the night before the New York opening of *The Birds* when the Museum of Modern Art sponsored a press-screening of the film. Hitchcock's "connection" with the Museum of Modern Art at around the time of *The Birds* illustrates that an understanding of the reputational process must take into account the reciprocity of self-serving relationships that can evolve between the institutions of the art world and the artist.

The day before *The Birds* opened in Manhattan, the media had announced that the Museum of Modern Art was organizing a large-scale retrospective of Hitchcock's work, which left the impression that the Museum was acknowledging Hitchcock's greatness as an artist. In truth, MOMA's film department was hardly a bastion for Hitchcock studies. Like MOMA's first film curator, Iris Barry (1935–50), whom he succeeded, Richard Griffith, who headed MOMA's film program, had long been an advocate for a socially responsible cinema, preferring films that dealt realistically with pressing social and economic problems to those preoccupied with escapism and subjective states (see Lounsbury 1973, 324–29). For him, the post–World War II film, *The Best Years of Our Lives* (1946) epitomized the type of socially aware filmmaking he most admired:

> This American masterpiece . . . came as near perfection as popular art contrives to be. . . . It showed Americans as they are, pre-

sented their problems as they themselves see them, and provided only such solutions—partial, temporary, personal—as they themselves would accept. The picture's values are values of the people in it. (Griffith and Mayer 1970, 381).

In addition to William Wyler, who directed *The Best Years of Our Lives,* other American directors for whom Griffith had expressed admiration over the years were John Huston, William Wellman, Billy Wilder, and Fred Zinnemann, all of whose films were exemplary of the realist aesthetic Griffith championed throughout his career. In 1958 Griffith had prepared a short monograph on Zinnemann in connection with a retrospective on the director he had organized for MOMA. A Billy Wilder film series was his last major project before retiring in 1965 from the museum (see Griffith 1950, 1958a; Museum of Modern Art 1964).

It should come as no great surprise, then, that Griffith was no fan of Hitchcock's. His distaste for the director is dramatically revealed in a 1951 publication, where he discusses Hitchcock's limitations and those of his genre. "This specialist in mystery stories," he wrote, "needed no roots in national life for the kind of entertainment he purveyed. The escapist appeal of the mystery is international; it need give no more than the barest simulacrum of reality to achieve suspension of disbelief" (Griffith 1951, 556–58). In Griffith's view, it was Hitchcock's calculated use of montage for shock effects that accounted for his early success in England. His films after coming to Hollywood, however, gradually declined, according to Griffith, as star values (as reflected in "pseudo-romantic conflicts involving the highlighting of principal players") overpowered his cinematic style—a view which, as we have seen, was fairly typical of how most intellectual critics responded to Hitchcock's films during the fifties. Like these critics, Griffith had also found *Vertigo* lacking in substance (Griffith 1958b). And shortly after the launching of MOMA's Hitchcock retrospective in spring of 1963, Griffith would admit privately how much he disliked *The Birds* (1963 Hitchcock Retrospective Exhibition file, MOMA).

Why then did MOMA and Griffith get involved in a Hitchcock retrospective in the first place? Actually, the idea originated with film journalist and critic Peter Bogdanovich. An early supporter of the auteur viewpoint, he had originally proposed a similar idea to the New Yorker repertory theater, a revival house specializing in movie classics, but the idea was rejected when the cost of the series proved prohibitive. Bogdanovich was more successful with the Museum of Modern Art, where he had already arranged two successful directorial retrospectives—one on Orson Welles in 1961 and the other on Hollywood cult director Howard Hawks (a favorite of the French auteurists) in 1962. As with the Hawks series, Bogdanovich, who would eventually direct Hollywood feature films, organized the Hitchcock retrospective in conjunction with the promotion for the director's latest film. The arrangement that Bogdanovich eventually worked out with MOMA is revealed in a letter (8 January 1963) from Griffith to William Blowitz, the head of the New York-based public relations firm handling publicity for *The Birds*. In the letter, Griffith confirms the recent understanding reached between the museum and Blowitz's office. The Museum of Modern Art agreed to present a film retrospective entitled "The Films of Alfred Hitchcock" with the understanding that Blowitz's office agreed to pay the costs of the exhibition, including "the writing, designing, and printing of a monograph to accompany the exhibition":

> Confirming our recent understanding, arrived at through Peter Bogdanovich: the Museum of Modern Art agrees to present, on or about June 1 but not later than June 15, 1963, a film exhibition entitled, "The Films of Alfred Hitchcock," such films to be borrowed from their owners by the director of the exhibition, Mr. Bogdanovich, with your assistance and that of Mr. Hitchcock. You on your part agree to pay the costs of this exhibition in the amount of $5000. Of this sum, $4000 will be assigned to pay for the writing, designing, and printing of a monograph to accompany the exhibition, of which five hundred copies will be delivered to you free of charge. The remaining $1000 will be assigned to cover the costs of transporting prints of the Hitchcock films from California, Britain, and elsewhere to New York. (Hitchcock Collection)

Approximately one week later, Blowitz sent a letter to the film's distributor, Universal Pictures. After spelling out the details of the monetary arrangement he had worked out with the museum, Blowitz adds, "It is also our intention to have a special preview showing of *The Birds* at The Museum approximately March 27, preceding the opening in New York on the 28th. There is great value in an exhibition of this sort running for six months in New York City. I believe we should get with it."

The Hitchcock publicity machine did get with it. Copies of the monograph (Bogdanovich 1963) were mailed to the press and leading members of the motion picture industry. (For example, Philip Scheuer, film editor of the *Los Angeles Times* received a copy.) In a memo to Hitchcock, dated 19 April 1963, Blowitz described the unusual procedure for mailing the monograph. "They will be mailed," said Blowitz, "from the Museum of Modern Art and not from our office." Thus, it was no accident that media coverage of the MOMA retrospective left the impression that the museum, under the supervision of its film curator Richard Griffith, had initiated the show as a way of sanctioning Hitchcock as a serious artist. Indeed, that was precisely the impression that Hitchcock and his publicists (including Bogdanovich) wished to create. And, with their considerable influence, they succeeded.

Since Hitchcock was not a personal favorite of Griffith's, one might wonder why he and MOMA would go along with Hitchcock's public relations move. Of major importance is that there were precedents for such an undertaking. Since the late 1930s, MOMA had presented film series on national cinemas, film movements or genres, and, less often, on directors such as D. W. Griffith (1940) and William Wyler (1962)—part of the Museum's original mandate, "to trace, catalogue, assemble, exhibit and circulate a library of film programs so that the motion picture may be studied and enjoyed as any other one of the arts" (Barry 1941, 3). Also, a year earlier, as we have seen, Bogdanovich had organized a series, similar to the Hitchcock series, on Howard Hawks, also tied to the promotional campaign for the director's latest film and costing the museum nothing (1962 Howard Hawks Retrospective Exhibition File, MOMA). Importantly, the Hawks series marked "the first time," as Andrew Sarris has correctly pointed out, "that MOMA had honored an out-and-out Hollywood cult director with no prominent place in the standard Anglo-American film histories published up to that time" (Sarris 1979). At this time Hitchcock was also a cult director of sorts. While his British films received some praise in the standard film histories, his American films were summarily dismissed, as were other Hollywood genre films. By launching a comprehensive series on Hitchcock, including all but two of his American films,[12] MOMA was once again acknowledging the artistry of a Hollywood cult director, or so it seemed.

Moreover, the museum would benefit in various ways from the Hitchcock series. MOMA and Griffith expected that the series would be profitable. In return for sanctioning the retrospective, the museum would present Hitchcock's films over a six-month period at no cost to the museum (correspondence from 1963 Hitchcock Retrospective Exhibition File, MOMA). In addition to generating income, the retrospective, according to Charles Silver of the MOMA Film Department, provided MOMA with the opportunity to expand its audience by attracting a different segment of the public to the museum (conversations with Charles Silver, spring 1990 and winter 1991). Another benefit to MOMA was that the Hitchcock series might facilitate future dealings between the museum and Hollywood distributors and producers over film rentals, loans, acquisitions, and outright gifts to the museum. The need to cultivate and maintain ties with the business sector of the film industry is reflected in a letter from Griffith to a Universal executive handling publicity for *The Birds,* where Griffith admitted to disliking *The Birds* while, at the same time, he complimented the executive for executing an extremely effective publicity campaign for the film. In the letter, Griffith attributed the film's commercial success not to its content but to the effectiveness of the publicity campaign. "To that and nothing else" was how he phrased it in the letter, implying that the film itself had no real merit (letter, Griffith to Universal executive, 18 April 1963, MOMA). The general public was led to see things differently, however. In the monograph which accompanied the museum's Hitchcock retrospective, for example, *The Birds* was characterized as sufficient evidence that Hitchcock belonged "among the giants of cinema" (Bogdanovich 1963, 7).[13]

Hitchcock realized another major promotional coup within the film art world when it was announced that *The Birds* would open the 1963 Cannes Film Festival, then, and still, the most prestigious of film festivals and also one of the major commercial events for the international distribution of films. In a 1960 interview, the festival's director, Robert Favre Le Bret, stressed the festival's dual purpose. "The first," he claimed, was "the artistic and cultural. We insist strongly on that aspect of international exchange which allows each country to show the level of technique it has attained and, incidentally, to give us a picture of its way of life." According to Le Bret, it was the Cannes Festival's "high standards that account[ed] for the solid achievements of the second aspect, which is, of course, economic" (French Film Office, 1960). The commercial importance of the Cannes Film Festival is echoed in a survey of American importers and distributors of foreign films who attended the 1962 festival. The respondents generally viewed Cannes as the "most important of all the many festivals held throughout the year, partly due to its strategic timing at the beginning of the summer festival season and mostly because of the international composition of the participants" (*Film Daily,* 14 June 1962).

During the early sixties, perhaps even more so than in recent years, the U.S. film industry paid mere "lip service" to festival participation, viewing Cannes and other international film festivals "as primarily extra outlets for publicity" (Alpert 1962b, 46). There were complaints that the Americans were not sending their best films because the major film companies worried that a poor showing at the festival would weaken a film's box-office potential (*New York Times,* 11 April 1962). Although the balance at Cannes between art and commerce has shifted back and forth over the years (see Perry 1981 and Sarris 1982), in the early sixties, artistic and cultural considerations still dominated over strictly commercial ones (Alpert 1962b). In Hitchcock's case, however, both considerations must have fed his desire to have *The Birds* open the 1963 Cannes Festival.

Several months before completing the film, Hitchcock received a letter from Odette Ferry, who had handled foreign publicity for many of his films. In the letter, she outlined in considerable detail a campaign for launching *The Birds* in Europe. The highlight of the proposed campaign was the idea of *The Birds* opening at Cannes.

> *The Birds* could be shown in Cannes for the Festival as "hors competition," i.e., the picture would not compete with the other films. The screening could take place either on the opening night of the Festival . . . or on the closing night. Personally, I would be in favor of opening night because the first day of the Festival is always much more widely publicized than the last one since at the end of the Festival people are exhausted of seeing too many pictures or reading about them. I am definitely sure that it would be very easy for me to get the film invited "hors competition" by Favre le Bret whom I happen to know quite well. (letter, Ferry to Hitchcock, 22 October 1962, Hitchcock Collection)

The official press release, dated March 1963, announcing that *The Birds* would open the 1963 Cannes Film Festival quoted from a cable sent to Hitchcock from the festival's director Favre le Bret saying, "I am happy and honored to present 'The Birds' at the festival inauguration. I consider it a masterpiece in every sense of the word." Also underscored in the press release was the news that the film would open the festival out of competition. Unlike the other films to be shown, *The Birds* would not compete for any of the top prizes. This placement probably appealed to Hitchcock for two principal reasons: it would generate a great deal of publicity for *The Birds* before the film's release in Europe and other foreign markets, and it might also improve Hitchcock's standing with the more serious critics because of the impression it would convey: *The Birds,* by being in a class by itself, was really above competition.

Hitchcock's personal correspondence with François Truffaut, particularly during the period of *The Birds* and *Marnie,* also reveals the active role that Hitchcock and his publicity machine played in maximizing the publicity value of Truffaut's infatuation with Hitchcock. It is understandable that Hitchcock would think that American highbrow critics would be impressed to learn that François Truffaut, one of the most esteemed of the directors associated with the new international art-cinema movement, viewed him as one of the supreme geniuses of cinema. Largely through the writings of the more intellectual critics "appearing regularly in the arts and leisure sections of the major metropolitan newspapers" (Gomery 1990, 348) and through such highbrow magazines as the *Saturday Review,* the European film director during the late 1950s and early 1960s "rose to the status of international celebrity, talked about in the same breath with noted novelists or composers. Fellini, Antonioni, Bergman, Truffaut, and Godard, to name but five, became stars within this new form of cinema" (Gomery 1990, 350). Therefore, it was reasonable for Hitchcock to assume that if the internationally acclaimed director of *The 400 Blows* and *Jules and Jim* expressed publicly his admiration for Hitchcock's work, then American critics would soon follow his lead and acknowledge Hitchcock's cinematic greatness.

On 12 August 1962, Truffaut arrived in Los Angeles to interview Hitchcock. Truffaut originally planned that the book resulting from the interview would be published by the end of 1962, that is, only a few months before the domestic release of *The Birds.* Accordingly, Hitchcock was prepared to charge all of Truffaut's travel-related expenses (e.g., air transportation from Paris to Los Angeles and back) to the publicity account for *The Birds.* However, Truffaut out-maneuvered Hitchcock, insisting that he would pay for all the expenses connected with his visit to Los Angeles. As a result, only minor expenses, such as limousine charges, were actually billed as part of publicity for *The Birds.*

Hitchcock's desire to exercise ultimate control over Truffaut's book surfaces in a draft of a letter that was never sent. In it, Hitchcock elaborates upon his conditions for cooperating. One of these was that the final manuscript, in whatever form, must be sent to Hitchcock prior to submission for publication and that Truffaut must agree "to make all changes and deletions in the text which I request provided I make the request to you in writing within forty-five days after I actually receive the text." And in the event that Truffaut failed to comply with this agreement, he must agree and promise to pay Hitchcock the sum of $500,000. I suspect that the letter was never sent because Hitchcock realized in the course of his informal exchanges that Truffaut's admiration for him was absolute and that, consequently, Truffaut would do almost anything to enhance Hitchcock's reputation. Under such circumstances, the letter would be redundant, not to say a trifle uncivilized (Hitchcock Collection).

As it turned out, the publication of Truffaut's *Hitchcock* was delayed a few years; the English edition was not published until summer 1967. However, Truffaut did complete the chapter on *The Birds* in time for the September 1963 opening of the film in Paris, and Hitchcock agreed to Truffaut's request to have it published at that time in *Cahiers du Cinéma*.[14]

By fall 1963, Hitchcock was already shooting his next film, *Marnie*, when he instructed the director of publicity at Universal to solicit and distribute a tribute from Truffaut elaborating on Truffaut's view of him as one of the greatest film directors of all time. Hitchcock's office received Truffaut's tribute in December of 1963. Truffaut's adulation of Hitchcock is captured in the following passage:

> He is an instinctive. In the fifty films he has made, he has presented a selective universe which belongs to him alone. He has in his head dreams, obsessions and preoccupations which are not those of the masses, but which he successfully transmits to the screen and then offers to the public. He practices a cinema which acts physically on the spectator. All creative artists dream of accomplishing such a goal. . . . By definition an artist is a man apart from society. To succeed he must not integrate himself with society. But he must impose his originality. In other words, an artist must make himself accepted by society without renouncing his artistic dreams. Alfred Hitchcock is the filmmaker who has best resolved the problem of communicating with the public. . . . (Original Truffaut letter in French dated 16 December 1963)

By January 1964, copies of Truffaut's solicited tribute had been sent to key journalists and critics. For example, a *Los Angeles Times* reporter who would soon interview Hitchcock on the set of *Marnie* received a copy. And in the spring of 1964, an English translation of an earlier article on Hitchcock by Truffaut (originally published in 1954), appeared in *Film Culture;* at Hitchcock's request, copies were sent to New York film critics. Hitchcock also identified a writer for the *New York Times* who had consistently praised him over the years as someone who should receive a copy and who might be willing to disseminate the article to other New York critics.[15]

During 1963, Hitchcock learned that the French government was planning to award him the Legion of Honor. On 27 December 1963, he wrote to the Universal executive in charge of foreign publicity for *Marnie* to inquire whether in connection with the *Marnie* campaign a good public-relations angle "could be found in the fact that I am supposed to be given the Legion of Honor." "Perhaps," added Hitchcock, "you might ask André Malraux what's been holding it up all this time!"

Even the official press kit for *Marnie* (issued to journalists and critics shortly before the release of the film in the summer of 1964) emphasized the idea of Hitchcock as creative genius. "The prestigious Museum of Modern Art in New York recently presented a cycle of the milestone productions which have come forth from his creative genius." The press information also mentioned that in France, where film is regarded as a serious art form, Hitchcock is "hailed with reverential esteem."[16] A marketing manual for theater owners also exploited this angle. The heading for one article read, "Alfred Hitchcock—Candid Close-Up of Hollywood's Master of Cinematic Art."

CRITICAL RECEPTION OF *THE BIRDS* AND *MARNIE*

Critical and popular reactions to *The Birds* and *Marnie* were to a large extent shaped by the marketing and publicity campaigns developed for the two films. As reported in the last chapter, many of Hitchcock's fans were confused, shocked, and even outraged about the tentativeness and lack of resolution of the final scene of *The Birds.* Advance publicity for the film had not really prepared them for such an ending. A number of middlebrow and highbrow critics were also quick to denounce the ending, complaining of its complicated and pretentious art-house slant on reality (see plate 20). "Fans hooked on Hitchcock," wrote a critic for *Time* magazine, "may be dismayed to discover that, after 38 years and more than 40 films, dealing mainly in straightforward shockery, the Master has traded in his uncomplicated tenets of terror for a new outlook that is vaguely *nouvelle vague.*" "The lovebirds," continued *Time's* reviewer, "ostensibly family pets, perching smugly in their cage throughout the attack, seem to know something. Are they spies for the gulls? Do they somehow madden other species? Or are they just a comment, a wry admonition that men should 'love birds?' Hitchcock does not tell, and the movie flaps to a plotless end" (*Time*, 5 April 1963; see also Hollis Alpert's commentary in the *New York Times*, 1963).

By the time of *Marnie's* release, film commentators continued to express annoyance over Hitchcock's recent flirtations with high culture. Indeed, some early reviews of *Marnie* related the film's shortcomings to Hitchcock's attempts to produce a more "arty" product. Hitchcock's *Marnie* was panned in the *New York Times* and, according to the reviewer (Bosley Crowther did not review it), many of the film's shortcomings could be related to Hitchcock's present infatuation with his so-called greatness as an artist:

> A strong suspicion arises that Mr. Hitchcock is taking himself too seriously—perhaps the result of listening to too many esoteric admirers. Granted that it's still Hitchcock—and that's a lot—dispensing with the best in acting, writing and even technique is sheer indulgence. When a director decides he's so gifted that all he needs is himself, he'd better watch out. (*New York Times*, 23 July 1964)

Most reviewers of *The Birds* and *Marnie*, however, were indifferent to the French view of Hitchcock as a significant artist and judged both films against the expectations that Hitchcock's old biographical legend had helped nourish, namely, that above all else a Hitchcock film ought to be a taut and tantalizing suspense thriller. A *New York Daily News* review of *Marnie* was representative of many mainstream reviewers: " 'Marnie' is an Alfred Hitchcock picture. But it is NOT what we expect from the mystery maestro, a tantalizing guessing game with sustained suspense and charming people pursued by crooks and killers" (*New York Daily News*, 23 July 1964; see also chapter 4 below). In other words, for reviewers who had enjoyed and admired Hitchcock's earlier Hollywood films, his romantic thrillers from the fifties became the bench marks for judging whether *The Birds* and *Marnie* were good films. Against such expectations, neither film faired too well. As for the debate among the more highbrow critics concerning Hitchcock's "artistic" standing, most rejected the auteur view and recommended that he return to making entertaining films in the spirit of his best English-made thrillers from the thirties (see Kael, *Film Quarterly*, 1963a, 1963b;

Knight 1963a, 1963b, 1964; Macdonald, *Esquire,* 1963; Kauffmann, *New Republic,* 1963a; and Archer, *New York Times,* 1964, 1965).[17]

CONSTRAINTS ON REPUTATION: HITCHCOCK'S LATER FILMS AND THEIR CRITICAL RECEPTION

After the commercial and critical failure of *Marnie,* the executives at MCA/Universal decided to exert more control over Hitchcock, insisting that he fall back on a proven or more commercial type of picture. One of the projects he started to develop in fall 1964 was a comic thriller centering on a Mafia type of family whose members all reside in a large New York hotel. Two successful writers of the New European art cinema, Agenore Incrocci and Furio Scarpelli, began work on the script, but the project quickly fizzled out.

Hitchcock was also considering at this time a film based on the notorious Burgess-MacLean spy case in England. What interested Hitchcock about this case of defection was the effect on a woman of her husband's treason. One of the first writers that Hitchcock tried to interest in the project was the great expatriate Russian novelist Vladimir Nabokov. In a letter to Nabokov, dated 19 November 1964, Hitchcock wrote, "The question I'm really interested in is what would be the attitude of a young woman, perhaps in love with, or engaged to a scientist who could be a defector." Despite expressing an interest in working with Hitchcock, Nabokov turned down this particular offer. Several months later Hitchcock met with the Canadian novelist Brian Moore, who agreed to assume the writing chores for what would soon be called *Torn Curtain.*

Hitchcock's decision in 1965 to return to the spy-thriller format must have seemed a reasonable and potentially lucrative one to the executives at MCA/Universal. Spy films, especially the Bond adventures, were doing big business at the box office.

The James Bond phenomenon of the sixties was typical of the "boom and bust" cycles that characterize the production of genre films. During the boom phase of a new cycle, dozens of films are released or re-released, and dozens more are in various stages of production. At the height of the boom, media gatekeepers regularly provide copy, programming, and features about the genre and the people associated with it. Ways of talking about the new genre or the latest expression of an old one become established, including the critical vocabulary and frames of reference that both story departments and critics will apply to appropriate projects.[18]

The first James Bond film, *Dr. No,* was released in America in 1963. However, it was not until 1964, after the appearance of the second film in the series, *From Russia with Love,* that the spy boom-period really arrived. The enormous success of both films quickly inspired imitators. On 18 February 1964, a story analyst at Twentieth-Century Fox reviewed a property describing the exploits of "Frank Bruce," "fearless, seemingly indestructible undercover agent of the CIA," an obvious American counterpart of the popular British undercover agent. And in June of the same year, soon after the hugely successful American release of *From Russia with Love,* the same reader evaluated a property introducing "Emily Wells," a female James Bond (Sage Collection).

1965 was another strong year for spy films, culminating in the remarkable box-office showing of the two latest James Bond thrillers, *Goldfinger* and *Thunderball.* Another landmark spy film that year was *The Spy Who Came in from the Cold,* a serious entry into the spy-film sweepstakes. Its seemingly realistic and no-nonsense approach to the "intelligence" community, in contrast to the hyperbole and escapism of the Bond series, offered a possible new direction for the spy genre. It never happened. Spy spoofs would prove more marketable.

The spy genre continued to flourish through 1966, the year that Hitchcock's *Torn Curtain* was released. One of the highlights of that year was *Our Man Flint,* a spy spoof that proved popular with audiences. However, by 1967, the market was so inundated with spy films of one kind or another that the production of such films fell off dramatically. By 1968, the fad for spy movies was over.

Hitchcock's awareness of the Bond phenomenon dates from the release of the first Bond picture, *Dr. No.* The film premiered in London on 7 October 1962; seven months later, it was released in the United States. Among Hitchcock's personal papers is a copy of *Film Daily's* enthusiastic review of the film, dated 19 March 1963, a portion of which reads: "Now here's a thriller with style, freshness and imagination. . . . *Dr. No* is an auspicious beginning of what looks like a thrilling series."

Considering that Hitchcock had established himself as a master of the spy thriller through his work in the thirties, forties, and fifties, it is not surprising that a new direction in the genre would attract his attention. Although Hitchcock had not made a spy film in nearly five years, his interest in the genre in 1963 was evident in his casting of Sean Connery (Agent 007) for the lead role in his 1964 psychological drama, *Marnie.*

On 22 October 1965, Hitchcock sent to François Truffaut an early version of the *Torn Curtain* script. In the accompanying letter, Hitchcock explained what motivated him to make the film:

> I came upon the thought in this way: in realizing that James Bond and the imitators of James Bond were more or less making my wild adventure films, such as *North by Northwest,* wilder than ever, I felt that I should not try and go one better. I thought I would return to the adventure film, which would give us the opportunity for some human emotions in situations that were not too bizarre.

The letter indicates Hitchcock's awareness of his own stature as originator of the spy thriller, and also some pique at being outdone. His response is an attempt to recoup his audience through injection of his standard formula of psychological drama into the adventure form. One month later, a *New York Times* reporter who had recently interviewed Hitchcock described the filmmaker's approach to his latest film:

> To Hitchcock, *Torn Curtain* . . . represents a happy throwback to *Notorious* and films of that genre—spy-suspense movies about believable people who are torn by personal conflicts. It is not, Hitchcock emphasizes, a James Bond-type "comic strip" film, with its invincible hero and mechanical gimmickry. In Hitchcock's view, successful moviemaking still hinges on character, point of view and personal involvement. (*New York Times,* 21 November 1965)

In subsequent interviews about *Torn Curtain,* Hitchcock continued to emphasize the important differences between his films and the James Bond series. For example, Hitchcock told Peter Bogdanovich (who had spent some time on the set of *Torn Curtain*) that in a Bond film killing a human being is simple and routine. So in *Torn Curtain,* Hitchcock concocted that grueling scene in which Paul Newman and a middle-aged female accomplice have a most difficult time trying to kill an enemy agent. Indeed, it takes clubs, a knife, and finally a gas oven to dispose of him. "It's not easy to kill a human being," the director explained to Bogdanovich. "It's very difficult—not like James Bond—bang, you're dead" (*Movies International,* July–August, September 1966). And in a Sunday *Los Angeles Times* article, Hitchcock claimed that unlike with his films, audiences who attend a Bond film don't really get involved; they remain spectators "no matter how exciting or bizarre the situation is." In a Hitchcock film, by contrast, audiences care about what happens to the characters; "the elements of suspense," added Hitchcock, "comes out of the characters" (*Los Angeles Times,* 10 July 1966).

The critical climate in which *Torn Curtain* was received in late summer 1966 was significantly different from that for earlier Hitchcock films. Merchandised as a spy-suspense film, *Torn Curtain* was judged in relation to recent developments in that genre. Hitchcock had established his reputation as the master of the espionage thriller with such films as *The Man Who Knew Too Much* (1934), *The 39 Steps* (1935), *Foreign Correspondent* (1940), *Notorious* (1946), a remake of *The Man Who Knew Too Much* (1956), and *North by Northwest* (1959). However, at the time of *Torn Curtain's* release, he had not made a spy film for nearly a decade and the vacuum, as we have seen, had been filled by James Bond and his imitators.

Hitchcock's earlier work still dominated most critical discussions of *Torn Curtain. New York Times* critic Bosley Crowther was typical of many critics when he lamented the film's solemness and stiffness and, above all, its lack of "the lively wit, imagination, and suspense" of Hitchcock's best spy films (31 July 1966). A majority of critics agreed with Crowther's criticism (see *Torn Curtain* reviews, Hitchcock Collection).

The then enormously popular James Bond (or Bond-inspired) adventure films also influenced how several reviewers responded to Hitchcock's latest entry in the spy genre. The majority of critics who compared and contrasted *Torn Curtain* to current spy films found it simpleminded and old-fashioned. Hollis Alpert complained to the readers of the *Saturday Review* that "having been inundated with spy novels and movies, many of them highly ingenious, we just can't accept such simple-minded stuff" (*Saturday Review,* 13 August 1966). In his Sunday commentary, *New York Times* critic Bosley Crowther characterized it as "ordinary," "sluggish" and "creaky," commenting that "alongside such Bondian adventures as *From Russia with Love* or *Thunderball,* it looks no more novel or sensational than grandma's old knitted shawl" (*New York Times,* 31 July 1966; see also *Christian Science Monitor,* 15 July 1966). *Newsweek's* review complained that the *Torn Curtain* saga was written with a "minimum of plausibility and none of the outrageousness that saves James Bond from being foolish" (*Newsweek,* 8 August 1966).

What went wrong with the film? Alpert speculated that "Hitchcock just hasn't been going to the movies lately. There's a lot he has to catch up on." Crowther believed that the film would have been more effective if Hitchcock had added some satiric touches and hyperbole, both

characteristics, incidentally, that "the Bondsman have liberally borrowed from Hitchcock's earlier spy films." "This is ironic and pathetic,"
noted Crowther, "for it was actually Mr. Hitchcock's great spy films, the
most recent of which was *North by Northwest* in 1959, that established
the pattern and the spirit of the succeeding Bond-type things and
projected the secret agent thriller into the realm of complete hyperbole."

These critical reviews of *Torn Curtain* at the time of its first release
illustrate how changing genre conventions can condition the critical
vocabulary and frames of reference used by critics in evaluating a film
which is perceived as an example of a currently popular genre. The complaint that *Torn Curtain* was too derivative of Hitchcock's other films
(while lacking their moments of gripping satire) and not enough like the
Bond films revealed the normative nature of the James Bond craze still in
force when the film was released. In the critical climate dominated by
the spy cycle, Hitchcock was unable to further his goal of elevating his
artistic reputation.

Hitchcock's frustration with the largely negative critical reception
of *Torn Curtain* in the United States is revealed in a memo Hitchcock
instructed his assistant to forward to the head of Universal's New York
office of publicity. Several enthusiastic French reviews of the film had
come to Hitchcock's attention. Understandably, he wanted the New
York critics to know of their existence. But in his typically oblique and
devious style, Hitchcock insisted that his New York publicist show the
French reviews to certain key critics without divulging Hitchcock's office as the source of them:

> I am enclosing here . . . some French reviews on *Torn Curtain*
> which were translated into English, and sent to us, by one of the
> heads of the publicity department of Paramount Pictures in
> Paris. . . .
>
> Hitchcock thought it might be fun if Bosley Crowther and
> Judith Crist could be amused by the French unanimity. If you do
> find the time to show these reviews to them—I know you will con-
> ceal the source of their origin as coming from Hitch. (*Torn Curtain*
> Publicity Files, no date)

It was not only the critical climate at the time of the release of *Torn
Curtain* that hindered Hitchcock's goal of improving his stature as a
filmmaker. A deeper problem had been his defensive response to the
James Bond phenomenon, no doubt fueled by MCA/Universal's in-
sistence after *Marnie* that he play it safe on his next project. Rather than

experiment, Hitchcock, as we have seen, cautiously returned to the genre conventions he had created and helped codify for his fans. It was for that reason that writer Brian Moore found working with Hitchcock on *Torn Curtain* so stifling. In an interview which appeared in *Cahiers du Cinéma* shortly before the release of *Torn Curtain*, Moore unequivocally dismissed the French view of Hitchcock as a serious artist: "You know, Hitchcock is strong, he knows his work. He knows that he does not create art and does not pretend. His only standard is totally anti-*Cahiers*. 'Will that make or not make money?'" (Hitchcock Collection, no date).

During the three and a half years between *Torn Curtain* (1966) and Hitchcock's next film, *Topaz* (1969), the journalistic discourse on American cinema significantly changed. The auteur theory, first introduced in France, England, and the United States during the 1950s, was clearly on the ascent as indicated by the increasing number of journalistic articles sympathetic to it (see Brown 1984) and by the fact that many young and influential journalistic film critics had embraced the auteur viewpoint (see, e.g., Sarris 1968a; Schickel 1969; Gardner 1969; Canby 1969a). It was not the concept of authorship per se that *Cahiers du Cinéma's* critics introduced in the early 1950s, as Bordwell and others have pointed out, "only a *politique des auteurs,* a policy favoring particular directors" (Bordwell 1989, 46). Hitchcock, Wells, Hawks, Preminger, and Lang were among the directors most frequently singled out (see Hillier 1985). Yet *Cahier*'s younger critics did ground their criticism on maxims established by their mentor, André Bazin, principally by "showing how a director's characteristic stylistic and dramatic patterns reflect underlying themes" (Bordwell 1989, 47). Andrew Sarris was the key figure in spreading auteurism to the United States. In the mid-1950s, as a regular contributor to the specialized periodical *Film Culture,* Sarris expressed a preference for "realist" directors over so-called "gimmicky" ones like Hitchcock. In his 1955 review of *To Catch a Thief* and *The Trouble with Harry,* Sarris characterized Hitchcock as "a director of shreds and patches, a technician of touches and highlights further than ever from the top rank of directors" (Sarris 1955, 31). Among those he ranked above Hitchcock were George Stevens, John Huston, William Wyler, Billy Wilder, Elia Kazan, Henri-Georges Clouzot, Roberto Rossellini, and Carol Reed—all favorites of the critical establishment of that period.

By 1960, however, Sarris had already embraced auteurism and Hitchcock. His rave review of *Psycho* appeared that year, inaugurating his nearly thirty-year stint as film critic for the *Village Voice* (see Sarris

1960 and 1961). After residing in Paris in 1961, he returned as a tireless promoter of the auteur viewpoint, championing Hitchcock and other directors favored by the *Cahiers* critics. By the early sixties, a number of other New York film critics (e.g., Eugene Archer, James Stoller, and Roger Greenspun) had embraced auteurism. The *New York Film Bulletin* and *Film Culture* are two film publications from this period that were instrumental in disseminating information about the auteur perspective to many future film reviewers and critics. Sarris's influential essay "Notes on the Auteur Theory in 1962" first appeared in *Film Culture*. At first, as we have seen, there was strong resistance to the auteur theory (see, e.g., Kael 1963a; MacDonald 1963; Knight 1963b; and Kauffmann 1963a). In fact, not until the late 1960s would there exist a critical mass of influential journalistic reviewers who in the years to come would prove to be staunch supporters of the auteur perspective.

Developments in film criticism at the *New York Times* epitomize this aesthetic shift. In 1968 Vincent Canby replaced Renata Adler, who one year earlier had replaced Bosley Crowther as head film critic for the paper. In contrast to Crowther, who saw "art" only in those quality Hollywood productions that dealt with serious social issues, Canby regarded the popular offerings of the Hollywood "dream machine" as potential works of art. While Crowther had routinely characterized Hollywood genre films such as the Hitchcockian thriller as mere entertainment, Canby would become an important champion of the view of Hitchcock as serious artist (see discussions of *Topaz* and *Frenzy* below).

Hitchcock's reputation was helped along by other developments. In spring 1968, the Academy of Motion Picture Arts and Sciences presented him with the Irving G. Thalberg Award "for the most consistent high level of achievement by an individual producer" (see plate 23). In a sense, the event made amends for a longtime oversight. Hitchcock had been nominated four times for a directorial Oscar but, as he frequently put it, he had "always been the bridesmaid." The Directors Guild of America also honored Hitchcock that spring with the prestigious D. W. Griffith Award for his directorial achievements.

During the late 1960s, American colleges and universities also paid tribute to Hitchcock. A Hitchcock retrospective (including the exhibition of all available films) was sponsored by the film society of Dartmouth College during the academic year 1965–66. And in 1968 the University of Southern California became the first American university to sponsor a film retrospective of Hitchcock's work.

Academic interest in Hitchcock reflected the rise of academic interest in film in general during the sixties. Charles Maland has described the social and political climate that led to the dramatic increase in the number of film courses offered at American universities during the mid- and late 1960s:

> Before the mid-1960s, college courses on film as an art form were nearly as rare as courses on the novel in universities before 1900. In the mid- and late 1960s a dramatic proliferation of film courses occurred. More widespread American release of European art films by directors like Bergman, Antonioni, Godard, and Fellini demonstrated that films could be as complex and ambitious as other narrative art forms. American movies (within limitations) also became more able to experiment in subject matter and film style, as television became the dominant medium of mass entertainment and film began to aim at more specialized audiences. Furthermore, college enrollments expanded dramatically as the baby boom generation came of age and as a college degree became a required credential for more and more jobs. And the social and political climate included a sense that education ought to be "relevant" to students' lives. Since moviegoing was often a regular part of those lives, film courses seemed to meet that demand for relevancy. Combined, these factors contributed to the rapid growth of film classes. (Maland 1989, 352)

Bordwell has reflected on the fact that film study entered the academy largely through the efforts of teachers in the humanities. "When film study entered the academy," he writes, "it could have become a subdivision of sociology or mass communication studies. It was instead ushered into the academy by humanists, chiefly teachers of literature, drama, and art. As a result, cinema was . . . subsumed within the interpretive frames of reference that rule those disciplines" (Bordwell 1989, 17).

By this time, Anglo-American New Criticism completely dominated the academic institution of criticism. According to Bordwell, the New Criticism was much more than simply one among several possible approaches to criticism vying for legitimacy during the fifties and sixties. "As a theory, it defined literature as neither scientific nor philosophical discourse, effectively creating a specialized domain of professional knowledge. Historically, New Criticism reconstituted the field of literary study and virtually created the academic institution of criticism as we know it. Whatever school, trend, or movement to which a critic pledges allegiance, the practice of interpreting a text proceeds along

lines laid down by New Criticism" (Bordwell 1989, 23). Stressing intra-
textual unity and the rejection of authorial intention as a guide to exegesis, the New Criticism also heralded the interpretive activity of
uncovering implicit meanings as central to understanding cultural texts
(cf. Bordwell 1989, 43).

The exegetical character of the New Criticism proved compatible
with French notions of directorial preeminence and authorship. For the
academic film analyst, French auteur criticism meant uncovering meaning through close analysis of a film. It also meant treating the films of
"favored" directors such as Hitchcock as the works of a single creative
mind. Hitchcock's "texts" would thrive in an academic setting dominated by auteurism and the New Criticism. His films became an ideal
showcase for academic practitioners of auteur theory who were drawn
to them precisely because they saw Hitchcock's career as a perfect
vehicle for illustrating their conviction that great cinematic art could
flourish within the Hollywood studio system.

Hitchcock's reputation received another shot in the arm when the
English edition of Truffaut's book on Hitchcock was finally published in
late 1967. As critic Andrew Sarris correctly predicted, the book was
widely discussed and quoted. For example, the brochure prepared for
the USC-sponsored retrospective of Hitchcock's films contained several
passages from Truffaut's study, including the following: "To reproach
Hitchcock for specializing in suspense is to accuse him of being the least
boring of film-makers; it is also tantamount to blaming a lover who instead of concentrating on his own pleasure insists on sharing it with his
partner" (Hitchcock Collection).

The year *Topaz* went into production, 1968, was a bad one for spy
films. The spy cycle was quickly coming to an end. While the espionage
angle was still evident in many television productions, only a few theatrical films clung to the spy motif. Between 1964 and 1967, the mass
media had overexploited the genre; by 1968, the media had lost interest.

At a May 1968 press conference in New York City, Hitchcock announced that he would direct the screen version of *Topaz*, Leon Uris's
best selling novel about international espionage. During the question-
and-answer period which followed, neither the press nor Hitchcock expressed much interest in discussing the project in relation to the recent
James Bond craze. The only reference to agent 007 was an oblique one.
A reporter asked Hitchcock whether he thought the recent avalanche of
spy films had caused audiences to grow tired of such films. Hitchcock,
reiterating his own special formula, replied "No, this one doesn't deal

with gimmickry . . . no special devices. *Notorious* had no gimmicks although it was a spy story. . . . It was treated on a personal basis and it's the same with this story" (*Motion Picture Exhibitor*, 15 May 1968). Hitchcock's answer, in other words, implied that audiences may have tired of Bondian-style gimmick films but not of Hitchcockian spy stories with their focus on personal relationships.

Subsequent promotion for *Topaz* made virtually no references to the recent James Bond phenomenon. Rather, the campaign emphasized that the book upon which the film was based was inspired by a real-life espionage incident which occurred during the Cuban missile crisis of the early 1960s. Consider the following passage from a Hitchcock letter sent to exhibitors, along with a copy of Uris's book, a week or so after the New York press conference: "It is with a great deal of pleasure that I send to you this copy of *Topaz,* my next Universal picture. It's the kind of book that created world headlines recently when it was revealed that its suspense, romance and intrigue are based on actual fact" (*Topaz* Production Files, 14 May 1968).

On the few occasions when promotional materials included a Bondian hook, journalists did not bite. For example, a lavishly put-together advertising, publicity, and promotion kit for *Topaz* mentioned that Frederick Stafford, who plays the key role in the film—a secret agent—had been considered as a replacement for Sean Connery in the James Bond series but turned it down:

> Rumor has it that the new European film idol, Frederick Stafford, turned down a huge salary to replace Sean Connery as James Bond, and also refused to play any more leads in the "Agent OSS-17" series, made abroad, which first brought him film prominence. He wanted no more "typecasting," he said. Instead Stafford happily accepted a starring role in Alfred Hitchcock's *Topaz.* . . . And what part does Stafford play? A secret agent naturally. Suave, sophisticated, and a dashing French government figure in Washington social life. But still a secret agent. (*Topaz* Production Files, no date)

Yet virtually none of the newspaper and magazine stories about Stafford to appear in connection with *Topaz* linked him to Bond or, for that matter, to the secret agent roles he had portrayed in the OSS-17 series.

Recall that during the promotional campaign for *Torn Curtain* three years earlier, when Hitchcock had seized upon every opportunity to emphasize how the film departed from the Bondian adventures, journalists were only too eager to report on the connection. After all, Bond in those days was a sociological event. But by 1968, Ian Fleming's creation was already passé and journalists were searching for other angles from which to discuss Hitchcock's latest film. For the remainder of the 1960s, a pervasive attitude in the media was that, if Hollywood was to continue manufacturing espionage films, they had better be serious ones in the tradition of *The Spy Who Came in from the Cold*. The new anti-Bond sentiment, partly a reflection of the mounting antiwar mood of the nation as well as of the counterculture, is captured in the following passage from a *New York Times* article appearing on 1 February 1970, just days after the opening of a New James Bond film:

> while I was standing in line on a recent weekend at the Waverly Theatre to see the latest Bond bundle, I noticed that I wasn't the only die-hard 007 fan. It was a young crowd which went into the theater smiling and came out looking perplexed. The formula didn't make it any more. . . . Like Superman and all other good super-heroes, James Bond had not changed. But since 1963, when all of us first caught sight of the dashing Mr. Bond, our heads had gone through more changes than you could shake a joint at. And it was astounding to realize how different we were at the start of the seventies! (*New York Times*, 1 February 1970)

Another promotional angle for *Topaz* which proved highly effective was inspired by the recent publication of François Truffaut's prestigious study of Hitchcock. Hitchcock's publicity machine was quick to capitalize on the propaganda value of Truffaut's latest tribute, referring often in promotional materials to the books as the "definitive" study of Hitchcock. The following passage appeared in a lavishly produced promotional kit for *Topaz:*

> Countless essays on Hitchcock's mastery of the film form have appeared in magazines and journals, as well as books by George Perry and Robin Wood, and finally, the prestigious volume "Hitchcock" by François Truffaut, with the collaboration of Helen G. Scott. This work, now in its second American printing, has become a handbook of film buffs the world over. (*Topaz* Production Files, no date)

With the spy cycle on the decline and auteurism on the ascent, the auteur viewpoint rather than a genre orientation framed much of the critical discourse on *Topaz* once the film was released at the end of 1969.

Reviews of *Topaz* were virtually devoid of any mention of the Bondian adventures or of other recent spy films. Instead, references to Hitchcock's earlier masterpieces completely dominated the critical discourse on the film. In one of the only reviews of the film which mentioned the Bond films the message was markedly different from the lesson drawn from those reviews of *Torn Curtain* which compared that film to the then popular Bondian-type adventure films. *Film and Filming's* critic found *Topaz* stylistically inconsistent and offered the following speculation to account for this:

> the manner is surprisingly uncertain for Hitchcock, who appears to be hovering between the glamour . . . of Bond and the elusive realism of spies who stay out in the cold. If perchance he is looking for something to imitate, all he needs to do is re-run *Foreign Correspondent, Notorious,* the 1956 version of *The Man Who Knew Too Much* and *North by Northwest.* (*Film and Filming,* January 1970)

A good deal of the critical discussion of *Topaz* centered on whether or not the film supported Truffaut's pro-auteur claim that Hitchcock was a serious artist. Joining Truffaut's camp was *New York Times* critic Vincent Canby, who characterized *Topaz* as a movie of "classic Hitchcock effects . . . beautifully composed sequences, full of surface tensions, ironies, absurdities [and] a cautionary fable by one of the most moral cynics of our time" (*New York Times,* 20 December 1969). In other words, Canby saw in *Topaz* many of the ingredients often equated with great art.

Prominent among the critics in the anti-auteur camp was *New Yorker* critic Pauline Kael, who in a series of influential and widely discussed essays and reviews from the early sixties had attacked the views of Sarris and other popularizers of the auteur perspective (see, e.g., Kael 1963a). (Other early critics of the auteur theory, as we have seen, included Arthur Knight [1963b], Stanley Kauffmann [1963a], and Dwight Macdonald [1963]). One of Kael's chief complaints had been that the American auteur critics (especially Sarris and Bogdanovich) extolled style and technique over content, leading them to favor "trash" over "substance." (By the late 1960s, Kael would be accused of the same heresy, a charge that her foes have repeatedly brought up against her—see chapter 6). According to Kael, the auteurists' preference for Hollywood action directors such as Hitchcock, Hawks, Walsh, and Aldrich over filmmakers of "substance"—Huston, Reed, Zinnemann, Bergman, etc.—

was sufficient proof that underneath it all the auteur critics were really lowbrows masquerading as highbrows:

> These critics work embarrassingly hard trying to give some semblance of intellectual respectability to a preoccupation with mindless, repetitious commercial products—the kind of action movies that the restless, rootless men who wander on Forty-Second Street and in the Tenderloin of all our big cities have always preferred just because they could respond to them without thought. These movies soak up your time. I would suggest that they don't serve a very different function for Sarris or Bogdanovich . . . even though they devise elaborate theories to justify soaking up their time. (Kael 1963a)

However, a few years later, in her much debated essay, "Trash, Art, and the Movies," Kael admitted that in addition to her opposition to commercialism, she too rejected so-called serious films of "substance":

> We generally become interested in movies because we *enjoy* them and what we enjoy them for has little to do with what we think of as art. The movies we respond to, even in childhood, don't have the same values as the official culture supported at school and in the middle-class home. At the movies we get low life and high life, while . . . the moralist reviewers chastise us for not patronizing what they think we should, "realistic" movies that would be good for us—like *A Raisin in the Sun,* where we could learn the lesson that a Negro family can be as dreary as a white family. Movie audiences will take a lot of garbage, but it's pretty hard to make us queue up for pedagogy. At the movies we want a different kind of truth, something that surprises us and registers with us as funny or accurate or maybe amazing, maybe even amazingly beautiful. ([1968] 1970, 102)

Audiences enjoy films like *Notorious* or *Morocco,* Kael claimed, because of their playfulness, not because of their complexity, depth, and solemnity. Yet, the auteur critics deceive themselves when they tell us in their "respectable museum publications" that the reason they enjoy Hitchcock or von Sternberg is because these directors are great artists:

> It's appalling to read solemn academic studies of Hitchcock or von Sternberg by people who seem to have lost sight of the primary reason for seeing films like *Notorious* or *Morocco*—which is that

they were not intended solemnly, that they were playful and inventive and faintly (often deliberately) absurd. And what's good in them, what relates them to art, is their playfulness and absence of solemnity. . . . It's a peculiar form of movie madness masquerading as highbrowism, eating a candy bar and cleaning an "allegorical problem of human faith" out of your teeth. If we always wanted works of complexity and depth we wouldn't be going to movies about glamorous thieves and seductive women who sing in cheap cafes. ([1968] 1970, 113–114)[19]

Kael directed her reviews and essays, especially after the mid-1960s, to a youthful, white, upper-middle-class, college-educated, and hip audience. Her readers, she assumed, were disaffected from mainstream society and identified with the bohemian life-style and leftist politics of the counterculture of the sixties. Also, she assumed that their knowledge about the movies meant that they would find pleasure in a film *because* it violated old movie conventions. That explained, according to Kael, why her readers found *Psycho's* shower scene so startling and pleasurable:

Hitchcock teased us by killing off the one marquee-name star early in *Psycho,* a gambit which startled us not just because of the suddenness of the murder or how it was committed but because it broke a box-office convention and so it was a joke played on what audiences have learned to expect. He broke the rules of the movie game and our response demonstrated how aware we are of commercial considerations. ([1968] 1970, 88)

On the other hand, according to Kael, when movies are bad and don't deliver, when "our hopes and expectations" are not met (including the expectation that a new movie might play around with old movie conventions), we feel alienated. Kael had felt that way about all of Hitchcock's post-*Psycho* films—*The Birds, Marnie,* and *Torn Curtain. Topaz* would be no exception.

Kael used her 1969 review of *Topaz* to reassert her position that Hitchcock had always been a master trickster and manipulator of audiences—never an artist. In the distant past, she conceded, he had been "the master entertainer of cinema" because he gave audiences pleasure. But now, argued Kael, "that he no longer gives pleasurable excitement there are no other dimensions to his work, there is not even craftsmanship! . . . The embarrassment of Topaz is that Hitchcock is lazy and out of touch" (*New Yorker,* 27 December 1969; see also

Alpert, 1969; *Nation,* 1970; and Mazzocco 1970). Unlike the auteur critics, Kael believed that, on some level, a really good film was a response to events and happenings in the wider society. During the late sixties and early seventies, the young warriors of the counterculture had denounced the cold-war ideology of their elders. Yet, here was Hitchcock unreflectively recycling these same old cold-war myths:

> I think he really expects us to identify with the waxwork Cuban rightists who are spying for the United States . . . and all the people who look like cutouts and behave like drab, enervated versions of spies in his earlier, better films. . . . The actors seem to have been selected to be stereotypes, but what Hitchcock thinks they represent may be a long way from what they mean to us. (Kael 1969)

Kael attributed Hitchcock's decline to a tendency that, she declared, has plagued most commercially successful directors: "they become deadened to their times and to new work in movies and the other arts." Still, Kael anticipated that the auteur critics would proclaim *Topaz* as another flawless masterpiece from Hitchcock, just as several auteur critics had done with *Marnie,* overlooking or explaining away many of that film's obvious flaws (see chapter 4).

Even the trade papers entered into the debate about auteur theory and Hitchcock. *Motion Picture Exhibitor*'s reviewer suggested that Hitchcock's recent highbrow and "intellectual" converts might find *Topaz* more to their liking than his "older, more demanding viewers":

> It used to be, in years gone by, that when an Alfred Hitchcock thriller was released, the same audiences that relished a Humphrey Bogart vehicle or a John Wayne shoot-'em-up would wait breathlessly for the film to play in their neighborhood theatre, while the "intellectual" film critics would grind out diatribes against the vulgarity and superficiality of the "master of suspense's" stylistics. Times have certainly changed. Now a Hitchcock film is considered a work of art (which, of course, it was all along) on the rarified plane of a Stravinsky symphony or a Picasso painting. (*Motion Picture Exhibitor,* 1969)

While a few auteur critics praised *Topaz* (e.g., Canby 1969; Sarris 1969; Belton 1970; McBride 1969–70), the majority opinion among reviewers was strongly negative (see *Topaz* reviews, Hitchcock Collection) Indeed, the critical consensus today is that *Topaz* is one of Hitchcock's weakest films. Therefore, it is not surprising that within the context of *Topaz*'s first theatrical release in late 1969, the debate about auteur theory and Hitchcock ended in a stalemate. One might speculate that had Hitchcock released a film at that time more reminiscent of *North by Northwest* or one of his other popular romantic thrillers of the 1950s, this would have tipped the scale in favor of the view of Hitchcock as a great movie auteur. Perhaps an additional reason why many American critics still refused to acknowledge Hitchcock as a significant artist is that the auteur theory, while gaining adherents between 1964 and 1969 (especially among academic critics), was still not that widely accepted among journalistic film critics. Many still clung to the belief that Hollywood films, because of their glaring commercialism, were incompatible with artistry and profundity (Brown 1984). As one journalist put it in a *New York Times* article published on 18 May 1969, "Some American critics still forget to mention who directed the film they've just seen, which is like writing a book review and not giving the author's name" (Brown 1984).

It was not until 1972 that Hitchcock released his next film, *Frenzy*. During the three years between *Topaz* and *Frenzy*, many more newspaper and magazine critics embraced the auteur theory (see Brown 1984) which by now had become firmly entrenched as the dominant theoretical perspective among academic film critics in the United States.[20] In fact, many of Hitchcock's films were now included as part of the core curriculum of university film programs.

A few weeks before *Frenzy*'s release, Hitchcock received an honorary doctorate from Columbia University. According to his biographer, Donald Spoto (1983), that event was "only the beginning of the greatest outpouring of adulation America gave Hitchcock in over a decade" (551). One observer reported that students attending an advance screening of *Frenzy* at the University of Southern California responded euphorically when the film ended (personal interview with former USC film student, spring 1986). The outpouring continued as critics nearly unanimously praised *Frenzy*.

By the time of *Frenzy*'s release, a significant number of influential U.S. critics had come to accept the "new" view of Hitchcock as a great artist.[21] Reflected in these reviews are many of the values that auteur critics look for: hidden meanings, personal vision, universality, reflexivity, and thematic and stylistic consistency and coherence (see plate 26). With *Frenzy*, reviewers would have a good vehicle for commenting on Hitchcock's artistry. Although perhaps not the great film that critics at that time claimed it to be, *Frenzy* was, at the very least, an entertaining one with some memorable Hitchcockian touches.

Many American critics agreed with the reviewer for *Newsweek* that *Frenzy* was not simply a great psychological thriller in the grand Hitchcock tradition but also a work of considerable artistry:

> he has created *Frenzy,* a psychological thriller that ranks among his very best and shows the 72 year-old director in triumphant command of his unmatched artistic powers. . . . As has always been the case, Hitchcock uses the vehicle of the thriller as a conveyance for more serious social and psychological material. . . . This is a fable about luck—Blaney's (and his ex-wife's) bad luck, Rusk's good luck. It is about the failures of friendship: all Blaney's old RAF buddies ultimately betray him. And the film is about the power of money, and the readiness of the world to judge events by their surface. (*Newsweek,* 26 June 1972)

Like other conventional practitioners of auteur criticism, the reviewer finds beneath *Frenzy*'s thriller surface a film rich in hidden or implicit meanings (see also Maslin 1972 and Belton 1972).

A number of reviewers also compared *Frenzy* favorably to recent works by such then-acknowledged masters of the international art cinema as Antonioni, Bergman, and Kubrick. As Bordwell has forcefully argued, "The art cinema accustomed critics to looking for personal expression in films, and no one doubted that it could be found in the works of Antonioni, Bergman, et al. Auteur critics went further and applied art-cinema schemata to classical Hollywood films" (Bordwell 1985, 232). For example, the critic for the *Hollywood Reporter* wrote: "Hitchcock seems to delight in making us aware of his craftsmanship—technique is flaunted the way it was in 'Blowup,' 'Persona,' and '2001.' And Hitchcock treats the audience as his intellectual equal; even when he's being coyly deceptive, he's really saying, 'The others may not catch on to this, but I'm sure you will!'" (*Hollywood Reporter,* 26 May 1972; see also Canby 1972). While few critics were in agreement as to what constituted cinematic art in *Frenzy,* a sizeable number acknowledged (either directly or indirectly) in their reviews that Hitchcock was a significant artist.

What struck *Life* reviewer Richard Schickel about *Frenzy* was "the way the moral universe we once thought existed only in Hitchcock's imagination has become reality" (Schickel 1972a), suggesting as the French auteurists characteristically did, that great film art transcends time and place (see also Champlin 1972). That is, many auteurists, as

Staiger maintains, "seek 'universality' and 'endurance,' which implies a transcendence of history. Sarris, for instance, criticizes those writers who argue that films are related to their historical circumstances, claiming that some of the most interesting films have nothing to do with the period in which they are made" (Staiger 1985, 12).

For *New York Times* critic Vincent Canby, *Frenzy* was a reflexive film: "Were Hitchcock less evident throughout the film 'Frenzy' would be as unbearable as it probably sounds when I report that the killer has to break the fingers of the corpse. Yet it is something more than just bearable because never for a minute does one feel the absence of the storyteller, raising his eyebrows in mock woe" (Canby 1972). A reviewer for *Rolling Stone* went even further, characterizing *Frenzy* as Hitchcock's first fully "retrospective" film, evoking his "entire body of work" (Paul 1972; see also Belton, 1972 and *Daily Variety* 1972).[22] "*Cahiers du Cinéma* and *Movie* frequently cited auteurs' works," says Bordwell, "as 'testaments,' ruminations on the essential conditions of the medium" (Bordwell 1989, 111).

According to *New York Magazine* critic Judith Crist, "it is . . . Hitchcock's far-from-simple art that makes the film work so splendidly. . . . So sure is the style that there is never a frenetic moment; the enthrallment is accomplished with care to its totality. 'Frenzy' is a complete entertainment for the viewer—and a total triumph for its creator" (Crist 1972). Crist's comments are consistent with the auteurist's search for consistency and coherence in cinematic works of art (see also Maslin 1972 and the *Hollywood Reporter* 1972). "In a way," as Staiger has observed, "this is related to the auteur's 'personal vision' rather than *visions* of the world. But it also derives from the requirement that the auteur has been touched with an enduring message, not one fragmented by historical, social, or idiosyncratic problems."[23]

Many of the reviewers who by the early 1970s had acknowledged Hitchcock as a significant artist—Richard Schickel, Vincent Canby, and Janet Maslin, to name but a few, were of a new generation, which had come of age in the late 1960s. Very few of those who raved about *Frenzy* in 1972 were among the same reviewers who had panned *The Birds* in 1963. While a few who had long admired Hitchcock's skills as a popular entertainer (e.g., Judith Crist) now embraced the new view of him as a consummate artist, others such as Arthur Knight, whose film criticism had appeared in the *Saturday Review* since 1949, resisted adopting the new label. Knight is an interesting case in point. In addition to his *Saturday Review* assignments, Knight had recently joined the staff of the *Hollywood Reporter,* while continuing to teach film at the University of

Southern California, where he had been affiliated since 1960. Long an admirer of Hitchcock's British thrillers, Knight (along with his former review partner at the *Saturday Review*, Hollis Alpert) had often expressed serious reservations about Hitchcock's Hollywood films, especially those he made for Paramount during the fifties (see chapter 2). An assistant curator at MOMA during the late thirties and early forties, Knight's subsequent writings—his influential cinema book, *The Liveliest Art (1957)*, and his numerous film reviews and commentaries—reflected the "realist" aesthetic to which he had been exposed as a young man while under the tutelage of MOMA's first film curator, Iris Barry (see Knight 1978). Not surprisingly, Knight had preferred the brutal realism of Clouzot's fifties thrillers to the glossy artificiality of Hitchcock's.

The good news about *Frenzy*, according to Knight, was not only that Hitchcock had returned to what he did best—exploring the "eccentric aspects of crime"—but that he had returned at the top of his form. Indeed, for Knight, *Frenzy* was "Hitchcock's best since *North by Northwest*"— a film he always considered among his "favorite Hitchcocks." However, for Knight, the film excelled solely as a clever thriller in the tradition of the "British school of mystery-fiction writing." At no point in his review did he approach *Frenzy* as an art work or Hitchcock as an artist (Knight 1972). For great film art, according to Knight, you would have to look beyond Hitchcock—to the works of Chaplin, Renoir, Griffith, Eisenstein, Murnau, Dreyer, Fellini, and Welles (see Knight 1988). As both critic and educator, Knight never wavered from this view. While a number of mainstream newspaper reviewers seemed to agree with Knight's assessment of Hitchcock (see the *Frenzy* review file, Hitchcock Collection), most of the more influential New York critics, as we have seen, had come to accept the new view of Hitchcock as a serious artist. And these critics would continue to crusade for Hitchcock, even after his death in 1980.

MAINTAINING A REPUTATION (1972–84)

In 1973 the popular public television series "The Men Who Made the Movies" highlighted the careers of eight master American film directors. The series finale on Hitchcock—which actually had been the pilot for the series—echoed the French auteur view of him as a serious artist whose work reflected on the darker aspects of the human condition:

> For over three decades people have been calling Alfred Hitchcock the master of suspense but he is more than that. In the age of anxiety he is the movie's great artist of anxiety. His wonderous tech-

nique is all directed to a simple end: staying in touch with his primal fears—the stuff of his childish nightmares and ours.

Indeed, our world, says Richard Schickel (who wrote, produced, and directed the series), "has come more and more to resemble the world that used to exist only in the anxious imaginings of Hitchcock's mind"—a world where evil is all pervasive and where all of us are "tainted by something like original sin." "History," continues Schickel, "has confirmed his vision. The only fantasy left is that he is just an entertainer."[24]

An understanding of how an artistic reputation is socially constructed must take into account the interlocking and self-serving relationships that can emerge between various representatives of the art world and the artist. In the case of Schickel's series, Hitchcock's artistic reputation would be maintained and reinforced through a project conceived as a vehicle for spreading the auteurist's view of Hollywood as a work-setting where a director could realize his or her personal vision. Hollywood, as would be expected, helped fund the project, much to Schickel's and Hitchcock's delight.

Schickel's first glimpse at the serious side of Hitchcock came during the summer of 1972 when he interviewed him for the TV program. That fall Schickel published an article on Hitchcock in the *New York Times Sunday Magazine* (29 October 1972). An important theme of the piece was that Hitchcock was more an artist than perhaps even Hitchcock realized. In an uncharacteristic letter, dated 8 November 1972, Hitchcock thanked Schickel for the article:

> You know, this is quite an occasion for me. This is definitely the only time in my whole career that I have ever written to a film writer—critic—adjudicator—you name it. I was propelled into writing because of the most fascinating and gratifying piece in the New York Times Magazine. I do sincerely thank you. (Hitchcock Collection)

While I do not question Hitchcock's sincerity, I suspect that by endorsing Schickel's view of him as a largely misunderstood genius, Hitchcock also hoped that the letter would persuade Schickel to incorporate this image of him into Schickel's TV profile of the director. After all, many more people would view the TV program than had read the *New York Times* piece.

Schickel also stood to gain a great deal from the Hitchcock TV profile. Soon after the release of *Frenzy* (a film which, as we have seen, Schickel greatly admired), Schickel had asked executives at MCA/Universal to provide him with the support money to produce a pilot program on Alfred Hitchcock for a projected series on American directors. Clearly the program would generate favorable publicity for Hitchcock, one of MCA/Universal's prized clients. In addition, Schickel pointed out to the executives that the proposed series would argue against the then widely held belief that Hollywood in the old days had stifled talent—a view that "had been propagated mostly by writers and by actors and directors who had been recruited from the stage and were convinced that the movies were a lesser art than the novel or the drama" (Schickel 1975, 6–7). By contrast, Schickel believed that broadcasting the recollections of such remarkable directors as Raoul Walsh, Frank Capra, Vincente Minnelli, George Cukor, Howard Hawks, William A. Wellman, King Vidor, and Alfred Hitchcock "would be a useful corrective to the . . . belief that Hollywood . . . had been universally ruinous to talent" (1975, 6). MCA/Universal executives liked Schickel's idea. Within a few weeks, the studio came up with the funds necessary to launch Schickel's project. Subsequently, Eastman Kodak Company agreed to underwrite the entire series. Without Hitchcock's endorsement and MCA/Universal's financial backing, the series probably would never have materialized.

This was not the first time that Hollywood capitalized on Hitchcock's preeminence. Hitchcock's personal papers reveal how the American film industry attempted throughout the sixties to exploit Hitchcock's high visibility and increasing stature in order to generate favorable press for the American film industry as a whole. Indeed, Hollywood was the major beneficiary of Hitchcock's improved stature as a filmmaker during the sixties and early seventies. Publicists for the industry could now point to Hitchcock's career as evidence that significant art could flourish within the American commercial cinema.

The publicity surrounding the 1976 release of Hitchcock's next and last film, *Family Plot,* was also slanted to flatter both Hitchcock and Hollywood. A press release announced that the film was selected to open the 1976 Los Angeles International Film Exposition (FILMEX) as a joint tribute to Hitchcock and the American cinema. As Arthur Knight put it (1976a), "In this Bicentennial year, I can't think of two American institutions more worthy of such a salute." Yet perhaps the most interesting aspect about the publicity and advertising campaign for *Family Plot* was how irrelevant it proved to be in shaping the critical response to the film. A more significant frame of reference for evaluating the film was the now widespread and deeply entrenched view among influential American critics that Hitchcock was an inspirational artist who could really do no wrong. For U.S. critics, *Family Plot* was additional proof that Hitchcock was a cinematic genius.[25] Only in this period, coinciding with the final stage of Hitchcock's filmmaking career, would the Matthew effect postulation, "the more one has, the more one gets" (see Merton 1968), be most dramatically revealed, with the reception of *Family Plot*.

By the mid-seventies, Hitchcock's artistic stature and renown had become so well-established among American critics that even with a film that today is viewed as inferior such as *Family Plot*, Hitchcock could accumulate more fame. This was achieved in two ways—through critics who praised the film and through those highly critical of it who used their reviews as an occasion for commenting on Hitchcock's illustrious career, highlighting his greatness as a cinematic artist.

While the present consensus among American critics is that *Family Plot* is a slight work, when first released in 1976 the film received generally favorable and even some enthusiastic reviews. Indeed, a number of influential critics such as Penelope Gilliatt of the *New Yorker* and Charles Champlin of the *Los Angeles Times* pointed to *Family Plot* as further evidence of Hitchcock's artistry and genius. Said Gilliatt (1976a), "Hitchcock has never made a strategically wittier film, or a fonder; and this in his seventy-seventh year." Champlin concurred. "It is atmospheric, characterful, precisely paced, intricately plotted, exciting and suspenseful, beautifully acted," said Champlin (1976) "and, perhaps more than anything else, amusing." On the other hand, those who found fault with *Family Plot* tended to blame not Hitchcock but his collaborators, especially his screenwriter, Ernest Lehman, whose screenplay provided a convenient scapegoat. As *New York Post* critic Frank Rich put it (1976a), "Given the script Hitchcock had to work with this time around, however, we should be grateful for small favors. . . . Lehman's contribution here, adapted from a novel by Victor Canning, is shoddy and, at times, downright sleazy. It's amazing Hitchcock has been able to get as much out of it as he has." Although Rich was less than enthusiastic about the film, his review reflected the momentum of Hitchcock's soaring reputation. Focusing scant attention on *Family Plot*'s weaknesses, Rich, instead, seized the opportunity to point to Hitchcock's more recent triumphs. In accord with the Matthew effect, Rich's review was structured more as a tribute to Hitchcock than as a condemnation of *Family Plot*. For example, Rich rhapsodized about how Hitchcock had become more interested in exploring the abstract possibilities of the medium than in simply telling a good story:

> Like many modern painters (such as Klee and Kandinsky), great movie directors often become more intrigued by the abstract possibilities of style as they get older—and Hitchcock's other '70s films, *Topaz* and *Frenzy* (like the late films of such other one-time storytellers as Ford, Hawks, Renoir, Buñuel and Chaplin), showed open disdain for many of the narrative conventions that had served his movies in the past. (Rich 1976a)

One astute American critic who was keenly aware of how Hitchcock's esteem had softened many of the reviews of *Family Plot* suggested conducting the following experiment as a way of sensitizing readers to the operation of the Matthew effect:

> Close your eyes during the opening credits of *Family Plot*. Then try to keep them open for the next two hours. Then close them through the final credits. Now tell me: who directed the film? If you say Alfred Hitchcock, it can only be because you spotted his familiar silhouette in one of the scenes, and not because *Family Plot* has any of the skillful storytelling or moral ambiguity associated with the Master of Suspense. To call this "a Hitchcock film" is to be an accessory to false advertising. *Family Plot* should be reported to the Consumer Protection Agency. (Corliss 1976)

By the time of Hitchcock's death in 1980, one would think that few still needed convincing as to his artistic preeminence and stature. Still, obituaries, remembrances, and commentaries following his death annoyed dyed-in-the-wool Hitchcockians. The epithet "master of suspense" had appeared far too frequently, especially in mass-circulation dailies such as the *New York Daily News* and the *New York Post*—ample proof for Richard Schickel and others that many of the "middlebrow" critics still regarded Hitchcock more as an entertainer or technician than as a serious or inspirational artist. As Schickel observed (1980) shortly after Hitchcock's death, "there were implacably middlebrow critics [still] insisting that Hitchcock never placed his impeccably subtle technique in the service of 'serious' matters." *New York Times* critic Janet Maslin also decried the "master of suspense" epithet for "offering a limited vision of his career" (1980). Instead, Hitchcock's long-time champions preferred referring to him as the "master of existential suspense" (Schickel 1980), the "poet of civilized suspense" (Canby 1980a), or simply "the Master" (Mark Crispin Miller 1980).[26] Of course, the less prestigious or intellectual publications were catering to more conventional filmgoers for whom Hitchcock was still only "the master of suspense."[27]

The Museum of Modern Art also acknowledged Hitchcock's importance as an artist. Earlier I described the 1963 Hitchcock retrospective at the Museum of Modern Art as a triumph in "impression management." By the time of his death in 1980, the aesthetic climate at MOMA's film department had dramatically changed. During the sixties and seventies, the department became increasingly more adventurous and less parochial than it had been during the forties and fifties. By the time of Hitchcock's death, the directorial retrospective at MOMA had become more the rule than the exception. Also, it became routine for MOMA's department of film to present film series on previously despised genre films or on directors formerly dismissed as not significant. Recent staff appointments at the Museum also reflected the growing acceptance of auteurism as a legitimate orientation to film studies (Study Center Files, MOMA). By the time of Hitchcock's death, MOMA's film department had also come to view Hitchcock as a major artist, as revealed in their condolence letter to the Hitchcock family:

> He was one of the supreme poets of the cinema. We believe that Sir Alfred, more than any of the other great filmmakers, always retained a sense of wonder about the possibilities of his medium. Every new film seemed an adventure in experimentation as Sir Alfred challenged himself to explore new territory. We all feel that we have lost a friend, but we are comforted by the treasure of his cinematic legacy. We extend our most sincere sympathy. (Hitchcock Study Center File, MOMA)

And a few weeks later, Charles Silver of MOMA's film department prepared a two-page tribute to Hitchcock for patrons which is excerpted below:

> Hitchcock's personal conservatism . . . was counterbalanced by the cinema's most creative experimental spirit. . . . His masterpieces (*Notorious, Strangers on a Train, Rear Window, Psycho, The Birds*) provide . . . a textbook on the cinema's potential for aesthetic expression beyond the limitations of literature, theatre, and the static visual arts. Although Hitch only occasionally bor-

rowed from others, he was able to absorb the advances of his contemporaries and incorporate them into his extraordinary personal body of work. . . . Directors like Ford, Hawks, and Chaplin became more pessimistic as they aged. In a sense, Hitchcock was always pessimistic and was, therefore, our most intrinsically modern filmmaker. . . . Since Robin Wood's *Hitchcock's Films* first appeared fifteen years ago, film scholars have been aware that no cinema artist has dealt with relationships in a more adult and serious manner than Hitchcock. If there is any salvation in our world, Hitchcock tells us, it is a personal one—forging an intimate relationship with another human being. (Hitchcock Study Center File, MOMA)[28]

Sociologists Kurt and Gladys Lang (1988) have suggested several reasons to account for the durability of a reputation, including "the availability of others who, after the artist's death, have a stake in preserving or giving a boost to that reputation [and] the artist's own efforts, in his lifetime, to protect or project his reputation" (Lang and Lang 1988, 86). The revival and reception of five "classic" Hitchcock films three years after the director's death provides a good illustration of this process. Of the fifty-four films that Hitchcock directed over a fifty-year period, he had commercial control over five of them—*Rope, Rear Window, The Trouble with Harry, The Man Who Knew Too Much,* and *Vertigo.* (Ownership rights reverted to Hitchcock eight years after the films were first released.)[29] These five films, dating from the ten-year period between 1948 and 1958, had been taken out of circulation by Hitchcock during the early seventies. According to Richard Schickel (1985), who had interviewed Hitchcock around that time, Hitchcock had decided to hold these five films "off of television and away from revival houses as a legacy for his wife, Alma, and his daughter, Patricia." Keeping the films off the market, Hitchcock believed, would increase their economic value. Another possibility, as Schickel has speculated (1985), is that Hitchcock's decision to keep these films out of circulation until after his death was related to his wish to maintain some control over his posthumous reputation. Once dead, Hitchcock could no longer control what might be published about him. Libel laws, for instance, could no longer protect him from slander. However, what he could do, before he died, was to prevent these films from being shown until after his death. It would then be up to the guardians of his estate to determine a propitious time for releasing them. And, as it turned out, the reissue of these films, starting in 1983, couldn't have been better timed for managing Hitchcock's posthumous reputation.

Three months before the reissue of *Rear Window*, the first of the five "lost" films to be released, Donald Spoto (1983) published his controversial biography, *The Dark Side of Genius: The Life of Alfred Hitchcock*. A long-time champion of the view of Hitchcock as a serious artist, Spoto in his new book characterized Hitchcock as a tormented artist with a dark and malicious streak. Behind Hitchcock's facade of high joviality and good-naturedness, Spoto claimed, was a tormented and mean-spirited individual with the sexual immaturity of an adolescent. This sexual immaturity and Hitchcock's cruelty, says Spoto, came to a head during the filming of *Marnie,* when he declared his affection for the film's star, Tippi Hedren, who rebuffed him. After that incident, according to Spoto, Hitchcock did all he could to ruin Hedren's career. While not rejecting his earlier view of Hitchcock as a serious artist (see Spoto 1976), Spoto's emphasis in his new study was on how these revelations about Hitchcock's stunted growth and cruelty as a human being provided insights into Hitchcock's art. While many reviewers interpreted Spoto's preoccupation with Hitchcock's character failings as a novel way of illuminating aspects of his genius, others hostile to the idea of Hitchcock as an important artist could also point to Hitchcock's "uncommon loathesomeness" as if that were proof enough that he could not possibly have been a significant artist (see, e.g., Richard Grenier [1983], who reviewed Spoto's book for the *New York Times* on 6 March 1983).[30]

Before Spoto's book could significantly damage Hitchcock's posthumous reputation, the five rediscovered Hitchcock films were reissued for theatrical release, starting with the popular 1950s film *Rear Window*. One outcome of releasing these by now critically acclaimed "masterpieces" was to undercut or cancel altogether the adverse effects that Spoto's book might have had on Hitchcock's posthumous reputation.

Among those involved in promoting these films was Hitchcock's daughter, Patricia Hitchcock O'Connell, who had appeared in three of Hitchcock's films, including *Strangers on a Train*. When asked by reporters to comment on the Spoto book (which she claimed never to have read), Pat Hitchcock came prepared with stories about her father which contradicted Spoto's thesis. For example, Spoto had charged that Hitchcock was a malicious prankster and bully. Among the many practical jokes described in the book is one Hitchcock reportedly played on his daughter while working on *Strangers on a Train*. According to

Spoto, Hitchcock had left her dangling high on a Ferris wheel, knowing that she was afraid of heights. Hitchcock's daughter denied the veracity of this story as well as all the other slanderous passages from the book she had heard about. "I've not read Mr. Spoto's book," she told one reporter, "but I have heard several quotes from it. So far I haven't heard one quote that is true" (Silverman 1984).

Others who had been close to Hitchcock also attempted to protect his public image from Spoto's allegations. At a New York press conference before the re-premiere of *Rear Window* at the New York Film Festival, James Stewart (who appeared in four of the five "rediscovered" films) was asked to comment on Spoto's revelations about Hitchcock's "dark side." According to Andrew Sarris, who had been present at the press conference, "Stewart said simply and graciously that he had never been aware of Hitch's 'dark side,' and doubted that Hitch could have hid it so successfully if it had actually existed" (Sarris 1983a).

The revival of these films also helped deflect the Hitchcock debate away from Spoto's "revelations" about Hitchcock's questionable conduct to the strength of the films themselves. Andrew Sarris, for example, seized the occasion of the re-release of *Rear Window* to denounce Richard Grenier for using Spoto to attack Hitchcock. Like others hostile to Hitchcock's art, said Sarris, Grenier has focused "on the 'dark' side of the title at the expense of the 'genius.'" Acknowledging the "sick side" of Hitchcock's art, Sarris argued that Hitchcock managed to "surmount this sickness time and time again with wit and humor and the most beautifully articulated feeling of which the motion picture medium was capable" (Sarris 1983a).

In 1983 with "the best" of the reissues, *Rear Window* and *Vertigo*, in the theaters, it seemed that "there was not a movie critic in the country who did not write an awed piece about Hitchcock's mastery of his form." As if by design, "the bright side of genius [had] banished the dark side to the edge of consciousness where it [belonged]" (Schickel 1985).[31]

Shifting Assessments of Hitchcock's Canonized Works

Academic film criticism, particularly during the 1970s when the auteur theory dominated film studies, has strengthened Hitchcock's reputation as a great "film artist." Films such as *Vertigo* (1958) and *Marnie* (1964), which were denounced by the vast majority of intellectual reviewers during their initial release, were rediscovered as forgotten masterpieces by academic and other more serious critics under the influence of the auteur theory. Despite the trend away from author-centered criticism, academic critics who approach meaning as lying "outside the conscious control of the individual who produces the utterance" (Bordwell 1989, 72) have continued to discuss Hitchcock's films (e.g., Mulvey 1975; Bellour 1977, 1979; Wollen 1982, 18–48; and Wexman 1986). Many feminist film critics, for example, have invoked Hitchcock's work to illustrate how women function as passive objects of spectacle for the sadistic pleasure of the male viewer in classical Hollywood cinema (see Mulvey 1975). Focusing on the shifting assessments of Hitchcock's films among journalistic and academic film critics, the present chapter shows how the criteria used by the auteur critics to evaluate Hitchcock's works from 1960 on were distinct from those that shaped both previous and later generations of critics.

To illustrate how changes in critical discourse over the past few decades have shaped the "meaning" of Hitchcock's works, I examine first *Marnie* and then *The Birds*—two films which have figured prominently in scholarly reassessments of Hitchcock's work.

The first generation of journalistic critics from the United States and England faulted *Marnie* (1964) for its loose plot, its simpleminded Freudian assumptions, and its numerous technical deficiencies.[1] Many early journalistic reviewers of *Marnie* complained that the film lacked the kind of taut plot so characteristic of Hitchcock's great romantic thrillers of the fifties. (Following the unrelenting gloom of *Psycho* and *The Birds,* many critics hoped Hitchcock would return to making films in the spirit of such works as *North by Northwest, Rear Window,* and *The Man Who Knew Too Much.*)[2] As one New York critic put it, "It has always been the dictum of Alfred Hitchcock that every single scene in a film, no matter how short or obscure, must be a step building toward the climax" and that "nothing can be omitted from one of his pictures because it would destroy the elaborate mosaic that makes a Hitchcock film." With *Marnie,* continued this critic, Hitchcock "seems to have deviated from his ideals, for there is a good deal of extraneous matter that could easily have been cut without affecting the highly charged climax at all." For example, according to this critic, Marnie's shooting of her horse Forio is an episode that did nothing to advance the suspense (Thompson 1964). (For a future generation of critics, on the other hand, Marnie's killing of Forio would be interpreted as a partial reenactment of her childhood trauma and, therefore, crucial in illuminating Marnie's kleptomania and frigidity.) As one critic perceptively pointed out, Hitchcock paid a price for concentrating on character: "by seeking to achieve an outstanding character portrayal for his star" he sacrificed "the famed Hitchcock suspense touch" (Greenberg 1964).

Many critics, both in America and abroad, also complained about the Freudian framework of the film, which they found simplistic and old-fashioned.[3] *New York Herald Tribune* critic Judith Crist, a long time admirer of Hitchcock, wrote:

> Somewhere along the plodding plot line of *Marnie* "Tippi" Hedren says to Sean Connery 'You Freud—Me Jane'—and there you have the 110 minutes of Alfred Hitchcock's new—or rather most recent—film. New it isn't in form or content. Mr. Hitchcock himself made this kind of movie nigh on to 20 years ago and made it a lot better. In the interim we've been so belabored on movie and television screens by five-cent psychiatry wrap-up in true romance and/or the annals of crime that *Marnie* can only strike us as pathetically old-fashioned and dismally naive. (Crist 1964)[4]

Critics were annoyed by the film's so-called technical deficiencies, for example, the phoney backdrops and the "poorly executed" process shots of Marnie riding her horse.[5] In his *Village Voice* column, Andrew Sarris wrote, "His fake sets, particularly of dockside Baltimore, have never been more distracting, and the process shots of 'Tippi' on horseback are appallingly dated" (1964). Reviewers proposed a variety of explanations to account for the film's technical shortcomings. Sarris felt that the "inability of the leads to hold the foreground" imposed "an extra burden on the background" ("Who cared if Rio were in process in 'Notorious' when Bergman and Grant held the foreground"), while others attributed the technical errors to Hitchcock's stint "in the shallow waters of TV films" and to personal laziness on his part.[6] A more frequent charge among critics both here and abroad was that Hitchcock was taking himself too seriously, with the result that he had dispensed with his best collaborators.[7] As a *New York Times* critic put it, "When a director decides he's so gifted that all he needs is himself, he'd better watch out!" (Archer 1964).[8]

Annoyance over what was perceived as Hitchcock's growing pretentiousness was a major reason why journalistic film critics responded so negatively to *Marnie* during its initial 1964 release. Thus, Hitchcock's efforts at the time of *Marnie* to transform his reputation from that of popular entertainer to serious artist affected not only the making of the film but also contributed to the film's negative critical reception. Most critics wanted a film consistent with what they had come to expect from the acknowledged master of suspense. From that vantage point, *Marnie* was not a "true" Hitchcock film.

The auteur phase of *Marnie* criticism began most visibly in 1965 with the publication of Robin Wood's *Hitchcock's Films* and lasted until roughly the late 1970s. Auteurist reassessments of *Marnie* during this period were overwhelmingly favorable and emphasized Hitchcock's total mastery of the film medium (see, e.g., Cameron and Jeffery 1965; Huss and Silverstein 1968, 40–43; Belton 1969; Spoto 1976, 397–413; Yacowar 1977, 265).

Unlike the heavily publicized appearance of Truffaut's *Hitchcock* in 1967, the publication two years earlier of Wood's study, the first book-length treatment of Hitchcock's films in English, went largely unnoticed by American journalistic critics. By contrast, academic film critics were quick to recognize Wood's work as a pioneering effort in the exegesis of Hitchcock's art. For example, in his introduction to *Focus on Hitchcock,* the first collection of critical readings on Hitchcock, published in 1972, Albert J. LaValley acknowledged the importance of Wood's study, describing it as "a key document in the Hitchcock controversy" and "essential reading for Hitchcock enthusiasts." Before we examine Wood's treatment of *Marnie,* it would seem appropriate, given the prominence of his study, to describe in some detail Wood's overall orientation.

He begins his book with the question: "Why should we take Hitchcock seriously?" His strategy, initially, is to clear away several "false preconceptions" about Hitchcock's work which he feels have adversely affected Hitchcock's reputation. According to Wood ([1965] 1977, 30), one reason critics have failed to appreciate Hitchcock's films is that they have failed to grasp the uniqueness of the film medium.[9] Echoing the position of the French auteur critics, he argues, in addition, that the commercial qualities of Hollywood filmmaking have also led critics to believe that "however clever," "technically brilliant," "amusing," "gripping," etc. they may be, Hitchcock's Hollywood films, especially his most popular ones, "can't be taken seriously as we take, say, the films of Bergman or Antonioni seriously" (Wood [1965] 1977, 30). As evidence of his concessions to the box office, critics have pointed to Hitchcock's tendency to return to the thriller genre for material, his use of established stars, his use of comic relief, and so on. As a partial rebuttal to this view, Wood ([1965] 1977, 31) reminds the reader, as academic auteur critics would so frequently do during the seventies, that Shakespeare too, whose work derived from "the sense of living contact with a popular audience," was unappreciated by contemporary critics for many of the same reasons as those given for disparagement of Hitchcock. He worked in an intellectually disreputable medium, the Elizabethan drama, and included bawdy scenes in his plays which undermined any high seriousness his works may have possessed. Another reason many critics have dismissed Hitchcock is his own apparent unwillingness to regard his work as serious ([1965] 1977, 33). As a corrective to those swayed by Hitchcock's public persona, Wood advises, paraphrasing D. H. Lawrence, "Never trust the artist—trust the tale," and recommends looking at Hitchcock's films in detail.

After clearing away these "false" preconceptions about Hitchcock, his work, and his medium, Wood outlines, in a manner that foreshadows many of the concerns of academic auteur criticism during the seventies, the following justification for treating Hitchcock as a serious artist. First, there is a unity to Hitchcock's work. Wood ([1965]1977, 36) believes that in his later films, especially, there is a consistent and deepening vision about the human predicament.[10] Second, there is tremendous variety to his work (Wood [1965] 1977, 36). For example, each of the five films he made between 1958 and 1964, *Vertigo, North by Northwest, Psycho, The Birds,* and *Marnie* is strikingly different in terms of "tone, style, subject-matter, [and] method." Third, the thematic content of Hitchcock's films is complex. Like other works of art, Hitchcock's films contain themes of profound and universal significance that inform not only the content but also the form and style of his films. Fourth, like other works of art, Hitchcock's films disturb, leaving a "nasty taste in the mouth."[11] Their disturbing features relate to Hitchcock's sense of a precarious moral order, most profoundly expressed in his later Hollywood films, especially *Rear Window, Vertigo,* and *Marnie.*

To further illuminate the moral dimensions of Hitchcock's work, Wood ([1965]1977, 40–41) identifies two threads which, he claims, "run through Hitchcock's later work." The first thread is what Wood (1977, 41) characterizes as "the therapeutic theme." A character "is cured of some weakness or obsession by indulging it and living through the consequences." The second thread is the extension of the "therapy" to the viewer "by means of encouraging the audience to identify." Much of Wood's book is preoccupied with showing how these threads run through Hitchcock's later films.

Following his introductory remarks, Wood concentrates on seven Hitchcock films, all made between 1950 and 1964—*Strangers on a Train, Rear Window, Vertigo, North by Northwest, Psycho, The Birds,* and *Marnie.* Except for *Strangers on a Train,* these are the films which Wood regarded as Hitchcock's masterpieces to date. Indeed, as Deutlebaum and Poague (1986) have correctly pointed out, these films have remained over the years at the core of the Hitchcock canon, having received more scholarly attention than his other works.

While early reviewers had charged that *Marnie* represented a serious falling off and decline in Hitchcock's development, Wood regarded the film as perhaps Hitchcock's most mature work. In the Marnie character, says Wood, Hitchcock "gives us the most definitive statement so far of that 'therapy' theme we have seen running through all his work." Every sequence in the film "is constructed as a necessary stage in the breaking down of Marnie's defensive barriers, of all that prevents her being fully alive." Hitchcock's preoccupation with the therapeutic theme is evident in the production information described in the previous chapter which revealed his attraction to psychoanalysis as an explanatory framework for making the behavior of his heroine credible to audiences and critics.

As further proof that *Marnie* is one of Hitchcock's richest films, Wood points to the film's moral and emotional complexity. For evidence of this, he describes the controversial rape sequence that precipitates Marnie's attempted suicide. While on their honeymoon cruise, Marnie reveals to Mark that she is frigid. Mark promises her that they will not have sex. He keeps his word for a few days. But under the influence of alcohol, he finally succumbs, forcing Marnie to have sex with him. "There is no more devastatingly beautiful scene in the whole of Hitchcock," says Wood, "and the beauty arises not merely from the fluency of expression but from the awareness of moral complexity that underlies it." Below is Wood's detailed "reading" of this controversial sequence, to which I shall return later in order to illuminate other interpretations of Hitchcock's work:

> Mark, who has been drinking heavily (to weaken the grip of his superego?), desperate from frustrated desire—which is both desire *for* Marnie and desire to help her—follows her into the bedroom. She asks him to leave if he doesn't want to go to bed; he replies that he "very much wants to go to bed." She understands, cries out "No!" in panic, and he rips off her nightdress. The sequence of shots is then as follows: 1. Marnie's bare feet and legs. 2. Her head and bare shoulders. Mark says, "Sorry, Marnie." 3. Both of them. He removes his dressing gown, wraps it round her. She stands stiffly, in a sort of tense, rigid resignation. He kisses her. 4. Overhead shot of the kiss. His hands stroke her tenderly. 5. Low-angle shot. We see his lips moving over her unmoving, expressionless face, her lips making no response whatever. She is like a statue. His protective gestures—the dressing-gown, his stroking hands, his tenderness—tenderness inseparable from sexual passion—combine with her hopeless, unresponsive immobility to give us that sense of a longing for the unattainable that is the essence of *Vertigo;* the angles—overhead shot to suggest protectiveness and solicitude, low-angle to reveal in detail the tenderness of the man's touch—add to the desolating sense of his helplessness, his inability to reach her. 6. Close-up, Marnie's face. She sinks down, the camera following her, peering into her eyes with their terrible, unfathomable emptiness, like the eyes at the beginning of *Vertigo.* 7. Close-up, Mark's face, huge and ominous, shadowed, the eyes seeming to bore into her. We share simultaneously his pity and desire and her terror, we see how in him desire for her and desire for power *over* her are not clearly distinguished. 8. Close-up, Marnie again. Then the camera pans round across the bedroom, coming to rest on a porthole. A sexual symbol, certainly, which conveys the sexual act; but more than that: for beyond the porthole is the sea, empty, desolate, grey, and the shot also com-

pletes our emotional response to the whole scene. The complexity here is both moral and emotional, conveying to the spectator a sense at once of the beauty and the tragic pathos of human relationships. The scene offers one of the purest treatments of sexual intercourse the cinema has given us: pure in its feeling for sexual tenderness. Yet what we see is virtually a rape. To the man it is an expression of tenderness, solicitude, responsibility; to the woman, an experience so desolating that after it she attempts suicide. Our response depends on our being made to share the responses of both characters at once. (Wood [1965] 1977, 147)

Much of Wood's praise of other aspects of *Marnie* was in response to earlier negative criticism of the film, especially from the English critics. For example, Wood elaborated that many reviewers complained that the film was "full of absurdly clumsy, lazy, crude devices, used with a blatant disregard for realism: hideous painted back-drop for Mrs. Edgar's street; ugly and obvious back-projection for Marnie's horse-riding (and during the hunt, for Lil Mannering's); zoom-lens for the final attempted theft; red flashes suffusing the screen every time Marnie has a 'turn'; thunderstorms arriving coincidentally at climactic moments" ([1965] 1977, 134). With this earlier criticism in mind, Wood then offers a justification for Hitchcock's use of each of these devices, including the backdrop of the ship and the rear projection used in the horse-riding sequence.[12] The "unreality" of the ship, says Wood, is a magnificent "inspiration," because a real ship on a real street "would have sacrificed the most important aspect of all: the constrictedness of Marnie's life belongs essentially to the world of unreality, the trap she is caught in is irrational and her prison will be finally shattered by true memory" ([1965]1977, 135). The back-projection also has purpose, says Wood, giving "a dream-like quality to the ride, but no sense of genuine release." This effect is achieved by editing. From the ride, we "cut immediately to the taxi driving up the mother's street toward the ship: change of 'vehicle,' apart, it is presented as part of a single movement, a single state" ([1965] 1977, 135). According to Wood, then, the direct use of all these devices—the backdrop, the rear projection, the zoom lens, the red flashes, and the thunderstorm always arriving at key dramatic moments—is "perfectly fitting in a film where every idea unerringly finds its most fluent, most economical, most direct expression, from the opening track on the yellow bag to the final long shot of the car turning away as it passes the ship" ([1965] 1977, 136). Wood's point once again is that Hitchcock can really do no wrong. With *Marnie*, he has created another seamless work of art (for a similar assessment, see Cameron and Jeffrey 1965).

While American and British auteur critics claimed to be not overly concerned with directorial intent, their search for artistic purpose and consistency often left the impression that their prized auteurs were in complete control of their material. The production information on *Marnie*, however, points to how the auteur critics' expectations of finding artistic purpose and consistency in the works of their favorite auteur directions could lead to exaggerated claims about a film's implicit meanings.

Hitchcock's production files strongly support the view that many but by no means all of the above-mentioned devices cited by Wood were intentionally implemented by Hitchcock to tap Marnie's subjective state. According to *Marnie's* production designer, Robert Boyle, who had worked in that capacity on a number of other Hitchcock films, including *Shadow of a Doubt, North by Northwest,* and *The Birds,* it was the subjective nature of the film which made it in many ways the most difficult film Hitchcock ever made. As production designer, Boyle was particularly close to Hitchcock's thinking during the preparatory stages of a film project. Boyle believed that *Marnie* was Hitchcock's most difficult film in that "Hitchcock was trying to get at something you couldn't see. He was trying to tell a story of things that are not all overt. That's why he got involved in those tricky solutions. He was trying desperately to really dig into the psyche of this woman" (personal interview, 16 April 1986). As Hitchcock told Tippi Hedren in a preproduction conference, he would attempt to make it clear to audiences that the red suffusions signified Marnie's inner turmoil rather than a technical flaw in the print (transcript of pre-production conference between Hitchcock and Hedren, October 1963, Hitchcock Collection).

With respect to the backdrops and process-shooting, on the other hand, the available production information strongly suggests, contrary to Wood and other auteur critics, that Hitchcock sought external realism but technical mishaps ensued. According to Robert Boyle, the backdrop of the ship was supposed to have looked very realistic. "We didn't intend it to look phony." It happened that one of the scenes which used the backdrop called for rain. With water on the backdrop, recalls Boyle, the ship as well as the painted bricks of the houses looked glossy. Robert Burks, the film's director of photography, agreed. So Boyle approached Hitchcock, almost pleading with him to reshoot the sequence. Much to his surprise Hitchcock didn't seem particularly upset with the backdrop sequences. In fact, Hitchcock said, "I don't see anything wrong with it, Bob. I think it looks fine" (Boyle interview). Also falling short of Boyle's and Burke's expectations were the riding sequences, but again Hitchcock appeared satisfied.[13]

As we have seen, the conventions of auteur criticism led Wood to argue erroneously that all of the so-called technical flaws of the film that had annoyed the early critics were really brilliantly executed expressionistic techniques employed by Hitchcock to convey to audiences what it must have felt like to be Marnie. Wood's polemical agenda led him astray in other ways as well. Because the film's early critics had failed to mention them, Wood and other auteur reviewers of *Marnie* (e.g., Cameron and Jeffrey 1965) tended to ignore the less dramatic but more subtle ways in which Hitchcock revealed Marnie's inner state.[14]

As an example of a less flamboyant moment in the film that beautifully conveys Marnie's inner turmoil, consider the scene that takes place immediately after Mark has forced Marnie to marry him. In this scene Hitchcock used very small shifts in the direction of Marnie's gaze to reveal the very large but concealed conflicts in her feelings. The setting is outside the Rutland family mansion. The marriage ceremony and reception are over. We see Marnie and Mark walking out of the mansion accompanied by Mark's father, his cousin Bob, Lil (his sister-in-law), and the minister who married them. On the surface, not much really happens here. About to embark on their honeymoon cruise, Mark and Marnie exchange pleasantries with Mark's father, cousin Bob, Lil, and the minister. However, what we actually see happening is far more important than what we hear.

The scene opens with an exterior shot revealing several cars parked outside the mansion. From the car that we infer will transport the newlyweds to the airport, the camera pans toward the front door which is closed as the shot begins. During the forward pan the door opens and Mark and Marnie start to come out. Our first glimpse of Marnie is before she steps out of the house. She is in profile, looking in the general direction of Mark's cousin; there is a smile on her face. Marnie and Mark are out of the house. From the viewer's perspective, Marnie is on the right and Mark on the left. While Mark engages his cousin in conversation, we notice that Marnie has an anguished look on her face that nobody except the viewer can see. Mr. Rutland comes out and says to Marnie: "Have fun, my dear." Marnie turns toward him and smiles. Mr. Rutland kisses her on the cheek. The minister has positioned himself to Marnie's right. Turning to him, she smiles and shakes his hand. She then resumes her position facing forward. The anguished look reappears on her face until Mark turns to Marnie to inform her that Bob is his father's old banking cousin. As a farewell gesture, Lil passionately kisses Mark on the mouth while Marnie in profile looks on, showing little emotion until after she turns away, faces forward again, and the anguished look returns. Discernible in the above scene is the following pattern: when facing one or more characters, Marnie either smiles or shows no emotion. However, when her face is visible only to the film audience, the anguished look reappears (see plate 27).

During the pre-production conference with Tippi Hedren mentioned earlier, Hitchcock discussed the importance of the above scene from the standpoint of Marnie's character: "I think what we should try and photograph, as subtly as we can is the inner person and her outward behavior. And I think the way to do it is when she feels that no one is looking at her, although it's hard to discover what moment she would be left on her own, but her face could lapse into a mood, then brighten up when, say, Mr. Rutland kisses her—so that she isn't constantly in an apparently happy marital mood—that we see her now and again with the shadow over her face—but she has to pull herself up and put on a front. . . . Generally speaking, I think that if we show that inside her she is going through the motions and externally it's kind of a forced show of happiness, for the benefit of everyone, you know. I think if she caught Mark's eye alone, it might be a little heavier, a little more of sort of a dead pan—only because continuity-wise, we've just left them in the car, although a lot has gone on. We mustn't feel that she's switched her mood or attitude to him, which we should still feel she is marking under his blackmail."

To summarize, the presuppositions of the early auteur critics led them to see a degree of artistic purpose and consistency in *Marnie* that the production information on the film simply fails to support. By assuming that Hitchcock was the quintessential auteur or movie author who "unerringly" gave expression to his ideas, the auteur critics were blinded from considering some of the other "voices" or factors of production out of which *Marnie* came. Moreover, their reactive response to earlier reviews led the auteurists to minimize less dramatic aspects of the film not discussed in the earlier reviews. Thus, for the auteur critics who embraced the view of Hitchcock as artist, *Marnie* was proof that Hitchcock was the complete filmmaker, uncompromising in his search for artistic perfection.[15]

Since the 1970s, a number of academic critics influenced by psychoanalytic and feminist film theory (e.g., Mulvey 1975; Flitterman 1978;

Bergstrom 1979; Bailin 1982; Silverman 1983; Piso 1986; Modleski 1988) have also been drawn to *Marnie*.[16] Unlike Wood and other auteur critics of *Marnie,* the feminist critics have tended to shift the focus from Marnie to Mark and the other male characters in the film. This development is understandable given that most feminist film criticism since the mid-seventies documents how women function as objects of spectacle in Hollywood cinema. As Judith Mayne (1985) has pointed out, "most feminist critics have assumed that the classical cinema is identified with a male vantage point and is addressed to a male spectator" (88). Moreover, they assume that the male point of view in a Hitchcock film is not strictly speaking Hitchcock's alone. In contrast to the auteur critics who glorified directorial authority, the feminist critics, influenced by post-structuralist thought, "implicitly challenge and decenter directorial authority by considering Hitchcock's work as the expression of cultural attitudes and practices existing to some extent outside the artist's control" (Modleski 1988, 3).

No work has had greater influence in steering feminist film criticism in this direction than Laura Mulvey's essay "Visual Pleasure and Narrative Cinema," which first appeared in the British journal *Screen* in 1975. Mulvey takes as her starting point "the way film reflects, reveals and even plays on the straight, socially established interpretation of sexual difference that controls images, erotic ways of looking and spectacle" (1975, 412). Mulvey's central argument has been nicely summarized by Marian Keane:

> Formally, Mulvey claims, film relies on a division or "split" between looking, which she calls the active role, and being looked at, which she claims is its passive opposite. On a narrative level, one of the ways in which this division is reproduced is by shots representing the view of one figure by another. In Hollywood films, she maintains, women occupy the passive position of being looked at, whereas men possess the active power of looking. (1986, 231)

According to Mulvey, many of Hitchcock's films, including *Vertigo, Rear Window,* and *Marnie,* rely on this division, thereby helping to maintain the "dominant patriarchal order." Mulvey's view of Hitchcock is at odds with the idea of him as an auteur director with a unique vision of the human condition. In her view, by contrast, there are aspects of Hitchcock's work which unwittingly reflect the patriarchal assumptions of the wider society.

Another major influence on feminist criticism of Hitchcock has been the work of Raymond Bellour, especially his complex analyses of several Hitchcock films, including *North by Northwest, Psycho, The Birds,* and *Marnie* (see Bellour 1969, 1975, 1977, 1979). In the influential *Marnie* essay, for example, Bellour extends Mulvey's notion of voyeurism to the film apparatus itself, showing in a detailed analysis of the film's opening sequences how Hitchcock's vision of the character Marnie is inscribed in the film by his male delegates or surrogates— Mark Rutland, Strutt, and Garrod. Critical to Bellour's reflexive reading of *Marnie,* is Hitchcock's early cameo appearance in the film which, according to Bellour, establishes Hitchcock as the enunciator of *Marnie's* story and the film's other male characters, mainly Mark, as Hitchcock surrogates (Bellour 1977).

A number of feminist film theorists have argued that Bellour's formulation of the cinematic apparatus of enunciation is particularly relevant for feminist analyses of film. Consider, for example, Sandy Flitterman's exegesis of Bellour's analysis of Hitchcock's walk-on in *Marnie.* "Bellour makes the point," says Flitterman, that "Hitchcock clearly intervenes as enunciator by inscribing himself in the chain of the fantasy" which begins with "Strutt's lustful description of her" (Marnie) and continues with "Mark's comments on her 'looks'":

> As Hitchcock appears in the hallway of the hotel, he looks first after Marnie and then turns to the spectator, addressing the camera and in so doing underlining his power as image-maker. By this intervention Hitchcock makes explicit the fact that the film, as discourse, is proceeding from somewhere, that it is he who is organizing the fiction and that he has delegated the look to his fictive surrogates (Flitterman 1978, 66–67).[17]

According to Flitterman, the point in Bellour's essay most critical to understanding how women function as the object of male desire through the operation of the look is when Bellour discusses "the shot in which Marnie, having just rinsed away a previous identity with her hair colour, looks jubilantly into the mirror." It is at that moment that the viewer first gets to see Marnie's face. What the viewer sees is Marnie imagining herself "in terms of her image reflected in the mirror, just as Mark, stimulated by Strutt's description and his own memories imagines her when he glances off-screen in the initial segment of the film." Marnie's preoccupation with "her own image here," continues Flitterman, "makes her an object of desire for the (male) spectator, for the source of the camera-wish-Hitchcock, and for the male characters.

For the woman spectator, it can only stimulate the identificatory desire to be the image, but never to possess it" (1978, 68).[18] Other feminist readings of *Marnie* (e.g., Bergstrom 1979) have also seen the film as a work made exclusively for the pleasure of the male spectator, reflecting not Hitchcock's distinct vision but rather the ethos of patriarchal society.

On the other hand, there has been a growing trend among feminist critics to concentrate on films which allow women's experiences to be "voiced" and "visualized." Consider, for instance, Tania Modleski's recent book on Hitchcock, *The Women Who Knew Too Much*, where she argues that "insofar as Hitchcock's films repeatedly reveal the way women are oppressed in patriarchy, they allow the female spectator to feel an anger that is very different from the masochistic response imputed to her by some feminist critics" (Modleski 1988, 5). Rebecca Bailin (1982), Kaja Silverman (1983), and Michele Piso (1986) have all approached *Marnie* from a similar vantage point, one which feminists have increasingly come to regard as more constructive and progressive than earlier styles of feminist film criticism.

Bailin, for example, maintains that the female "voice" or "discourse" in *Marnie* is about violence in women's experience. From that perspective, she argues that the film is a particularly important text for the "female spectator." According to Bailin, the enunciation of a women's discourse in *Marnie* recognizes violence as a social and not a natural phenomenon. Moreover, it recognizes violence against women in its most traumatic and sadistic forms and shows how violence shapes and defines a woman's life. Finally, the women's discourse in *Marnie* recognizes the trauma resulting from violence as "something to be responded to, questioned, 'cured'" (1982, 27).

Bailin argues that Marnie's illness is conceived as social in origin, "not mysterious, biologically derived, intrinsically 'feminine,' or unknowable." She is ill because of "something that happens to women at the hands of men" (1982, 27). Not only is Marnie's stealing connected to her trauma but it is also shown as a response to sexism. Indeed, as Bailin points out, in the film's opening scene there is the suggestion that Strutt has sexually harassed her (1982, 28).

Like other cultural products in a sexist society, according to Bailin, *Marnie* also contains a "patriarchal enunciation" which in significant ways undermines the depiction of Marnie responding to her traumatization. Mark's apparently successful efforts at "curing" Marnie undercut the indictment of patriarchal society by saying that the recognition of women's oppression "is, in and of itself, enough" (1982, 29). Moreover, Mark's transformation into a "real" and "partially motivated" person in the narrative signifies the rebirth of the patriarchal order as nonoppressive.

From a similar dual perspective, Silverman introduces the film as part of a general critique of Freud's and Lacan's arguments which "attempt to justify or naturalize the privileged position of the paternal within our culture" (1983, 131). As a progressive text, *Marnie* dramatizes the breakdown of the mechanism whereby the female subject "takes into herself the values of inferiority and powerlessness embodied by the mother rather than those of superiority and power embodied by the father" (1983, 147). Critical to Silverman's analysis of *Marnie* is the revelation near to the end of the film of the traumatic episode responsible for Marnie's unorthodox behavior:

> What the flashback sequence brings to the manifest level both of the film and of Marnie's psychic existence is a "perversion" of the Oedipal scenario, in which the hostile energies both of the mother and of the daughter are directed against a male figure who temporarily occupies the place of the father, resulting in his death. Marnie not only indulges in the "masculine" wish to kill the father, but she fulfills that wish: she thus violates the Oedipal norm in two ways. In addition, and perhaps most radically, she organizes her desires not around the father, but around the mother. (1983, 147)

This "perversion" of the Oedipal scenario explains the matriarchal character of the Edgar household as it is introduced early in the film. The household consists of Marnie, her mother, and Jessie, a young girl who spends her afternoons with Mrs. Edgar while the girl's mother works. Marnie's mother, says Silverman, "is the dominant figure in this miniature matriarchy" and is perceived as "powerful and adequate." According to Silverman, "Marnie's transgressive impulses have their origin in her adoration of her mother, and the latter's usurpation of the paternal position" (1983, 147). Because she has never learned the crucial lesson of her "castration," Marnie "shows herself capable of exercising control in areas—guns, money, identity papers, inter-sexual relations, and even narrative—where that control is traditionally denied to women" (1983, 148).

Nonetheless by the end of *Marnie*, argues Silverman, patriarchy reemerges triumphant. Like other Hollywood films which seem to question conventional family structures, *Marnie* ultimately reasserts the dominance and rightness of the patriarchal order. "For instance, in *Marnie*," says Silverman, "a 'false' coherence (the coherence of a matriarchy) gives way to a 'true' coherence (the coherence of a patriarchy). As in other seemingly anti-establishment Hollywood films (e.g., *It's a Wonderful Life*), "the new order always turns out to have been the original order, temporarily interrupted" (1983, 221).

More recent feminist critiques of Hitchcock's work have claimed that the psychoanalytic models central to the vast majority of earlier feminist interpretations of his work (e.g., Mulvey 1975; Silverman 1983; and Modleski 1982) are too narrow and need to be combined with other theoretical models such as the Marxist to yield a more definitive or holistic reading of his films. Virginia Wexman, for example, argues that "Hitchcock's recurrent preoccupation with psychoanalysis in his films has often served as a 'Maguffin' (to use his term), distracting the viewer's attention from other, more hidden aspects of the text, his shrewd co-optation of a popular discourse that could locate the roots of social dis-ease in psychological rather than economic causes" (1986, 36).

Michele Piso's 1986 essay on *Marnie* attempts to integrate feminist concerns within a Marxist framework. According to Piso, the film's central tension and particular pathos is not really psychological or Oedipal at all but "the class antagonism between Mark and Marnie, with her mother standing not only for a purely private and hideous past but also as the twisted embodiment of social repression and sexual exploitation" (289). According to Piso, Mark's desire to possess Marnie relates to his class position as owner of a mid-sized publishing firm; that is, Mark is a man of considerable property. Moreover, his unquestioned view of himself as a capitalist, argues Piso, leads him to rape Marnie. "So accustomed is he to owning, so synonymous is his sexuality with social power, that he assumes he can possess Marnie too, violate her, break her down, and then build her back up (in his image, his language, in the image of the 'normal' female) in much the same way that he rebuilt the Rutland business" (1986, 297–98). Not surprisingly, Piso views Marnie's marriage to Mark not as salvation, recuperation, and recovery, as did Wood from his therapeutic perspective, but as the "deepening of a wound that won't close" (1986, 302). To support her interpretation, Piso points to the film's ambiguous ending. In her view, Marnie's remark, "Will I have to go to jail? I'd rather stay with you," conveys that Marnie's marriage to Mark will be a kind of imprisonment. Moreover,

Piso "reads" the Baltimore street urchins' chant "Mother, mother, I feel worse," to mean that there is really no hope that Marnie will ever recover from her childhood trauma.

Piso's analysis lacks the subtlety possessed by some of the earlier-mentioned feminist studies of *Marnie,* especially Bailin's (1982). Indeed, Piso comes dangerously close to presenting Hitchcock as a merciless and unrelenting critic of patriarchal and capitalist society. Consider, for example, Piso's unambiguous reading of Mark's rape of Marnie compared to Bailin's (and earlier Wood's [1977]) more multilayered analysis. Unlike Bailin, Piso fails to acknowledge the textual ambiguity of the presentation of the events leading to the rape (see plate 28). In fact, virtually all that Piso really tells us about the rape is that Mark's unquestioned view of himself as a capitalist is what leads him to rape Marnie. Approaching *Marnie* from the perspective of how the film "speaks" on violence against women *and* how the film mirrors patriarchal society, Bailin's more ironic reading attributes the film's "powerful density," especially in the rape and trauma scenes, to the fact that it is a work of more than one enunciator. Bailin's analysis, reminiscent of Wood's earlier one, shows how the rape scene alternates between generating disapproval and approval of Mark's actions. After ripping off Marnie's nightgown, Mark apologizes and takes off his robe to cover her bare body. Immediately before the shot, from Marnie's perspective, of Mark's intent to violate her, Hitchcock inserts a low-angle shot, suggesting the tenderness of Mark's lovemaking. At the same time, Hitchcock sets up the viewer (especially the female spectator) to feel distanced from Marnie and "to question that she is actually being violated." Indeed, the very "sexiness" of Sean Connery "undermines identification with Marnie as violated." For Bailin, the resurfacing at this point in the film of the "erasing enunciation" largely cancels out the female voice of the text which has shown Mark, contrary to his promise, violating, humiliating, and traumatizing Marnie, leading to her attempted suicide. Even the suicide attempt, according to Bailin, is doubly enunciated:

> The scene is enacted from Mark's point of view (he discovers her missing from bed, then runs to find her in the pool—it is a scene of *his* fear), and when revived, Marnie jokes about her own suicide, seeming to trivialize it. Yet the joke too is double-edged; she says, "I wanted to kill myself, not feed the damn fish," as though she had anticipated and is aware that her death might be in fact trivialized. (1982, 30)

Other textual evidence not cited by Bailin supports her double enunciatory interpretation but not Piso's more one-dimensional reading. Consider, for example, the juxtaposition of scenes leading to the rape sequence. We recall that, during the first night of the honeymoon, Mark learns that Marnie is frigid. Immediately after he promises not to sleep with Marnie, there is a forty-second sequence, consisting of three brief scenes set in a dining room, a sun deck, and a lounge, respectively. According to Hitchcock, these "small scenes" were inserted to represent the passage of time (three more nights of the honeymoon cruise with the marriage act still unconsummated) and to illustrate Mark's effort to be patient with Marnie. At a pre-production conference, Hitchcock told Hedren, "He's not going to rush into the second night, or the third night, or the fourth night. He's quite patient with her." Thus, before breaking his promise and forcing her to submit, Mark is shown to have allowed Marnie to maintain her sexual independence.

The dinner-party scene also supports Bailin's double enunciatory interpretation of the film. Mark has agreed to give a dinner party as a way of introducing his new wife to local society. The party sequence occurs immediately after the famous "You Freud—me Jane?" scene which has ended with Marnie acknowledging her illness and pleading for somebody (Mark?) to help her. Marnie is unusually composed during the party. At one point, she tells Mark that she feels relaxed. What she says is consistent with what we see. At all times, regardless of whether she is facing someone or is manifesting a facial expression not visible to others in the film, we see her animated and with a big smile on her face. Absent here is the vacillation between her public and private presentation of self so evident in earlier scenes. Clearly, Hitchcock wants the viewer to conclude from her altered behavior that Mark's earlier efforts to help Marnie with her psychological problems have produced some beneficial results. In one of their pre-production conferences, Hitchcock explains to Hedren that the pleasure Marnie "flashes" during this sequence is "real." Why is she feeling so good? "She's recovered, you see." Now she "*is* the mistress of Wyckwyn." Unfortunately, Marnie's improved mental state is short-lived. With Strutt's unexpected appearance at the party, Marnie is again made to feel like a hunted animal. Still, the revelation of Marnie's brief moment of inner calm at the party can be viewed from Bailin's interpretive scheme as a sign that the patriarchal society can be "reborn" as "nonoppressive." From this perspective, the dinner-party scene functions to "erase" some of the "wrongness" of the patriarchal order which Mark's earlier entrapment of Marnie had signified.

To summarize, a number of feminist film critics have used *Marnie* to illustrate how filmmaking practices themselves construct sexist images of women. From this perspective, *Marnie* has been treated more as an accurate reflection of film practices in a patriarchal society than as a "progressive" text articulating the concerns of real women, thereby diminishing Hitchcock's reputation in the process. Other feminist film critics, by contrast, have found a "progressive" or feminist voice in the film. One proponent of this viewpoint (Piso) has even gone so far as to claim (I think erroneously) that the progressive voice in *Marnie* is the only true voice in the film. From Piso's perspective, Hitchcock emerges from *Marnie* as an uncompromising and unambiguous critic of patriarchal society. As I have tried to demonstrate, the feminist interpretations most faithful to the *Marnie* text (e.g., Bailin's) have approached the film from both vantage points, concluding that *Marnie* is a doubly enunciated or multivocal text, containing both progressive and reactionary elements.

By comparing reviews of Hitchcock's *Marnie,* I have attempted to show how the film was interpreted in three different periods of criticism in light of Griswold's (1987) thesis that meaning is constituted or "fabricated" through the interaction of viewer and film. The *Marnie* case revealed how the presuppositions of three different generations of critics differed and how they shaped the film's critical reception. To one group of critics, *Marnie* was an old-fashioned psychological melodrama about a female thief, while another group highlighted the film's cinematic qualities to demonstrate Hitchcock's total command as an artist. A third group found it to be about male dominance in a patriarchal social system.

One of the principal findings from the *Marnie* case history is that Hitchcock's efforts at the time of *Marnie* to transform his reputation from that of popular entertainer to serious artist affected not only the making of the film but also contributed to the film's negative critical reception. Most critics wanted a film consistent with what they had come to expect from the acknowledged master of suspense. From that vantage point, *Marnie* was not a "true" Hitchcock film. For the auteur critics, on the other hand, who embraced the view of Hitchcock as artist, *Marnie* was proof that Hitchcock was the complete filmmaker, uncompromising in his search for artistic perfection. Among the feminist film critics, no consensus existed as to Hitchcock's reputation. While some characterized him as a shameless misogynist, others saw him as a merciless critic of patriarchal society. These results point to the importance of a filmmaker's publicized persona (or established track record) in shaping how critics and, by extension, audiences respond to his or her latest work. They also underscore how a change in a filmmaker's persona may affect how the same film is evaluated years later by changing the "horizon of expectations" (Jauss 1982) against which the filmmaker's work is interpreted by critics and audiences.

On the other hand, one should not conclude from the *Marnie* case that films or other cultural objects are a blank sheet or "Rorschach equivalent" onto which viewers simply "project their concerns" (Griswold 1987, 1110). Cultural works, I suggest, vary in their ability to sustain a relative diversity of interpretations. Griswold maintains that a cultural work has power and enters a canon upheld by a cultural elite in proportion to its ability "to elicit relative consensus on what it is about plus its ability to sustain a relative divergence of interpretations" (1987, 1106). According to Griswold's criterion, *Marnie* is a powerful film.[19] Whether it has greater "power," in the Griswoldian sense, than other Hitchcock works can only be ascertained by examining the range of interpretations that other Hitchcock works have elicited.[20]

The Birds is one Hitchcock film that has not fared as well over the years as *Marnie*. By comparing and contrasting the critical reception over time of *The Birds* relative to *Marnie*, we can gain additional insights about the factors which shape canon formation in the arts.

The critical reception of *The Birds* in 1963 was generally better than *Marnie's* in 1964. While a number of critics expressed serious reservations, complaining about the film's weak characterizations and the split between the "human" story and the terror of the bird attacks (see Macdonald 1963; Scheuer 1963; Winsten 1963; and *Variety* 1963), others found much to praise about *The Birds*, especially the effectiveness of its terror sequences (e.g., Crowther 1963 and Knight 1963a). In addition, *The Birds* (unlike *Marnie*) received strong initial endorsements from virtually all of those who, as we have seen, had actively campaigned during the sixties to elevate Hitchcock's stature as an artist—Peter Bogdanovich (1963), Andrew Sarris (1963), Robin Wood (1977), and François Truffaut (1967).

In a monograph prepared for the Museum of Modern Art's Hitchcock retrospective, Bogdanovich singled out *The Birds* as one of Hitchcock's greatest and most fully realized works:

> *The Birds* is, in every way, a more serious, more thoroughly conceived film [than *Psycho*]; an excellent blending of character and incident, of atmosphere and terror. If he had never made an-

other motion picture in his life, *The Birds* would place him securely among the giants of cinema. And that is where he belongs. (1963, 7)

Reviewing *The Birds* for the *Village Voice*, Andrew Sarris (1963) characterized it as "a major work of cinematic art [which] finds Hitchcock at the summit of his artistic powers. His is the only contemporary style that unites the divergent classical traditions of Murnau (camera movement) and Eisenstein (montage). . . . If formal excellence is still a valid criterion for film criticism—and there are those who will argue that it is not—then *The Birds* is probably the picture of the year" (Sarris 1963).

To illustrate Hitchcock's allegiance to the principles of pure cinema, Sarris describes the motorboat sequence following Melanie Daniels' delivery of the love birds to the Brenner house. Back in the motorboat that brought her there, Melanie is hurrying across the bay while Mitch Brenner in his car is racing to intercept her on the other side:

> This race, in itself pure cinema, is seen entirely from the girl's point of view. We see only what she can see from the boat. Suddenly, near shore, the camera picks up a sea gull swooping down on our heroine. For just a second the point of view is shifted and we are permitted to see the bird before its victim does. The director has apparently broken an aesthetic rule for the sake of a shock effect— gull pecks girl. Yet this momentary incursion of the objective on the subjective is remarkably consistent with the meaning of the film. (1963)

In his assessment of the film in 1965, Robin Wood (1977) was more equivocal than either Sarris or Bogdanovich had been, confessing that at first he had found it a major disappointment. But after repeated viewings, he concluded that *The Birds* was "among Hitchcock's finest achievements," representing yet another "mature" expression of Hitchcock's therapeutic theme. On the other hand, Wood warned that, to appreciate *The Birds,* one must break down a number of preconceptions regarding the relationship between this film and Hitchcock's preceding works, especially *Psycho*. In *Psycho,* Wood explained, we become Marion Crane, while in *The Birds* we are kept at a distance from Melanie Daniels. In *Psycho,* when Marion Crane drives from Phoenix to California, says Wood, audiences are "restricted almost exclusively to her vision and emotions"; in *The Birds,* by contrast, "the tendency to identification is offset by certain endistancing effects." Hitchcock's use of back-projection in the motorboat sequence, says Wood, whether intentional or not, "has the effect of giving an air of unreality to her [Melanie's] situation, of isolating her from the backgrounds, of stressing her artificiality by making it stand out obtrusively from natural scenery" ([1965] 1977, 119). A case can be made, argues Wood, that Hitchcock's use of back-projection in *The Birds* was deliberate rather than a mere convenience.[21] After all, he points out, whenever back-projection shots are interspersed with sequences which were clearly shot on location, the shots are always of Melanie. The effect on viewers is that we can simultaneously understand Melanie's attitudes and motives while recognizing their insufficiency:

> Hitchcock here is undertaking something more delicate and difficult to realize than the direct identification demanded by *Psycho:* the precise controlling of a partial and intermittent response to Melanie's attitudes, balanced by a sense of their insufficiency. We identify with Melanie enough to understand her, and enough to become aware of our own proneness to admire the sort of smart "cleverness," with its trivialising effect on relationships, that she represents. Instead of encouraging a deep involvement that the spectator will only later be able to judge, Hitchcock here makes involvement and judgement virtually simultaneous. (Wood [1965] 1977, 119–20)

The Birds dominates the discussion in Truffaut's *Hitchcock* (1967), receiving far more coverage than any of Hitchcock's other films. In addition to including an entire chapter on *The Birds*, the Truffaut book contains many references to the film scattered throughout the text. Hitchcock's interest in *The Birds* is understandable, considering that he was still working on the film at the time Truffaut interviewed him for the book. As I showed in chapter 3, Hitchcock envisioned the book as a vehicle for promoting not only himself but also *The Birds*. Hitchcock's comments to Truffaut about *The Birds* had the desired effect, influencing many auteurist "readings" of the film published over the next decade.[22]

One example of such a reading is Elizabeth Weis's (1982) interpretation of Hitchcock's use of sound in *The Birds*. In the introduction to her book-length study of Hitchcock, Weis reveals the auteurist assumption of her own work—that "Hitchcock was to a great extent in creative control of his work despite the collaborative nature of filmmaking." To justify this assumption, she cites the authority of Truffaut's *Hitchcock*, which she characterizes as "the most thorough discussion [to date] of Hitchcock's responsibility for his work" (Weis 1982, 26). References to the Truffaut book are a recurring feature of her study, especially in her chapter on *The Birds*. We are informed, for example, that Hitchcock had told Truffaut that "Until now we've worked with natural sounds, but now, thanks to electronic sound, I'm not only going to indicate the sound we want but also the style and nature of each sound" (1982, 136). Moreover, Weis habitually inserts Truffaut's observations about the film to add credibility to some of her bolder claims concerning Hitchcock's use of sound in *The Birds:*

> By the time of *The Birds,* screeches are even more important than visual techniques for terrorizing the audience during attacks. Indeed, bird sounds sometimes replace visuals altogether. Moreover, Hitchcock carefully manipulates the sound track so that the birds can convey terror even when they are silent or just making an occasional caw or flutter. As Truffaut points out, "The bird sounds are worked out like a real musical score." Instead of orchestrated instruments there are orchestrated sound effects. If in *Psycho* music sounds like birds, in *The Birds* bird sounds function like music. (1982, 138)

Hitchcock's opportunity to influence the reception of *The Birds* both before and after the film's release may partly account for the greater number of auteur-inspired accounts of *The Birds* than for *Marnie,* about which Hitchcock said little publicly after the film's release. That Hitchcock was upset with *Marnie,* choosing not to discuss it in any depth after it came out, could account for the relative paucity of auteurist accounts of the film. When Hitchcock first spoke to Truffaut about *Marnie* in 1962—well before the film went into production—he was quite animated about its prospects, especially as a character study of Marnie. However, none of his pre-production comments about *Marnie* appear in Truffaut's book. At Hitchcock's urging, Truffaut kept the space devoted to *Marnie* to a minimum. We know from Truffaut's later testimony that, after *Marnie* was released, Hitchcock had not wanted to discuss his relationship with Tippi Hedren. By talking almost exclusively about the inadequacies of the Mark character, Hitchcock could avoid talking about Tippi Hedren altogether. With *The Birds,* on the other hand, Hitchcock continued voicing enthusiasm for the film long after its initial release.

While a number of feminist film theorists have written about *The*

Birds, the sheer volume of reviews and commentaries on the film from a feminist perspective is significantly less than for *Marnie.* Those feminists who were initially drawn to *The Birds* pointed to the film as evidence of Hitchcock's misogyny and membership in a patriarchal society. As with *Marnie,* a major influence on the early feminist readings of *The Birds* was the work of Raymond Bellour (1969), in particular his detailed analysis of the Bodega Bay sequence. This has become a virtually "canonized" sequence largely as a result of Bellour's influential essay combined with the efforts of the early auteur sponsors of the film and the first generation of feminist critics who wrote about the film. According to Bellour, the sea gulls attack Melanie as punishment for her sexual aggressiveness. In his view, the birds function as representatives of the men in the film (Mitch in particular), of its director, Hitchcock, and of all men in our culture. The birds are a plot device through which Mitch is able to work out his Oedipal problem. A feminist critic, Jacqueline Rose (1976–77) has questioned Bellour's Oedipal interpretation, arguing that the film also speaks to the problems of the psychosexual development of women. What about the psychological condition of Melanie Daniels, who has regressed to a state of dependency by the time the film is over? Doesn't the film make much of the fact that Melanie's mother abandoned her when she was eleven? Doesn't this suggest that *The Birds* is not simply about a male protagonist working out his Oedipal problems?

In another more aggressively feminist account of the film, Susan Lurie stresses how classical narrative cinema castrates women, such as Melanie Daniels in *The Birds,* not because of their lack of the phallus, as Bellour (1969) and Rose (1976–77) had argued, but rather because of their perceived strength and wholeness which trigger dread in the male (see plate 29). A number of feminist critics have also commented on the bizarre family structure that has been reconstructed by the time the film has ended: Mitch and Lydia are the mature couple while Cathy and Melanie (whose independent spirit has been destroyed) function as their children (see Horwitz 1982; Rose 1976–77).[23]

On the other hand, *The Birds* has not generated the kind of continuing interest among feminist-oriented critics that *Marnie* and many of Hitchcock's other works (e.g., *Vertigo, Rear Window, Notorious,* and *Psycho*) have sustained. Comments on the institutional norms that govern academic life help to illuminate why feminist critics have not paid as much attention to *The Birds.* As film historian Janet Staiger (1985) has implied, textual critics are often more interested in sporting a

16. Truffaut interviews Hitchcock (August 1962).
Photograph by Philippe Halsman. © Yvonne Halsman.

17. Hitchcock's standard
portrait, created in the
early sixties and appear-
ing in promotional mate-
rials over the next decade.
Hitchcock Collection, Academy
of Motion Picture Arts and
Sciences.

18. Hitchcock's standard portrait incorporated in a theater display for *Frenzy* (1972).

Hitchcock Collection, Academy of Motion Picture Arts and Sciences.

19. The marquee for the Broadway opening of *The Birds* emphasized Hitchcock as the principal element of the film (1963).

Hitchcock Collection, Academy of Motion Picture Arts and Sciences.

20. The final sequence from the controversial
ending of *The Birds* (1963).
Museum of Modern Art Film Stills Archive.

21. Tippi Hedren with a cardboard lobby display for *The Birds* during a foreign tour (1963).

Hitchcock Collection, Academy of Motion Picture Arts and Sciences.

22. Production still from *Marnie* suggesting the disturbed psychological state of the film's heroine (1964).
Museum of Modern Art Film Stills Archive.

23. Lew Wasserman presents Hitchcock with the Irving G. Thalberg Memorial Award at the fortieth annual Academy Awards Ceremony (April 1968).

Hitchcock Collection, Academy of Motion Picture Arts and Sciences.

24. Hitchcock's appearance on a Los Angeles television talk show (1970).
Hitchcock Collection, Academy of Motion Picture Arts and Sciences.

25. Hitchcock becomes a Chevalier de l'Ordre de la Légion d'Honneur with his wife, Alma, at his side in Paris (1971).
Hitchcock Collection, Academy of Motion Picture Arts and Sciences.

26. The critics find in *Frenzy* a thriller rich in hidden
or implicit meanings (1972).
Museum of Modern Art Film Stills Archive.

27. Marnie, the troubled heroine, on husband Mark's
family estate following their marriage (*Marnie*, 1964).
Museum of Modern Art Film Stills Archive.

28. Textual ambiguity surrounds the events leading to Mark's
rape of Marnie (*Marnie*, 1964).
Museum of Modern Art Film Stills Archive.

29. By the end of *The Birds*, the film's heroine has been reduced to a helpless child (1963).
Museum of Modern Art Film Stills Archive and Sciences.

30. The controversial rape and murder of Brenda Blaney
(Barbara Leigh-Hunt) (*Frenzy*, 1972).
Museum of Modern Art Film Stills Archive.

31. Doris Day at the piano in *The Man Who Knew Too Much* (1956).
Paramount Collection, Academy of Motion Picture Arts and Sciences

novel theoretical or methodological approach—a key to career advancement in academia—than in really elucidating the film under their scrutiny:

> Competition for jobs, for better salaries, for higher professorial ranking, for endowed chairs, competition for publishing contracts or research grants hinges on the academic establishing an exchange-value by proving that her or his critical methodology, history, or theory is not only worth financial support but, in an era of a tight economy, worth it more than others are. As a student, one must master not only the canon of films on a filmography list, but a canon of articles and books, so that one can supersede that work and be admitted into the group of professional canon-makers and canon-analyzers. One re-reads canonized works not only for providing another interpretation, but usually to make one's name with a new methodology. One resurrects a film to claim it as an unnoticed masterpiece. One may survey a genre, a national film output, a historical period, or a stylistic group to show how other scholars have misunderstood, simplified it. One applies rigorous analyses of theories and methodologies to indicate fallacious reasoning of predecessors. (Staiger 1985, 18).

If *The Birds* had been more congenial or amenable to a progressive, feminist reading, later feminists probably would have been more inclined to use the film to illustrate how a progressive film could be an inspiration for the women's movement. Alas, *The Birds* was not such a film. While many feminists perceived Marnie as a kind of social bandit—stealing from the rich (her employers) and giving to the poor (her mother), Melanie Daniels, by contrast, was no present-day Robin Hood. Rather she had all the mannerisms associated with a rich socialite. Indeed, in a pre-production conference with Tippi Hedren, Hitchcock described the character as "very well appointed, very well dressed . . . smart, sophisticated" (Transcript of a taped conference between Hitchcock and Hedren, ca. 1962, Hitchcock Collection).

I suggest that an additional reason why relatively few psychoanalytically oriented feminist critics were drawn to *The Birds* is that the film lacked the psychological richness of many of Hitchcock's other works such as *Marnie*. The interconnecting production histories of *The Birds* and *Marnie* suggest why feminist textual critics may have found Melanie Daniels to be a less appealing character for study than Marnie. While filming *The Birds*, Hitchcock was also working out with his screenwriter the psychological dynamics of Marnie, the tragic heroine of his next project. His attention to the psychological verisimilitude of the Marnie character caused Hitchcock to worry about how critics might respond to the underdeveloped characters in *The Birds*. Accordingly, he instructed his official and unofficial writers, as we have seen, to improve the connections between characterizations and actions. For example, Hitchcock requested one of his ghost writers to incorporate into the script of *The Birds* the fact that Melanie had been abandoned by her mother at the age of eleven. In order to effectively convey the deepening of the relationship between Melanie and Lydia, Hitchcock added Melanie's point-of-view shots to the scene with Lydia and the broken china, replacing the earlier more objective rendering of the sequence. Apparently, these changes were too piecemeal, too after the fact. For as we have seen, many critics expressed dissatisfaction with *The Birds*, charging that the characters were underdeveloped. It is conceivable, following Staiger's reasoning, that feminist critics concluded that "psychoanalyzing" Melanie Daniels would not be as effective a vehicle for advancing their academic careers as focusing on Marnie or some other complex Hitchcock heroine.

In recent years, even auteurist interest in *The Birds* has waned. In 1972 Wood expressed growing dissatisfaction with the film (see Kaplan [Wood] 1972) while Truffaut, after Hitchcock's death, hinted about having reservations as well (Truffaut 1984, 323). Brill (1988), in his recent book on Hitchcock, hardly mentions it at all. On the other hand, close analysis of selected sequences from the film continue to appear in books on cinematic style (see, e.g., Sharff 1982, 9–19; Bordwell and Thompson 1986, 200–210).

The historical reception of *Frenzy* provides another interesting variation to the critical trajectories of Hitchcock's films. When it was first released in 1972, many reviewers characterized *Frenzy* as one of Hitchcock's greatest films, surely his best since *North by Northwest*. The film, however, has not fared well over time. Prominent film scholars have found serious fault with it. Neither Robin Wood nor William Rothman, for example, rank *Frenzy* among Hitchcock's major achievements. In a 1983 article, Wood expressed serious reservations about how women are treated in the film. According to Wood (1983), a number of Hitchcock's films (e.g., *Rear Window* and *Vertigo*) contain a relatively uncontaminated feminist discourse which, in his view, *Frenzy* does not. In fact, the misogynistic tendency in Hitchcock's work, says Wood, is "at its grossest in *Frenzy*," in particular "the rape and murder of Barbara Leigh-Hunt (see plate 30) and the notorious potato-sack scene—the latter the more disturbing in that Hitchcock clearly supposed it to be funny." Other commentators have faulted the film on similar grounds (see, e.g., Spoto 1983; Allen 1985). For Spoto, one of the great strengths of Hitchcock's earlier works, where violent behavior occurred, most notably in *Psycho,* was his stylization of violent acts:

> The act of murder in Alfred Hitchcock's films had always been stylized by the devices of editing and . . . photographic wizardry. [But in *Frenzy*] Hitchcock insisted on all the ugly explicitness of this picture, and for all its cinematic inventiveness, it retains one of the most repellent examples of a detailed murder in the history of films." (Spoto 1983, 545; see also Allen 1985)

Although there are signs that *Frenzy* could be reinstated among Hitchcock's canonized works in the not too distant future (see, e.g., Modleski 1988; Brill 1988; Sharff 1991), the recent downgrading of this film demonstrates the power of both feminist thought and critical attitudes concerning cinematic stylization and restraint in shaping recent assessments of Hitchcock's work. (In the next chapter we see how similar preconceptions have affected the production, dissemination, and reception of horror thrillers during the late seventies and early eighties.)

How have developments in "Hitchcock scholarship" affected journalistic film criticism? Which of the two dominant scholarly approaches to Hitchcock's work since the 1970s—auteur theory or the feminist orientation—has had the greater impact on journalistic reviewers? While the auteur perspective dominated the critical response to *Frenzy* in 1972, has that perspective continued to hold sway among film reviewers in the United States? What about the feminist perspective? Has it gained adherents among journalistic critics? The re-release of Hitchcock's so-called "lost" films in 1983 and 1984 provides an opportunity to find out.

In a number of the reviews of *Rear Window* that followed its reissue, I found evidence of a backlash against the "Hitchcock" of Hitchcock scholarship. Several critics pointed to the exhilaration they experienced from their latest viewing of *Rear Window* to remind their readership of Hitchcock's consummate skills as a popular entertainer; this, as we recall, was how reviewers initially responded to the film in 1954. Echoing Pauline Kael's anti-auteur views, these contemporary critics charged that much of the so-called serious criticism had overinterpreted the film, too zealously advancing the image of Hitchcock as a serious artist at the expense of considering how his films functioned as entertainment. As *New York Times* critic Vincent Canby put it, "*Rear Window* enchants us immediately, and need not be analyzed to death to achieve its place in the Pantheon" (1983). David Chute of the *Los Angeles Herald-Examiner* made a similar point, chiding the pro-Hitchcock and anti-Hitchcock forces for their extreme positions, which caused them to miss much of what Hitchcock really accomplished. Said Chute, *Rear Window* is "still one of the most sheerly enjoyable American movies ever made. Hitchcock was an entertainer, all right, but there was nothing 'mere' about him and this much pure pleasure can sometimes matter more to us than whole truckloads of Great Art" (1983).[24]

Several commentaries on *Rear Window* also focused on thematic issues related to voyeurism and self-reflexivity, reiterating the concerns of earlier auteurist accounts of the film (e.g., Douchet 1960; Wood [1965] 1977; and Truffaut 1967). Under that influence, Chute commented on the connection between the wide-screen VistaVision process used in shooting and displaying the film and the windows of Jeffreys' apartment building, which "are the same shape." Continuing the analogy with the cinema, Chute wrote that Jeffreys transforms his neighbors whom he is spying on into "realistic movie characters," a point that Wood had developed more fully in his 1965 book. Chicago critic Dave Kehr raised similar issues about the film in a detailed commentary that appeared first in the *Chicago Reader* and then was revised for *American Film*. *Rear Window* is really a meditation on art, argued Kehr, with Jeffreys, the photo journalist, filling in for Hitchcock, the director (see Kehr 1984; cf. Stam and Pearson 1983).

While feminist concerns about sexual differences in patriarchal society and problems of spectatorship have also figured prominently in much of the Hitchcock scholarship over the past fifteen years, one would hardly sense this from the vast majority of newspaper and magazine commentaries on *Rear Window*. When critics brought up the issue of voyeurism and Peeping Tomism, it was as if the viewer inscribed in the film was sexless, subject to the voyeuristic instinct in all of us. After all, isn't that what attracts us to the cinema in the first place? But "the spectatorship inscribed in the film," as Wood correctly argues in his 1983 *American Film* article, "is by no means neutral. It is unambiguously male." It is the Jimmy Stewart character (Jeffreys) who does most of the watching. According to Wood, the film is as much about the projection of male anxieties as it is about spying. Afraid of getting too involved with his girlfriend, the Stewart character projects these anxieties onto his neighbors, whose lives, for the most part, reflect negatively on both marriage and bachelorhood. Yet only a few critics addressed the issue of voyeurism and spectatorship from the perspective of sexual difference. Not surprisingly, among those who did was Andrew Sarris, who in addition to his weekly movie column for the *Village Voice,* taught film courses at Columbia University. Unlike other commentators on *Rear Window,* Sarris unabashedly acknowledged those strands of "Hitchcock scholarship" that had most influenced him: the early French auteurists—Rohmer and Chabrol, Truffaut, Jean Douchet, and Jean-Luc Godard—and Robin Wood's *Hitchcock's Films.* In addition, he informed his readers about which developments in film scholarship he didn't much admire, especially the "recurring assaults of antiseptic practitioners of 'textual' criticism." In his commentary on *Rear Window,* Sarris also assessed, as I mentioned in chapter 3, Spoto's *The Dark Side of Genius,* which had just been published. Although critical of the book, Sarris admired Spoto's effort "to elevate Hitchcock to a kind of Baudelairian Pantheon by making him seem romantically evil," an effort that prompted Sarris to reflect on the perverse side of *Rear Window's* sexual politics, namely, that Jeffreys becomes most aroused by his girlfriend when her life is in jeopardy.

Turning to *Vertigo,* we find the whole spectrum of auteur interpretations of that film represented following its 1983 reissue (see, e.g., Kehr 1983; Wilmington 1983; Gleiberman 1983). In addition, several of the reviews also reflected sensitivity to feminist concerns (see, e.g., Wilmington, 1983). Shortly before the film's re-release, Wood (1983) published his revisionist essay on *Vertigo* and *Rear Window* where he offered an affirmative answer to the question, "Can Hitchcock be saved for feminism?" In light of Wood's "feminist" reading of *Vertigo* and Spoto's recently published "revelations" about Hitchcock's hostility toward women, it is understandable that a feminist reading of *Vertigo* would make sense to a number of reviewers. However, even for reviewers most receptive to the film's uncompromising indictment of romantic love, the feminist viewpoint functioned as but one of several ways of illuminating the film. Without the recent contributions from Wood and Spoto, film reviewers would probably have neglected raising feminist-related issues just as they had done three months earlier with *Rear Window.*[25]

Of the five Hitchcock films reissued in the mid-1980s, the one that generated the most unexpected response among reviewers in the United States was the 1956 *The Man Who Knew Too Much*. Long regarded by Anglo-American reviewers and scholars alike as "minor" Hitchcock, this film came to be viewed by American reviewers as one of the major "revelations" of the Hitchcock "revival." A review of the history of critical response to this film in the United States and England will launch a more general discussion about the possible cultural variations in the diffusion of Hitchcock's artistic reputation and of those stellar or canonized works behind that reputation. Differences in the perception of "Hitchcock" in the United States and England also shed light on the connection between Hitchcock's improved stature as a filmmaker in America and the reputation of the thriller genre.

When first released in 1956, *The Man Who Knew Too Much* received generally positive reviews in the United States, especially among reviewers writing for the average filmgoer. For those most favorably disposed to the film, the 1956 version contained an effective blending of the various elements which had recently come to be associated with the Hitchcock Hollywood thriller—spine-tingling suspense, relief through humor, exotic locations, box-office stars—all shot in color and displayed on a wide screen. On the other hand, the critics for more sophisticated publications such as the *New Yorker* or the *Saturday Review,* who typically compared the film to the earlier British version, tended to be more critical of the remake, preferring the quickness of pace and surface realism of the original to the slowness and greater subjectivity of the remake (see, e.g., Alpert 1956). In England, by contrast, the vast majority of critics, regardless of type of publication, compared the new version unfavorably to the 1934 original. For them, the remake violated all the rules governing their model of perfection—the British thriller form (see, e.g., Lejeune 1956; Pearson 1956; Brien 1956; Houston 1956). C. A. Lejeune, who had reviewed the original when it first came out, put it this way, "the first *The Man Who Knew Too Much* was stronger in every way." During the fifties, America's more intellectual critics shared with most British reviewers the view that Hitchcock's American films were inferior to his British output (especially when compared to the six "classic" espionage thrillers, including the original *The Man Who Knew Too Much,* he made for Gaumont between 1934 and 1939).

In contrast to the Anglo-American critics who, as a whole, viewed the American version as "minor" Hitchcock, were the French critics of the *Cahiers du Cinéma,* especially Jean-Luc Godard, Claude Chabrol, and Eric Rohmer, who became early champions of the film. In their

1956 book, *Hitchcock: The First Forty-Four Films,* Rohmer and Chabrol characterized the 1956 version as vastly superior to the 1934 film, singling it out as "one in which the Hitchcockian mythology finds its purest, if not its most obvious expression" (Rohmer and Chabrol 1979). For the French, the Hitchcockian mythology referred to the film's metaphysical trappings of a world where "salvation can only be obtained through the combined interplay of Fate (but isn't it rather Providence?) and Free Will" (Rohmer and Chabrol 1979, 141; see also Godard 1956).

While American reviewers and critics would have few opportunities to write publicly about *The Man Who Knew Too Much* until after its posthumous re-release almost thirty years later in 1984, English critics had occasion to remain outspoken about the film. In championing Hitchcock, the French auteur critics had argued that Hitchcock's Hollywood films, especially those made during the fifties, were better-made than his British ones. For the English critics, especially those connected with the British Film Institute publication, *Sight and Sound,* the two versions of *The Man Who Knew Too Much* became central to their debate with the French auteurists over the relative stature of Hitchcock's British and American films. For many British critics, the 1934 version of *The Man Who Knew Too Much* held a special place in their hearts, representing not only a major turning point in Hitchcock's career (which indeed it was) but also an important new direction for British cinema. With this film, said Peter John Dyer in a 1961 *Sight and Sound* article, Hitchcock broke away from his reputation, as "a model of compliance" and as a "critic's director" to make thrillers for "the unsophisticated"—a viewing echoing C. A. Lejeune's much-quoted review of the film when it first came out:

> Now at last he has thrown critics and intellectuals overboard with one of his incomparable rude gestures, and gone in for making pictures for the people. . . . For my own part, I am very happy about *The Man Who Knew Too Much.* It seems to me, because of its very recklessness, its blank refusal to indulge in subtleties, to be the most promising work that Hitchcock has produced since *Blackmail,* and quite possibly the best picture he has ever made. (Lejeune 1934).

In addition, Lejeune had hoped that the film would encourage English filmmakers to be less pretentious and make more movies with "quick action and robust playing" or in the tradition of the Hollywood genre film with its easily recognizable types. Twenty years later, on the eve of a special screening of the 1934 film, an English critic commented on how this version, in addition to being one of the yardsticks by which critics have measured Hitchcock's subsequent work, also "blueprints the British comedy-thriller so long the standby of our studios" (Winnington 1953).

Not surprisingly, Ian Cameron, the editor of *Movie,* the English magazine which spoke for the French auteur view, defended the Hollywood version on the occasion of its reissue in 1962. In response to earlier complaints that the 1956 version was slow-moving, Cameron explained that Hitchcock had done that on purpose so that audiences could get to "like the couple whose child is kidnapped. Hitchcock knows better than his critics and he sets out to use our liking for the couple to help break down our resistance to suspense. It is a measure of his astounding skill that one is still thrilled when one knows what is going to happen" (Cameron 1962b; see also Cameron 1962a, 1963). Not so, according to more traditional critics such as *Sight and Sound* editor Penelope Houston (1963) who, in responding to Cameron, argued that Hitchcock had broadened or loosened the film for commercial considerations. ("I can't but feel that this long introduction is precisely what one might have expected at that moment in Hollywood history, when the pressure was on to exploit both stars and locations.") Judged as a thriller, the original, according to Houston, was a superior film. But that, said Houston, is not how the remake was being judged. Rather, several critics (mostly French but also a growing band of English renegades as well) had judged the Hollywood version to be superior precisely because it transcended the lowly thriller form. As Houston sarcastically put it, "But can't we *see,* we may be asked, that [the Hollywood version is] so much more than a thriller. . ." Seventeen years later, Houston hadn't modified her view of the film, although by then she conceded that a number of Hitchcock's other Hollywood films such as *Strangers on a Train, Rear Window, Vertigo, North by Northwest,* and *Psycho* were at least as good as anything he had ever made in England (Houston 1980).

The 1934 version of *The Man Who Knew Too Much* remained an important yardstick for a majority of English reviewers when the Hollywood remake was reissued in 1984. This time the British reaction to the American film was more varied than it had been in 1956. A sizeable minority of London movie reviewers wrote favorably if not enthusiastically about the film. Although not one of Hitchcock's masterpieces, the

1956 Hollywood version, they thought, was clearly superior to contemporary thrillers such as *Indiana Jones and the Temple of Doom* and *Friday the 13th* (see, e.g., Malcolm 1984; Andrews 1984). That is, for movie reviewers who compared *The Man Who Knew Too Much* to other thrillers then in circulation, Hitchcock's was the best available at that time. Still, a majority of British reviewers remained highly critical of the film, especially those who professed some familiarity with the original (Collection of Film Reviews, British Film Institute).

Typical of the majority position was Philip French's (1984) commentary in the *London Observer,* echoing Houston's perennial reservations about the film. According to French, a frequent contributor to *Sight and Sound,* the problem with the remake was that, unlike the original, the 1956 version was simply not a well-designed thriller. The unattractiveness of the American couple, argued French, was what made the remake so "heavy and oppressive." By contrast, "the balance between character and dramatic incident in the economic, unpretentious earlier film," said French, "makes for a far better thriller." The real heavy in French's indictment of the 1956 remake was Doris Day, whose "querulous, pouting homemaker who pops pills and saves her son by sitting down at the piano to sing a doleful pop tune" ("Che sera, sera"), is no match for the international crack-shot played by Edna Best who "saves her daughter with a well-aimed bullet in the 1934 version" (see plate 31). Judging the remake against the benchmark of the classic British thriller, French and other English critics (e.g., Castell 1984; Bergson 1984) concluded that the 1956 version was no match for the 1934 original—that prototype of the thriller form.

On the other hand, the American reviewers who saw the 1956 *The Man Who Knew Too Much* as much more than a thriller were also much more enthusiastic about the reissued film. While aware of its long-standing reputation among Anglo-American critics as a "minor" work from Hitchcock, several American reviewers, under the influence of auteur criticism, now asserted that the remake was actually one of Hitchcock's greatest artistic triumphs. A key promoter of this revised view of the film was Andrew Sarris, who wrote:

> Alfred Hitchcock's *The Man Who Knew Too Much* (1956) is, along with *Vertigo* and *Rear Window,* one of the major revelations of the current Hitchcock series. (*The Trouble with Harry* and *Rope* emerge as comparatively minor.) Don't miss it just because of any lingering prejudice against Doris Day. I shall analyze it in

greater detail, as well as compare it with Hitch's 1935 original, when I am sure that I cannot "spoil" it for anyone by giving away the plot, which I have to do in order to redeem its reputation from its persistent detractors. (Sarris 1984a)

In his follow-up reflections on the two films, Sarris (1984b) argued that along with the "genre conventions of guns and chases" there coexisted in both versions "a very lucidly realized world of family feelings." In the 1956 remake, however, Hitchcock's relationship with his players was "less intimate and more ironic," enabling him to explore the darker side of his not so wholesome All-American couple, while moving beyond the thriller form.

Whereas the British critics had tended to regard the Hollywood remake as far less than a great film because it was not a fully realized thriller, the American critics, heavily influenced by the principles of auteur criticism, tended to view the remake as a superior film precisely because, if one took the trouble to dig beneath the film's thriller surface, one would discover something more than a mere thriller. As a critic for the *Philadelphia Inquirer* put it:

> Here, beneath the masterfully handled suspense, is an extraordinary richness of theme and a serving of Hitchcock's dolorous view of the world. In this story of an American family in Morocco that becomes unwittingly involved in an assassination attempt against an international leader, Hitchcock found many elements that engaged him on a profound level.
>
> It is possible, as a result, to enjoy *The Man Who Knew Too Much* as a drama of excruciating superficial tension. It is also a movie, like *Rear Window* and *Vertigo,* that offers great rewards to those prepared to look beneath the surface. (Ryan 1984; see also Blowen 1984; Sheehan 1984; Denby 1984a)

To increase the credibility of their own favorable reassessments of the 1956 remake of *The Man Who Knew Too Much,* a number of U.S. critics (e.g., Blowen 1984) invoked Hitchcock's now famous remark to Truffaut about the differences between the 1934 original and the 1956 remake: "the first version is the work of a talented amateur, and the second was made by a professional" (Truffaut 1984, 94). This view of Hitchcock as a serious auteur which, as we have seen, Hitchcock himself came to embrace, had been the dominant perspective among American journalistic reviewers since *Frenzy* in the early seventies and has continued right up to the present. By contrast, the vast majority of England's mainstream reviewers never really adopted the view of Hitchcock as a serious artist. Rather, they have continued to feel more comfortable with the Hitchcock who made those entertaining "little British comedy thrillers" back in the thirties. Symptomatic of this bias was their assessment of Hitchcock's last two films—*Frenzy* and *Family Plot*. We recall that American reviewers were in general agreement that *Frenzy* was a film of importance and substance, while *Family Plot* was entertaining but lacked depth. The British reviewers sharply disagreed with the Americans, overwhelmingly preferring *Family Plot* to *Frenzy* precisely because the former was more entertaining than the latter.

Frenzy had made the British critics uncomfortable because of its unflattering portrayal of the English as well as its artistic flourishes, which were perceived as pretentious. The *Listener*'s critic complained, "What is so curious about this effort is that while it freely, and offensively, takes advantage of recent permissiveness, it also portrays the English as stifled by sexual inhibition. An unmarried couple has to bribe the desk clerk at the Coburg Hotel, Bayswater, to hire a double room" (*Listener,* 1 June 1972). The film, in other words, reflects bad taste and unnecessary nastiness. On the other hand, the reviewer for the *New Statesman* was made uneasy by the film's overtly artistic flourishes, most notably the long virtuoso camera movement "out of a room, down some stairs, out of the front door, to pull back and look blankly at a house front"—which this critic found only "tricky," lacking any deeper purpose (*New Statesman,* 2 June 1972).

By contrast, when *Family Plot* was released four years later, the English critics proclaimed it the triumphant return of Hitchcock's magical touch, which in their eyes had made him a great entertainer but not an important artist. Typical is the following excerpt from a review which appeared in the *Daily Mail:*

> For all its neatly engineered tensions, his latest film is primarily a comedy rather reminiscent of his underrated *The Trouble with Harry.* . . . After the mixed-up *Frenzy,* which tried to combine a modern permissiveness with vintage Hitchcock style, *Family Plot* is a delightful return to form. . . . "Hitch" himself has never quite understood the fussing idolatry he has provoked in his old age. He marvelled to me, for instance, at the subtle nuances Truffaut and Claude Chabrol found in his films. . . . All he is concerned with is giving the customer a good night out at the movies. . . . .

Hitchcock is still the best screen entertainer in the business. (18 August 1976)

As the English auteur critic Ian Cameron astutely put it (1976), the fact that *Family Plot* has been unanimously praised by the English critics "signals" that it must be a "lightweight work."

This English view of Hitchcock as essentially a "lightweight" persisted, leading British reviewers in 1984 to include different works on their list of preferred Hitchcock films. While *Rear Window* was favored among the reissued films, *Vertigo* ran a distant third with many critics viewing it as highly overrated. In contrast to their American counterparts, British reviewers who liked *Vertigo* tended to concentrate on matters relating to plot construction and the building of suspense rather than on thematic concerns or mise-en-scène. That is, the British were more interested in reassessing *Vertigo's* effectiveness as a thriller than in exploring the implications of its probings into psychopathology and its indictment of romantic love. When *Vertigo* was first released in 1959, England's premiere critic, C. A. Lejeune, had attacked Hitchcock for prematurely revealing the murder plot to audiences. In the eighties, English critics applauded Hitchcock for doing this. By sharing information about the conspiracy with audiences, Hitchcock was being perfectly consistent with his much-publicized views on how to make a successful thriller. Applying Hitchcock's distinction between suspense and surprise, the *London Times* critic explained that "the audience knows more than Stewart and the spectator's interest in the final part of the film is that much greater, following Stewart's gradual realization of the truth, than if the information had been held back." Not surprisingly, a number of British reviewers preferred *The Trouble with Harry*—a film Hitchcock had often described as characteristically English—to *Vertigo* and *The Man Who Knew Too Much*. American critics, on the other hand, continued to assess *The Trouble with Harry* as a relatively minor Hitchcock film.

In sum, British critics have continued to assess Hitchcock's work against the high standard, they claim, he set with his early British thrillers. By contrast, American reviewers, because they were more inclined to embrace auteurism than their British counterparts, came to view Hitchcock less as a thriller director and more as a serious artist whose work, they believed, often transcended the thriller form.

In addition to embracing auteurism, American reviewers seemed generally more knowledgeable about Hitchcock scholarship than British critics who, it is my impression, lack the training in film studies of their American counterparts. Compared with the American critics, for example, "very few" British film reviewers "have produced books on the cinema" (McArthur 1985). While the institution of film reviewing has recently come under attack in both countries for functioning as little more than a consumer guide to new films (see, e.g., Corliss 1990; McArthur 1985; cf. Ebert 1990), I would argue that this charge is less applicable to American reviewers, especially those working out of major cities such as New York, Chicago, and Los Angeles. In my own reading of journalistic criticism from both countries, I find that American reviewers are not as likely to pander to audience prejudices as is the case in England. (For a similar view on British film reviewing see McArthur [1985].) Occasionally American critics even serve to educate the public about cinema. As much as TV reviewers Gene Siskel and Roger Ebert have been attacked for their "thumbs-up-thumbs-down" approach, the fact remains that their weekly television series has periodically featured programs that reflect critically on certain harmful tendencies in American cinema, for example, how Hollywood's block-buster mentality routinely ignores the offbeat projects of such highly innovative filmmakers as Robert Altman. Many mainstream reviewers in the United States now and then discuss film in relation to the wider society. Several were attuned to the sharp debate in feminist circles about the "slasher films" of the eighties (see chapter 5). Not so in the film columns of British newspapers where, according to McArthur, there were no "glimmerings of awareness of the sharp debate in the feminist presses about 'stalk and slash' movies such as *Dressed to Kill*" (1985). American reviewers have also been more vocal than their British counterparts about the place of Hitchcock in film culture. Hitchcock's legacy in America is the subject of the next two chapters.

FIVE

Hitchcock's Posthumous Reputation and the Contemporary Thriller

One of the fundamental correlations in auteur criticism is that between neglected directors and neglected genres. To resurrect Ford and Hawks, it is necessary also to resurrect the Western. To take Minnelli seriously, it is necessary to take musicals seriously.

(Sarris 1985, 29–30)

Although all the arts develop genres that perpetuate themselves, this activity is intensified in the movie business due to a problem endemic to the industry, namely, <u>uncertainty about the future tastes of the mass audience</u>. To reduce this uncertainty, the movie studios, like other mass entertainment industries, try to gauge which genres are "alive" or "dead." Whether a particular genre finally is produced depends on how organizational gatekeepers at various stages of the film production process assess the product in relation to their perception of the audience's future tastes. Hollywood decision-makers have often attributed the unexpected commercial success of a particular film to its generic features or to characteristics which by virtue of their being repeated in subsequent films become the prototype for a new genre or subgenre. The film *Little Caesar* (1931) functioned as such a prototype for the short-lived cycle of popular gangster films during the early 1930s.

Two cycles of thriller films appeared during the 1980s: horror thrillers aimed at younger audiences and domestic thrillers targeted for more mature audiences. Each cycle resulted from the unexpected success of a film which became a prototype for films within the cycle (*Halloween* and *Jagged Edge*). Hitchcock's work and reputation shaped the making and marketing of several of the films in both of these thriller cycles and also entered into the critical debate about them.

Using the concept of the "film cycle" as a way of integrating information on Hitchcock's legacy in filmmaking, film packaging, and film criticism, this chapter examines Hitchcock's posthumous reputation against the backdrop of developments in the thriller genre over the past decade. It also assesses the impact of Hitchcock's reputation on the production and critical reception of thriller films relative to other factors, such as the increasing vocalization of feminist concerns within the film art world. The revival during the late 1980s of the adult thriller offered critics better opportunities for reflecting on Hitchcock's artistry than did the horror films that preceded them. Therefore, it is especially with respect to the critical evaluation of the adult thriller that I will assess the applicability of Becker's (1982) thesis that the upgrading of an artist's reputation might in time also improve the stature of the genre and the medium in which the artist worked.

THE YOUTHFUL HORROR FILMS (1978–83)

Beginning in 1978, a new cycle of horror films emerged which would last until around 1983.[1] Although the impact of Hitchcock's work on the making of these films was for the most part minimal, his legacy was frequently summoned as *the* standard against which to evaluate current films in the cycle. In addition, the generic labels commonly associated with the Hitchcock canon, such as "psychological thriller" or "suspense film," were routinely invoked to facilitate the marketing of horror films made during this period.

Horror has been one of the most enduring of Hollywood film genres.[2] The decade of the 1970s was no exception. Three top-grossing films, *The Exorcist* (1973), *Jaws* (1975), and *Halloween* (1978), probably did more than anything else to assure that the horror-film genre during the 1970s and early 1980s would enjoy the kind of long-term popularity it had experienced throughout the 1930s. The enormous success of *The Exorcist,* for example, resulted in each major studio reaching out to make another film about demonic possession. But by fall 1978, the popularity of such films had already peaked. Horror films were leaving studios in the red, and it would have come as no surprise had Hollywood temporarily stopped making them altogether. The meteoric arrival of the low-budget horror film *Halloween* in October 1978, after the genre had supposedly peaked, assured that studio executives would continue to back horror-film projects. *Halloween* earned over $50 million in box-office receipts after costing under $400,000 to produce. And it performed well in both domestic and foreign markets.

The brief synopsis of *Halloween* which follows foregrounds

those aspects of the film that critics would allude to as reminiscent of Hitchcock's *Psycho* as well as those elements that the film studios subsequently concluded were responsible for the film's unexpected commercial success. *Halloween* is about a male psychopathic killer who terrorizes the teenagers of a small midwestern community. The film makes considerable use of the subjective camera. In the prologue to the film, for example, we observe a brutal killing from the perspective of the killer himself. Not until we cut from the killer's perspective to an objective shot of him holding the blood-soaked knife he has just used to kill his sister do we learn that he is a male child of only ten or so. Following the prologue, we jump ahead fifteen years to 1978, the year in which the remainder of the film takes place. We learn that the boy (Michael Myers) has been placed in a mental institution. He escapes and returns to his hometown, where the earlier murder was committed. We see him tormenting and eventually eliminating several local teenagers. The film is punctuated with several suspenseful sequences along with a number of surprise shocks (see plate 32).

Press coverage about the making of *Halloween* frequently invoked Hitchcock. Director John Carpenter told a reporter that he was shooting some scenes to resemble those in Hitchcock's films. Journalist Lee Grant (1978) pointed out that a character in *Halloween*, Sam Loomis, had the same name as the John Gavin character in *Psycho*. And *Halloween*'s producer, Debra Hill, told the press, "The trick in scriptwriting for horror films is to keep intercutting between the victim and the threat. You manipulate the audience. One moment they think they're safe and then you introduce the threat. The old Hitch[cock] trick of the victim getting into a car, starting it up while a hand creeps up over the back seat, and driving off not knowing anyone is in the car is a trick we used in *Halloween*" (Mizell 1980).

Although *Halloween* opened to mostly negative reviews, one notable exception was a review by *Village Voice* critic Tom Allen, who championed the film. Characterizing *Halloween* as "an instant shlock horror classic," Allen (1978) further enshrined it as the only horror film of the last decade that belonged in the same company as *Night of the Living Dead* (1968) and, before that, *Psycho* (1960). The most obvious connection between *Halloween* and *Psycho*, he observed, is that both films feature a "knife-wielding madman." But Allen pointed to other parallels as well. John Carpenter "has attempted to stretch the shower sequence [from *Psycho*] into as much a feature film as the traffic will allow." In addition, *Halloween* evoked "that unique mix of subliminal threat and contrapuntal physicality employed by Hitchcock." While not the "disciplined director of narrow strategies and high aims like Hitchcock," conceded Allen, Carpenter nonetheless "does blow imitators like Brian De Palma and all his works off the screen." Several other critics also noticed the Hitchcockian virtues of *Halloween,* including *New York Times* critic Vincent Canby, whose commentary, "Chilling Truths about Scaring," acknowledged *Halloween*'s indebtedness to the Hitchcock legacy. What apparently had prompted Canby's piece was the release of three new films—Peter Weir's *The Last Wave,* Philip Kaufman's remake of the *Invasion of the Body Snatchers,* and Carpenter's *Halloween,* all of which, in Canby's words, were "evoking the Hitchcockian legacy" but with only "mixed results." While Canby found merit in these films, his major point was that none of them were really on par with *Psycho,* that "model of scare filmmaking" where Hitchcock "set standards . . . that have never since been equalled." For one thing, commented Canby, they lacked Hitchcock's "easy, graceful command," a symptom perhaps of trying too hard to imitate the Master. Notwithstanding his characterization of *Halloween* as "plodding moviemaking" compared to *Psycho,* Canby also praised the film for its Hitchcockian elements. Carpenter, like Hitchcock, is "fascinated by the technical ingredients that make an audience scream"; like his mentor, he subordinates "characterization" and "plausibility" to his principal task—causing audiences "as much distress as possible." Still, Carpenter along with the other contemporary directors cited in the article fall short of Hitchcock, said Canby, because of their inability, as yet, to transcend "pure film." "What [Hitchcock] has to say," wrote Canby, "is the manner in which he says it. This is something his students obviously know, though they have yet to find their own voices" (Canby 1979).[3]

Film companies—first the minors and then the majors—were quick to cash in on *Halloween*'s commercial success. Film executives extracted from *Halloween* the elements or formula they believed to have been responsible for its success: (1) the male psychopathic killer terrorizing teenage girls in their social milieu (the world of babysitters, prom queens, and camp counselors) and (2) the graphic depiction of blood and violence (indeed, more explicit than permitted at that time on prime-time television). Over the next two years film companies produced a large number of films so similar to the *Halloween* formula that a new subgenre of horror emerged, what has been termed "knife-kill," "splatter," "slasher," or "dead teenager" movies. From *Prom Night* and *Friday the 13th* to *Terror Train* and *Friday the 13th Part II,* each film contained successively more graphic depictions of violence, blood and gore. The "slice and dice" horror film had been born.[4] Somehow lost in the shuffle during the production of these films were the Hitchcockian virtues of suspense and understatement which early critics had found so much in evidence in *Halloween*.[5]

During this period, horror projects received considerable coverage from the mass media. Executives at Pickwick/Maslansky/Koenigsberg (PMK)—a public relations firm whose horror-film clients during the horror boom included directors Brian De Palma, George Romero, and John Carpenter, producer Debra Hill, and actress Jamie Lee Curtis reported that at the height of the horror craze, media gatekeepers "were all jumping on our horror films," that is, were willing to plug them in various ways. Said accounts executive Katie Sweet, "We really got involved with the whole business of horror after *Halloween*. . . . We started handling John Carpenter and for whatever reason we became the office for handling a lot of this genre of film" (Personal interview, fall 1981). According to Sweet, at the height of the horror-boom period, PMK could bring together many of its clients working in horror and have them talk to the media about their work. For example, one night on NBC's now defunct Tomorrow Show, Rona Barrett moderated an entire segment which brought together horror directors John Carpenter and George Romero to discuss their work. "In those days," recalled Sweet, "there was ease in getting the media to cover horror; it was just not that difficult." Invariably Hitchcock came up in these discussions. In a 1980 interview, Carpenter was asked whether it was valid for critics to compare him with Hitchcock. Carpenter thought not. "Hitchcock is an artist and master of film, which I am not, so there's no comparison. He is one of the great innovators in movies. He has influenced almost every filmmaker who's now making films. Mostly people say that because I tend to work in the thriller genre. But I'm not at all like Hitchcock. He never makes people jump. His whole concept is suspense—the bomb under the table that the audience knows about and agonizes over while the people at the table go on with their conversation unaware that it's going to explode. My way of scaring people is to have it blow up unexpectedly—taking the audience by surprise" (Olddie 1980).

Another characteristic of the horror-boom period was that there were no organized crusades against horror films.[6] In fact, it became chic among some journalistic and academic film critics to like horror— a trend traceable to the rise of auteur theory in the late 1960s; to the growing sense of "the American Cinema's dense intertextuality" (Ray,

1985); and to the attempts of high-culture critics in the 1970s to apply self-sufficient and self-referential aesthetic criteria (derived from high-culture criticism) to popular genres.[7] As we have seen, one outcome of this shift in critical standards was that by the late 1960s a number of films of popular genre filmmakers such as Alfred Hitchcock and Howard Hawks were considered works of art. This tendency was broadened during the 1970s to include other popular genre filmmakers as well. Indeed, at the start of the horror-boom period of the late 1970s, critics who ordinarily regarded horror with disdain were arguing that with the right director (e.g., Hitchcock in *Psycho,* Carpenter in *Halloween,* or Brian De Palma in *Dressed to Kill*) a work of considerable artistry could be achieved within that genre (see, e.g., Ansen 1978; Canby 1979; Kael 1980).[8] Apparently, the *New Yorker* agreed with the early assessments of Carpenter's work because in winter of 1980 it featured a lengthy profile of Carpenter (Stevenson 1980).[9]

While Hitchcock was often brought up in critical discussions of horror films during this period, his style of filmmaking had little bearing on the actual production of horror films made early in the cycle.

The production of *Fear No Evil,* a horror film conceived in 1979, shot in 1980, and released in early 1981, illustrates how the favorable climate for horror between 1979 and 1981 affected filmmaking at that time. It also exemplifies how during this period non-Hitchcock elements dominated Hollywood's thinking about horror. In fall 1978 the film's director, Frank LaLoggia, started work on a love story but ended up with a horror movie. At that time, according to LaLoggia, "Horror films were doing very well and we were looking for a first project that our money people could get behind, and so we developed an idea for a horror fantasy, approached them with that, and were able to raise about a half million dollars" (Personal interview, fall 1981).

With that money the director was able to complete principal photography for the film but still needed about $250,000 to add the visual and sound effects. So he took the picture in rough-cut form to Avco Embassy—a major distributor of horror films at that time—which agreed to supply the money to complete the film. Recalled the executive who subsequently advised the director on the project, "The sales department thought they could take it to Cannes and get $1 million right off the top in foreign rentals" (*Los Angeles Times,* 1980). Convinced that it was a safe investment, Avco agreed to cover post-production costs, but with certain strings attached.

Avco Embassy executives wanted more shots of high school students at school because they believed they could sell the film from the exploitative angle of young people in danger. Yet the film's story line really had little to do with youth in jeopardy. The film centers on three archangels—Michael, Gabriel, and Raphael—who periodically return to earth in the guise of humans to do battle with the latest incarnation of Lucifer, the fallen angel. The premise of *Fear No Evil* is that Lucifer comes to earth in the form of a high school student who is then pursued by the archangels. According to LaLoggia, in the film's original form the high school environment was not central to the story. "We included that environment because the horror films that were making it theatrically seemed to revolve around high school kids. When we brought the film to Avco the first time, they found the high school setting the most appealing aspect of the picture." Therefore, Avco insisted that the high school element be more dominant and that more blood and guts be added whenever possible. The director had shot several scenes involving high school students that were absent from the rough-cut form that Avco saw. Recalled LaLoggia, "I'd shot the material primarily as a safeguard and sure enough when they began to ask for it, it was a good thing we had it around, because not having the footage might have jeopardized the deal. That's just the way they were thinking at the time." More relevant than how audiences were thinking at the time of the horror-boom period was how studio executives were thinking about that audience. According to the studios, it was the escalation of the gore and not the subtle building of Hitchcockian suspense through restraint that youthful audiences found especially enticing about these films.

By early fall 1980, it appeared to some well-placed industry observers that the domestic market was once again saturated with horror and that the low-budget horror film was on a downslide (Harmetz 1980). Accordingly, worried marketing executives concentrated on positioning the horror films that were already finished, releasing them when national or regional markets were not already glutted with horror.

In January of 1981, the next wave of horror started with Avco Embassy's *Fear No Evil* and *Scanners*. *Fear No Evil* opened in Florida and Texas on January 16 and did good business. The film's good showing in the South did not escape the notice of the other studios. In a matter of weeks, many of the other horror films that had been sitting on the shelves were released. By the time *Fear No Evil* opened in New York in February, for example, *Scanners* and *Maniac* had already opened, and *My Bloody Valentine* was to premiere the next week. Soon to follow were *Blood Beach, The Boogey Man,* and a rerelease of *The Texas Chain-Saw Massacre.*

The 1981 mini-boom in horror provoked a media backlash. Leading the assault of the critics were Chicago reviewers Gene Siskel and Roger Ebert, who devoted an entire "Sneak Previews" television show to denouncing knife-kill movies, while (paradoxically) defending Carpenter's handling of similar material in *Halloween.* The Siskel-Ebert complaints focused on both the explicit and exploitative violence of these films as well as on their rampant misogyny (the victims often were independent young women who, the films implied, were asking for it). Other critics and journalists quickly followed suit (Newspaper clipping file on horror films, Academy Library). Indeed, by late 1982, many newspapers and national magazines had stopped reviewing low-budget horror films altogether.[10]

During this period, it became common for critics of gore to enlist the Hitchcock legacy in their crusade. References to Hitchcock's artistry figured prominently in the critical backlash against horror, with many critics commenting on Hitchcock's unusual restraint in such shock classics as *Psycho, The Birds,* and *Vertigo.* In an article appearing in the *Los Angeles Sunday Times* entitled "Horrors! It's Getting To Be No Joke!" Laurie Warner wrote, "Even the grand master of edge-of-their-seats suspense, the late Alfred Hitchcock, gave audiences nightmares with films like *Psycho, Vertigo,* and *The Birds* without ever resorting to excessive gore" (Warner 1980, 5). A month later, an essay in *American Film* expressed a similar sentiment, "The best horror films avoid overwhelming us with gore and violence, which can easily turn comical when overdone, or be pointlessly punishing to the audience. Both Carpenter and De Palma work more by suggestion, like their acknowledged master, Hitchcock, and like some erotic filmmakers who eschew hard-core sex for being too literal and unimaginative: organ-grinding rather than fantasy" (Dickstein, 1980).

The critical attack on low-budget horror movies extended to big-budget productions which were more dependent on the good will of critics and other journalists as they sought a broader appeal. Not only did most of the big-budget horror films released in 1981 and 1982 (e.g., *Ghost Story, Cat People,* and *The Thing*) receive terrible reviews, they also performed poorly at the box office. Failing to attract a broader audience, these films received most of their business from fans of low-budget horror (Newspaper clipping file, Academy Library).

It also became more difficult for horror films to get free media coverage, a result not merely of the backlash or crusade against horror but of the fact that "horror" was no longer perceived as "newsworthy." One might expect free publicity for any type of genre film to be easier to obtain earlier in a cycle than later. According to public-relations executive Neil Koenigsberg, whom I interviewed in 1981, "You can no longer go in and say, 'Oh we have this horror picture.'" He then cited as a hypothetical case the prospects for getting *Life* magazine to do a story on John Carpenter's *The Thing*—a horror film that was scheduled for release the summer of 1982. Because it was perceived as a horror film, a story about its production would not get published. What might work, Koenigsberg said, was a story about "this incredible career of a young person named John Carpenter. Look at the career and look at what makes him tick, because that means eventually getting into *The Thing*."

An additional assault against horror films came from the Classification and Rating Administration (CARA) of the Motion Picture Association of America, which assigns the ratings to Hollywood films. After the arrival of the slasher films in 1978, CARA got tougher on violence. For instance, some movies that would have received an R three years ago were assigned X ratings during the period of the backlash. One movie that received the dreaded X on its first screening for CARA was the sequel to *Halloween*.[11]

Despite the chill, horror films continued to be made. The difference was that now skittish directors and producers started to put some distance between themselves and the genre. An early indication came in late October 1981 when critic Stephen Farber hosted a weekend "Harvest of Horror" course at UCLA. At the opening session, Farber apologized to his students for the failure of a number of invited guests to show up and discuss their work. "We had invited Christopher Lee," said Farber at the time, but "he decided he no longer wanted to be associated with horror films. He felt that he had transcended the genre."

Farber went on to cite similar reactions from other industry people he had contacted. Filmmaker Paul Schrader, who was completing his remake of *The Cat People,* told Farber that his film wasn't horror but "a phantasy in the tradition of Cocteau." Many producers insisted their movies were "suspense thrillers," "supernatural tales," "intense psychological dramas"—anything but horror films (Field notes, 30 October 1981).

Producer Edward Feldman is typical of those who worked on horror projects during the 1981–82 downturn period and called horror by any other name. "Horror to me always connotes a low-budget maneuvering of the audience," he said. "It is graphically violent. It appeals to a much lower educational level." According to David Madden, who was feature-story editor at Twentieth Century-Fox in fall 1981, Feldman's film, *The Sender,* was Fox's only horror project then in development (Personal interview, fall 1981). Not surprisingly, Feldman disagreed with Madden's characterization of his film—insisting that his unfinished picture was more suspenseful than graphically violent. While not directly mentioning Hitchcock by name, Feldman discussed *The Sender* in a manner recalling Hitchcock's distinction between suspense and surprise. "There is much more intellectual violence. It's more in your mind and in your emotional state. You don't see people chopping people up. You walk a fine line in these kinds of movies. If you don't intellectualize a little and make them more a dramatic vehicle, as *The Exorcist* or *The Shining,* you've got what is known as a 'quick-in and quick-out movie,' which opens in a thousand theaters and you pray for one or two good weekends. We're trying to make a movie that has some substance" (Personal interview, fall 1981).

In spring 1980 when plans to make a sequel to *Halloween* got underway, the boom in low-budget horror films was in full swing. However, by fall 1981, when *Halloween II* was about to be released, industry uncertainty about the marketability of horror had become widespread and the media backlash against horror films had reached its zenith. The making of this film illustrates that audience uncertainty among filmmakers and studio marketing people intensifies as it becomes less and less clear whether the genre cycle in question will continue to boom or suddenly bust.[12] It also reveals how filmmakers and critics alike increasingly brought up Hitchcock's more restrained style as an alternative to the recent excesses in horror films.

According to its producers, the challenge of *Halloween II* was to make a film that would end the slasher cycle but would not be as bloody as recent films in the genre. The game plan was to create a thriller or suspense film rather than simply a horror film. The director, Rick Rosenthal, said he was hired for *Halloween II* because of his work on a short, *The Toyer,* which "was not a horror film but a psychological thriller" in the Hitchcock tradition.

Coproducer Debra Hill concurred that the premise of the sequel as with the original was to build fear and suspense—Hitchcockian virtues—rather than repulse the audience with graphic displays of blood and guts. At the same time, the filmmakers recognized that because of recent developments in the horror genre, the sequel would have to be more graphic and violent than the original. Indeed, the original script was most compatible with this strategy, calling for no less than a dozen grisly killings.

Co-writer and coproducer John Carpenter, who had directed the original *Halloween,* visited the set on only two occasions, but his presence was felt throughout the shooting, especially by director Rosenthal. Working closely with cinematographer Dean Cundey, Rosenthal tried to make the film consistent with Carpenter's style in *Halloween,* such as the use of the moving or subjective camera to convey the killer's presence and point of view, and the creation of images that are shocking in themselves—that grab the viewer viscerally but are not necessarily bloody or violent.

Although Rosenthal was clearly the person in command on the set, there were limits to what he could do. While staging a particular scene he might be reminded by the line producer (Hill) or the cinematographer (Cundey) that Carpenter would not have done it that way. Or if he tried to add anything new, it would be called to his attention that it was not in the script and that he had better keep in mind the shooting schedule. Nonetheless, there were certain touches in the final film that were distinctively Rosenthal's, particularly the Germanic or *film noir* look. He and art director Mike Riva had a visual concept of what the film should look like—hard-edged shadows, people either in the light or in the dark. Cundey affirms that during the shooting, as well as at the dailies, Rosenthal had considerable control. "John was at the dailies to offer Rick encouragement but pretty much allowed him to do what he wanted" (Personal interview, fall 1981).

On the few occasions when Cundey strongly disagreed with Rosenthal's handling of a particular shot, he would try to persuade Rosenthal to shoot it differently. Interestingly, we find that behind these occasional creative differences were differing approaches to the audience. Although both the artistic and marketing strategists agreed that *Halloween II* should be directed toward those people who saw the original, the filmmakers themselves also tried, in varying degrees, to identify their audience in terms of its emotional response to filmic manipulation and to study how these responses may change over time. Alfred Hitchcock's shadow frequently loomed behind their discussions about how to deal with audience expectations.

Except for the twenty-minute suspense film he had made while still a student at the American Film Institute, Rosenthal had little experience working in the horror-film genre. His lack of experience is reflected in the following remark he made to one of my research assistants regarding the audiences for his films: "Maybe I am wrong about this, but I don't think you should make films for audiences. I think you should make a film that entertains you, that you want to make, and that you have to hope that the film finds an audience." In contrast, cinematographer Dean Cundey seemed always aware of creating something for someone other than himself. Before *Halloween II,* he had worked on a number of low-budget horror films, including the original *Halloween, The Fog,* and *Dark Star* and has since worked on *The Thing* (1982), *Halloween III* (1983), and *Psycho II* (1983). Accordingly, Cundey has a remarkable knowledge of how to affect audiences, particularly experienced horror-film buffs. In discussing the mechanics of scaring an audience, Cundey commented that if you repeatedly set up scare scenes the same way, you end up building a resistance to the scares. Consequently, "you have to be inconsistent in your consistency."

These differing approaches to the audience are reflected in many of the occasional creative differences between Rosenthal and Cundey that arose during the filming. One scene in the film provides an excellent example of how these alternative views can affect the final product. In it a scare is to be delivered by having a nurse find a dead body. On the day it was filmed there was a great deal of discussion between Rosenthal and Cundey over how to stage it so that the body would be revealed with maximum impact on the audience. The script originally had called for the dead man's head to be propped up by a lamp, with the nurse then pushing him back to explore his fatal wounds. However, Rosenthal decided that it would be impossible to prop up a man's head on a lamp realistically, and that the revelation should instead be accomplished by having him sitting in an armchair with his back to the nurse, and then having her reach across a desk and spin the chair around to reveal him.

Even though this routine was not unique, having been used so effectively by Hitchcock in *Psycho,* Rosenthal felt that because horror films are, in his words, "a chilling suspension of disbelief," it would nonetheless work. Cundey, on the other hand, felt that a scene staged like that would only distract audiences:

> If a scene draws the audience out for a moment, if they are suddenly looking at a flaw or a hackneyed gag, if it is running contrary to what you are trying to create, then it is bad. . . . My feeling is if you are going to ask an audience to believe the impossible you have to made it as believable as possible. You have to answer all their questions.

Rosenthal (and Hitchcock) prevailed.

After shooting the film, the director was given about five weeks to prepare his cut or version of the film. Once his rough cut (minus a sound track) was completed, the producers, still unsure about what audiences hoped to find in their film, proceeded to show the unfinished film to high school students, soliciting their opinions. And, according to one of the producers, the students wanted more blood and guts. As the director described it, the producers became scared that there wasn't enough gore in their film, so they went out and shot a few new scenes that were extremely violent. Although the rough-cut version of the film did include a dozen or so brutal killings, none of the victims was a teenager girl. Killing off at least one teenage girl had become a staple of the genre. So a new scene was shot and inserted early in the picture depicting the fatal slashing of a high school girl. Also, the producers drastically shortened several scenes where there were no immediate payoffs, that is, where no gory killings occurred. One of the scenes tampered with was, in its original form, reminiscent of the typical Hitchcock suspense sequence (the bomb that doesn't go off) in which the audience has knowledge not available to the film's protagonists.

Late in the film, one of the female characters is trying to escape from the killer. She gets in a car, tries to start it, can't start it, and gets out. In the director's original cut, the scene lasts several minutes and functions to build suspense in the audience. "It goes on and on and on when I cut it," the director told us. "The viewer is supposed to think, 'Oh shit, the car doesn't start' and then you say 'Wait a minute. This isn't a scene about a car not starting. He's in the back seat. Get out! Get out of the car!' And just when you are saying, 'Oh no! He's coming out of the back seat,' she gets out of the car." According to the director, because there was no payoff in the scene, that is, the girl was not brutally murdered, the producers shortened it. In the final version, she gets in and gets out of the car in a matter of seconds—not long enough for the audience to say, "Look Out!" (Personal interview, fall 1981).

Shortly after the film was completed, two students of mine discussed the film with Rosenthal and asked him to comment on some of the weaknesses in his direction of the film. A shortcoming, he felt, was that he had been too preoccupied with trying to replicate Carpenter's style in order to achieve stylistic continuity between *Halloween* and the sequel. The film, he volunteered without any coaxing from the interviewers, would have benefited from more Hitchcockian touches. "You know," said Rosenthal, "Hitchcock really is the master. He's the best. And, we can't copy him. But we can learn from him."[13] Referring to

Carpenter's style, Rosenthal pointed out that in *Halloween* there was very little cutting. Often the killer made his appearance from behind a door. "One of the things that Hitchcock did so well," says Rosenthal, "was that he would set up the cut by using a nice wide shot where people are small and vulnerable." He would then cut to a very big image or closeup of the killer and his weapon (see, for example, the shot of the gun at the end of *Spellbound*). Said Rosenthal, "it would have tremendous impact, like a volt of energy." Rather than have the killer pop in behind the victim, "I think it might have been more effective to pop a real giant close-up of the shape."

Halloween II was released on Halloween weekend 1981. By that time, as mentioned earlier, horror had become a *genre non grata* in Hollywood. But if movies about psychotic killers with an eye for teenage camp counselors and baby-sitters still score high at the box office, what is a distributor or public relations firm to do?

Avco Embassy, which had become identified with horror through its distribution of *The Howling* and *The Fog*, gave some indication of the strategy for handling horror during a period of backlash when in early October 1981 it released a film called *Dead and Buried*. The ad featured a graveyard with a skull, an obvious horror motif. But the press kit did not once refer to the movie as a "horror film." It was characterized as a "bizarre new suspense thriller" or "terrorizing mystery" from "the creators of *Alien*." It seems that the title and ad campaign were meant to attract one audience—horror-film enthusiasts—and the press kit was directed at another—critics and other journalists who might be persuaded to promote it as a Hitchcockian thriller, thereby helping it to find a more sophisticated audience.[14]

Universal's strategy for handling *Halloween* resembled Avco Embassy's approach. The ad for *Halloween II* featured a skull superimposed upon a pumpkin, an unmistakable horror motif. While Universal's press kit for the film did not hide the fact that *Halloween II* was a horror film (how could it?), it did stress that the film was more a quality suspense film than a "slice and dice" horror film. For example, Universal Pictures took up this theme in its production notes, quoting Debra Hill as saying, "People don't seem to realize that we showed next to no blood in the first picture. You think you're seeing a lot more than we're showing you. Chopping off people's limbs isn't scary or entertaining, it's disgusting."

Following a preview screening of *Halloween II* at Farber's weekend course in horror at UCLA, Rick Rosenthal and Debra Hill, who were present, responded to questions concerning the film. One member of the audience complained about the cardboard characters and silly dialogue in the film. Defending her film, Hill argued that, in a thriller film, what a character says is often irrelevant, especially in those sequences where the objective is to build suspense. Shallow characterizations in horror films "are a by-product of the pace and suspense the genre demands," Hill said. To illustrate her point, Hill invoked Hitchcock's well-known story about the ticking bomb. A scene where several people are talking, claimed Hill, is not nearly as suspenseful as when the same scene is inter-cut with shots of a bomb ticking away. In the latter case, "the audiences aren't listening to the characters talk," Hill said. Rather, it is the audience doing the talking. And "they're saying, 'Get the hell out of there.' It's one of the rules of suspense; that's a choice we made as filmmakers" (Field notes, 30 October 1981).

Halloween II was a big success at the box office but nearly all reviews of it were strongly negative. In fact, the vast majority of horror films released in 1981 and 1982 were panned, including several that many of today's critics admire (e.g., *Deadly Blessing,* 1981; *The Thing,* 1982; and *The Entity,* 1982). One of John Carpenter's best films, *The Thing,* was "reviled by critics as loathsome, disgusting and horrible" (Pollock 1982).[15] A number of critical essays also appeared decrying the current crop of horror films and pointing out what was wrong with them. Within this context, Hitchcock's name again was frequently invoked.

Despite the backlash, horror remained a potentially big winner at the box office. While film rentals for horror were somewhat down in 1981, they climbed to a record high in 1982. Horror films performed badly at the box office in 1983, a trend which continued more or less right into the nineties. Domestic film rentals in 1983 declined by over 50 percent from 1982 levels. "In absolute dollar terms, not correcting for inflation," reported *Variety* (1984), "this represented the worst performance for shock pictures since 1976." In addition, none of the horror films released by independent producers earned over $5 million dollars, while virtually all the big-budget horror films flopped. In fact, the only commercially successful horror films were the moderately budgeted and well-publicized projects from the major distributors (*Jaws 3D, Cujo, The Dead Zone, Christine,* and *Psycho II*).[16]

After several years of discussion, a sequel to *Psycho* finally went into production in 1982—a low-budget joint venture involving Universal Studios and a cable company.[17] Given the stature of *Psycho,* the film's director, Richard Franklin, felt that his film would not have to trade on the works of contemporary horror directors such as Carpenter and De Palma. Meditating on the original would be sufficient. At the same time, simply copying *Psycho* would not work either. According to Franklin, *Psycho II* had to capture the excitement and experience of seeing the original when it first came out. As we have seen, during the height of the backlash against horror films, critics had frequently invoked *Psycho* as a model of restraint compared to the gory slasher films which dominated the horror market at that time. Ironically, as we remember, the reception of *Psycho* in 1960 had emphasized the film's lack of moderation. Only in light of subsequent excesses would it be viewed as a model of classical restraint. Aware of these shifts over time in the critical reception of *Psycho,* Franklin felt that it would be consistent with the original to at some point really shock the audience. "When one goes back to the original reviews of *Psycho,*" Franklin told me, "one discovers that the general impression of the time was not as it is now thought a picture of restraint. Rather, the feeling was that the picture was very over stated and blood thirsty. So I felt that it would not be inconsistent with *Psycho* to at some point . . . shock the audience" (Personal interview, spring, 1986).

Expressing no interest in topping some of the gore that had recently splattered the screens, Franklin decided to pepper his film with "visceral shocks that would turn your stomach," such as when Norman stabs Vera Miles through the mouth or with the image of Norman closing his hand around a sharp knife. In *Psycho II,* the real shocks don't come until the beginning of the film's third act. Franklin's rationale for postponing the violence is interesting, illustrating how *Psycho*'s legacy shaped the overall structure of *Psycho II:*

> *Psycho* had changed direction totally at the end of the first act when Janet Leigh got killed. And the second and third act were a different story. So I figured I can't switch direction there because . . . that is where everyone would be expecting me to shift direction if they knew anything. So what I have to do is I will set up a *modus operandi* and then I will pull the rug out from the audience, which is exactly what the original *Psycho* did. But I elected to do it at the beginning of the third act. (Personal interview, spring, 1986)

To summarize, Franklin's decision to make *Psycho II* shocking was influenced less by the conventions of the then current slice-and-dice films than it was by his feeling that *Psycho II* would not be a true sequel to *Psycho* if it did not jolt the audience in new and unexpected ways.

The Hitchcock legacy also became a key element of *Psycho II*'s promotional campaign. The production notes, for example, emphasized that, like *Psycho,* the sequel would also demonstrate that it was possible to make a quality film on a low budget. As with the original, this was hardly an experiment, since economic necessity dictated that *Psycho II* be made on a low budget. At the time the sequel went into production, well-placed industry observers perceived that horror films were doing poorly at the box office. Despite the fear that *Psycho II* might attract only fans of low-budget slasher films, the whole thrust of the studio press releases emphasized *Psycho II* as a quality film.

One way of establishing the film's pedigree was to show that the personnel working on the film had deep roots in the Hitchcock tradition. The promotional materials on Franklin, for example, emphasized his impeccable credentials. After all, he was a serious student of Hitchcock. While studying film at the University of Southern California, he organized a major retrospective of Hitchcock's works which resulted in Franklin meeting Hitchcock. Later Hitchcock would invite Franklin on the set of *Topaz.* Franklin's studio biography also stressed that his work had been exclusively in the thriller genre. In fact, his first thriller, *Patrick* (1978), had won awards at several film festivals.

Moreover, the film's production notes informed journalists and critics that the film's producer, Hilton Green, had worked as Hitchcock's first assistant director on several episodes of Hitchcock's television series, as first assistant director of the original *Psycho,* and as production manager on *Marnie.* Audiences were also informed that Tony Perkins and Vera Miles would update their renowned roles from *Psycho.*

In interviews published before the release of *Psycho II,* Franklin repeatedly reminded the press that, like any effective avant garde film, Hitchcock's *Psycho* had shocked audiences when first released and that, therefore, to simply imitate it would not evoke the kind of response generated by the original. Rather than show more gore, Franklin said he would try to redirect the genre along different lines, hoping to recapture the kind of experience he had when he first saw *Psycho* at the age of twelve. Imitating the marketing strategies used in promoting other horror films of the period, Franklin insisted that neither *Psycho* nor *Psycho II* were really horror films.

Despite Franklin's promotional strategies, most reviews of *Psycho II* were negative, ranging from lukewarm to outright hostile, with many decrying the film's explicit bloodiness and the full-frontal gore. While the reviewer for *Variety* (1983b) saw these excesses as an asset with respect to the film's box-office potential, most other commentators on the film condemned the practice, citing Hitchcock's relative restraint in the original *Psycho*. Particularly irksome to hostile reviewers was the slice-and-dice flavor of the film's finale. As *Newsweek* reviewer Jack Kroll put it, "You don't have to be a Hitchcock idolater to see this dumb, plodding pseudo-camp bore is a callous, commercial parasite." After dismissing the cheap and recombinant horror thrills of the first part of the film, Kroll cynically referred to the inspirational filmmaking of the final portion of the film where screenwriter Holland and director Franklin introduce such innovative touches as "a knife plunging into a woman's screaming mouth, with appropriate orthodontic noises" (Kroll 1983). Other critics were more explicit in their condemnation of the film's escalating violence, linking it to the recent excesses of the slasher cycle. According to *New York Magazine* reviewer David Denby, "as it goes on and on, and the stabbings and murders pile up, the gruesome stupidity of today's horror film mentality overwhelms Hitchcock's spirit of comic ghoulishness" (Denby 1983; see also Stack 1983; Sterritt 1983; Kenas 1983). Indeed, as *Christian Science Monitor* critic David Sterritt was anxious to point out, Hitchcock in *Psycho* followed a plan of diminishing violence. "After the notorious 'shower scene' with its jolting knife attack," writes Sterritt, "other violent sequences are briefer and show less mayhem. Once he had the audience's imagination worked up, Hitchcock felt that there was no need to overdo things" (Sterritt 1983).

At the same time, a number of critics did enjoy the humorous mood of the first part of *Psycho II,* which they compared favorably to the black humor of the original. Indeed, many became disappointed when Franklin's film shifted from a humorous to a more macabre mood in the second half. Commenting on the "comic ghoulishness," the "black comedy," and "droll, stiletto-tipped wit" of the original, most critics seemed unaware of the extent to which *Psycho* had angered those who experienced the film when it first came out. While there is a good deal of black humor in *Psycho,* the fact remains that much of this humor was lost on viewers during the film's initial run in 1960. Then it had been extremely rare for reviewers to refer to the film's "droll wit" or "comic ghoulishness." As one person who saw the film in 1960 told me, "Nobody laughed. We were all too busy gasping and shrieking" (Personal interview, June 16, 1989).

As for the minority view that *Psycho II* had some real merit, it is ironic that several of these reviewers had been outspoken sponsors and enthusiasts of Hitchcock's work during the sixties and seventies. In his review of *Psycho II, Time* critic Richard Schickel stressed the overall good-naturedness of the film, including its finale. Wrote Schickel, the ending "is genuinely surprising and, like much of the rest of *Psycho II,* it has a certain sly wit about it. Indeed, there is a rather good-natured air about this not overly scary picture which pays homage to Hitchcock's most famous (but not best) work without trying either to rip it off or knock it off" (Schickel 1983; see also Sarris 1983b).

In this section, we have seen how Hitchcock's mastery of the thriller form was frequently brought up in critical discussions of horror films released during the late seventies and early eighties. Reviewers and commentators often invoked his work as the standard against which to evaluate current films in the cycle. During the backlash against slasher films, for example, it became common for critics of gore to comment on Hitchcock's unusual restraint and ironic use of humor, especially in *Psycho*. Throughout the backlash period, critics were remaking Hitchcock by claiming that he was a classicist. Also around this time, filmmakers working in horror declared similarities between their films and Hitchcock's, hoping to cash in on Hitchcock's preeminence. However, exploiting memories of Hitchcock's legacy to market horror films released late in the cycle could not offset the critical backlash against the genre.

THE REVIVAL OF THE ADULT THRILLER (1985–88)

The revival of adult thrillers in the late 1980s provided critics with far richer opportunities for reflecting on Hitchcock's versatility and range as a director than did the horror films of the early eighties, which often did little more than spark a brief comment about Hitchcock's classic distinction between suspense and surprise. Since Hitchcock's stature as both a thriller director and as a serious artist affected both the development and critical evaluation of many of these films, their release provides a good context for exploring the thesis, implied by Becker (1982), that the upgrading of an artist's reputation might also improve the stature of the genre in which the artist works. I use the critical response to these films, compared to the reaction to pre-1970 thrillers, to gauge the extent to which the more serious newspaper and magazine critics have increasingly come to treat the thriller as a legitimate vehicle for serious art. In addition, I determine whether the available evidence supports the claim that the transformation of Hitchcock's reputation from popular entertainer to serious artist caused the status of the suspense thriller to improve in comparison with other Hollywood genres. As I will show, while critics routinely measured these new thrillers against the work of the old master of suspense, they also judged them on the basis of other considerations, such as the way women are represented in Hollywood cinema.

The theatrical re-release during the mid-eighties of Hitchcock's five so-called "lost" films did not directly stimulate the revival of the adult thriller in the late 1980s. The catalyst, according to several Hollywood marketing experts, was the unexpected success of the 1985 romantic courtroom thriller, *Jagged Edge*—a film that few Hollywood professionals regarded as a potential blockbuster (Hannerz 1988). For one thing, it featured no big box-office stars. Yet the film grossed over 40 million dollars. Speculating as to the source of *Jagged Edge*'s success, Hollywood executives and film packagers agreed that the real key was the film's generic pedigree. It was an adult thriller—a genre which, except for the commercially successful recycling of Hitchcock's work, had long been perceived by Hollywood packagers as dead. For Paramount production executive David Madden, the success of *Jagged Edge* was evidence that "there was life in a genre where people thought there wasn't much." Moreover, *Jagged Edge*'s success came at a time when Hollywood had become less hesitant about making films for adults. "There was a time," said thriller producer Laurence Mark, "when it seemed that wasn't done. It's a real grab bag now" (Thompson 1987).[18] After *Jagged Edge*'s unexpectedly good performance in the marketplace, the commercial success and the overall success two years earlier of the re-release of Hitchcock's "lost" films took on new significance. Confident that there now existed a sizeable market for the Hitchcock-type thriller, Hollywood's development mills started grinding out Hitchcock imitations, spawning the nearly two dozen suspense films which were released in 1987 and early 1988.

Critical response to an early thriller in the cycle, *The Bedroom Window* (1987), reveals some of the negative consequences for a director perceived to have fallen too much under the Hitchcock spell. While a number of reviewers quickly dismissed *The Bedroom Window* as little more than a Hitchcock clone which ultimately didn't measure up as an effective old-fashioned suspense thriller, several other reviewers, though also critical, presented a more subtle critique of the film, illustrating how journalistic appraisals of Hitchcock's work had deepened over the past twenty years.

Newspaper and magazine ads for *The Bedroom Window* made no bones about the film's Hitchcockian roots, announcing it as a "romantic thriller in the tradition of the master of suspense" (see plate 33). A few weeks before its release, the executive in charge of marketing *The Bedroom Window* had described the film to a columnist for the *Hollywood Reporter* as "an old-fashioned Hitchcock-style thriller with the added benefit of having the humor that Steve Guttenberg brings to the character. It's not so much a whodunit as a how-do-you-catch-him-and-then-what-happens-to-him kind of movie" (Grove 1987). The columnist, who had already seen the film, reiterated the more widespread view of Hitchcock as "master of suspense":

> As a Hitchcock buff I found in "Window" many of the classic elements developed by the Master of Suspense—including the innocent person swept up by events out of his control in a crime that the police think he committed but that the audience knows he's innocent of; the murder in an important public place of the only person who can clear the hero; the awareness of the audience very early in the film as to who the killer is; the pursuit of the hero by both the police and the villain; and the hero's ultimate realization that only he can save himself by setting a trap for the killer with the aid of the lady that events have brought him together with. Naturally, much of this action takes place in true Hitchcock fashion in darkness, shadows and rain. (Grove 1987)

This fifties view of Hitchcock was echoed in several reviews of *The Bedroom Window*, especially those appearing in the trade papers (see *Variety*, 1987) and in more mass-oriented publications (see Carroll, *New York Daily News*, 1987).[19]

On the other hand, reviewers heavily influenced by the auteur theory were more inclined to comment on the film's thematic richness. *Chicago Tribune* critic Dave Kehr, for example, thought the film's director (Curtis Hanson) should be commended for developing "one of the most mysterious and personal of Hitchcock's themes—the exchange of guilt between two characters that occurs in *I Confess, Strangers On A Train* and *Frenzy*" (1987a).[20] At the same time, Kehr underscored Hanson's difficulties in executing his ideas. Evoking the image of Hitchcock as classicist, he argued that Hanson "can't imitate Hitchcock's sense of structure, proportion and rhythm."

In his review of *The Bedroom Window*, *New York Magazine* critic David Denby (1987a) made a similar point, alluding to Truffaut's discussion about "plausibility" in Hitchcock's films:

In the course of François Truffaut's magisterial, book-long interview with Alfred Hitchcock, Truffaut occasionally raises the mundane issue of plausibility. Would people in danger really behave the way they do in Hitchcock's films? Hitchcock usually responds in cynically pragmatic terms: If the characters had acted plausibly and called the police, there wouldn't have *been* any movie.

As far as Hitchcock was concerned, the audience's demand for plausibility was an irritating case of philistine literal-mindedness. On the surface, he was contemptuous of it. But if you look at the films closely, you can see how much he respected this garden-variety element of audience psychology—how he alternately seduced, tricked, kicked, or charmed us out of our unquenchable longing to see characters pick up the phone and scream, "Help!"

One of Denby's chief complaints about Hanson's film was that its plot lacked the plausibility that had kept audiences sufficiently glued to a Hitchcock film, enabling the master to explore his theme about the transfer of evil. "One of the many fascinating things about his movies," said Denby, "is the elaborate secondary machinery of the plot—all those awkward and funny reasons why James Stewart and Doris Day had to rely on their wits rather than ring Scotland Yard. No matter how far he jumped into lurid fantasy, Hitchcock never left the recognizable world behind."[21] "He knew we wouldn't follow him," said Denby, "unless he revered our plodding common sense." After establishing "his web of circumstances," Hitchcock would then explore his "theme of the transfer of evil," providing "striking insight into the universality of criminal desires."

A few critics also expressed the view that a fully realized thriller in the post-Hitchcockian era must transcend Hitchcock. Pointing to the dangers to filmmaking if too many young directors continued to fall under the spell of Hitchcock, Kehr observed: "Alfred Hitchcock was a very great filmmaker, but these days the most frightening aspect of his work is the way in which it seems to have colonized the consciousness of two or three generations of young directors." Hanson, in Kehr's view, was yet another casualty of this style of thinking. While Kehr thought that Hanson was a talented filmmaker, he also felt that there was "nothing in *The Bedroom Window* to compare to the force and originality Hanson displayed in his last feature, the underrated 1983 *Losin' It*." "*The Bedroom Window* is not at all an unskilled film, but that, in some ways, is what is most discouraging about it: Hanson is more than good enough to do something of his own. In its drive to imitate the past, Hollywood is leaving itself without a present" (Kehr 1987a). A critic for the *Los Angeles Times,* Michael Wilmington, argued that post-Hitchcock thrillers needed to update Hitchcock. "Hitchcock, as much as Raymond Chandler, really belongs to a specific period, a different era's private romanticism and public morality. And *The Bedroom Window*—like dozens of others—never succeeds in updating him" (Wilmington 1987).

More in touch with the times, according to many critics, was Bob Rafelson's *Black Widow,* also released in 1987. This thriller focuses on Catherine (Theresa Russell), a glamorous female psychopath who seduces, marries, and then murders a series of rich and powerful men. Her case attracts federal investigator Alex Barnes (Debra Winger), who is determined to track her down. Barnes's motivation for getting involved in the case is what many critics found so fascinating about the film.[22]

In reviewing this film as well as *The Bedroom Window* and Arthur Penn's *Dead of Winter, Time* critic Richard Corliss (1987) singled out *Black Widow* as the one among the three that came closest to meeting the Hitchcock standard. What Corliss especially liked was the film's feminist approach to the Hitchcockian theme of the transference of evil and the preoccupation with the double. According to Corliss, when Alex Barnes, who is obsessed with her work, discovers that Catherine is equally obsessed with hers (which happens to be murder for profit), what Alex really discovers is "a freer, more dangerous part of herself. Could she become her own evil twin? Catherine would like the world to think so." Said Corliss, "Russell and Winger make movie history: a detective and a villain, both women. Together, they fuse as a feminist femme fatale" (Corliss 1987).[23]

Another admirer of the film's feminist slant was *Los Angeles Herald Examiner* critic Richard Natale, who argued that the murderess's sexist husbands got what they deserved. "Russell never preys on the weak, her target being the rich and famous, men with overinflated egos and delusions of potency; she mates with and murders males who regard her as yet another manifestation of their material success, a handsome acquisition like a new Ferrari or a fast speed-boat—their droit de seigneur. But this beauty is no dummy. She's smarter, more cunning than any of the men she marries, capable of letting them believe they're chasing her, until she snares them. They wind up dead. She winds up their beneficiary. This 'Black Widow' is the avenging angel of sexism" (Natale 1987).

While lauding the film's feminist touches, many critics felt that *Black Widow* ultimately missed its mark by not being daring enough in its exploration of the relationship which develops between the two women (see Anson 1987). Speculating on what would have happened if Hitchcock had directed it, *New York Magazine* critic David Denby wrote, "I hate to keep coming back to Hitchcock (as if no one else could make a thriller)," said Denby, "but if he had been directing, the virtuous Winger would have approached Russell with a mixture of excitement and moral nausea bordering on the uncontrollable; and no doubt Russell would have felt that Winger could kill her, too. But we don't feel anything of the sort. *Black Widow* is far too civilized for its subject" (Denby 1987b).

One reason viewers do not develop any real feelings about Catherine (Russell's character), argued *New Yorker* critic Pauline Kael, is because her murderous behavior lacks motivation.[24] As another New York critic put it, "surely Hitchcock wouldn't have done it that way." While the film's script "is greatly indebted to Alfred Hitchcock, . . . it ignores Hitchcock's biggest concern—psychological motivation." To illustrate Hitchcock's skill at establishing psychologically motivated characterizations, Weinberg (1987) compared *Black Widow* to Hitchcock's *Marnie,* in which the central character "embezzles money from an employer, dyes her hair, and changes her identity, and then moves on to her next victim. The hair dying has a peculiar, haunting resonance which establishes Marnie's mental instability and her lack of a solid personality. For all the character swapping in *Black Widow,* Rafelson and Bass [the film's screenwriter] set up no such link between Catherine's interior and exterior world. The viewer is left as emotionally uninvolved as Catherine is with the men caught in her web" (Weinberg 1987).[25]

Other critics also raised the issue of plausibility with respect to *Black Widow,* again citing Hitchcock as the uncontested master-designer of plausible thriller plots. "When Hitchcock was at his best," said *Wall Street Journal* critic Julie Salamon, "and that was often, he propelled the story forward by means of clearly calculated, powerful im-agery reinforced by his cannily casted actors Later, on a second or third viewing, one might pay attention to the implausibilities of a given plot. But the first time around, Hitchcock could usually lull audiences into ignoring the things that didn't 'make sense.' He played lots of tricks but rarely with the elements that mattered: a precise—and rich—vision of time, place, character. *Black Widow* director Bob Rafelson hasn't man-aged to put at bay that nagging suspense-snuffing rumination: 'Now why would she do that? That doesn't *make sense.*' In fact, this movie's plot holes might as well be surrounded by blinking neon, they glare so brightly. That's a shame, because between the gaps, which come with increasing frequency as the story winds down, the director has staged a provocative tease" (Salamon 1987b).

Judging from the range of critical response to it, the one thriller from this period that seemed to succeed on many different levels was *The Stepfather,* directed by Joseph Ruben and released later in 1987. Here was a Hitchcock-style thriller which most critics could agree was a fitting homage to Hitchcock. To a considerable degree, the critical response to *The Stepfather* mirrored the full range of interpretations that Hitchcock's films had elicited over the past forty years. While some reviewers praised the film for its successful build-up of suspense, others singled out the director's artistry, especially his thematic concerns, in particular, his swipes at patriarchal society.

Several newspaper reviewers liked *The Stepfather* for many of the same reasons that their colleagues from the fifties had admired such Hitchcock films as *Rear Window, The Man Who Knew Too Much,* and *North by Northwest.* One West Coast critic, for example, likened the "stepfather" character to the proverbial "bomb" in *Sabotage.* Said the critic, "Jerry is like the character in Hitchcock's *Sabotage* who's unknowingly delivering a package with a bomb in it—except this time the bomb's ticking away in Jerry's skull" (Goldstein 1987). While audiences know it will go off, they don't know when or under what circumstances. Another reviewer commented on how the build-up of suspense in *The Stepfather* was similar to how it usually unfolded in a Hitchcock film. "One of the hallmarks of the Hitchcock style," according to this reviewer, "was that the audience always knew who was going to do what to whom and then spent the film waiting for the inevitable to happen. And that's exactly what happens in *The Stepfather*" (*Los Angeles Magazine,* 1987). Critics of this bent seemed satisfied if a contemporary thriller met their narrow conception of Hitchcock as "master of suspense," a view which had been the dominant image of Hitchcock during the fifties and much of the sixties. Although this earlier view of Hitchcock still had its adherents among a minority of journalistic critics, it had, as we have seen, been superseded by the auteur viewpoint, which stressed the "thematic profundity" or "self-reflexivity" of his films over their "storytelling virtuosity" (cf. Palmer 1986, 4).

Those approaching the film from a more auteurist viewpoint saw *The Stepfather* as not simply a good thriller but also as a legitimate work of art. An almost ideal-typical distillation of the auteurist viewpoint can be found in Dave Kehr's review. Three weeks earlier, Kehr had criticized the director of *The Bedroom Window* for slavishly imitating Hitchcock rather than developing his own directorial voice; now he was lavishing great praise on Joseph Ruben, the director of *The Stepfather* for having achieved virtually everything that his counterpart on *The Bedroom Window* had failed to achieve. While not mentioning Hitchcock by name, Kehr seemed to do so by implication. Referring to the "generic conventions" that Ruben so completely reworked, Kehr possibly had Hitchcock in mind. The following passage from his review of *The Stepfather* exemplified Kehr's auteurist-inspired approach to film criticism:

> *The Stepfather* represents the kind of filmmaking achievement available only to the American cinema at its best, drawing as it does on the broad genre traditions that define our popular culture and re-forming those traditions into a striking and original artistic statement. *The Stepfather* is a nearly perfect work of popular entertainment. A thriller about a psychopathic killer, it is absolutely terrifying. At the same time it is a highly personal work, the expression of a gifted individual. (Kehr 1987b)

For Kehr, like his French counterpart, there was nothing inherently incompatible between working within a popular generic tradition such as the thriller film and producing a significant work of art.

Other reviews of *The Stepfather* reflected more ambivalence about the thriller form. Consider, for example, Terrence Rafferty's commentary in the *Nation*. Rafferty begins by acknowledging the thriller's potential as a medium for artistic expression, describing it as an "abstract stylized form" rich in metaphoric possibilities. In a thriller such as *The Stepfather,* which explores the psyche of a mass murderer, the killer, he continued, can function as a "fabulous metaphoric figure, radiating meaning like a perfect conceit in a sonnet." At the same time, Rafferty cautioned the reader that thrillers can also be confining, like a torture chamber. And that, he implied, was one of Hitchcock's failings as an artist. However, by putting a satiric spin on the conventions of the thriller, the *Nation*'s critic added, Ruben and his screenwriter have succeeded in lifting the viewer "outside the tight little world of the thriller." Their film, he argued, is reflexive in a way that the average thriller never is. It is as satire that the film really excels, subverting "the way the family has turned into ideology in 1980s America" (Rafferty 1987). In viewing *The Stepfather* as trenchant social commentary, the *Nation*'s critic was not alone. For those responsive to the film for similar reasons, *The Stepfather*'s rootedness in Hitchcockian tradition seemed largely irrelevant. More important was its wry commentary on the sources of American ideology—its uncompromising indictment of patriarchal society.

While it had recently become fashionable among academic critics to rank as Hitchcock's greatest films those which are most critical of patriarchal society, journalistic critics tended to steer away from such interpretations of Hitchcock's work. This, however, did not deter a number of reviewers from praising *The Stepfather* for its originality in representing some of the excesses of American ideology. The following synopsis accentuates what many such liberal or progressive-minded reviewers would find so original about the film. It is because the film's central character, Jerry, believes so completely in the American dream, especially the idea of the happy nuclear family in suburbia, that he has become a mass murderer. When the existing family he has married into no longer conforms to his expectations of family bliss, he massacres them. Before then, he has already made plans to relocate, having found a new family which he expects will meet all his conditions.

Many critics praised *The Stepfather* for its ironic treatment of the cause of Jerry's psychosis, presenting him as really believing in the rose-colored picture of family life portrayed on his beloved old TV sitcoms:

> It's not the culture's violence that drives people mad, the film implies, but its fake harmony—especially the sunny world of TV sitcoms where every crisis is handily resolved (in 26 minutes), every family is a "bunch," and every father knows best. Ruben and writer Donald E. Westlake have drawn a clean line from *Father Knows Best* to *Friday the 13th*. No wonder Jerry Blake, the patriarch with dwindling power over his wife and daughter goes mad—he's living in the wrong universe. (Edelstein 1987)

Other critics also admired *The Stepfather* for being sensitive to feminist issues. Jerry's wives are also fatally flawed, according to Richard Natale, for believing in sexual stereotypes:

> his wives have all the earmarks of classic victims, women who think a man is the solution to all their problems. These ladies are so blinded by their own needs they fall for the first decent (or maybe even not so decent) *homo erectus* that comes along, failing to notice flaws even a child can (and in this instance, does) sense. (Natale 1987)

In much the same vein, Pauline Kael pointed admiringly to a scene between the mother and daughter where "we see the solidity of their affection for each other and understand how muddled they both get when Jerry comes between them" (Kael 1987b). Commenting on *The Stepfather* as well as several other domestic thrillers of the 1980s, *Village Voice* social critic Ellen Willis points out that it is the women, mother and daughter, who finally kill Jerry, not the two male characters we think might come to their rescue. As Willis sees it, the film ends amidst the imagery of "self-sufficient matriarchy" (Willis 1987). Among the journalistic critics and commentators of this bent, there was no attempt at legitimating their progressive readings of recent thrillers by pointing to similar tendencies in Hitchcock's more fully realized works.[26]

In this section, I have suggested that intellectual critics have increasingly come to regard the suspense thriller as a legitimate vehicle for art. This means that if one were to actually compare the post-1970 reviews of thrillers with earlier reviews of comparable thrillers, one would expect to find that the serious critics from the seventies and eighties were more likely to recognize the thriller's potential for artistic expression than were their counterparts from the forties, fifties, and sixties. Reviews of non-Hitchcock thrillers from this earlier period indicate that it was extremely rare for highbrow critics to acknowledge the thriller's potential for artistic expression.[27] Consider, for example, *The Wages of Fear,* which in 1953 won the Grand Prix at the Cannes Film Festival. When American highbrow critics reviewed *The Wages of Fear,* they acknowledged it as a great thriller but hesitated to refer to it as a great film. A *New Yorker* reviewer, who had just seen the film at Cannes, put it this way, "*The Wages of Fear . . .* is now being hailed by Parisians as a truly great French film. It is certainly a great cinematic thriller" (16 May 1953). And Bosley Crowther, who complained that *The Wages of Fear* might have been a better film if it hadn't been reduced by forty-five minutes for its American release, wrote that "though quite a thriller, [it] would not seem to merit a festival award" (Crowther, *New York Times,* 20 February 1955). Not until the late sixties and early seventies, as I have suggested, would a significant number of critics come to recognize the thriller's potential for artistic expression.

But why this shift in critical evaluation? Was it because of the change in attitude toward Hitchcock or because of some other variable? To illuminate this issue, consider the timing of the discovery of the film noir thrillers among Anglo-American critics. Generally speaking, "film noir" refers to a body of Hollywood films which when released during the 1940s and early 1950s were perceived by Anglo-American critics as little more than low-budget crime thrillers. As Root has put it, critics' dislike of these films when they were first released "was compounded by economic snobbery: the low budgets and 'B' film status of many film noirs was seen as a priori proof that the films were 'trash' (1986, 93). Even Fritz Lang's "noir" thrillers were initially dismissed as rather routine potboilers by the more serious Anglo-American critics (see, e.g., Crowther's 1946 review of *Scarlet Street*); they were casualties (along with his other Hollywood films), says Lang scholar Stephen Jenkins, of the "critical establishment's refusal to deal seriously with the bulk of the product of the American cinema" (Jenkins 1981, 2). During the 1950s French critics discovered the "noir" films, especially Lang's, and elevated them to the status of art (Borde and Chaumeton 1955; Mourlet 1959; Demonsablon 1959; see chapter 7 for more on Lang). Not until the early 1970s did American and, with some reluctance, British critics begin to embrace the French view of these films (see, e.g., Schrader 1972; Place and Peterson 1974; McArthur 1972). The fact that this reevaluation of 1940s crime thrillers occurred shortly after Hitchcock's reputation changed would suggest that Hitchcock's change in reputation was one of the causes of the change in attitude toward that type of thriller.

On the other hand, one cannot rule out the possibility that the change in attitude toward Hitchcock and toward earlier as well as more recent thrillers were *both* consequences of other factors, such as changes in the aesthetic discourse on film. Indeed, there is considerable evidence from a variety of sources that starting in the early seventies, other traditional Hollywood genres, such as the musical and the family melodrama, were also reevaluated as potentially "artful" (see, e.g., Grant 1986). That is, the shift in aesthetic discourse brought about by the adoption of the auteur viewpoint and other developments in film aesthetics in the late 1960s and early 1970s resulted in a general upgrading in the stature of traditional Hollywood genres such as the gangster film and musical relative to nontraditional ones such as the social-problem film and the art film.[28] These additional developments included a growing awareness among critics and audiences alike of the rich intertextuality of popular Hollywood films and the increasing practice among the more serious critics of valuing those genre films that were self-conscious of stock generic conventions and ideological assumptions, as evidenced in films with "heavy doses of irony, parody, and camp" (Ray 1985, 256). Best of all, according to these critics, were those self-reflexive genre films which discredited the conventions of standard genres (e.g., the gangster film—*Bonnie and Clyde*, 1966; the western—*McCabe and Mrs. Miller*, 1971; the musical—*New York, New York*, 1977). *New Yorker* critic Pauline Kael, for example, championed the careers of a number of directors, e.g., Arthur Penn, Robert Altman, Martin Scorsese, and Brian De Palma, who made self-conscious and highly stylized films of this type.

One director noticeably absent from the ranks of those involved in thriller projects during the late 1980s was Brian De Palma, who for over a decade had specialized in making films that were meditations on the Hitchcock thriller. For much of this period, however, critics had attacked him for relying too heavily on Hitchcock for inspiration. In fact, by the mid-1980s, De Palma had decided to stop making thrillers altogether. Clearly, his preoccupation with the Hitchcock tradition had hurt his career. The events leading to De Palma's decision to pull out of the thriller will be the subject of the next chapter.

Coping with the Hitchcock Legacy: The Case of Brian De Palma

To the usual coordinates fixing the individual's position—his temperament and his training—there is also the moment of his entrance, this being the moment in the tradition— early, middle, or late—with which his biological opportunity coincides. Of course, one person can and does shift traditions, especially in the modern world, in order to find a better entrance. Without a good entrance, he is in danger of wasting his time as a copyist regardless of temperament and training. From this point of view we can see the "universal genius" of the Renaissance more simply as a qualified individual bestrid-

Over the last decade, the contemporary filmmaker most often associated with the Hitchcock legacy is American director Brian De Palma. His attraction to the Hitchcock thriller has affected the direction of his career and his stature within the film art world. While many critics have commented on the Hitchcockian elements running through his films, I shall focus instead on the critics themselves and how Hitchcock's preeminence in the thriller field has shaped their response to De Palma's work. In addition, I shall explore how De Palma has managed his own reputation in light of the Hitchcock legacy.

In his book *The Shape of Time*, art historian George Kubler (1962) proposes conceptualizing an individual artist's lifework in terms of the position that the artist occupies within an artistic tradition or genre.[1] Kubler's view of an artistic tradition is "a linked succession of prime works with replications, all being distributed in time as recognizably early and late versions of the same kind of action." According to Kubler, the moment of the artist's entrance in that tradition—early, middle, or late—is crucial to how the artist will be judged by the art world. In the history of Western art, Leo-

ing many new tracks of development at a fortunate moment in that great renovation of Western civilization, and traveling his distance in several systems without the burdens of rigorous proof or extensive demonstration required in later periods.

(Kubler 1962, 6–7)

nardo and Raphael acquired towering reputations, while their followers, Bernardino Luini and Guilio Romano, did not. Though talented artists, Luini and Romano ran into bad luck: "They came late," says Kubler, "when the feast was over through no fault of their own" (1962, 7). Samuel Johnson evidently had thought about the same issue, for when Boswell asked him why no later authors had rivaled the poets Homer and Virgil, he replied, "Because, sir, they came first."[2]

Kubler's time-of-entry perspective is applicable to De Palma, who became a director of Hitchcockian thrillers during the mid-1970s, when Hitchcock had for decades been the acknowledged master of the form. The danger of working in a genre at such a late stage of its development, according to this perspective, is that critics will tend to view the recent entrant's work as imitative and unoriginal. "[W]ithout a good entrance," says Kubler, even the highly talented artist is "in danger of wasting his time as a copyist regardless of temperament and training" (Kubler 1962, 6; see also Rodden 1989, 97). By the time he entered the thriller field, De Palma had already acquired a formidable reputation as an independent filmmaker with a distinctive style and vision bordering on the avant-garde. Accordingly, this chapter addresses the question: How did De Palma's preoccupation with Hitchcockian concerns coupled with his early reputation as a maverick filmmaker shape critical response to his thriller films? One might expect that, once De Palma became identified with the Hitchcockian-style thriller, he would be perceived as a mere imitator regardless of his artistic merit. To explore this issue, I trace De Palma's "reputation history," showing how the critical reception of his thrillers affected his public image at different phases of his directorial career. Hitchcock's renown in the thriller field, I show, adversely affected the critical response to a number of De Palma's thrillers (e.g., *Obsession,* 1976; *Dressed to Kill,* 1980; and *Body Double,* 1984) *and* seriously damaged his public reputation as well. On the other hand, contrary to Kubler, Hitchcock's legacy could also be beneficial to De Palma's reputation, especially when certain champions of his work, like Pauline Kael, impressed with the high reflexivity of his art, intimated that De Palma, especially as a satirist of film history, was actually more gifted and daring than Hitchcock.

In addition to time of entry, that is, the constraint of Hitchcock's perceived preeminence in the thriller field, what other factors have shaped or conditioned the critical response to De Palma's thriller films? And how important are they relative to time of entry? In addressing this broader issue, I show how shifting critical fashions were especially crucial in shaping the critical reception of De Palma's works. I also chronicle De Palma's own efforts at managing his reputation. To a considerable extent, then, this chapter provides another testing ground for hypotheses about the constraints on artistic reputation first introduced in earlier chapters of the book.

In what follows, I have conceptualized De Palma's reputational career as falling into four distinct phases: the American Godard or irreverent independent and avant-gardist (1965–75); the new master of suspense (1976–80); brilliant "sicko" and former critical favorite (1981–86); and respectable director of grade A films (1987–present).

THE AMERICAN GODARD (1965–75)

On the eve of the opening of his first nationally distributed thriller, *Sisters* (1973), thirty-one-year-old Brian De Palma was already well known in the film art world. As an independent filmmaker trained in New York, he had made five feature films, only one of which, however, had been both produced and distributed by a major Hollywood studio. Several of his earlier films such as *Greetings* (1968) and *Hi, Mom!* (1970) had been praised by the critics for their irreverent, anarchic, and exuberant spirit (see, e.g., Winsten 1968; Sheed 1969; Greenspun 1970; Schickel 1970; Thomas 1970a). Already these facts and evaluations had become part of De Palma's biographical legend and public reputation. From the beginning of his directorial career, the promotional materials on De Palma also highlighted his elite background and precociousness. In addition to mentioning that his father was an orthopedic surgeon, the early studio biographies emphasized how as a high-schooler pursuing an interest in science De Palma had won second prize in the National Science Fair for his "Critical Study of Hydrogen Quantum Mechanics Through Cybernetics." His studio biographies also listed his two prestigious educational degrees—a bachelor's in film from Columbia and a master's in writing from Sarah Lawrence College. The early promotional materials stressed that not until he was at Columbia did De Palma become interested in filmmaking. But he learned quickly. While still a student, he had made a series of short films, including *Wotan's Wake,* which in 1962 won the prestigious Rosenthal Foundation Award for the best fictional film that year by an American under twenty-five (Production Files, Academy Library).

During the late sixties and early seventies, a number of critics championed De Palma's work. To these critics, he was an example of a new breed of film director—fiercely innovative and independent—whose entrance at this time was part of a "technological and aesthetic revolution in movies" which would "inevitably restructure human consciousness and understanding" (Gelmis 1970, ix). Critic Joseph Gelmis assumed that greater access to the means of production along with changes in distribution and exhibition would soon democratize the movies so that there would be "thousands made every year instead of just hundreds. And the independent filmmaker, whether he's working in Super 8 or 70-mm Panavision, [would] be the nexus of the change to come" (Gelmis 1970, ix). De Palma seemed to fit this picture of the maverick independent trained outside the studio system who made films his own way while maintaining a certain distance from Hollywood. In fact, it was quite common for journalists to characterize De Palma as a filmmaker with roots in New York's underground film scene.

One of the films that helped nourish De Palma's reputation as an underground filmmaker was *Greetings.* Released in 1968, *Greetings,* like other underground films of the period, satirized many aspects of American life in the late sixties—U.S. involvement in Vietnam, antiwar protestors, sexual politics, paranoia over the assassination of John F. Kennedy, and media coverage of the war. It is not surprising that critics such as Pauline Kael, who sympathized with De Palma's countercultural or bohemian-leftist view of the world, would be among the most enthusiastic supporters of his earlier work. His novel use of long takes, jump cuts, multiple-frame imagery, and other infrequently employed cinematic devices (many of which he borrowed from New Wave directors like Godard and Truffaut) also revealed that De Palma, like other avant-garde filmmakers, was fascinated by the film medium itself. A number of reviewers and commentators (e.g., Winsten 1968; Mishkin 1968; Bayer 1969; Mayerson 1969) wrote admiringly of De Palma's cinematic know-how and inventiveness. Indeed, film historian Thomas Gomery's characterization of American underground cinema's infatuation with the medium would seem also to apply to De Palma:

These filmmakers prided themselves on seeking to understand what was essentially cinematic and on forcing the medium beyond what Hollywood held were its proper limits. Thus, Andy Warhol made films in which there was no movement . . . Robert Breer took on frame-by-frame cutting . . . Tony Conrad made flicker films by simply alternating black and white frames. Stan Brakhage painted on film, deliberately scratching individual frames. To these artists, a film was like a musical composition, filmmaking a process by which to explore the basic parameters of the medium rather than to tell a Hollywood-like story. (Gomery 1991, 340)

On the other hand, if by an underground filmmaker we mean an artist, like Stan Brakhage or Jonas Mekas, who was *unconditionally* dedicated to the avant-garde and the abstract *and* who did not pursue a Hollywood career, then De Palma was no underground filmmaker. In contrast to these filmmakers (such as those associated with Jonas Mekas' New American Cinema movement in New York) who made films primarily for themselves and other artists, De Palma was willing to work for Hollywood. In that respect, he was like many other independents of that period. Like them, he wanted to describe the world and make films as he saw it, while at the same time attracting a large audience. After making a few short films, two independently produced feature films, and a number of documentaries during the sixties, De Palma worked briefly for the story department at Universal Studios in Hollywood. It was because he was unable to get studio backing for any of his projects that he sought financing for *Greetings* (1968) in the then growing independent-film market.[3] Although De Palma was not part of Jonas Mekas' New American Cinema movement, before finding an independent distributor for *Greetings,* he and his partner did consider "opening it at Jonas Mekas' basement (the New York Filmmakers' Cinematheque)" (Gelmis 1970, 30).

To summarize, while not an underground filmmaker, De Palma was perceived as a maverick director. Given his early successes and affiliations (several then-prominent New York-based independents—Robert Downey [*Putney Swope*], Jim McBride [*David Holzman's Diary*], and Paul Williams [*Out of It*] were friends of De Palma), it is not surprising that journalistic critics frequently characterized him as a boldly independent director with roots in the New York underground cinema movement.

De Palma actively cultivated this view of him as an unconventional director. In 1970, he told Gelmis that French director Jean Luc Godard, arguably the most daring and experimental of the New Wave directors, had been a major influence on him:

> Godard's a terrific influence, of course. If I could be the American Godard, that would be great. I think there are more interesting social and political things going on here in the United States than in France. And if we can have some kind of sounding board through movies, if Chuck [Charles Hirsch, De Palma's producer and partner on a number of films] and I could develop that material and evolve a structure and a style for it, that's the millennium (Gelmis 1970, 29).

When De Palma turned to making Hitchcock-inspired films in the early 1970s, it is interesting that in spite of major, generally recognized borrowings from Hitchcock, these films were perceived as lighthearted and avant-garde rather than imitative. De Palma never masked his admiration for Hitchcock, declaring it in several interviews. In 1970 he told a *Los Angeles Times* critic that one of his next projects, *Sisters,* would be "a very Hitchcock thriller" in the spirit of *Psycho.* The thriller film, De Palma said, was the type of movie he felt compelled to make at this stage of his career because it would force him "to try new things." At the same time, he stressed the thematic continuity between *Sisters* and his earlier work, especially his fascination with voyeurism (Thomas 1970b).

Sisters was the first De Palma film to generate considerable discussion about De Palma's indebtedness to Hitchcock. Following its premiere in 1972 at a trade show in Los Angeles, the film received excellent notices in the trade papers, where reviewers compared it favorably to *Psycho.* For example, the *Hollywood Reporter* described *Sisters* as "the most genuinely frightening film since Hitchcock's *Psycho*" (Lovell 1972).

The advertising and promotional materials for *Sisters* sold the film in two major ways—as a low-budget horror film and as a suspense thriller. While the bulk of the ads stressed the film's "shocker" value, press releases emphasized the Hitchcock connection. Among the references to Hitchcock in the press book was the following: "As reporter Grace Collier in *Sisters,* Jennifer [Salt] is the sole witness to a murder. In trying to convince others that the event really happened, she becomes involved in a series of bizarre, suspenseful happenings in the best Hitchcockian tradition" (see plate 34).

The overall critical response to *Sisters* when it was released in the spring of 1973 was favorable. Most of the reviews in the major metropolitan newspapers and weekly and monthly national magazines praised the film. *Time* magazine critic Richard Schickel (1973b), for example, pointed out that *Sisters* was more a loving tribute to Hitchcock than a run-of-the-mill shocker. "*Sisters* is being promoted as a routine shocker of the kind that has made its distributor, American-International, rich and infamous. But it is something more—and more interesting—than that," says Schickel. "It is a homage by a gifted, if erratic, young director, Brian De Palma (*Hi Mom!, Greetings*), to one of cinema's genuine masters, Alfred Hitchcock." While Schickel and many other reviewers saw obvious parallels between *Sisters* and Hitchcock's work, especially *Psycho* and *Rear Window* (e.g., Thomas 1973; Canby 1973), only a few complained about De Palma's "borrowings" from Hitchcock (e.g., Oster 1973). Rather, critics were more inclined to praise De Palma for his wonderful blending of the macabre with black humor. In addition to characterizing *Sisters* as the most frightening film since *Psycho,* the *Hollywood Reporter* review described the film as "the most compelling black comedy of the year" (Lovell 1972). In fact, several critics even characterized *Sisters* more as a "Hitchcock parody" or "dark comedy" than as a pure horror or suspense film—a view especially prominent among those most familiar with De Palma's earlier work in comedy (see Thomas 1973).

Speaking before a group of students attending a spring seminar at the American Film Institute, De Palma was emphatic that *Sisters* was a suspense picture—not a comedy. "The only way I used comedy there," insisted De Palma, "was to relieve the tension. The beginning was a little funny, but again it has to be funny within the context of the characters and situations, but it never becomes a comedy" (De Palma 1978). De Palma also told the students that he had pushed hard to make *Sisters* because he thought it would be good for his career. Unlike his earlier films, which he characterized as fragmentary in structure, *Sisters* had forced him to work within a very strict preestablished form—the Hitchcockian thriller. Throughout his AFI seminar, De Palma spoke of how *Sisters* had been influenced by Hitchcock's art.

De Palma's next film was the *Phantom of the Paradise* (1974), which reviewers were more inclined to view as a satire on the record industry than as a monster or horror picture. While De Palma's penchant for lifting memorable shots and whole sequences from movie classics was much in evidence throughout the film, this did not seem to annoy the critics. Rather, *Phantom of the Paradise* reinforced the strong impression many critics already had of De Palma as a free spirit who made films his own way, unencumbered by the more conventional ways of making a film. In her review of *Phantom of the Paradise, New Yorker* critic Pauline Kael, who would become a tireless champion of De Palma's artistry, wrote that he was "the only filmmaker to have come up from the underground and gone on for years working the same way with a larger budget" (Kael 1974). Like other underground filmmakers, De Palma has remained fascinated with the film medium and its history. With *Phantom of the Paradise,* for example, he accomplished something that, according to Kael, underground filmmakers have been trying for decades to pull off, namely, to create "a new Guignol, in a modern idiom, out of the movie Guignol of the past." What he concocted, says Kael, is "a rock horror show about a composer, Winslow . . . who is robbed of his music, busted for drugs, and sent to Sing Sing—all at the instigation of Swan . . . the entrepreneur of Death Records, who has made a pact with the Devil for eternal youth. Winslow escapes from prison, is maimed by a record-pressing machine, and haunts Swan's new rock palace, the Paradise, where Phoenix . . . , the girl he loves, becomes a star." Not content with merely mixing "The Phantom of the Opera" and "Faust," he throws on, in addition, "layers of rock satire, and parodies of 'The Cabinet of Dr. Caligari,' 'The Hunchback of Notre Dame,' 'Psycho,' and 'The Picture of Dorian Gray'—and the impacted plots," asserts Kael, "actually function for him." On the surface, it would appear that De Palma was no different from other student filmmakers who have also shown a fascination with old movie conventions and clichés. Not according to Kael, who argues that unlike most student filmmakers, who are "gullible," harboring a "naive belief in the clichés they parrot," De Palma lovingly satirizes old movie conventions "for their shameless, rotten phoniness." Instead of simply "reproducing" the grotesque effects of classic horror-film sequences, he redeems their phoniness through his humor. Like the works of other filmmakers of the seventies whom Kael championed, such as Robert Altman, Arthur Penn, Sam Peckinpah, and Roman Polanski, De Palma's films, in her view, were also deliriously self-conscious and reflexive, especially with respect to old movie genres and conventions.

Following the release of *Phantom of the Paradise,* this impression of De Palma as an offbeat, irreverent, and fiercely independent filmmaker and satirist would remain the dominant view of him for the next couple years—a view which De Palma himself would continue to actively cultivate (see, e.g., De Palma 1974).

By 1976, the promoters were ready to exploit De Palma as an artist. Capitalizing on his growing reputation among college audiences as one of the most important of the young American directors, Columbia, the distributor of De Palma's next film, *Obsession,* generated a number of promotional materials which emphasized his artistry. One of the exploitation articles appearing in an advertising manual for the film was entitled "Brian De Palma—Big Man on Campus." In the article De Palma is categorized as a "new wave" director who along with Martin Scorsese, Francis Ford Coppola, and George Lucas has made a "significant impact on high school and college campuses." While acknowledging that most filmgoers would enjoy *Obsession* because of its "crackling suspense," the article accentuated the film's special appeal to youthful cineastes who would also be "talking about De Palma's use of flashbacks, soft focus and directorial touches worthy of the 'master' himself, Alfred Hitchcock." The message for film exhibitors was simple: "Make the most of De Palma's youth-market appeal." In a related promotional gimmick, the article proposed that exhibitors stage a contest in which a professor of a college film class invites students to write critical essays about De Palma's cinematic style, using *Obsession* to illustrate their points. The winning critique (presumably favorable to *Obsession*), could then be "excerpted in a newspaper ad, aimed at the college crowd," and if strong enough, "reprinted as a lobby display" (Production Files, Academy Library).

Other promotional materials circulating around the time of *Obsession*'s release emphasized the film's roots in the Hitchcock tradition. Before the release of the film, both De Palma and Paul Schrader (who coauthored the screenplay) told journalists that the film was intended as an homage to Hitchcock. Of course, the single-word title echoes such Hitchcock titles as *Spellbound, Notorious, Frenzy, Psycho,* and *Vertigo.* In addition, stories circulated about the composer of the film's music, Bernard Herrmann, pointing out that he had been a long-time associate of Hitchcock's, having scored all of Hitchcock's feature films between 1955 and 1964 (see Production Files, Academy Library). Once the first wave of reviews were out, all subsequent ads for *Obsession* included a quote from critic Rex Reed's rave review, "Like Hitchcock at the top of his form" (Reed 1976).

Overall, this promotional strategy backfired, with a number of critics concluding that the film fell considerably below the high standards set by Hitchcock (e.g., Canby 1976a; Sarris 1976a; Kauffmann 1976; Gilliatt 1976b). Vincent Canby, critic for the *New York Times,* articulated the feelings of many reviewers who had responded negatively to the film:

> Brian De Palma, the director, and Paul Schrader, the writer, have made a mistake, I suspect, in allowing *Obsession* to be identified as an *hommage* to Hitchcock. It puts a needless strain upon them, and upon us, who thus come to expect something more complex, more terse and more stylish than the film they've made. To be blunt, *Obsession* is no *Vertigo,* Hitchcock's witty, sardonic study of obsession that did transcend its material, which wasn't all that bad to start with. (Canby 1976a)

By making so much of the film's indebtedness to the Hitchcock tradition, the promotional campaign for *Obsession* prompted several reviewers like Canby to conclude that *Obsession* was second-rate.

The circumstances of De Palma's roots as an independent filmmaker also entered Canby's negative reading of *Obsession.* Concluding his mildly critical review of the film, Canby admitted to preferring De Palma's earlier anarchic comedies over his more recent efforts, which involved larger budgets and, in the case of *Obsession,* was being distributed by one of the major studios, Columbia: "With *Obsession* Mr. De Palma is moving into the big time. He's a very talented director and one must be glad for him, though I still prefer those films he made on shoestrings (*Greetings, Hi, Mom!, Sisters*), when he didn't hesitate to give a Bronx cheer to the Establishment that he now aspires to join" (Canby 1976a).

Like Canby, Andrew Sarris used his review of *Obsession* as an excuse for rhapsodizing about *Vertigo,* comparing the De Palma film unfavorably to other homages by Resnais and Truffaut, who had drawn on Hitchcock's content rather than mimicking his style. Though faithful to its original, *Obsession*'s convoluted plot, lack of stars, and lack of humor made it, according to Sarris, merely "a mannered cerebral exercise" (1976a).[4]

Even more critical of De Palma's latest career move was the *New Republic*'s critic, Stanley Kauffmann, who dismissed *Obsession* as "garbage of a special stench." Kauffmann, who was no fan of Hitchcock, had been one of the few to have seen De Palma's 1968 film *Murder a la Mod,* and had remembered De Palma once referring to it as a film from his "Hitchcock period." "Now he has returned to filming a Hitchcock imitation," said Kauffmann, but this time with a big budget which has allowed him the luxury of wrapping his Hitchcock imitation in "figurative mink." The result? "Even as parody, which it isn't," continued Kauffmann, "it would be rotten" (1976).[5]

De Palma defended his borrowings from Hitchcock in several newspaper and magazine interviews appearing within a month after the release of *Obsession*. For example, he told a *Los Angeles Times* reporter:

> My films are inspired by Hitchcock, of course. . . . Hitchcock is the grammar of cinema; he's made all the film connections. I'm just trying to learn the vocabulary. But I've made a conscious attempt to develop my own grammar. I have a strong stylistic orientation; I'm strongly aware of images. I think film is a graphic art form. The advent of sound attacked that a lot and films became a recording media. The silent directors had learned how to sell stories in a completely visual way and sound overwhelmed a lot of that. You have to create the story so that the audience can see it instead of being told about it. Hitchcock developed this point of view—giving the audience the same information as the character. But that takes a lot of thought and few directors know what it's all about. (Taylor 1976)

Decrying the politics of fame, De Palma attacked those critics who routinely evaluated his films by comparing them unfavorably to Hitchcock's. A major reason why critics picked on him, De Palma insisted, was that, like Hitchcock, he was a visual director. Until recently, critics had discussed Hitchcock in literary rather than in cinematic terms, feeling more comfortable analyzing recurring themes in his work than his visual style:

> The critics are just now picking up on it—on the visual impact— but now when a director expresses things clearly or precisely, he's immediately compared to Hitchcock! Of course, he's done it better than anyone; he's the giant. But it's really distressing when they take you apart on the basis of comparing you to an old master. (Taylor 1976)

Finally, De Palma attacked the critics for continuing to rave about the older director's most recent films even when, according to De Palma, they were really pretty bad. Echoing Richard Corliss's critique of *Family Plot* (see chapter 3), he asserted, "Anyone who says that Hitchcock's last film ("Family Plot") was a masterpiece is a fool. The man has clearly lost his sense of timing, of cinema. He's 75! You can't be a genius forever" (Taylor 1976).

Only three months after the release of *Obsession,* De Palma came out with his next film, *Carrie.* As if to defy his detractors, he helped engineer a promotional campaign for the film which presented him as a "new master of suspense"—rivaling the old master, Alfred Hitchcock (Biographical sketch of De Palma in *Carrie* Press Kit, 1976, Academy Library).

While the press materials emphasized that *Carrie* was based on Steven King's best-selling novel about a teenage wallflower of a girl who is possessed with telekinetic powers, they also stressed the film's generic roots as a "chilling suspense picture." As one press-book entry put it, "With *Carrie,* director Brian De Palma demonstrates why he is hailed as one of the country's finest and most versatile young directors displaying a mastery of the suspense shocker in the best Alfred Hitchcock tradition." Following Kubler's line of reasoning, one might have expected that another Hitchcock-inspired effort from De Palma would precipitate an even greater backlash against him.

To the contrary, several commentators stressed that it was *Carrie* that firmly established Brian De Palma as one of America's best young directors. In fact, it was only after critics first began commenting on this film that De Palma's reputation as the new master of suspense really emerged. Unlike *Obsession, Carrie* received mostly favorable reviews with no discernible pattern in the incidence of favorable reviews by type of publication. Regardless of whether critics were writing for prestigious or esoteric publications such as the *New Yorker* or the *Soho Weekly,* or for a more mass-oriented readership such as the *Los Angeles Times,* the reviews ranged from favorable to wildly enthusiastic. Arthur Knight (1976b) called it "a movie that marks the final emergence of yet another major young directorial talent, Brian De Palma." Other critics who quickly followed suit included Pauline Kael of the *New Yorker* (1976), Richard Schickel of *Time* (1976), and Steven Farber of *New West Magazine* (1976). Even Andrew Sarris (1976b), a long-time nemesis of De Palma's, was moderately impressed, "For all its contrivances, *Carrie* is warm and affectionate." (For one of the few negative assessments, see Canby [1976b].)

In addition to praising De Palma as a first-rate director, reviewers also acknowledged him as a masterful director of thrillers. For instance, Kael (1976) described *Carrie* as "a terrifying lyrical thriller" in which

De Palma "has mastered a teasing style," made up of "a perverse mixture of comedy and horror and tension, like that of Hitchcock or Polanski, but with a lulling sensuousness."

Why the critical accolades for *Carrie*?[6] The hostile response to *Obsession* three months earlier may have had something to do with it. As *New West* critic Stephen Farber (1976) put it, "*Carrie* is especially surprising and gratifying coming just a few months after the limp, ludicrous *Obsession*."

The major problem with *Obsession*, as mentioned earlier, had been that most critics saw it as a mindless imitation of Hitchcock, devoid of humor. *Carrie*, too, had its share of borrowings from Hitchcock (Carrie attends "Bates High," after "The Bates Motel" in *Psycho*, and there is a shower scene—a variation of the famous one in *Psycho*), but critics did not see it as a mere Hitchcock clone. Rather, they saw the film's Hitchcockian elements converging with other elements to create an astonishingly original work. As Stephen Farber succinctly put it, with *Carrie*, unlike *Obsession*, "De Palma's interests—in satire,[7] Hitchcockian horror and gothic romance—finally converge[d] in a fully integrated, iconoclastic work."[8]

What the more intellectual or highbrow critics seemed to enjoy the most about *Carrie* was that it marked the return of De Palma as a satirist of American life, especially of its popular culture. Indeed, for Kael, it is pop culture, namely, "old movie trash" and "soft-core pornos" which provides *Carrie* with its heart and soul. (Recall that Kael [1970] explained her attraction to movie "trash" in a late sixties essay entitled "Trash, Art, and the Movies.") In her view, audiences root for Carrie, the film's teenage heroine, because of the "banal teen-age movie meanness" that her classmates show toward her:

> If De Palma were an artist in another medium—say, fiction or poetry—he might be a satirist with a high reputation and a small following. Everything in his films is distanced by his persistent adolescent kinkiness; he's gleefully impersonal. Yet, working in movies, he's found his own route to a mass audience: his new trash heart is the ultimate De Palma joke.

For critics like Kael who were practicing a nascent form of postmodern criticism at this time, De Palma seemed very much the prototype of the postmodern artist: out of the junk heap of our pop culture (which unlike the modernists he does not reject), he forged a rich, satirical, and highly reflexive art whose real subject was art itself.

Like Hitchcock before him, De Palma openly discussed his principles of suspense and terror with reporters. In a *New York Times* article appearing at around the time of the release of his next film, *The Fury* (1978),[9] De Palma was quoted as saying: "I operate on the principle of escalating terror"; how to orchestrate the terror is the crucial problem. At the same time, he did not regard his films as "particularly horrible." "To me," De Palma remarked, "they deal with a stylized, expressionistic world that has a kind of grotesque beauty about it." On Hitchcock's influence, De Palma noted, "he is the one who distilled the essence of film. He's like Webster. It's all there. I've used a lot of his grammar" (Dunning 1978).

De Palma also reminded interviewers of his unflagging commitment to independent filmmaking, which he lamented had been in decline since the late 1960s. His latest independent venture, he told them, would be a feature-length film he was currently making with students at Sarah Lawrence College, where for the past several months he had been giving a course in filmmaking. "The kids have to understand the practical problems. In the course I'm teaching, we're *making* a movie, not just sitting around talking about it."

A broader implication of Kubler's thesis, namely, that an artwork's reception is primarily a function of its "time of entrance," is well demonstrated in the critical response to De Palma's next film, *Dressed to Kill* (1980). Critics were not lukewarm about this film; they either loved or hated it. Among the most important factors shaping the negative critical response to *Dressed to Kill*, especially among newspaper reviewers, was Hitchcock's death, coming a few months before the release of the film, and the emergent backlash against the recent proliferation of low-budget horror films. On the other hand, for the more serious critics, the key factor shaping their response to *Dressed to Kill* was how the film fit into the current debate concerning the ascendancy of a more extreme version of auteurism in which "pulp," "sleazy," "trash," and "lurid" had become fashionable as terms of praise. This critical reaction to *Dressed to Kill*, especially among the more serious critics, proved to be a turning point in De Palma's reputation history. After this film, the lines were clearly drawn. De Palma was either a consummate filmmaker or a rip-off artist.

Following Kubler's line of reasoning, one might have expected that Hitchcock's death three months before the release of the film would have adversely affected the critical response to *Dressed to Kill*. Indeed, many of the critics who wrote obituaries and articles in tribute to Hitchcock did eventually review *Dressed to Kill* and were quite hostile to it. The promotional campaign for the film advanced the view of De Palma as the new master of suspense. The mere suggestion that De Palma was the rightful heir to Hitchcock annoyed reviewers still mourning over Hitchcock's passing. Many echoed *New York Magazine* critic William Wolf's point that "the level to which the current suspense films have sunk makes us realize how much we are going to miss Alfred Hitchcock" (1980). The contemporary thriller directors most frequently attacked were John Carpenter and Brian De Palma. Wolf, for example, seized Hitchcock's death as an opportunity to attack two of De Palma's recent films—*Carrie* and *Obsession:*

> De Palma, who went from promising young director of such offbeat films as *Greetings* and *Hi, Mom!* to purveyor of slick, sick horror, resorts in *Carrie* to the climactic stunt of a hand rising suddenly from the grave to make audiences scream. The muddled pretentiousness of *Obsession* was made even more noticeable because the film was meant as an homage to Hitchcock. (Wolf 1980; see also Corliss 1980; for a more favorable assessment of De Palma in relation to Hitchcock see Arnold 1980)

Recent developments in the thriller genre also shaped how critics would respond to *Dressed to Kill*. The unexpected success in 1978 of the low-budget shocker *Halloween* precipitated a horror-film boom which reached its zenith in 1979 and 1980. At the time of *Dressed to Kill*'s release, the film market was inundated with slasher films, and a great deal of media attention was addressed to the horror phenomenon. By the summer of 1980, there was agitation by groups hostile to the blood-and-gore content of these films and to what was perceived as their misogynistic sentiments. A feminist organization called Women Against Violence Against Women had already organized boycotts against a number of horror films. *Dressed to Kill* would be on the hit list of several such organizations (see Mackinnon 1970).[10]

Dressed to Kill opened in August 1980, generating strong reaction from critics. Those hostile to the film condemned it for many of the same reasons critics had denounced *Obsession* four years earlier. The popular press was particularly hostile to De Palma for stealing from Hitchcock. Rex Reed's syndicated review, for example, characterized *Dressed to Kill* as a "Hitchcock ripoff about a transvestite maniac who slashes women to death with a straight razor." De Palma is so much under the spell of Hitchcock, said Reed, that "he doesn't borrow from his master anymore; he just rips him off until there's no joke, no parody, no fun in even spotting the parallels" (Reed 1980; for a listing of other critical reviews see *Variety*, 30 July 1980, 6). Others attacked *Dressed to Kill* for being both imitative of Hitchcock and derivative of the then currently popular slasher films. These critics condemned De Palma for drawing inspiration from what they characterized as the "basest" forms of popular culture (see, e.g., Schaefer 1980; Winsten 1980). As *US Magazine* critic Stephen Schaefer put it, "You would think by 1980 that a filmmaker like De Palma who is now being billed 'as the modern master of the macabre,' would transcend exploitation and attempt material that is more than the corny, old-fashioned schlock that shows up everywhere" (1980).

On the other hand, a majority of reviewers from more prestigious and sophisticated publications, such as Canby of the *New York Times* (1980b), Kael of the *New Yorker* (1980), David Denby of *New York Magazine* (1980), and J. Hoberman of the *Village Voice* (1980) became strong advocates of *Dressed to Kill* and of De Palma's artistry. In fact, their enthusiasm for the film would precipitate a critical backlash against their opinions involving a number of highly respected critics, including Sarris (1980a, 1980b), Kauffmann (1980), and Farber (1981), who attacked both De Palma and his defenders.

For many serious reviewers, especially those based in New York, *Dressed to Kill* confirmed De Palma's stature as a genuine auteur. Unlike reviewers in other parts of the country, New York critics had had the opportunity two months before the release of the film to see De Palma's anarchic comedy, *Home Movies*[11] which rekindled their appreciation for the more anarchic strains of his artistry. Reviewing *Dressed to Kill* in the *New York Times*, Vincent Canby (1980b) observed that, until that film, there had been really two Brian De Palmas—the maker of formless, anarchic comedies such as *Hi Mom!*, *Greetings*, and *Home Movies*, and the maker of psychological thriller and horror films—both of whom had "functioned side-by-side only in uneasy peace." "Now," says Canby, "the two De Palmas can settle down to work together with most entertaining results." Kael's (1980) enthusiastic review also described how the various sides of De Palma's personality were seamlessly blended in *Dressed to Kill*. A similar sentiment was echoed in J. Hoberman's (1980) rave critique, which appeared in the *Village Voice* on the same page as Sarris's strongly negative assessment of the film.

Sarris (1980a), whose review was almost identical in tone to his earlier hatchet job on *Obsession*, dismissed *Dressed to Kill* for being little more than derivative of Hitchcock. When he renewed his attack in a subsequent column entitled "Dreck to Kill" (Sarris 1980b), it became apparent that not only De Palma's reputation was on the line but also the direction that film criticism would be taking in the years to come. Other negative assessments of the film, such as those from Corliss (1980), Kauffmann (1980), and Farber (1981), indicated that among the more serious critics, the controversy over *Dressed to Kill* really transcended that film. For them, what was really at stake were their reputations as film critics and opinion leaders, as well as the direction of film aesthetics.

According to Kael and others in her camp who championed the film, such as David Denby,[12] *Dressed to Kill* demonstrated De Palma's superiority to Hitchcock. In her enthusiastic review, Kael praised *Dressed to Kill* as De Palma's finest film to date, his coming-of-age picture, where he has become a "true visual story teller." While acknowledging voyeurism as a recurring motif in De Palma's work, Kael pointed out that it was not an end in itself but rather "fuels his satiric art." De Palma understands that "voyeurism is integral to the nature of movies." While Hitchcock had similar concerns, Kael does not acknowledge them here, thereby strengthening her case that De Palma is an artist with a unique vision. As for De Palma's indebtedness to Hitchcock, Kael preferred instead to accent how De Palma had altered the Hitchcockian "with a funky sensuousness that is all his own." (As Kael was quick to point out, De Palma had also learned a great deal from Welles, Godard, Polanski, and Scorsese.) He also takes more risks, she added, than Hitchcock ever did. "[H]e does what Hitchcock always said he wanted to do—such as have Cary Grant really be a murderer at the end of *Suspicion*." One example of De Palma's risk-taking is his ironic use of sentimental conventions. Once he explodes these conventions, those in the audience most vulnerable to romantic assumptions "feel hurt—betrayed—and can't understand," declared Kael, "why the rest of us are gasping and laughing." Like Hitchcock, De Palma has a prankish sense of humor. But unlike Hitchcock, who used humor to relieve tension, De Palma, insisted Kael, uses jokiness to make the horror more intense. While both Hitchcock and De Palma employ visual storytelling to tap the "currents of sexiness and fear and guilt that were the hidden strength of the great silent horror films," De Palma plays around with those currents for a different end than did Hitchcock. According to Kael, De Palma "replays film history as farce. Having kept the dirty fun of a bad boy at the center of his art has given his work a lurid, explosive vitality." Consider, for example, that late scene in *Dressed to Kill* where the psychotic killer's behavior is explained. According to Kael, it resembles the explanation scene in *Psycho*. The kicker, however, argued

Kael, is that in the De Palma film, "it's an homage to—arguably—Hitchcock's worst scene." The parody then comes in the restaurant scene, where another conversation explaining the lurid behavior of the killer takes place, but this time is overheard by an elderly woman who, judging from her facial contortions, is clearly shocked by what she hears.

In Kael's view, De Palma did not have to move beyond thriller material to demonstrate that he was an artist. "In his hands," she maintained, "the thriller form is capable of expressing almost everything—comedy, satire, sex fantasies, primal emotions." Her comment is particularly interesting considering that she had never accepted the view of Hitchcock as a serious artist.

Denby's (1980) review of *Dressed to Kill* echoed many of Kael's sentiments about De Palma and Hitchcock. With this film, Denby thought, De Palma did more than merely match Hitchcock's skills; he topped them. "Even at his most outrageous," claimed Denby, "Hitchcock could not have been entertaining as this." Minimizing De Palma's borrowings from Hitchcock, Denby emphasized how De Palma satirized Hitchcock. While acknowledging that Hitchcock was the dominant influence on *Dressed to Kill*, Denby also detected the legacy of an even "greater master," Luis Buñuel, "in the subversive reality-or-fantasy games and in the way that De Palma sees women's sexual fantasies as both dangerous and funny."

In contrast to the more sociologically oriented critics, Denby saw as one of De Palma's greatest strengths his lack of temperament to be a socially responsible filmmaker. De Palma's is a "deliciously lurid style," maintained Denby, which "has infinitely more authority than that of directors working in culturally respectable forms." De Palma's indulgence is trashy subject matter such as pornography or female soap-opera fantasies, notes Denby, liberates his imagination and his lawless sense of play, freeing him to explore more formal aspects of the film medium. Given his pursuit of "beautifully bloody thrills" only to draw humor out of them, De Palma cannot be concerned, argued Denby, "with socially responsible statements or even with our feelings about his characters." To complain about the absence of fully rounded characters and about highly implausible plots in De Palma films, said Denby, is like "seeing a great opera and complaining that the plot isn't very satisfying." What one must ultimately bear in mind about De Palma is that he "plays with the medium, with the audience, and with the masters who have formed him."

While both Kael and Denby seemed intent on teaching audiences how best to appreciate De Palma's art, Andrew Sarris set out to expose De Palma as a shameless imitator and fraud. In his initial review, Sarris attacked *Dressed to Kill* for its weak characterizations, implausible plot, and ultimately sophomoric spirit. But most of all, he attacked it for being shamefully derivative of Hitchcock. What seemed to have turned Sarris against *Dressed to Kill* was his "discovery" that the film "was a shamefully straight steal from *Psycho,* among other things." Accordingly, much of his review was preoccupied with pointing out the "Hitchcockian parallels in the plot"—the most obvious being the sudden elimination of the Angie Dickinson character a third of the way into the film, paralleling Janet Leigh's demise in *Psycho*. While Kael and other defenders of *Dressed to Kill* also had acknowledged De Palma's indebtedness to Hitchcock for this particular plot device, Sarris along with others hostile to the film found it infuriating, especially in light of the other borrowings in the film from *Psycho* and from other Hitchcock classics such as *Vertigo*.[13]

Sarris pointed to other serious problems with the film. He faulted the central characters, who remained "mysteriously motivated and psychologically undeveloped." The Angie Dickinson character is as much a mystery just prior to her death as she was during the dream sequence which opened the film. In addition, he found the plot structurally weak and inconsistent. The only continuity in the opening three sequences of the film—the dream, the conversation between the mother and child, and the museum tour, according to Sarris, was Angie Dickinson, who appeared in all three scenes. However, Sarris's most serious charge against the film was its schizophrenic quality, which he claimed was one reason why De Palma's Hitchcockian flourishes didn't work. "They do not mesh," said Sarris, "with De Palma's obtrusive facetiousness." When Nancy Allen and Keith Gordon team up to solve the murder, we have left "the frightening world of kinky grown-ups" and have entered the "cuddly cosmos of delayed adolescence to which De Palma retreats at the slightest opportunity." When the grown-up and adolescent worlds collide, as they do earlier in the film in the sequence involving Keith Gordon and Angie Dickinson, it is as if we are in two different movies. "Angie Dickinson and Keith Gordon act together as if they had bumped into each other on the way to two different movies, Angie's being a glossy thriller in Dolby Sound, and Gordon's an 8mm feature for a college course." After conceding that the film was not all that bad, Sarris then closed his review with the observation that *Dressed to Kill* left De Palma's artistic reputation in "the same problematic position it has occupied throughout the '70s."

Two months later, Sarris devoted an entire column to those critics who had reacted so positively to *Dressed to Kill*. What especially upset him was how Kael and Denby had manhandled Hitchcock in their reviews. As we have seen, both Kael and Denby had virtually proclaimed De Palma superior to Hitchcock as a director. They "punish Hitchcock posthumously," insisted Sarris, "for having once made films that show up De Palma's shot-by-shot replicas for the cheap, skimpy imitations they are." They are cheap imitations, according to Sarris, because De Palma lifted Hitchcock's privileged moments without building up to them.

Sarris was particularly riled by Kael's characterization of De Palma's art as enshrining the visual over the verbal—a position which Sarris found hypocritical. Since the early sixties, Kael had attacked Sarris and other auteur theorists for exaggerating the importance of the visual over the verbal. In *The "Citizen Kane" Book* (1971), Kael had argued that Orson Welles was no true auteur when one considers that Herman J. Mankiewicz—not Welles—did most of the writing for *Citizen Kane*. "It is ironic," asserted Sarris, "that Kael wrote thousands and thousands of words trying to demonstrate that the late Herman J. Mankiewicz could write Algonquin circles around Orson Welles, and yet will not devote a full paragraph to the self-evident proposition that De Palma has no ear for the cadences and textures of spoken words."[14]

Several months later, critic Stephen Farber (1981) perceptively placed the critical debate about *Dressed to Kill* within the broader framework of film aesthetics and how they had radically changed in recent years. The subject of Farber's essay was what he characterized as the new fashion in movie criticism in which "words like 'pulp,' 'sleazy,' 'dirty,' 'lurid,' 'decadent' are frequently used as terms of praise," while words like "liberal," "social problem oriented," "classical humanist," and "sociological" are routinely used as terms of derision. A result of auteurism taken to its logical extreme, this new critical fashion, argued Farber, had its roots in the reactions during the sixties of both Sarris and Kael to the then prevailing standards of criticism, which overemphasized "sociological analysis." In Farber's view, the once provocative auteur argument that had instructed critics to "look for artistry in unfashionable American movies" had degenerated into a "rigid and untenable catechism." Moreover, he maintained that the auteur premise that a good director could overcome a "pulp" or "bland" plot with a virtuoso visual style (a minority view during the sixties) had "overpowered all other movie criticism." For evidence that this development had become dominant, Farber pointed to the overall glowing reviews that *Dressed to Kill* received from so-called sophisticated New York critics. Echoing Sarris's objections, Farber argued that these critics had "blithely overlooked the narrative gaps, flimsy characterizations, and manipulative crudeness" of the film. (For an interesting feminist attack of the film, see Asselle and Gandhy [1982].)

In interviews with the press, De Palma once again tried to reshape the critical debate about his thriller films. His defensiveness was a sign that the debate in film circles over the reputability of the thriller form would remain a hotly contested issue throughout the eighties. At a press conference in New York City just prior to the release of *Dressed to Kill*, De Palma told journalists that most critics didn't really understand film aesthetics very well because if they did, he reasoned, they wouldn't have attacked him for the so-called explicit violence in many of his films. "I think the people who talk about explicit violence in this movie just do not like horror and suspense pictures. People reject these films because they don't understand that [the essence] of film is the ability to stir an audience with images. That's what movies are." De Palma reminded the journalists that Hitchcock too had been attacked and misunderstood. For most of his career, De Palma argued, Hitchcock was regarded as a light entertainer who worked in a genre that the film industry did not respect. The attitude in the business, said De Palma, was that when you became an important director you no longer made suspense films. To really make it in this business, he asserted, you have to graduate to "message" pictures—films about Three Mile Island. Look what happens, said De Palma, when a serious director like Stanley Kubrick or John Schlesinger makes a thriller or horror film. They show little respect for the form: "they think it's a sleazy form and they're doing it to make money so they can go out and make more message pictures. They condescend to the genre, they don't understand it, they have no passion for it. And so they make terrible movies. I mean I was amazed by *The Shining*, right from the first job-interview scene" (Chute 1980). In a number of interviews conducted shortly after the release of *Dressed to Kill*, De Palma reiterated his hostile views toward certain critics and filmmakers, angering many journalists.[15]

BRILLIANT "SICKO" AND FORMER CRITICAL FAVORITE (1981–86)

By this stage in De Palma's career, the critical response to his films had become predictable. Consider, for example, how reviewers reacted to his next film, *Blow Out* (1981). While still a thriller, the film was somewhat of a departure for him—a political thriller involving a coverup with resonances of Watergate, the Kennedy assassination, and Chappaquiddick. It is clear from the advance press information that with this film De Palma was attempting to broaden his base of critical support. Press materials emphasized that *Blow Out* was not a standard De Palma suspense film combining "a perverse mixture of horror, comedy, and tension" but rather a thriller "based on a mysterious incident that results from a political cover-up" (Production Files, Academy Library). As De Palma told one reporter, "After *Dressed to Kill*, . . . I felt that I had pushed the horror/suspense genre as far as I could go." *Blow Out,* he claimed, was intended more as a character study, in contrast to his earlier films where the characters were "trapped inside the design of the film" (Hinson 1981).[16]

By the time of *Blow Out*'s release, the critical lines were clearly drawn with respect to De Palma's perceived worth as a filmmaker. The reviews of *Blow Out* were somewhat more varied than for *Dressed to Kill,* but, overall, those who had liked *Dressed to Kill* also liked *Blow Out,* whereas detractors of the earlier film came down at least as hard on the later film.

Accepting De Palma's prerelease claims about his new film, Kael described it as his best yet. With this film, declared Kael, De Palma has transcended genre. What moves us about the film, asserted Kael, is "an artist's vision." "Seeing this film," she continued, "is like experiencing the body of De Palma's work and seeing it in a new way." In moving beyond genre, he is "investing his work with a different kind of meaning. His relation to the terror in *Carrie* or *Dressed to Kill* could be gleeful because it was Pop and he could ride it out; now he's in it. . . . This is the first film he has made about the things that really matter to him" (Kael 1981).

De Palma's long-time detractors, however, were not any more impressed with *Blow Out* than with *Dressed to Kill*. To them, De Palma was still lifting plot structures and whole sequences from other films. For example, Sarris saw De Palma as once again appropriating "privileged moments" from classic films, not just Hitchcock's *Vertigo, North by Northwest,* and *To Catch a Thief* but also Antonioni's *Blow Up* and Coppola's *The Conversation*. Not surprisingly, Sarris found the originals "infinitely superior" (Sarris 1981). Other De Palma foes also attacked his genre of choice: "If he made superior thrillers, as his idol Hitchcock often did," argued Stanley Kauffmann, "we could all be appropriately grateful, But to fail at a pop genre seems to me about the most wretched of failures for a would-be artist" (1981).

The current backlash against the excessive violence and rampant misogyny in recent horror films also hurt De Palma's efforts to broaden his base of critical support. The manner in which the crusade against horror affected critical response to De Palma's latest work is revealed in an incident that occurred in the late summer of 1981 when the Writers Guild Film Society screened *Blow Out*. One member of the society, Harlan Ellison, walked out of the screening, and subsequently complained in a letter to the group's selection committee, urging it to use "restraint in showing films that consciously, gratuitously debase the human spirit." In another passage from the letter, Ellison judges the De Palma film as basically no different from the low-budget slasher films that had gutted the market since 1979. "As a craftsman who works seriously at the holy chore of screenwriting," Ellison adds, "I think it's time we examine more responsibly the nature of the cheap-jack predators prowling through our industry. . . . Every time another woman gets an ice pick in her eye in the course of one of these films, all of us get tarred by the same brush." As a result of Ellison's crusade, the selection committee altered its policy. Films provided by the studios which were deemed as excessively violent by committee members would not be shown to members. Subsequently, critic Arthur Knight, a member of the Film Society committee, excerpted Ellison's letter in his Hollywood Reporter column, where he added, "We booked *Blow Out* for our society without a single member of our committee having seen it; it was enough that De Palma's name was on it. Not any more. Somewhere along the line, someone has to say, 'Hold, enough! We simply won't run any more of these violent, vicious, dehumanizing, degrading movies.' And that's precisely what we did last week" (Boyer 1981).

The misogynist charge also surfaced in a number of reviews of *Blow Out*. What Sarris had found most distasteful about the film was De Palma's obsessive dedication to reaffirming the thesis that "all women are hookers and bimbos, and deserve to be punished for their sinfulness and stupidity" (Sarris 1981). On the other hand, a number of reviewers defended De Palma against the charge of misogyny, including Veronica Geng, whose review in the *Soho News* was appropriately titled "Brian De Palma Loves Women" (Geng 1981).

Between *Blow Out* and his next thriller, *Body Double,* De Palma directed *Scarface,* a gangster film which weakened his reputation further. A remake of Howard Hawks' 1932 classic, the film's excessive violence turned off most critics. While the film did damage De Palma's reputation, one could argue, as a few critics did, that *Scarface* was not really a De Palma picture, since he neither wrote nor produced it. That same excuse, however, could not be made for his next project, *Body Double*.[17]

The advance publicity and promotion for *Body Double* is important to consider as background for examining the film's critical reception and subsequent impact on De Palma's then flagging reputation. The press kit made it clear that *Body Double* was a De Palma film all the way—directed, produced, and based on an original story and screenplay by him. It also emphasized that with this film De Palma had come back to familiar territory. "Returning to the suspense genre after directing the hard-action box office hit *Scarface*,[18] De Palma reaffirms his devotion to the format in which he is arguably America's most accomplished living auteur." Moreover, the press kit commentary singled out *Dressed to Kill* as the film responsible for firmly placing De Palma in the "pantheon of contemporary suspense directors."

Several months before the release of *Body Double*, De Palma once again antagonized the critics. In a widely quoted interview in *Esquire,* he announced his grandiose plans for the film. "If they want an X, they'll get a real X. . . . They wanna see suspense, they wanna see terror, they wanna see sex—I'm the person for the job" (Hirschberg 1984). These remarks were proof enough that De Palma had become defiant of those who had criticized his films for their explicit treatment of violence and sex.

In addition to De Palma's own blunders as publicist for his film, the political climate in the early eighties was not conducive for a film like *Body Double*. The recent crusades against slasher films, pornography, and media violence, which had been building momentum since 1980, would reach a crescendo in 1984. In the year that *Body Double* opened, a statute was passed in Indiana declaring pornography a violation of a woman's civil rights. These moralistic movements reflected not only the raised political consciousness of women during this period but also the more conservative political climate symbolized by the Reagan White House.

The vast majority of *Body Double* reviews were strongly negative. But for our purposes, what is striking about them is that they were also strongly critical of De Palma's character. It is clear from the tone of the reviews that many critics had made up their minds before seeing *Body Double* that they would find it repugnant. Consider, for example, the following excerpt from *Box Office*'s review:

Brian De Palma is back to offend women, the memory of Alfred Hitchcock, anti-violence proponents and anyone with an ounce of sense. He's still the same superb technician who could once divert a critic's attention from the sadism and plagiarism with his dazzling camera work. But his reputation has fallen since the days of *Dressed to Kill,* and *Body Double* should complete the descent. This time around he lifts characters, motivations, plots, and scenes from *Vertigo,* along with a thing or two from *Rear Window.* And violence? Let's just say the movie's center piece involves a woman being drilled to the floor. (Summers 1984)

Many of De Palma's staunchest supporters joined his detractors in attacking *Body Double* as a shallow exercise in style. Peter Rainer of the *Los Angeles Examiner,* for example, wrote, "The movie is just what his detractors always accused him of: a hollow exercise in style. Except that *Body Double* isn't so very stylish" (1984). David Sterritt, the critic for the *Christian Science Monitor,* warned that unless he replaced his "cold style" with "a new and deeper vision," he would remain a second-rate director for good (1984). Still others referred to his work as "mean," "misogynistic," "sleazy," "sadistic," "cynical," and "spiteful." Although a few critics felt that the picture had merit, the backlash against *Body Double* (and *Scarface* before it) was so widespread that it prompted one critic to refer to De Palma as "a former critical favorite." The erosion of De Palma's reputation was now complete. Most critics must have felt that the view of De Palma as a "brilliant sicko" with a limitless capacity for filmic wickedness was an apt characterization of him. Apparently, audiences agreed. *Body Double* flopped at the box office.

RESPECTABLE DIRECTOR OF GRADE "A" FILMS (1985–PRESENT)

During the latest phase of his reputation history, De Palma has attempted to regain some commercial and artistic credibility. With his next film, a Mafia comedy called *Wise Guys* (1986), critics could not accuse him of repeating himself. De Palma's sensitivity to that kind of charge surfaced after a press conference to publicize the film, where he told a journalist, "This time, no one can accuse me of ripping off Hitchcock." After completing this film, Paramount offered De Palma the opportunity to direct *Fatal Attraction,* but he declined. Since the screenplay for *Fatal Attraction* borrowed generously from Clint Eastwood's *Play Misty for Me* (see chapter 7), De Palma feared (I think quite rightly) that if he made the film, critics would once again accuse him of plagiarism. Another reason he turned his back on *Fatal Attraction* was his decision, following the uproar over *Body Double,* to stop making suspense movies. "I don't think you can make movies any longer where you put women in peril that way," he told a reporter in 1987. "The media and the audience don't accept it and it gets categorized in the press as being violent against women and sexist" (Darling 1987). What the media fails to realize, De Palma added, is that when you are "making a suspense movie, women are sometimes very good focuses for characters in peril."[19] In another interview, De Palma went further, insisting that in the suspense genre "women in jeopardy . . . work better than *men* in jeopardy. It's a convention of the form. But it's something that's sort of gone out of fashion" (Loder 1987). So instead of a thriller, De Palma chose as his next project a gangster story based loosely on the popular TV crime series *The Untouchables.*[20]

Given the conservative mood of the country, which De Palma complained was stifling creativity in the arts, it must have seemed to him more prudent to make a film with resonances of John Ford than of Hitchcock. Accordingly, he promoted *The Untouchables* as "probably different from anything [he had] done in the past, because it is a traditional American picture, like a John Ford picture, with a tremendous amount of integrity in the characters" (Loder 1987). Here was a relatively safe project, especially after his recent string of critical misses and commercial failures.

The Untouchables was an enormous critical and popular success. Reviews like the following one helped rehabilitate De Palma's tarnished image, "This is a gangster picture so there is violence, and it is a De Palma picture so the violence is vivid. But there is nothing like the exhuberant gore (limbs sliced off by chainsaws, women pierced by electric drills, for example) that has in the past won Mr. De Palma as many detractors as admirers. Fans may miss his wild cackle, the darkly absurdist tilt on the world that distinguished most of his work. But *The Untouchables* lets him show that he isn't just a brilliant sicko. Now he has also made a big, absorbing crowd pleaser" (Salamon, 1987c). Even De Palma's veteran detractors gave the film favorable reviews, among them Andrew Sarris, who saw "sheer craftsmanship" finally win out over "expressive eccentricity" (1987).

On the other hand, a few critics who had championed his earlier works, including many of his controversial thrillers such as *Carrie, Dressed to Kill,* and *Blow Out,* expressed serious reservations about *The Untouchables.* Here was a film, they argued, for people who don't like De Palma films. A number of these critics used their reviews of *The Untouchables* to reflect on what they had found so "great" about De Palma's more personal films. "He isn't the voluptuary satirist here," says Kael, "that he is in *Carrie* or *Dressed to Kill* or the hallucinatory *The Fury;* he isn't the artist that he is in *Blow Out.*" With *The Untouchables,* De Palma has made a conventional genre film. According to Kael, the film was "more like an attempt to visualize the public's collective dream of Chicago gangsters; our movie-fed imagination of the past is enlarged and given a new vividness. De Palma is a showman here" (Kael 1987c). Many of his well-wishers hoped that the enormous commercial success of *The Untouchables* would provide De Palma with the financial freedom to make a more personal film again. As the reviewer for the *Nation* put it, "This picture is his movie-industry merit badge; if we're lucky he'll find a way to twist it into a deadly weapon next time out" (Rafferty 1987).

By the time his next film, *Casualties of War* (1989) was to be released, many critics had concluded that with the enormous popular and critical success of *The Untouchables* coupled with the obvious seriousness of *Casualties of War,* De Palma had successfully traveled the road from "bad" boy to "respectable 'A' director." For a number of these critics, it was clear that with *Casualties of War* De Palma was seeking artistic respectability as well. His remark to a reporter, "I think it has a real moral and political statement to make," seemed to confirm this view of De Palma trying to negotiate a new reputation as a serious and responsible artist.

One of the lessons exemplified by De Palma's reputation history is that specializing exclusively in thrillers or other popular genres was by the late 1980s still not considered a sufficient career path for a director seeking artistic respectability. To solidify one's artistic credentials, one still had to move on to what critics regarded as more serious subjects. On the other hand, De Palma did more than simply make thrillers, and, hence, other pertinent features of his filmmaking observed by critics also shaped his critical reputation. As we have seen, many critics commented on his tendency to recycle old movie plots and classic movie sequences, while others were sensitive to his portrayal of women. Critics attracted to a postmodern sensibility were less offended by De Palma's penchant for recycling old movie plots and classic scenes than were more conventional critics who often attacked him for not creating new suspense plots. While the debate over whether De Palma was a misogynist remained unresolved, what is undisputed is the impact that feminist concerns have had on films aesthetics and filmmaking, especially during the early eighties. In fact, a strong case could be made that the feminist outcry against his thriller films is a principal reason why De Palma stopped making such films.

Beyond Hitchcock

I have explored how reputations emerge and change in the art world of film using Hitchcock and the thriller genre to illuminate the process. In this, the final chapter, I will assess the broader significance of the reputational patterns reported in the book. Using the method of controlled comparison (see Smelser 1976), I will extend the discussion beyond Hitchcock and the thriller case to other film directors whose reputations have also fluctuated dramatically over the years. As described by sociologist Neil Smelser, the technique of controlled comparison is an analytical strategy in which the selection of additional "case histories" is guided by the logic of experimental design. "[P]otential sources of variation are converted into parameters by selecting cases that resemble one another in significant respects. The resemblances can then be regarded as 'ruled out' as explanatory factors, and explanations based on other variables can be generated within the framework provided by the resemblances" (Smelser 1976, 215). By comparing the reputational careers of directors who resemble one another in significant ways, I can both further check on the reasonableness of my interpretation of Hitchcock's reputational trajectory and gain further insight into the process of reputation building.

The sixties and early seventies marked a watershed for Hitchcock as well as for other directors of his generation. It was during the early sixties that François Truffaut, Andrew Sarris, Peter Bogdanovich, Robin Wood, and other auteur critics actively sought to elevate Hitchcock's stature as a serious artist. While their efforts eventually succeeded, the transformation of his reputation from "master of suspense" to serious auteur proceeded slowly. The campaign to improve Hitchcock's reputation was part of a general movement to promote directors who fit the new criteria for filmmaking. In advancing their views, the auteur critics constructed a new pantheon of directors wherein certain directors were singled out for special praise while the rest were demoted or ignored (see Sarris 1986a; cf. Wollen 1969, 166–67).

For the old-guard intellectual critics (e.g., Bosley Crowther [1967],

Dwight Macdonald [1969], Arthur Knight [1957], Hollis Alpert [1962a], and Richard Griffith [1950]), the major dividing line for directors was American versus European or, more precisely, Hollywood directors versus the Europeans they favored—Ingmar Bergman, Michelangelo Antonioni, Jean Renoir, and others. Among the relatively few American directors singled out as significant by the critical establishment were John Huston, George Stevens, Billy Wilder, William Wyler, and Fred Zinnemann (see, e.g., Alpert 1962a, 130; Knight 1957, 184–88; and Griffith 1950). "In January 1956," reports film historian Robert Ray, "*Newsweek* offered a mid-decade appraisal of the American popular film occasioned by John Huston's about-to-be-released *Moby Dick*. Including Huston, the article named 'the top five directors in the industry' as William Wyler, George Stevens, Fred Zinnemann, and Billy Wilder" (Ray 1985, 141–42).

The young American auteurists of the sixties, as we have seen, countered the established pantheon with one of their own choosing, reflecting their belief that there were directors such as Hitchcock, Hawks, Ford, Lang, and Welles who, despite having worked within the old Hollywood studio system, had somehow managed to maintain in their work a personal vision not entirely limited by space and time. On the other hand, Huston, Wyler, Stevens, Zinnemann, and Wilder were all dismissed as second- or third-rate by the auteurists, and, as Ray has pointed out, "all but Stevens [were] eventually included in American auteurist Andrew Sarris's most damning category, 'Less Than Meets the Eye'" (1985, 142). In contrast to these directors, Hitchcock was an ideal showcase for the American practitioners of auteur theory. Not only did his work span forty years, it also traversed two continents—Europe and North America. As we have seen, according to the critical establishment circa 1955, Hitchcock's British films were superior to those he made in Hollywood. To many veteran critics, Hitchcock had sold out to Hollywood—selling his artistic soul for the commercial dollar. By contrast, the auteur critics, believing that they could demonstrate that his Hollywood films actually surpassed those he made in England, saw Hitchcock's career as a perfect vehicle for illustrating their conviction that great cinematic art could flourish within the Hollywood studio system.[1]

In spite of support from the auteur critics and Hitchcock's own massive efforts at self-promotion, the campaign to elevate his artistic reputation required over ten years to achieve success. The evidence reported in this book strongly indicates that it was the prevalence through much of the fifties and sixties of a critical discourse favoring "realism" over the artificiality of Hollywood genre films that was principally responsible for delaying his reception as an artist. In addition, I would suggest that Hitchcock's deeply entrenched celebrity status as master of suspense also worked against him. That is, the very success of Hitchcock's self-promotional activities during the fifties may have actually hurt the later campaign initiated by the French auteur critics to enhance his reputation. Perhaps, had Hitchcock not cultivated a public reputation *and* not been perceived by critics as a master of self-promotion—in other words, had he maintained a relatively low profile—his reputation as an important artist probably would have advanced more quickly. As a check on this interpretation, I turn to the filmmaking career of Howard Hawks.

Virtually unknown outside the film industry before 1960, Hawks came to be regarded by the late 1960s and early 1970s as one of Hollywood's greatest directors. In fact, my strong impression is that by the late 1960s, the critical consensus on Hawks' stature as a significant artist even surpassed Hitchcock's (see, for example, the clippings file on Howard Hawks and the reviews of what proved to be his last film, *Rio Lobo* [1971], MOMA). Today, while critics might still debate the elements of Hawks' artistry, few would question applying the artistic label to his work. Why did Hawks' reputation advance more smoothly and quickly than Hitchcock's during the early sixties? Before answering this, I will establish the extent to which Hawks' filmmaking career is comparable to Hitchcock's.

Like Hitchcock's, Howard Hawks' career spanned over forty years. One of Hollywood's most successful directors, he had worked, unlike Hitchcock, in a variety of popular genres—gangster films such as *Scarface,* crime stories such as *The Big Sleep,* comedies such as *Bringing up Baby,* musicals such as *Gentlemen Prefer Blondes,* and westerns such as *Rio Bravo.* Like Hitchcock, Hawks presented himself publicly as a popular director, never as a serious or significant artist. However, unlike Hitchcock, Hawks maintained a low profile through most of his career; rarely did he publicly discuss his views on filmmaking. Indeed, before 1960, no one had asked him to do so. Nor did he have the audience recognition that Hitchcock had enjoyed throughout his career. For established critics, Hawks went practically unnoticed. Rarely did they mention his name when reviewing one of his films. As Sarris put it in 1962, "Howard Hawks is the least known and least appreciated giant in the American cinema" (Sarris 1962b, 20).

Many of the early French, English, and American auteur critics who embraced the view of Hitchcock as a serious artist also crusaded on behalf of Hawks. The French auteurs who sponsored both directors came to be known as the "Hitchcock-Hawksiens." Jacques Rivette wrote a ground-breaking essay on Hawks for *Cahiers du Cinéma* which appeared in 1953. Three years later *Cahiers du Cinéma* published an extended interview with Hawks conducted by Truffaut, Rivette, and Jacques Becker. While Hawks' films were frequently reviewed and discussed in French newspapers and periodicals from the early 1950s on, it was not until the early sixties that American critics started to write seriously about his work. In the summer of 1962, roughly a year before Bogdanovich organized the Hitchcock retrospective for the Museum of Modern Art, he put together a similar one on behalf of Hawks for which he also prepared a monograph consisting of an introductory essay and a lengthy interview touching on many of Hawks' films. Later that summer, Andrew Sarris published a two-part essay on Hawks for the British film journal *Films and Filming*. At the end of the year, another British journal, *Movie,* devoted an entire issue to Hawks with articles by several critics including Robin Wood and V. F. Perkins. And in early 1963, *Cahiers du Cinéma* put out a special issue on Hawks which included abridged versions of Rivette's original essay and Bogdanovich's monograph along with essays by other critics. Robin Wood also published a book-length study of Hawks in 1968 (see also Poague 1982 and McBride 1972).

Much of the early scholarship on Hawks resembled the critical scholarship on Hitchcock's work during the sixties. Champions of Hawks raised the question: why was Hawks invisible to the public and why did he receive so little attention from the media? As Gerald Mast pointed out, Hawks had a tremendous reputation within the film industry, enjoying great freedom from the power of the individual studios (and he worked for all the major ones). Says Mast, "no other Hollywood director—not Ford, not Capra, not Hitchcock, not Lubitsch (the directors with whom Hawks liked to be compared)—enjoyed greater freedom from the power of an individual Fox, Paramount, or MGM than Hawks" (1982, 116).

While honoring Hawks with favorable contracts, the film industry withheld from him any artistic awards, at least until late in his career. Hawks was not even listed on *Who's Who* until 1971. Why was a filmmaker who today is acknowledged as one of the great masters of the cinema so neglected throughout most of his career? One reason, according to the Hawksians, was that he worked in so-called minor genres such as adventure films, gangster films, private-eye melodramas, westerns, musicals, and screwball comedies, "the sort of things," said Sarris, that "Hollywood has done best and honored least" (Sarris 1962b, 20). While it may have been true that Hawks had made possibly the best film in each of the genres he had worked in, wasn't it also true that these films were simply vehicles for entertaining audiences rather than for edifying them as serious art might? (See plate 36.)

As Wood, Sarris, and other auterists have pointed out, earlier film critics tended to view art and entertainment as distinct and unbridge-able provinces, analogous to those assigned to high art and popular culture. Rejecting this critical bias, Wood argued in the introduction to his book on Hawks that "A work is 'entertaining' in so far as we spontaneously enjoy it and 'art' in so far as it makes intellectual and emotional demands on us" (Wood 1968, 7). Applying this distinction between entertainment and art to music, Wood argues that many of Mozart's works, for example, a number of his divertimenti and serenades, "were composed for social gatherings at which the listeners wandered about and conversed during the music: 'art' or 'entertainment'?" (1968, 7). When Mozart's operas were first performed, most notably *The Marriage of Figaro* and *The Magic Flute,* audiences were entertained right from the beginning. Arias became popular hits of the day. Turning to Elizabethan theater, Wood maintains that Shakespeare enjoyed the same kind of rapport with audiences that Mozart enjoyed. According to Wood, the works of both Shakespeare and Mozart represent "conservative" as distinct from "revolutionary" art. Revolutionary art, such as works by Joyce and Beckett, says Wood, "deliberately breaks with the immediate past, inventing entirely new forms and new methods of expression," while conservative art "develops out of the immediate past, using forms and language already evolved" (1968, 8). For Wood, Hollywood genre films belong to this latter category and Hitchcock and Hawks are two notable examples of genre filmmakers. While Hitchcock concentrated on thriller films, Hawks worked in a variety of genres. Though not originating any of them, Hawks did produce, says Wood, "probably the best work within each genre he . . . tackled" (1968, 12). Hawks, like Hitchcock, in Wood's view, lacked the excruciating self-consciousness of most modern artists. Two years earlier, in *Hitchcock's Films,* Wood had made much the same point about both directors, "It seems clear that the relationship of a Hitchcock or a Hawks to his art is much more like Shakespeare's than is that of a Bergman or an Antonioni; the sense of communication on many levels precludes the self-consciousness of the artist that besets the arts today and fosters true artistic impersonality" (Wood [1965] 1977, 32).

What many auteur critics found most compelling or instructive about Hawks' work was that it provided a crucial test case for the auteur theory. Having worked in virtually all of the popular Hollywood genres, Hawks, according to these critics, still had managed to sustain a considerable degree of thematic and stylistic distinctiveness and consistency throughout his body of work. Influenced by the auteur-inspired Hawks scholarship which appeared in the early 1960s, Wood (1968), for example, pointed out that, while Hawks' adventure films and his comedies might seem to move in opposite directions, they actually shared the same tragic vision of the world.[2] This sentiment that Hawks' films, regardless of the genre in which he was engaged, reflected essentially the same personal vision about the human condition is also echoed in Peter Wollen's widely disseminated 1969 essay on Hawks, where he writes:

> Hawks has worked in almost every genre. He has made westerns (*Rio Bravo*), gangsters (*Scarface*), war films (*Air Force*), thrillers (*The Big Sleep*), science fiction (*The Thing from Another World*), musicals (*Gentlemen Prefer Blondes*), comedies (*Bringing up Baby*), even a Biblical epic (*Land of the Pharaohs*). Yet all of these films (except perhaps *Land of the Pharaohs*, which he himself was not happy about) exhibit the same thematic preoccupations, the same recurring motifs and incidents, the same visual style and tempo. In the same way that Roland Barthes constructed a species of *homo racinianus,* the critic can construct a *homo hawksianus,* the protagonist of Hawksian values in the problematic Hawksian world (Wollen 1969, 81).

To summarize, the auteur critics, as we have seen, responded similarly to both Hawks and Hitchcock. Notwithstanding Hitchcock's apparent edge as self-promoter, the auteurists' efforts to improve Hawks' reputation, as I have suggested, proved initially more effective than their early crusade on Hitchcock's behalf. It was Hawks' relatively low public profile, I would argue, that gave him an important edge in the initial stages of the campaign to elevate his reputation. Unlike Hitchcock, Hawks did not have a deeply ingrained public image (not as master entertainer or as self-promoter) to overcome. As Sarris once put it, " 'Who the hell is Howard Hawks,' became a recurring refrain in English and American film journals. It was different with Hitchcock. Everyone knew who *he* was and what he did. The only argument was whether he was a major artist or a minor entertainer. With Hawks, the movies were more prominent than the man" (Sarris 1978). Since the secondary literature is virtually silent about Hawks' role in improving his reputation among the critics, future research will have to rely on primary sources to determine the extent of Hawks' own involvement in reshaping his directorial reputation. Even if we should learn that Hawks, too, was covertly involved in elevating his reputation, the fact still remains that he was more successful than Hitchcock in keeping such involvement a well-guarded secret.

In many respects, Frank Capra's early reputation history paralleled Hitchcock's more closely than did Hawks'. Capra made popular films which general audiences recognized clearly as his. He became a media celebrity but sought recognition from highbrow critics as well. Comparing the reception of Capra's films with Hitchcock's, I found striking similarities in how their reputations shaped both the popular and critical response to their films. I shall discuss those similarities, and, in addition, I shall explore why the auteur critics were less likely to embrace Capra's work than Hitchcock's.

If the fifties were the decade in which Hitchcock solidified his generic contract with audiences, then the thirties were surely when Capra achieved a comparable standing with the American public. Following the enormous success of *It Happened One Night* in 1934, Capra became one of the most popular and sought-after directors. With his next film, *Mr. Deeds Goes to Town* (1936), he found the formula upon which his reputation in the thirties and forties is largely based, the romantic fable extolling the virtues of the "little man." Like Hitchcock, Capra affixed his name to newspaper and magazine articles in which he conveyed to audiences the type of film he wanted the public to associate with his name (see, e.g., Capra 1936). Between 1934 and 1939, he also became a media celebrity. Capra was discovered as a media personality by various pressure groups and packagers of public opinion. In 1938 he was the subject of a cover story in *Time* and a photo essay in *Life*. As president of the Academy of Motion Picture Arts and Sciences from 1935 to 1939 and as head of the directors' guild from 1938 to 1939, he championed the cause of directorial preeminence and autonomy. One of his goals was to secure for the director the "name above the title," a goal he defended in articles appearing in major newspapers, including the *New York Times*.

When Hitchcock settled in America in 1939, Capra was the director to whom he was often compared in terms of reputation. In 1939 a film-revival house in New York City offered a joint Capra-Hitchcock series. In Preston Sturges's self-reflexive comedy, *Sullivan's Travels*, the traveling companion of a famous movie director asks him about other famous directors, including Capra and Hitchcock:

THE GIRL: Is Capra nice, or don't you know him?
SULLIVAN: Very nice.
THE GIRL: Is Hitchcock as fat as they say he is?
SULLIVAN: Fatter.
THE GIRL: Do you think Orson Welles is crazy?
SULLIVAN: In a very practical way.

A filmmaker with a well-established reputation must manage that reputation each time he is about to release a new film. Hitchcock's biographical legend by the mid-fifties was such that when audiences thought about a Hitchcock film, they had something quite specific in mind. In order for his films to perform well in the marketplace or to receive acceptable reviews, it became incumbent upon Hitchcock to take into account the extent to which his latest film deviated from what viewers expected from him at that point in time. It is recalled how the overall weak commercial showing of *Vertigo* when first released in 1958 was in part attributed to the impression—a misleading one as it turned out—that audiences had of that film based on prior publicity and promotion. The commercial fate of Capra's 1946 film, *It's a Wonderful Life*, was similar to that of Hitchcock's *Vertigo* twelve years later.[3]

The film's box-office returns did not live up to Capra's expectations. In fact, after one year of release, it had barely broken even. A major reason, I believe, was the inappropriateness of the advertising campaign. The film was sold in three ways: (1) as a Frank Capra film; (2) as a happy family story; and (3) as a romance (see plate 37). In none of the advertising materials did the word "suicide" appear. As the curator of the Capra archives Jeanine Basinger has put it, "Looking at newspaper ads and lobby cards and posters outside theaters, the moviegoer got the impression that the movie was a happy-go-lucky, warm love story, reminiscent of the screwball comedies of the thirties—in particular Capra's own 'You Can't Take It With You,' which also starred Stewart and Lionel Barrymore. . . . There was no suggestion of the darker aspects" (Basinger 1986, 54).

And yet today many regard the film as Capra's crowning achievement, much in the same way as Hitchcock's *Vertigo* has been reassessed. Undoubtedly, Capra's own self-promotion helped create a receptive audience for the film. For example, starting in the late 1960s, Capra became involved in film education, lecturing on filmmaking and on his career at colleges where he discovered a new and sympathetic audience for his films. When asked about his career, he would tell students that *It's a Wonderful Life* was his personal favorite.

During the late thirties and early forties, Capra, like Hitchcock in the sixties, had also fretted that his films were not receiving the kind of critical acclaim that he felt they deserved. In his 1972 autobiography he wrote, "No, it wasn't the existence of critics that really riled me. It was their supercilious attitude that got under my skin. I had made seven smash hits in a row. Had I performed that feat on Broadway I would have been canonized. Shubert Alley would have been renamed Via Capra. As it was, not one of my last three films—*Lost Horizon, You Can't Take It With You,* and *Mr Smith Goes to Washington*—had made the New York Critics Annual Poll of their selected "ten best" films. . . . And so, *Meet John Doe,* my first completely independent film venture, was *aimed* at winning critical praises" (Capra 1971, 297).

In a number of ways, *Meet John Doe* was Capra's *The Birds*. In both instances, a director was appealing to New York critics who they felt had snubbed them in the past. Both Capra and Hitchcock struggled with the ending of their film and both found themselves "negotiating" with audiences about their ending. Like Hitchcock with *The Birds,* Capra directed *Meet John Doe* to two constituencies—his fans and the so-called serious critics. His struggle with the film's ending highlights this dual focus. In fact, Capra changed the film's ending so that it would be perceived as more satisfactory by his fans. This decision ultimately hurt the film's critical reception not only at the time of the film's initial release but right up to the present (see Wolfe 1989). By contrast, Hitchcock defended his controversial ending for *The Birds.* However, as we have seen, he did renegotiate the "meaning" of the film with his fans, reflecting ultimately his growing disenchantment with the mass audience.

We might ask why Capra has not enjoyed the critical esteem of other American directors such as Hitchcock or Hawks. A major reason is that the French auteur critics did not champion Capra's films. His work did not fit their aesthetic nearly as well as Hitchcock's or Hawks'. According to these critics, the individual "auteur" was the sole source of a film's meaning: the auteur's personal vision transcended "reality," "history," and "society." While American auteur critics like Sarris acknowledged Capra as a genuine auteur (he had a personal vision), they criticized the content of his vision for being little more than a crude reflection of the idealism of his middle-class audience. That is, according to the auteur critics, Capra's films were simply too sociological. This charge has some validity. A number of sociologically oriented film scholars have treated his films, especially those made between 1934 and 1941, as a barometer of the times (see, for example, Bergman 1971, 132–48; Sklar 1975; Schatz 1981). In his history of American films during the thirties, Andrew Bergman examined Capra's post-1934 films partly as a reflection of America's search for unity under the New Deal and partly as mythmaking:

> To see the Capra films from 1934 to 1941 is to learn more about a nation's image of itself than one has any right to expect. How much did Capra create, and how much did he respond to? His classlessness was an obvious fantasy, but the myth obviously was dear to Americans. He created a tradition in effecting the screwball social peace of *It Happened One Night* and responded to tradition in *Deeds* by neutralizing the shyster world, a world very much Hollywood's creation. Once the thirties had been crossed with the nation's basic institutions intact and relatively unscathed, Capra was free to argue from greater strength; fascism was neither his nor Hollywood's creation. (Bergman 1971, 147–48)

On the other hand, it has been extremely rare for Hitchcock's films to be examined as a reflection of society, although the deconstructionist bias of much feminist criticism of Hitchcock does point to the wider patriarchal society as an important source of meaning in his films. Overall, critics have found Hitchcock's darker vision of the human condition more to their aesthetic liking than Capra's sentimental populism, although a number of recent film scholars maintain that Capra's work is far more complex than earlier critics believed (see, e.g., Glatzer and Raeburn 1975; Poague 1975; and Carney 1986).

I turn next to Viennese-born director Fritz Lang (1890–1976), best known for *M* and other suspense films. Lang, who early in his career gained recognition as both a serious and innovative artist within the international film community, was less successful than Hitchcock in maintaining that reputation over the years (see plate 38).

By the time Hitchcock directed his first film, Lang was already one of the most revered European filmmakers, having directed eleven films, including such acknowledged classics as *The Spiders* (1919), *Dr. Mabuse the Gambler* (1922), *Die Nibelungen* (1923–24), and *Metropolis* (1926). Despite the fact that many of his early films were in the crime genre, critics regarded Lang as one of the supreme artists of the silent cinema. When Hitchcock's *The Lodger* was released in 1927, a number of British critics compared it favorably to the work of Lang and of other directors associated with German expressionism. Twelve years later, after Hitchcock had made six successive thrillers, Lang's reputation in England still exceeded Hitchcock's. As one critic put it, "Hitchcock is our native Fritz Lang, and in many ways a true disciple of the master. . . . Like [Lang], he is a superb craftsman. . . . But often the sum-total of a Hitchcock film is a sense of disappointment, based in the realisation that the film's intellectual substance is too slight to hold it together" (quoted in Spoto 1983, 206–7).

In 1933, after Goebbels asked him to head the German film industry, Lang fled from Nazi Germany, finally settling in Hollywood in 1934. Like Hitchcock, Lang would encounter problems with the more serious critics, who came to view his Hollywood films as inferior to his earlier output. At that time, as we have seen, serious film criticism, both in England and the United States, was dominated by a social realist aesthetic. Verisimilitude and social significance were the rallying points of these critics. At least Lang, unlike Hitchcock, had started off in Hollywood on the right foot with these sociologically oriented critics. His first film, *Fury,* because of its unrelenting "sociological" treatment of a lynching, was enthusiastically received by the important critics. For example, *New York Times* critic Frank S. Nugent wrote:

> Let it be said at once: "Fury" . . . is the finest original drama the screen has provided this year. The theme is mob violence, its approach is coldly judicial, its treatment as relentless and unsparing as the lynching it portrays. . . . This has been a completely enthusiastic report, and such was our intention. Hollywood rarely bothers with themes bearing any relation to significant aspects of contemporary life. When it does, in most cases, its approach is timid, uncertain or misdirected. "Fury" is direct, forthright and vehement. That it is brilliantly executed as well makes it all the more notable. (*New York Times,* 6 June 1936)

Lang's later films, however, never fulfilled the promise that the pre-auteur critics like Nugent had read into *Fury.* Many were thrillers and, like Hitchcock's, were attacked for their subject matter—pulpy crime stories, implausible plots, sketchy character delineations, and overall oppressiveness and rejection of the idea of social betterment and progress. The principal charge against both filmmakers was that their works lacked verisimilitude.

The next generation of auteur critics, however, found more value in Lang's Hollywood films. The French auteur critics were first to champion his American work, which they found philosophically more challenging than his German films. Like Hitchcock, Lang was an ideal case for the French auteur critics because, in their view, his unique vision and style achieved greater expression in America than in Germany.

One critical difference between Lang and Hitchcock was Lang's inability to establish rapport with his admirers. He lacked Hitchcock's wit and seemingly carefree attitude. As one of his collaborators put it:

> Lang had his own special brand of humor which he expressed in subtle ways. He took pleasure in observing people's weaknesses or when a person did something for expediency. I think he was basically cynical. During the making of a picture he had no peripheral vision. He did not socialize a great deal, but kept to himself. Away from the picture, after hours, he was cordial but never familiar and, even in the best of spirits, never effusive. But I liked working with him; others did not. They saw only the Teutonic side, but, in general, he was respected by the crew and this, I think, counted most to Lang. (quoted in Ott 1979, 44)

Unlike Hitchcock, Lang was often abrasive with people, even with those who hailed his work. For example, in the late 1960s, Peter Bogdanovich interviewed Lang for an article in *Esquire* magazine. When the article evolved into a book, Lang became furious, denouncing Bogdanovich for misleading him (Lang Collection, University of Southern California). At the time, Lang's long-time friend Lotte Eisner was also writing a book about him. Possibly Lang was concerned that Bogdanovich's book might up-stage Eisner's effort. It should come as no surprise that after this flare-up, Bogdanovich did not remain so visible a champion of Lang's art and career. Bogdanovich is not an isolated case. In 1967, Paul M. Jensen, who was completing his monograph on Lang (Jensen 1969), sent a draft to Lang for his comments and suggestions. Unwilling to alert the author to any errors or offer him suggestions on how to improve the study, Lang wrote back a nasty reply, denouncing the entire project:

I don't think that I have the right to criticize what someone writes about me, may it be negative or positive. However, your paper is full of obvious errors and inaccurate data concerning myself and the films I have made, errors and inaccuracies which, with a little more careful research could easily have been avoided. If I were to comply with your request, I would be forced to re-write almost every page, which I certainly do not have the time to do. I cannot afford and do not want to be connected with your essay in any way. (Letter, Fritz Lang to Paul Jensen, 11 November 1967, Lang Collection)[4]

Lang's shortcomings as a self-promoter prevented him from establishing the kind of linkages to critics and writers which would have inspired them to remain active Langians, even after his death. By contrast, as we have seen, Hitchcock had charmed his foot soldiers to remain devoted Hitchcockians to the bitter end. Many who championed Hitchcock—Sarris, Bogdanovich, Canby, Schickel, Wood, and Truffaut —continued to actively promote his work, even after his death. While receiving recognition among his peers within the film art world, Lang never gained the renown or celebrity status with the average American citizen that Hitchcock had achieved.[5]

We have seen how the critical standing of Hitchcock, Hawks, and Lang improved in the sixties as the auteur perspective came to dominate both journalistic and academic discourse on the cinema. To gain further insight into the reputation-building process, one might examine directorial reputations that evolved during the 1970s and 1980s—when the idea of the director as the major source of meaning remained powerful among mainstream reviewers. That is, by looking at reputation histories from their inception in the 1970s up to the present, one is able to explore what factors have been important in shaping the reputation-building process at a time when the auteur perspective remained largely uncontested. Clint Eastwood is a case in point. Like Hitchcock, Eastwood became an enormously successful commercial filmmaker, then overcame a public image that initially conflicted with his quest for artistic respectability. He achieved recognition as a significant film artist far more quickly than did Hitchcock. What might explain the relative speed of Eastwood's rise to artistic fame?

In the late 1960s and early 1970s Clint Eastwood starred in a series of action-adventure films, first westerns and then cop thrillers, which firmly established him as one of the world's most popular film actors. The role that forged his public image was Harry Callahan, the fiercely independent hard-hat detective he introduced in Don Siegel's *Dirty Harry* (1971). In this film and its sequels, *Magnum Force* (1973), *The Enforcer* (1976), *Sudden Impact* (1983), and *The Dead Pool* (1988), Eastwood portrays a tough San Francisco cop who stalks criminals with his 44-Magnum revolver, at the same time fighting against the bureaucratic structures that protect criminals. Extremely popular with audiences, these films, from the outset, were denounced as right-wing propaganda by many of the serious critics who, despite the shift to an auteur aesthetic, continued to pay attention to what they perceived to be the social implications of a film. Reviewing *Dirty Harry,* Pauline Kael set the tone for other critics when she wrote:

> *Dirty Harry* is obviously just a genre movie, but this action genre has always had a fascist potential, and it has finally surfaced. If crime were caused by super-evil dragons, there would be no Miranda, no Escobedo; we could all be licensed to kill, like Dirty Harry. But since crime is caused by deprivation, misery, psychopathology, and social injustice, *Dirty Harry* is a deeply immoral movie. (Kael 1972)

Eastwood's notorious portrayal of Harry Callahan would adversely affect his reputation as a director. He launched his directorial career in 1971 with the psychological thriller *Play Misty for Me.* Released before *Dirty Harry,* the film did well commercially and received generally favorable reviews. On the other hand, the next several films he directed —*High Plains Drifter* (1973), *Breezy* (1973), *The Eiger Sanction* (1975), *The Outlaw Josey Wales* (1976) and *The Gauntlet* (1977)— received generally poor notices, especially from the more serious critics, who judged these films against the shadow of Dirty Harry. For example, Richard Schickel, who panned *High Plains Drifter,* characterized the film's cowboy hero as "part Dirty Harry in cowboy boots, a good cop trying to do his duty in a world ungrateful for his sadistic efforts" (1973). David Ansen's pan of *The Eiger Sanction* was even more hostile to Eastwood's star persona:

> Eastwood may be a lame actor, a dull director and a moral pigmy —but he knows his audience. The smug violence and grating arrogance are as essential to his persona as Cagney's pugnaciousness or Monty Clift's shivering sensitivity. Eastwood understands his

symbolic role: he's the current kind of unrepentant macho—the inarticulate knight errant to a vast audience of action-loving, women-hating fans. If he seems a touch overeager for the kill, well, that's our rambunctious Clint. . . . Clint Eastwood hasn't refined his art, but he's mastered his market research. With a steely eye on the box office he serves himself up: tough, spicy, and just rotten enough to delight the hungry hordes. (Ansen 1975)

Yet, by the mid-eighties, many critics were writing more favorably about Eastwood, including some, like David Ansen, who earlier had denounced him. While not proclaiming Eastwood a great American moviemaker, Ansen was willing by 1985 to concede that many of Eastwood's films had been underrated:

The Gauntlet (1977) is terribly underrated. It's great comic-book fun, with Eastwood as a dumb, drunken cop and Locke as a smart, tough hooker—the first of the noticeably strong women who have emerged in recent Eastwood movies . . . . *The Outlaw Josey Wales* (1976) is the most ambitious and emotionally rich of the Eastwood-directed Westerns. There are also those memorable movies he made with Don Siegel . . . including *Dirty Harry* (1971)—a zinger of a crime movie, whatever you think of its politics." (Ansen 1985)

Other critics, such as Vincent Canby, went even further in their rethinking about Eastwood. Reviewing *Pale Rider* (1985), Canby confessed, "I'm just now beginning to realize that, though Mr. Eastwood may have been improving over the years, it's also taken all these years for most of us to recognize his very consistent grace and wit as a filmmaker" (Canby 1985).

What demands explaining is the swiftness of Eastwood's achievement in advancing his reputation as a director. Earlier I argued that Hawks had achieved artistic respectability more easily than Hitchcock because Hawks did not have to overcome a prior reputation as a popular filmmaker and personality. Like Hitchcock, Eastwood had such a reputation. His right-wing macho image was a formidable obstacle to overcome.

On the surface, the process through which Eastwood improved his critical reputation seemed to parallel Hitchcock's. The French critics were early champions of his work and have remained more supportive of his career than have their American counterparts. When the French in

1985 honored Eastwood with a film retrospective at the Cinémathèque Française in Paris, the tribute ran every day for four months, compared to the one-day tribute sponsored by the Museum of Modern Art five years earlier.

Before it became fashionable, there were those who championed Eastwood's work in the United States, including film critics Andrew Sarris, Tom Allen, Molly Haskell, and Dave Kehr, and novelist Norman Mailer, who in a 1983 article in *Parade* magazine "confessed" that Eastwood was an artist—"the most important small-town artist in America":

> Eastwood knows the buried buttons in his audience as well as any filmmaker around. Is it out of measure to call him the most important small-town artist in America? One of the buried secrets small-town life is about is knowing how to press other people's buttons—that is, the ones concealed from themselves." (Mailer 1983, 7)

And, as Mailer pointed out, "You can see the man in his work just as clearly as you see Hemingway in *A Farewell to Arms*" (1983, 5).

Arts organizations also honored Eastwood, starting in 1980 with the one-day tribute at the Museum of Modern Art in New York. Highlighting the MOMA tribute were screenings of his directorial debut in *Play Misty for Me*, as well as *Bronco Billy* (1980), his latest critically acclaimed film.

The year 1985 stands out in Eastwood's reputation history, paralleling, in many respects, the year 1963 in Hitchcock's career (see plate 39). There were the international museum tributes at the Cinémathèque Française in Paris, the Filmmuseum in Munich, and the British Film Institute in London. (In 1963 Hitchcock had been honored with a retrospective of his work at MOMA). Eastwood's latest film, *Pale Rider*, opened the 1985 Cannes Film Festival (Hitchcock's *The Birds*, we recall, inaugurated the 1963 festival). And newspaper and magazine articles about Eastwood mushroomed. An important difference distinguished the critical perceptions of the two directors in 1963 and 1985. A number of the articles on Eastwood already viewed him as a serious artist, including a cover story in the *New York Times Magazine*, fittingly titled "Clint Eastwood, Seriously" (Vinocur 1985). Not until 1972 with *Frenzy* did the debate about Hitchcock's artistic status tip noticeably in favor of the French view of him as a serious auteur.[6]

Did Eastwood actively work to make 1985 a milestone in his reputation history? The fact that in 1984 he had placed a one-page ad in the *New York Review of Books* to promote his latest film, *Tightrope,* strongly suggests that, in addition to perfecting his craft, he also endeavored to improve his reputation as a director through strategies of self-promotion. While the circumstantial evidence implies that Eastwood is every bit as clever and cunning a promoter as Hitchcock, documenting this claim is beyond the scope of this chapter.

What is demonstrable is that the critical climate during the seventies and eighties was receptive to the view that genre filmmaking, especially meditations and reflections on a popular genre, could yield important films. (Consider, for example, the enthusiastic critical response to Francis Ford Coppola's first two *Godfather* films, which while respectful of the conventions of the classic gangster cycle, reworked them in interesting ways.) When Eastwood started directing in the early seventies, most critics did not need to be convinced of the compatibility between genre filmmaking and artistry. The films of Hitchcock, Hawks, and Ford were testimony of this compatibility. Rather, Eastwood's problem, as his directorial career evolved, was overcoming the strong political bias against his earlier work—the charge that his films were "fascist" and "sexist." It would not take long for critics to come around to admiring how Eastwood played with and reworked his star persona through his films, which were viewed increasingly as highly reflexive works. This critical reevaluation occurred partly because Eastwood was seemingly making all the right career moves in reshaping his reputation without the constraint of a critical discourse hostile to his efforts. Another reason is that critics, writing during a more conservative period, could acknowledge that the earlier charge that Eastwood was a fascistic director had been greatly overstated. Influenced by the women's movement, several critics now discovered in Eastwood's films a sensitivity to women's issues. The critical reception of *Tightrope* reflects these developments.

In his commentary on the film, *New York Times* critic Vincent Canby identified both Alfred Hitchcock and John Ford as directors who had discovered new ways of revitalizing the generic traditions of the thriller and the western, respectively. Hitchcock's specialty, Canby reminded us, was the "chase" film. "Only Hitchcock could have made a great chase film like *Rear Window,*" said Canby, "in which the hero spends most of his time in one room in a wheelchair." While directors like Hitchcock and Ford did not actually transcend the genre in which they worked, they did, according to Canby, "enrich its possibilities."

Tightrope also functions that way in relation to the Dirty Harry films. Here is a film, says Canby, where Eastwood (and his director) "know exactly when to meet the expectations of the Eastwood fans and when to do something a little different" (Canby 1984). *Tightrope*'s departure from the conventions of the Dirty Harry pictures, as Canby and many other critics would observe, was to make visible "certain disturbing aspects" of the Dirty Harry character. Specifically, the cop in the film has the same psychological problem, a fear of women, as the rapist-killer, who functions as the cop's double or *doppelganger* (see Hoberman 1984). Many viewers also commented on the strength and independence of the film's major female character—the rape counselor played by Genevieve Bujold, who ably assists the Eastwood character in tracking down the killer. As reviewers pointed out, she is also responsive to the cop's own personal problems. "When these two get together," said David Denby, "I feared we might hear a hammy male chauvinist-feminist debate, but the movie is smarter than that. Bujold, authoritative and tender as always, finds this suffering man rather touching—another movie with Eastwood and she might bring something remarkable out of him" (Denby 1984b).

In sum, for the critics *Tightrope* was proof that Eastwood was the model genre filmmaker, respectful of the conventions of genre yet bold enough to rework them, with sometimes dramatic results. When reexamining his earlier work, critics would discover that Eastwood had been doing these things for some time—intermittently parodying his macho image in films such as *Bronco Billy* (1980) and including in most of his films strong and independent female characters. Through interviews with the press, Eastwood would make sure that the critics spotted these continuities running through his films.

With his 1988 film *Bird,* about legendary jazz saxophonist Charlie Parker, critics would agree that Eastwood had finally transcended genre altogether. Only then was a critical consensus reached that Eastwood was indeed a serious artist. Crucial to the film's success were Eastwood's promotional activities, which helped nourish the view that *Bird* was a non-genre film. Eastwood carefully promoted the film to maximize its chances of being judged an art film. It competed in the Cannes Film Festival, with Forest Whitaker winning the best-actor award; it opened the New York Film Festival; and, a few weeks before the film's national release, it was announced that two film archives had been set up to preserve Eastwood's work—one at the Museum of Modern Art which would hold the original prints of his films, starting with *Play Misty for*

Me, and the other at Wesleyan University Cinema Archives which would preserve production materials and other papers and memorabilia relating to his career. The nearly unanimous acclaim that *Bird* received from American critics strongly suggests that for a film to be perceived as a truly great one, it must, in the vast majority of cases, be seen as having moved beyond genre. Indeed, many of the reviews of *Bird* attempted to demonstrate just that. Consider, for example, *Village Voice* critic J. Hoberman's enthusiastic review, which emphasized how *Bird* was more in the style of an avant-garde art work than simply a contemporary version of an old-fashioned Warner Bros.-styled bio-picture. To support his claim, Hoberman attempted to establish that the film's subject matter— how popular culture through Charlie Parker and his jazz associates "produced its first avant-garde," was highly self-reflexive. Did Eastwood, one of Hollywood's most successful filmmakers, see himself *via Bird* joining the ranks of the avant-garde (Hoberman 1988)?

For Hoberman, the film contained many more perverse reflections and inversions on Eastwood's career as well. For example, *Bird's* Parker is "spontaneous," "self-destructive," "dependent," and "explosive"— the antithesis, one might say, of Eastwood, who has the reputation of having everything under control. In a more recent film, *White Hunter, Black Heart* (1990), Eastwood is less obliquely self-conscious, for his subject matter is no less than cinema itself. Here he plays a director modeled after John Huston, whose persona was romantic, impulsive, and extravagant, another character at odds with the Eastwood persona, which is pragmatic, controlled, and penny-pinching (see Kehr 1990). Like De Palma with *Casualties of War* (1989), Eastwood had come to realize that the drive for artistic respectability might begin with a genre property but to actually achieve and maintain that respectability one must move beyond the generic.

How applicable are these findings to other art worlds? There are numerous examples of popular artists and performers in other entertainment industries such as popular music, who after achieving celebrity status, sought acceptance of their work from the more elitist critics. American composer George Gershwin, once known principally for his Broadway show tunes, wrote his opera *Porgy and Bess* with that objective in mind. More recently, Barbra Streisand has tried her hand with the classical repertoire, achieving a mixed critical response.

Unlike the more audience-oriented media such as commercial filmmaking and pop music, classical music and other more creator-oriented art forms appeal to a more highly educated and elite public. Yet within the art world of classical music there are the familiar divisions between "serious" and "less serious" composers, compositions, and performers. There are musicians who appeal exclusively to audiences knowledgeable about their specialty and others who attract wider audiences, including those not typically involved in consuming classical music but who have heard about the performer by virtue of his or her reputation as a celebrity. George Gershwin, Arturo Toscanini, Jascha Heifitz, Luciano Pavarotti, Leonard Bernstein, Van Cliburn, and Vladimir Horowitz were all eventually successful in straddling different taste cultures (see Gans 1974). In a recent study of Arturo Toscanini, Joseph Horowitz traces how the U.S. marketing of the Italian-born conductor was aimed at a more middlebrow than elite audience. In the process of appealing to a wider public, as the author points out, Toscanini's artistry was watered down and vulgarized (Horowitz 1987). More analogous to Hitchcock are those classical music performers such as Vladimir Horowitz and Van Cliburn, who early in their careers established broad popular appeal but who were rarely acknowledged as serious artists by the critical establishment.

Russian-born pianist Vladimir Horowitz (1903–89) carved out a reputation history which in many ways resembled Hitchcock's. While still in his twenties, Horowitz developed the reputation as one of the most electrifying concert pianists of all time, a reputation he never had to relinquish in the course of a long career. At the same time, throughout his career, critics were reluctant to rank him among serious musicians. Concerned about his critical reputation, Horowitz attempted on many different occasions to improve his standing among the serious music critics. In examining Horowitz's reputation history against the background of our discussion of Hitchcock, I will highlight how the management of Horowitz's reputation was affected by features peculiar to the medium of solo classical performance. In so doing, I hope to suggest what a "replication" of the present study might look like transposed to an art world other than film.

Specializing in the romantic literature (especially the works of Chopin, Liszt, Schumann, and his compatriot Rachmaninoff) Horowitz is said to have been capable of achieving instant rapport with an audience. Before he turned thirty, there were Horowitz fan clubs throughout Russia and Europe. While critics marvelled at the digital dexterity, the thunderous sonorities, and dramatic intensity of his playing, many had reservations about his artistic depth. As evidence of his artistic shallowness, critics pointed not only to the superficiality of many of his interpretations of the compositions in the romantic piano literature but also to his decision not to perform more serious compositions, especially the works of such staples of the Germanic classical literature as Hayden, Mozart, Beethoven, and Schubert, echoing the pre-auteur criticism of Hitchcock's innocuous "little thrillers." While extremely rare, Horowitz's performances of the classical Germanic literature were generally not praised by the critics.

After settling in the United States in 1939, Horowitz attempted to maintain his celebrity status with classical music audiences while, at the same time, winning the respect of the more serious critics, paralleling Hitchcock's efforts in the 1960s, but with one important difference. Unlike Hitchcock, who always presented himself publicly as a popular showman, Horowitz often presented himself before the public as a serious, searching, and discriminating artist.

Between 1934 and 1938, Horowitz had stopped concertizing altogether and was uneasy about returning. "After a five-year absence from the concert platform in the United States and only a modest roster of European appearances in 1938 and 1939," says Horowitz's biographer Glenn Plaskin, "Horowitz was nervous about the upcoming season" (1983, 201). To enhance his reputation, which had suffered somewhat during the period of his "retirement," Horowitz's manager, Arthur Judson, issued press releases prepared by his publicity staff at Columbia management, projecting Horowitz as a considerably more mature artist than he had been before his retirement: "Horowitz is still in his thirties, a simple, natural person, without affectation, who has traveled a long way from the very young man who loved loud ties, luxurious bathrobes and elaborate automobiles" (quoted in Plaskin 1983, 201). The "new" Horowitz was portrayed not only as a family man (husband and father) but also a collector of fine art (Picasso, Rouault, Pissarro) and a connoisseur of literature (Racine, Molière, Tolstoy). Another of his propagandists was New York Times critic Howard Taubman, "whose masterstroke," according to Toscanini biographer Joseph Horowitz, "was to make Horowitz as much like 'Toscanini' as possible" (Horowitz 1987, 384). In a 1948 article on Horowitz for the New York Times Magazine, Taubman wrote: "The wild volatile virtuoso of 20 years ago has become one of the most mature, responsible musicians." In Taubman's view, Horowitz had achieved "objectivity about his performances," an outgrowth of his newly acquired belief in the supremacy of the composer. Shortly after Taubman's article appeared, Horowitz and

Toscanini collaborated in a performance of Brahm's musically demanding second piano concerto. A critic for *Time* magazine characterized the event as a concert to remember, noting that listeners "had lately found a new maturity and depth—if not real warmth—in the playing of Vladimir Horowitz."

On the other hand, Horowitz's habit, especially during the forties and early fifties, of closing his recitals with one of his flashy and fiercely difficult arrangements of a popular classical work such as the Liszt Hungarian Rhapsody no. 15 contradicted his posturings as a serious artist. (Hitchcock's detractors had often felt that his bravura suspense sequences in such films as *The Birds* undermined any interest he may have had in making a serious statement about the human condition.) Horowitz's most famous arrangement, which he often presented as an encore during the war years, was not based on a strictly classical piece at all but on John Philip Sousa's march, "The Stars and Stripes Forever." As Plaskin reports, Horowitz's audiences "were likely to be restless during Scarlatti, Bach-Busoni, Schumann, or Mendelssohn, keenly anticipating the moment when, as one writer put it, 'the characteristic sound and fury would be turned loose [and] Horowitz would stop being respectful of the classics and start being his unafraid self'" (Plaskin 1983, 248).

The inconsistency between his style of public performance and public image weakened Horowitz's efforts through the forties to improve his artistic reputation among the serious music critics. Indeed, throughout this period, the press attacked Horowitz for catering to the lowest common denominator of taste. As B. H. Haggin of the *Nation* put it, "one of the instrumentalists I stopped going to hear was Horowitz, whose prodigious mastery of the piano was not enough to keep me from being bored beyond endurance by the musical limitations evident in the program" (Plaskin 1983, 247).

Frustrated with his reputation as "an acrobat," Horowitz decided for his 1957 silver jubilee recital to program one of the most musically challenging works in the classical piano repertoire, the great Schubert posthumous Sonata in B-flat major. Few critics, however, were impressed with his performance. In fact, most New York reviewers considered the performance as "an instance of temperamental miscasting" (*Saturday Review,* 26 December 1953; see Plaskin 1983, 271). That is, Horowitz's virtuosity and overripe sonorities had corrupted Schubert's classical proportions and design. As the critic for the *Saturday Review* put it, in order to play the piece in a classical style, Horowitz "would have to find a way of arising on a given morning, reducing all the gradations of his internal amplifying system, like the dials on a machine, for the impending occasion." The poor critical reception of the jubilee recital at Carnege Hall contributed to Horowitz's decision to take another sabbatical from the concert stage. Little did he realize that his second retirement would last for twelve years.

Horowitz's long periods of inactivity as a live performer call attention to differences in the meaning of career interruption for a film director and a solo concert artist. The dictum, "You're only as good as your last film," is a fact of life for film directors, including the most successful (see Faulkner 1983). Even Hitchcock lost some of his autonomy at Universal following the commercial failure of *Marnie*. Without a new project in the works, it becomes virtually impossible for a director to publicly promote his or her career. We recall that it was within the context of promoting his latest film that Hitchcock during the 1960s and early 1970s sought to reshape his reputation. Like most movie directors and other creative personnel within the film industry who are employed on a freelance basis, a classical solo performer's career is often punctuated by long periods of inactivity. Among less-established performers the absence of bookings in major cities can quickly bring a halt to a promising concert career. Long absences from concertizing are also fairly common among star performers, arising from psychological problems related to stage fright and from physical ailments resulting from the routines of practice. Some impaired performers take up teaching. (Horowitz took on a few students during his "sabbatical" years.) Others hope to maintain their public reputation as performers primarily through recordings. Such was the case with Horowitz.

We have seen how Hitchcock used the television medium to promote his motion pictures as well as to shape audience expectations about differences between his TV show and his feature films. Whether he emphasized the similarities or differences between his TV and film work depended on the type of film he was working on at the time. With a movie like *North by Northwest,* Hitchcock emphasized how much grander in scale were his movies. With other films, like *Psycho* or *The Wrong Man,* he designed them to resemble his TV work and used that in promoting them (recall Hitchcock's personal appearance at the beginning of *The Wrong Man*). Like television for Hitchcock, recordings for Horowitz were also tied to various strategies for managing his reputation.

Horowitz once told an interviewer that the reason he decided to resume his recording career was to remain visible to his public, "I said to myself, 'OK. I will do it so the public will know I am not dead or something is wrong with me'" (Plaskin 1983, 283). However, his choice of esoteric repertoire for his RCA recordings during the early years of his "second" retirement strongly suggest that he also hoped that these recordings would enhance his standing with serious critics and musicians.

Horowitz's first recording was devoted solely to the works of Muzio Clementi, a relatively obscure eighteenth-century Italian composer who, as Horowitz attempted to demonstrate with this recording, was an important influence on Beethoven. Next, Horowitz decided to focus on the works of another relatively unknown musician, the nineteenth-century Russian composer, Alexander Scriabin. He attempted to show that Scriabin's temperament was reminiscent of Chopin's, a composer who, like Scriabin, wrote almost exclusively for solo piano. Here was another instance of Horowitz engaged in adventurous programming that seemed geared more to serious critics and connoisseurs of unusual keyboard music than to the general public. As Horowitz put it, Scriabin's music was "difficult for the general public even though it's Romantic. This is supersensuous, superromantic, supermysterious. Everything is 'super'; it is all overboard. From the spiritual and emotional point of view, it is one of the most difficult chunks of music in the literature" (Plaskin 1983, 287; see Dubal 1984, 195).

While his choice of repertoire for these two RCA recordings impressed the critics, it caused great concern among RCA executives, who wanted Horowitz to record more popular pieces such as George Gershwin's "Rhapsody in Blue." Horowitz refused.[7] His contract with RCA about to expire in 1961, Horowitz decided to sign a lucrative three-year contract with Columbia Masterworks.

During this phase of his career, recordings would function differently than they did ten years earlier. By this time, Horowitz had been absent from the concert stage for almost a decade. One of his chief worries was the existence now of a younger generation of concertgoers who had never heard him. If he was ever to resume his concert career, he would have to inform this new generation about his art. Unlike the more cerebral pianists such as Rudolph Serkin or Arthur Schnabel, Horowitz had never prepared recitals featuring the works of a single composer. With an eye to the youth market, Horowitz and Columbia agreed that Horowitz's first recording for them should spotlight a varied repertoire, mirroring the general format of his live recitals. His choice of repertory for the album delighted Columbia. As the director of artists and repertoire at Columbia Masterworks put it, "One look and I knew that he had chosen cannily, with an eye on the largest public. There was something for everyone who knew his work—Rachmaninoff, Chopin, Schumann, and Liszt—a perfect recital program for the home and maybe, just maybe, for the concert hall" (Plaskin 1983, 319).[8]

When he resumed his concert career in the late sixties and seventies, Horowitz continued to make recordings that would motivate those purchasing them to want to hear him live. One of his strategies involved releasing recordings of his "live" concerts. In addition to his performances, these recordings also featured the audience's thunderous applause, which Horowitz hoped would lure listeners to his live recitals. While Horowitz promoted these recordings as historical documents, the truth is that many had been "doctored." One example must suffice. In 1976 at a special Carnegie Hall concert commemorating the fiftieth anniversary of his American debut, Horowitz performed the Rachmaninoff third piano concerto with Eugene Ormandy and the New York Philharmonic. This "historic" performance was recorded and released a few months later. According to a number of observers, Horowitz's playing that night was extremely uneven with more than a sprinkling of wrong notes, irregular tempi, and banging. While some of his lapses are documented on the recording, many others had been surgically removed and replaced by the cleanly executed passages which Horowitz had rerecorded in the studio. Horowitz's record-buying public knew none of this. The promotion for the album misled them into believing that this was an authentic replication of Horowitz's golden jubilee concert—mistakes and all.

Hitchcock's strategies in the 1960s to improve his standing among the critics came up against the realist aesthetic, which temporarily nullified his efforts. Only with the shift to the auteur perspective in the late 1960s would Hitchcock finally be accepted as an artist. The prevailing critical climate also influenced Horowitz's critical reputation. In the performance of classical music, a recurring aesthetic issue is the relationship between the performer and the composer. Until the 1930s, classical performance was dominated by a romantic style which emphasized the emotional content of music more than adherence to the printed page. Performers and critics alike valued highly personalized interpretations or re-creations over those claiming fidelity to the text and subservience to the composer's intentions. By the thirties and forties, however, this romantic performance aesthetic had been supplanted by one which

32. A scene from *Halloween*, the prototypical slasher film (1978).
Museum of Modern Art Film Stills Archive.

33. An ad for *The Bedroom Window* described the film as "a romantic thriller in the tradition of the master of suspense."
Academy of Motion Picture Arts and Sciences.

34. Hitchcock legacy exploited in trade advertising for
De Palma's *Sisters* (1973).

35. De Palma in a publicity still for *Dressed to Kill*. This photograph was distributed with a caption heralding his "world-wide acclaim for macabre and suspenseful films" (1980).

Museum of Modern Art Film Stills Archive. © Orion Pictures Corporation.

36. Humphrey Bogart and Lauren Bacall in Howard Hawks's *The Big Sleep* (1946).

Museum of Modern Art Film Stills Archive.

37. Theater display for Frank Capra's *It's a Wonderful Life* (1946).
Wesleyan University Film Archive.

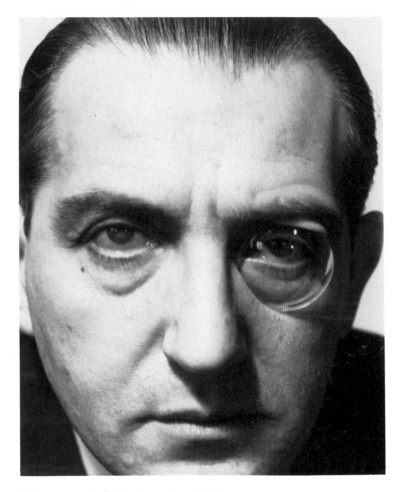

38. A monocled Fritz Lang (ca. 1930).
Museum of Modern Art Film Stills Archive.

39. Clint Eastwood meets the press in Paris after being awarded the medal of Chevalier des Arts et des Lettres (1985).

Bettmann Archive

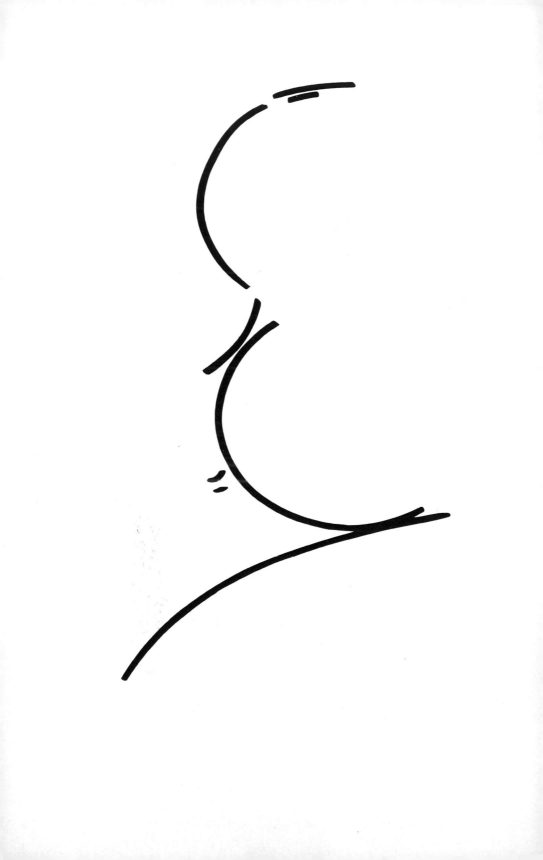

stressed anti-romantic literalism and textual fidelity. Now it was believed that the true goal of performance was fidelity to the composer's intent. Toscanini and his popularizers in the United States were major exponents of this view of faithfulness to the classical scores. In this climate, Horowitz and other romantic stylists were frequently discredited for their exaggerations and distortions of the printed page. One strategy employed in the management of Horowitz's reputation during the forties, as we have seen, was to characterize him as a performer who served the composer rather than himself. Reviewing one of Horowitz's recitals in the forties, *New York Times* critic Olin Downes, a champion of both Horowitz and Toscanini, characterized Horowitz as one of the "few musicians today before the public who so reverently and objectively approach the music of masters they interpret" (*New York Times,* 4 February 1947).

Thirty years later, critics were decrying what they saw as the tendency of conservatories to turn out unimaginative performers blindly striving for textual fidelity in performance at the expense of highly personalized interpretation.[9] As part of their reaction against this tendency, critics singled out Horowitz and only a handful of other classical performers as fiercely independent artists who, in the words of *New York Times* music critic Donal Henahan, have "asserted their rights as re-creative artists who challenge the composer's right to control every detail of the score" (5 August 1990). Horowitz, in the recording notes to his next to last recording, presents himself precisely that way—as a musician who from the beginning of his career "considered music of *all* periods romantic." Of course, there is "an objective, intellectual component" in musical structure, says Horowitz, "but when it comes to performance, what is required is not interpretation but a process of subjective re-creation" (Horowitz 1989). While highly personalized interpretations were always part of the Horowitz arsenal, his extraordinary technical accuracy, especially earlier in his career, sometimes obscured the fact that his basic approach to piano playing was diametrically opposed to the canon of textual fidelity.

Like Hitchcock, Horowitz's towering reputation proved to be a difficult act to follow, especially during the 1950s and 1960s when, according to critic Harold Schonberg, "all the world's pianists wanted to be Vladimir Horowitz" (*New York Times,* 12 November 1989). If Horowitz recorded a relatively obscure work like Schumann's "Kreisleriana," within a year or so, it would seem, every young pianist was programming the piece. While many would attempt to match

Horowitz's performance in terms of technical accuracy, virtuosity, phrasing, and coloration, none succeeded, as critics of that time were quick to point out.

During the fifties, the contemporary pianist most often associated with the Horowitz legacy was his pupil Byron Janis. As with De Palma's infatuation with Hitchcock, Janis's association with Horowitz was a mixed blessing for his career. While the publicity he gained as Horowitz's prized pupil enabled him to launch a concert career without entering competitions, his playing often came under attack for being too imitative of his mentor's. Like other pianists of his era, Janis had difficulty matching Horowitz's sheer accuracy, especially at high speeds. Today, there are commentators who would maintain that a whole generation of American pianists was damaged by choosing Horowitz as a role model (see, e.g., Horowitz 1987).

In recent years, as we have seen, a number of critics came to view Horowitz as "the last Romantic," linking him to the romantic performance tradition and its idea of the power of the re-creative artist to communicate profoundly with audiences. Part of the Horowitz legacy in the years to come may be to upgrade the reputation of the romantic performance style, just as, in a limited way, Hitchcock's artistic reputation improved the stature of the thriller genre.

This book contributes to the ongoing debate concerning whether an artist's fame is earned or unearned. One view argues that an artist's reputation is based on works. If an artist is famous, it is because of enduring qualities intrinsic to the person's work. For example, Shakespeare scholarship has repeatedly invoked the test-of-time criterion—hundreds of years in the limelight—as irrefutable proof of Shakespeare's greatness as a playwright. In much the same way, Richard Posner (1990) has recently argued that Benjamin Cardozo's reputation as one of the greatest jurists of all time stemmed primarily from the rhetorical or "literary" brilliance of his writings and only incidentally from factors extrinsic to his work such as his attractive personality, his attempt to cultivate the good opinion of others, or his appointment to the U.S. Supreme Court. Using a citation methodology, Posner shows that Cardozo's opinions "were not cited [by legal scholars] appreciably more frequently (relative to contemporaneous opinions by his colleagues) after he was appointed to the Supreme Court" (1990, 128), thus supporting the view that Cardozo became eminent because of the intrinsic merits of his work, not because of any aura or "halo effect" emanating from his tenure on the Supreme Court.

The more standard approach to studying reputation and reception these days, however, is to show how extrinsic factors, usually of political import, cause certain works and artists to become canonized and others to be demoted or ignored. In his wildly irreverent study, *Reinventing Shakespeare*, Gary Taylor (1989) argues, for example, that Shakespeare's fame was largely if not entirely unearned—a function of an unusual series of historical accidents such as the rise of Great Britain as an imperialist power. Therefore, as Taylor suggests, Shakespeare's future claim to fame would be very much in question should the English language be replaced as the dominant language of our international culture (see also Tuchman 1989, on Victorian novelists; and Rodden 1989, on George Orwell). Unlike these earlier studies, my work led me to determine which of a number of nontextual factors—changing aesthetic codes, self-promotion, and sponsorship by others—was the most important in increasing Hitchcock's stature as a filmmaker.

I found changing aesthetic codes to be the most important of these considerations, particularly the rise of auteur criticism. When auteurism became the dominant aesthetic discourse among film critics in the late sixties, Hitchcock's self-promotional efforts succeeded in ways inconceivable in the pre-auteur era. According to the auteur viewpoint advanced by Sarris and practiced by numerous others, all the works of a major auteur, including even minor efforts, are more interesting than the best work from a lesser director. That is, acceptance of the auteur view of Hitchcock as a serious artist produced its own kind of halo effect. Under that condition, a seriously flawed Hitchcock film like *Family Plot* received generally enthusiastic reviews while many of his earlier works were reappraised upward. On the other hand, a Hitchcock work from the pre-auteur period such as *Vertigo*, which a significant number of critics would subsequently claim as one of his masterpieces, was dismissed by many early critics on the grounds that it failed to measure up to the standards set by Hitchcock in his great English thrillers from the late 1930s.

Other findings from my study also suggest the important role that textual elements play in making and sustaining an artist's reputation. I would argue that Hitchcock's reputation has survived for over sixty-five years partly because of the great range of his work but also because many of his films have been able to sustain a diversity of interpretations. In his study of Cardozo's reputation, Posner speculates about those textual qualities of a reputee's work that help sustain a reputation even after the reputee's death. "Posthumous reputation," says Posner, "is facilitated by the generality, variety, and ambiguity of the reputee's work, or in short by its adaptability to social, political, and cultural change" (1990, 60–61). Among those, he asserts, whose extraordinary fame rests to a "significant extent" on the variety and ambiguity of their work are Shakespeare, Kafka, Nietzsche, Wittgenstein, Orwell, and Oliver Wendell Holmes. The wide diversity of response to Hitchcock's films strongly indicates that his work too deserves high marks for variety, ambiguity, and, even, contradictoriness. For example, the broad range of interpretations elicited by *Marnie* provides compelling support for this argument.

My study also chronicles an interesting period in the history of taste. The "great divide" in the history of Hitchcock's reputation is the sixties, roughly coincident with the historical turning point described by Andreas Huyssen (1986) in his widely discussed book, *After the Great Divide*. Associated with the rise of French, British, and American auteurism in the sixties was the emergence of a new aesthetic in Western society, what various commentators have called "the postmodern." According to Huyssen, "the most significant trends within postmodernism have challenged modernism's relentless hostility to mass culture" (1986, 188). The pop movement in American art, the literary criticism of Susan Sontag and Leslie Fiedler, and the architectural writings of Robert Venturi all involved, according to Huyssen, a break with high modernism and an "expousal of the commercial vernaculur of consumer culture" (1986, 187; see also Naremore 1990). Yet, as James Naremore puts it, these events maintained a "sometimes baffling mixture of elitism and populism." Whereas Sarris applied high-culture criteria to Hollywood pop films, Kael, by contrast, attempted to assess pop films from a pop perspective. Kael's championing of De Palma over Hitchcock during the seventies and eighties revealed the extent to which her aesthetic orientation was compatible with a postmodern sensibility, while Sarris's defense of Hitchcock over De Palma revealed how much closer Sarris's aesthetic was to the precepts of modernism than of postmodernism. The cultural significance of these developments in film aesthetics, as in the other arts, is that they reflect a growing cultural eclecticism in American life as the old cultural categories—"high" versus "low"—have lost their meaning for many artists and critics. In her defense of this cultural shift, Susan Sontag wrote, "it is important to understand that the affection which many younger artists and intellectuals feel for the popular arts is not a new philistinism (as has so often been charged) or a species of anti-intellectualism. . . . It reflects a new, more open way of looking at the world, our world. It does not mean the renunciation of all standards. . . . The point is that there are . . . new standards of beauty and style and taste. The new sensibility is defiantly pluralistic" (Sontag [1966] 1982, 302–4; see also Levine 1988, 243–56). This view is compatible with Kael's aesthetic stated in her classic essay "Trash, Art, and the Movies."

The ups and downs of Hitchcock's marketing campaigns, as reported here, have implications for the study of the reception of advertising. Hitchcock's self-promotional activities powerfully illustrate how difficult it is to determine the effectiveness of an advertising campaign for a film. Throughout his career, Hitchcock had the reputation of being the most effective self-promoter in the film business. Yet, as we have seen, there were limits to what even he could accomplish. Hitchcock's ill-fated marketing campaign for *The Wrong Man* and *Vertigo* illustrate that the conditions of advertising reception are complex and that, therefore, assessing the effectiveness of an advertising campaign requires a multivariate approach. A simple stimulus-response model will just not do (cf. Staiger 1990).

The meaning of an art work, as this book has documented, is the result of an ongoing exchange between the art work and the receiver. As the receivers change, so does the meaning. While a number of film scholars (e.g., Brown 1982; Leff 1987; Schatz 1988, 271–94, 381–407) have emphasized the contributions of individual collaborators in their discussions of specific Hitchcock films, I have accented instead how the "meaning" of a Hitchcock film was also a product of an ongoing exchange between Hitchcock and his audience of fans and critics, especially during the fifties and sixties when he solidified his reputation as the master of suspense.[10]

This study, therefore, is relevant to the debate, mentioned earlier, about the role of the audience in popular-culture creations. According to the reflection perspective, Hollywood's audience is sovereign because, by choosing the films it attends, the audience reveals its preferences to the Hollywood studios which, in turn, produce films reflecting audience desires. By contrast, the art-world orientation maintains that the audience's influence has less impact or authority since it is filtered through conflicting perceptions of the audience's future tastes, interorganizational decisions regarding expanding and contracting markets, and other in-house conflicts endemic to the film business. As to this debate, my study supports aspects of both viewpoints since my findings on Hitchcock and his audience (including critics) suggest a reciprocal relationship.[11] As we have seen, Hitchcock and his publicity machine appeared to be successful in the fifties in shaping audience expectations regarding his genre of film—the thriller. However, when Hitchcock's films deviated sharply from the formula he taught them, audiences chose to stay home despite his efforts to persuade them otherwise. While Hitchcock was generally successful with the mainstream American reviewers, especially during the fifties, he was less so with the more intellectual critics. Although he ultimately achieved and sustained the stature and reputation he sought in the film art world, Hitchcock's attempts (like Horowitz's) to manipulate his public and the serious critics were frequently resisted, as in the failure of *The Wrong Man, Vertigo, The Birds,* and *Marnie* to generate the response he desired.

The aesthetic contract that Hitchcock established with audiences and critics, as we have seen, shifted over the course of his career. Tracing that contract over time has been my strategy for estimating the strength of Hitchcock's commitment to making films in the thriller genre. In contrast to other genre studies which ignore altogether how genre films are disseminated in the marketplace, mine has called attention to the role that journalists play in bringing such films and their categorization to the attention of audiences. Part of Hitchcock's genius, unlike De Palma's, was his ability through much of his career to maintain a good working relationship with the media. His reputation history provides a vantage point from which to see clearly the reputation trajectories of other filmmakers such as Clint Eastwood, Steven Spielberg, and Woody Allen, who, like Hitchcock, have straddled the line between popular genre movies and films with a more elitist intent.

THE FILMS OF
ALFRED HITCHCOCK

SILENT FEATURES (1925–1929)

The Pleasure Garden (A Gainsborough-Emelka Picture, prod. 1925/
rel. 1927).
The Mountain Eagle (A Gainsborough-Emelka Picture, prod. 1925/rel. 1927).
The Lodger: A Story of the London Fog (A Gainsborough-Emelka Picture,
prod. 1926/rel. 1927).
Downhill (A Gainsborough Picture, prod./rel. 1927).
Easy Virtue (A Gainsborough Picture, prod./rel. 1927).
The Ring (A British International Picture, prod./rel. 1927).
The Farmer's Wife (A British International Picture, prod. 1927/rel. 1928).
Champagne (A British International Picture, prod./rel. 1928).
The Manxman (A British International Picture, prod. 1928/rel. 1929).

SOUND FEATURES (1929–1976)

Blackmail (A British International Picture, prod./rel. 1929).
Juno and the Paycock (A British International Picture, prod./rel. 1930).
Murder! (A British International Picture, prod./rel. 1930).
The Skin Game (A British International Picture, prod. 1930–1931/rel. 1931).
Number Seventeen (A British International Picture, prod. 1931/rel. 1932).
Rich and Strange (A British International Picture, prod./rel. 1932).
Waltzes from Vienna (A Tom Arnold Production, prod./rel. 1933).
The Man Who Knew Too Much (A Gaumont-British Picture, prod./rel. 1934).
The 39 Steps (A Gaumont-British Picture, prod./rel. 1935).
Secret Agent (A Gaumont-British Picture, prod. 1935/rel. 1936).
Sabotage (A Gaumont-British Picture, prod./rel. 1936).
Young and Innocent (A Gaumont-British Picture, prod. 1937/rel. 1938).
The Lady Vanishes (A Gaumont-British Picture, prod. 1937/rel. 1938).
Jamaica Inn (An Erich Pommer Production, prod. 1938/rel. 1939).
Rebecca (A Production of the Selznick Studio, prod. 1939/rel. 1940).
Foreign Correspondent (A Wanger Production, prod./rel. 1940).
Mr. and Mrs. Smith (An RKO Radio Picture, prod. 1940/rel. 1941).
Suspicion (An RKO Radio Picture, prod./rel. 1941).

This list has been adapted from Spoto 1983.

Saboteur (A Frank Lloyd Production for Universal, prod./rel. 1942).

Shadow of a Doubt (A Jack H. Skirball Production for Universal, prod. 1942/rel. 1943).

Lifeboat (A 20th Century-Fox Picture, prod. 1943/rel. 1944).

Spellbound (A Selznick International Picture, prod. 1944/rel. 1945).

Notorious (An RKO Radio Picture, prod. 1945–1946/rel. 1946).

The Paradine Case (A David O. Selznick/Vanguard Film, prod. 1946–1947/rel. 1947).

Rope (A Transatlantic Picture, prod./rel. 1948).

Under Capricorn (A Transatlantic Picture, prod. 1948/rel. 1949).

Stage Fright (A Warner Bros.-First National Picture, prod. 1949/rel. 1950).

Strangers on a Train (A Warner Bros.-First National Picture, prod. 1950/rel. 1951).

I Confess (A Warner Bros.-First National Picture, prod. 1952/rel. 1953).

Dial "M" for Murder (A Warner Bros.-First National Picture, prod. 1953/rel. 1954).

Rear Window (A Paramount Release, prod. 1953/rel. 1954).

To Catch a Thief (A Paramount Picture, prod. 1954/rel. 1955).

The Trouble with Harry (A Paramount Release, prod. 1954/rel. 1955).

The Man Who Knew Too Much (A Paramount Release, prod. 1955/rel. 1956).

The Wrong Man (A Warner Bros.-First National Picture, prod./rel. 1956).

Vertigo (A Paramount Release, prod. 1957/rel. 1958).

North by Northwest (An MGM Picture, prod. 1958/rel. 1959).

Psycho (A Paramount Release, prod. 1959–1960/rel. 1960).

The Birds (A Universal Release, prod. 1962/rel. 1963).

Marnie (A Universal Release, prod. 1963–1964/rel. 1964).

Torn Curtain (A Universal Release, prod. 1965–1966/rel. 1966).

Topaz (A Universal Release, prod. 1968–1969/rel. 1969).

Frenzy (A Universal Release, prod. 1971/rel. 1972).

Family Plot (A Universal Release, prod. 1975/rel. 1976).

TELEVISION FILMS (1955–1962)

Unless otherwise noted, all were filmed for the series "Alfred Hitchcock Presents."

"Breakdown" (prod. Sept. 7–10, 1955; broadcast on CBS Nov. 13, 1955, as the 7th episode).

"Revenge" (prod. Sept. 15–17, 1955; broadcast on CBS Oct. 2, 1955, as the premier episode).

"The Case of Mr. Pelham" (prod. Oct. 7/8/10, 1955; broadcast on CBS Dec. 4, 1955, as the 10th episode).

"Back for Christmas" (prod. Jan. 13/14/16, 1956; broadcast on CBS Mar. 4, 1956, as the 23rd episode).

"Wet Saturday" (prod. Aug. 22–24 1956; broadcast on CBS Sept. 30, 1956 as the 40th episode).

"Mr. Blanchard's Secret" (prod. Oct. 18/19/22, 1956; broadcast on CBS Dec. 23, 1956, as the 52nd episode).

"One More Mile to Go" (prod. Jan. 9–11, 1957; broadcast on CBS Apr. 7, 1957, as the 67th episode).

"The Perfect Crime" (prod. July 17–19, 1957; broadcast on CBS Oct. 20, 1957, as the 81st episode).

"Four O'Clock" (prod. July 29–Aug. 2, 1957; broadcast on NBC Sept. 30, 1957 as the premier episode of the series "Suspicion").

"Lamb to the Slaughter" (prod. Feb. 18–19, 1958; broadcast on CBS Apr. 13, 1958, as the 106th episode of "Alfred Hitchcock Presents").

"Dip in the Pool" (prod. Apr. 15–16, 1958; broadcast on CBS June 1, 1958, as the 113th episode of the series).

"Poison" (prod. Aug. 21–22, 1958; broadcast on CBS Oct. 5, 1958, as the 118th episode).

"Banquo's Chair" (prod. Mar. 25–26, 1959; broadcast on CBS May 3, 1959, as the 146th episode).

"Arthur" (prod. July 7–9, 1959; broadcast on CBS Sept. 27, 1959, as the 154th episode).

"The Crystal Trench" (prod. Aug. 25–27, 1959, broadcast on CBS Oct. 4, 1959, as the 155th episode).

"Incident at a Corner" (prod. Feb. 8–12/15–17, 1960; broadcast on NBC Apr. 5, 1960 as the 27th episode of the series "Ford Startime").

"Mrs. Bixby and the Colonel's Coat" (prod. Aug. 17–19, 1960; broadcast on NBC Sept. 27, 1960 as the 191st episode of the series "Alfred Hitchcock Presents").

"The Horseplayer" (prod. Jan. 4–6, 1961; broadcast on NBC Mar. 14, 1961 as the 212th episode).

"Bang! You're Dead" (prod. July 25–27, 1961; broadcast on NBC Oct. 17, 1961 as the 230th episode).

"I Saw the Whole Thing" (prod. July 23–27, 1962; broadcast on NBC Oct. 11, 1962 as the 4th episode of the series "The Alfred Hitchcock Hour").

NOTES

1. Of course, Gitlin identifies even more closely with the "polemical" or critical sociologies associated with the Frankfurt school.

2. For a good overview of the art-world (or institutional) orientation to art, see Danto (1964), Dickie (1975), Carroll (1979), and Wolff (1983). See also DiMaggio's (1982) historically grounded and sociologically insightful examination of the institutionalization of so-called high culture in the United States.

3. For a reader-oriented approach similar to the one I have adopted for this study, see Bennett (1982) and Bennett and Woollacott (1987). Bennett (1982) emphasizes how meaning derived from a text (including a film) is conditioned by "everything that has been said or written about the text," such as advertisements, reviews, other texts of the same author or genre, and so forth.

4. For key texts on reader-oriented literary criticism, see Culler (1981); Fish (1980); Barthes (1977); Eco (1977); Jauss (1982); and Iser (1978). Suleiman and Crosman (1980) and Tompkins (1980) have produced excellent anthologies of reader-oriented literary criticism. For applications to film and television, see Allen and Gomery (1985) on film and Allen (1987) on television.

5. The concept of "realization" was developed by Wolfgang Iser (1978, 68–9), one of the most influential theoreticians of reader-oriented literary criticism. According to Iser, the realization of meaning involves a dynamic interaction between the reader and the text. "The text," says Iser, "can never be grasped as a whole—only as a series of changing viewpoints, each one restricted in itself and so necessitating further perspectives. This is the process by which the reader 'realizes' an overall situation" (1978, 68). Compare Allen and Gomery (1985, 74–76).

6. Jauss (1982) is the author of the concept of "horizon of expectations." For a good sociologically-informed account of Jauss's position, see Swingewood (1987). The concept of "horizon of expectations," says Swingewood, points to the fact that "aesthetic value is not the result of a reader's state of mind but is determined by historical/social/cultural elements such as knowledge of genres, antecedent art-forms and themes, and distinctions between poetic and ordinary language" (1987, 143).

7. On the other hand, several critics, including John Simon, have pointed to De Palma's many "borrowings" from Hitchcock as evidence of how "unfaith-

ful" De Palma has been to his early talent. Said Simon, "De Palma has been a critics' darling ever since his early irreverently anomic movies made on a shoestring and wildly diverting [sic]. But fidelity to De Palma's early talent from the critics seems absurd when one considers how unfaithful to it De Palma himself has been" (Review of *Carrie, New York Magazine,* 6 December 1976).

8. This assertion is based on an examination of reviews of the following Hitchcock spy films—*Saboteur* (1942), *Notorious* (1946), *The Man Who Knew Too Much* (1956), and *North by Northwest* (1959). (Collection of newspaper clippings of moving picture criticism, Lincoln Center Library for the Performing Arts, New York City.)

9. Before the 1930s, much of what was considered artistic had to do with stylistic or formal considerations (see Budd 1986; Lounsbury 1976). I am indebted to Janet Staiger for bringing these works to my attention.

TWO

1. Another influential film person who occupied a similar position, straddling the worlds of "film art" and entertainment, was film exhibitor Sidney Bernstein. A member of the British Film Society, Bernstein became both a business colleague and lifelong friend of Hitchcock's.

2. Already Hitchcock was developing the reputation of an "artistic maverick in a commercial jungle," who like the American director John Ford had "the ability to turn his hand to the assignments imposed upon him by the studio system," while at the same time "developing his own conception of cinema" (Ryall 1986, 88).

3. "As Montagu himself has said 'long titles especially came as an interruption to the sort of hypnotism of the silent film' . . . Film makers such as Murnau, for example, were trying to make films which abandoned the use of titles altogether and depended on the visual images to recount the narrative. The stress on the visual aspects of the film implied by the reduction of the titles is credited to Montagu yet Hitchcock himself understood narrative cinema in primarily visual terms and this aesthetic position becomes clearer in his attitude towards the introduction of sound in the late 1920s" (Ryall 1986, 89; see Montagu1972, 77).

4. These reviews reflected the prevailing critical discourse on film from the British point of view (see Rotha 1951).

5. Hitchcock kept a scrapbook of reviews, commentaries, and press releases relating to the 1927 release of *The Lodger* (see *The Lodger* Scrapbook, Hitchcock Collection).

6. To illustrate his point, Montagu mentioned a sequence from a film involving a husband, his wife, and her lover returning from the theater. Hitchcock "wanted to show the lover and the wife touching knees in the taxi. He showed a shot from above. But he used the wrong lens and you would have been viewing from a helicopter, if you'd had a helicopter in those days, with no roof on the

taxi and to my mind it destroyed the illusion entirely. I always used to quarrel with him on those sort of grounds but it didn't matter to him, everyone would have said, 'what a wonderful and original shot.' And he was right. As you could tell from Danston's audience questionnaire: 'Who is your favorite director?'— the only English director the public had heard of was Hitchcock. Most of the others were American names that had been publicised. The public generally did not know who directed the films they saw, but they had seen Hitchcock's name in the Press" (Montagu 1972, 80).

7. The popular and critical success of his post-1933 British thrillers, as Patricia Ferrara (1987, 79) has persuasively argued, also "kept him working in the genre" (see also Hark 1990, 9). Earlier, "the increasingly negative reception of Hitchcock's more downbeat B.I.P. films from 1930 to 1933," says Ferrara, had been "influential in pushing Hitchcock into light spy thrillers" (Ferrara 1987, 79).

8. Hitchcock continued to exploit his weight problem after settling in America (see, e.g., Creelman 1939; Hitchcock 1943; Johnson 1946; Skolsky 1948). During the making of *Lifeboat* (1943), for example, he had dieted, shedding nearly 100 pounds or roughly one-third of his original weight. Photos taken before and after were printed in a mock-up newspaper which constituted his cameo appearance in the film (see plate 5). When Hitchcock lost considerable weight, as he did during the mid-fifties, a number of feature stories appeared about his successful regimen of dieting. In one article, dated 11 November 1954, Hitchcock offered tips on how to effectively lose weight. The key to a successful diet, he explained, is to "spend your calories as though they're pocket money. If you have 100 calories to spend, better to spend them on half a broiled chicken than on a dish of ice cream" (Connolly 1954). Whenever Hitchcock started gaining weight again, as he did in the late fifties, stories would appear emphasizing that he was not really a big eater at all but that he suffered from low metabolism. In other words, the stories tried to convey that Hitchcock was not responsible for having been overweight most of his life.

9. On the other hand, as Schatz has pointed out, Selznick's experience with Hitchcock during the making of *Rebecca* made Selznick "acutely aware" that Hitchcock "was a filmmaker whose work he could not prepare, control, and reshape to suit his own tastes." Schatz describes how Hitchcock's ability to "cut with the camera" threatened Selznick's control over the final cut:

> The standard procedure of most directors was to shoot a "master scene," usually a wide shot including all the principal action in a given sequence, and then to "cover" the sequence from various angles in medium shots, medium close-ups, and tight shots. During the editing process the shots would be assembled and reassembled to satisfy the demands of dramatic, temporal, and spatial continuity. Thus the amount of "coverage" shot during production—often called "protection," for obvious reasons—

determined the range of options available during editing. Because Hitchcock so carefully conceived and preplanned his pictures, he shot very little coverage, getting only what he envisioned as essential to the final cut. (Schatz 1988, 283)

10. The considerable range of films that Hitchcock made in Hollywood during the 1940s also strongly supports the view that his earlier work in the thriller format during the mid-to-late 1930s was more out of necessity than personal conviction. While his forties output included a number of straightforward thrillers (*Foreign Correspondent*, 1940; *Suspicion*, 1941; *Saboteur*, 1942; and *Notorious*, 1946), it also included a screwball comedy (*Mr. and Mrs. Smith*, 1941), a costume drama (*Under Capricorn*, 1949), an antiwar film (*Lifeboat*, 1944), and a middlebrow theatrical adaptation (*Rope*, 1948).

11. While at Warner Bros., Hitchcock cultivated some important professional relationships (see Schatz 1988). A number of creative personnel he worked with there (e.g., cinematographer Robert Burke, who would work on all but one of Hitchcock's films between 1953 and 1964), joined his production unit at Paramount. It was also at Warners that Hitchcock first worked with actress Grace Kelly in *Dial M for Murder*.

12. Journalistic reviews of Hitchcock films released between 1954 and 1960 were drawn from the files of newspaper and magazine clippings of motion picture criticism at the Lincoln Center Library for the Performing Arts, New York City, and the Margaret Herrick Library, the Academy of Motion Picture Arts and Sciences, Beverly Hills. These reviews included those appearing in the major New York City and Los Angeles newspapers as well as in national magazines. All assertions of critical consensus made in this chapter are based on assessments of film reviews drawn from these two collections unless otherwise indicated. When a review from a major New York or Los Angeles newspaper or New York-based periodical was missing from these collections, I attempted to locate the review from some other source such as the New York Public Library Newspaper Collection or the Film Study Center of the Museum of Modern Art. Using this procedure, I collected all the reviews of Hitchcock films released from 1954 to 1960 to appear in the *New York Times*, *New York Herald Tribune*, *New York Daily News*, *New York Post*, *Los Angeles Times*, *Los Angeles Examiner*, *Time*, *Newsweek*, *Life*, *Look*, *New Yorker*, *Saturday Review*, *Nation*, and *New Republic*.

13. Crowther believed that, with few exceptions (e.g., *Spellbound*, 1945, and *Notorious*, 1946), Hitchcock's Hollywood films were inferior to his classic thrillers from the thirties (see, e.g., Crowther's reviews of *Suspicion*, 1941; *Saboteur*, 1942; *Shadow of a Doubt*, 1943; *Lifeboat*, 1944; *Rope*, 1948; and *Strangers on a Train*, 1951).

14. In previous reviews of Hitchcock's work, Crowther had expressed the hope that Hitchcock might some day evolve into a "significant" artist. A few years earlier, in his review of *Strangers on a Train* (1951), Crowther lamented Hitchcock's apparent unwillingness to make a socially responsible film:

Just why it is that Mr. Hitchcock is watering his pictures down to the thinness of mere exhibitions of his known virtuosity—just why it is that he doesn't latch onto some good, meaty yarn that would make some significant contact with the world in which we live—eludes this unhappy observer. Certainly the commerce of films needs today all of the substance that its talented artists can provide. Mr. Hitchcock would do well to ponder Nero, another corpulent man who applied his dexterity to mere fiddling at a time when the heat was on. (Crowther 1951)

15. Promoted as an "exciting suspense drama" (Production Notes, c. 1955), *To Catch a Thief* was a Technicolor and wide-screen production featuring big-name stars Cary Grant and Grace Kelly in gorgeous settings along the French Riviera. Released in August 1955, the film, like its predecessor, garnered strong box office, but met with, at best, mixed reviews. Two months later came the release of yet another Hitchcock film, *The Trouble with Harry*—a film which for Hitchcock exemplified the kind of macabre humor he sought for his television series, which premiered later that fall.

16. MCA was the largest talent agency in the world. In the late 1940s Hitchcock became one of their major clients. Soon after joining the agency, he came to be represented exclusively by Wasserman, who in 1946 had become president of MCA. It was Wasserman who helped set up a multipicture deal for Hitchcock at Paramount in 1953 which would prove to be a turning point for Hitchcock's career.

17. In fact, as Howard Prouty (1984) has astutely observed, "Even the 'twist' ending with which the Hitchcock series was to become so strongly identified [had become] somewhat old-hat by 1955."

18. From 1953 to 1956 he made six feature films: *Dial M for Murder; Rear Window; To Catch a Thief; The Trouble with Harry; The Man Who Knew Too Much;* and *The Wrong Man*.

19. One of the stumbling blocks in the negotiations was that Hitchcock's Paramount unit was not equipped for telefilm production.

20. A later program, "An Unlocked Window" (1965), offered a similar twist. A series of murders are committed by a male masquerading as a female. At the end of the show, Hitchcock returns to report that T. C. Jones, the actor portraying the female impersonator, today tried to murder someone else, who happened to be a policeman in disguise.

21. More likely, women found him physically unattractive: short, fat, and bald.

22. Palmer (1979) has approached the literary thriller from a similar perspective. "The plot—the story—," says Palmer, "is the process by which the hero averts the conspiracy and this process is what provides the thrills that the reader seeks" (1979, 53). The connection between the literary thriller and the cinematic thriller is made explicit by Ryall (1986): "In referring to 'process' i.e. the operation of reading in relation to the thriller, Palmer introduces an essential format component of the genre, its dependence for generic identity on the

creation of suspense for the reader. . . . It is this quality which is of supreme importance to the genre in the cinema" (1986, 121).

23. Hitchcock discusses the principles of the TV thriller in "Alfred Hitchcock Presents a Variety of Views On . . . ," a press release, dated 17 November 1958, CBS Television Network (Hitchcock Clipping File, Lincoln Center).

24. As Becker (1982) has put it, "Members of art worlds coordinate the activities by which work is produced by referring to a body of conventional understandings, embodied in common practice and in frequently used artifacts. The same people often cooperate repeatedly, even routinely, in similar ways to produce similar works, so that we can think of an art world as an established network of cooperative links among participants. If the same people do not actually act together in every instance, their replacements are also familiar with and proficient in the use of those conventions so that cooperation can proceed without difficulty. . . . Works of art, from this point of view, are not the products of individual makers, "artists" who possess a rare and special gift. They are, rather, joint products of all the people who cooperate via an art world's characteristic conventions to bring works like that into existence" (Becker 1982, 34–35).

25. See n. 10 above.

26. It is not that the American highbrows faulted Hitchcock's films for not being art but rather for not being as "thrilling" and enthralling as his earlier British output. For these pre-auteur critics writing in the forties and fifties, what counted as "art" were films of "social significance." For that reason they did not consider Hitchcock's films to be art, but that is not why they panned them. Even *New York Times* critic Bosley Crowther, who in the 1940s had hoped that Hitchcock would graduate to more significant subject matter, reviewed favorably a number of Hitchcock's fifties films (e.g., *Rear Window, The Man Who Knew Too Much,* and *Vertigo*) to the extent that they measured up to the standards Hitchcock himself had established earlier.

27. So did the review in the more middlebrow *Time* (21 May 1956).

28. Appealing here to Hitchcock's TV fans made sense. The second week before the release of *The Wrong Man,* "Alfred Hitchcock Presents" (37.5) was the Nielson's fourth top-rated network TV show. Ahead of it were "I Love Lucy" (46.5), "G. E. Theater" (41.2), and "The Ed Sullivan Show" (38.1) (*Time,* 14 January 1957). Each figure in parentheses is the percentage of the nation's TV homes within reach of the show that was tuned in to it on the night of 31 December 1956.

29. *The Wrong Man* Review File, Warner Bros. Archives. The file included well over one hundred newspaper and magazine reviews with a heavy concentration of reviews from major U.S. metropolitan newspapers and mass magazine periodicals. I also examined reviews from the sources listed in endnote n. 10 above.

30. The art-house patron belonged to what Herbert Gans has described as

"upper-middle culture"—"the taste culture of the vast majority of America's upper-middle class, the professionals, executives, and managers and their wives who have attended the better colleges and universities" (Gans 1974, 81). This taste public, according to Gans, is exposed to "the so-called class media or quality mass media," including *Time, Newsweek,* and other newsmagazines, the *New Yorker,* the *Saturday Review,* and *Harper's* among others (Gans 1974, 84). One would expect the politically liberal or progressive members of this public to be more likely to read the *Nation* or the *New Republic* than the more conservative weekly newsmagazines.

31. Bosley Crowther did not review *The Wrong Man.*

32. The reviewer for *Time* also panned it (14 January 1957). The *Newsweek* review was favorable but low-keyed (7 January 1957).

33. Another publicity article stressed the Hitchcock-Stewart connection, pointing out that while their three previous films together—*Rope, Rear Window,* and *The Man Who Knew Too Much*—had attained high standards of entertainment, with *Vertigo* Hitchcock and Stewart "seem to have attained even higher peaks of perfection in the art of suspense." Moreover, the article very misleadingly characterizes Stewart's role as fitting "Hitchcock's description of the kind of hero a true suspense film should have—'an average man to whom strange and bizarre things happen . . . the innocent fellow who gets involved in something he can't control'." Hardly an average kind of guy, Scottie is as strange and bizarre as the things that happen to him. However, one would never know this from the publicity generated for the film.

34. *Vertigo* placed second at the box office during its first week, dropping to third the following week. By this time, Paramount had replaced the Bass-inspired ad with their more conventional one showing pictures of Stewart and Novak. During its third week, *Vertigo* jumped back to second place. But by its seventh week, it had dropped to twelfth place.

35. *The Motion Picture Exhibitor's* review suggested another possible reason why *Vertigo* would be a difficult film to sell. It "will prove most confusing to all who see it other than from the beginning. It is certainly no picture to walk in on, if it is to make any sense to the viewer" (14 May 1958). Two years later, with a structurally similar film, *Psycho,* Hitchcock implemented the policy that no one would be admitted to the theater after the film started.

36. See, for example, John McCarten's reviews of *The Wages of Fear, New Yorker,* 26 February 1955 and *Diabolique, New Yorker,* 26 November 1955. Another favorite of the highbrows was British director Carol Reed, whose concern with character development and "sound psychological motivation" they preferred over Hitchcock's tendency to sacrifice plausibility in favor of maximizing audience effects. For example, in his review of *Strangers on a Train* (1951), *Saturday Review's* critic wrote:

> Perhaps one should allow Mr. Hitchcock the ultimate in suspension of disbelief in order to get full benefit of the surprises and chills he works for.

But a British counterpart of his, Carol Reed, by concentrating on characterization and sound psychological motivation, as he did in *Odd Man Out,* has shown that he can get with similar material into a dimension seemingly impossible for Hitchcock to reach. Hitchcock, on the other hand, too readily sacrifices these dependable ingredients in favor of plot development that will maintain the suspense at a keen level. You then find a kind of facileness and artificiality that you did not get in Henry Hathaway's *Fourteen Hours,* where the suspense grew more naturally out of the characters and situation. (14 July 1951)

37. Attacked by highbrow and middlebrow journalistic reviewers, *Vertigo* was ignored entirely by academics. The two existing American journals engaged in serious criticism, *Film Quarterly* and *Film Culture,* did not even review it. The films of French thriller-director Henri-Georges Clouzot (*The Wages of Fear* and *Diabolique*) were more to their liking (see *Film Culture,* May–June, 1955).

38. That idea, says Stefano, got him the job.

39. In another published interview, Hitchcock admitted that *Psycho* did break with the conventions of the Hitchcock thriller film by resorting to the depiction of physical violence. As if to reassure readers, the article ends with the suggestion that with *Psycho* Hitchcock would not repeat the mistake of *Sabotage,* where a bomb explodes, killing the innocent child who is carrying it through the streets of London, "He [Hitchcock] has long since concluded that people are enthralled by the chills and thrills of a roller coaster, but want the assurance of being able to exit laughing" (Masters 1960).

40. *Psycho* grossed around $7 million from its first 3,750 engagements in the United States, and an estimated $6 million from foreign markets. By the end of its first year alone, the film had grossed around $18 million in the U.S. and Canada (*Variety,* 9 November 1960).

41. According to writer Joseph Stefano, "Hitch was annoyed the picture had gotten some bad reviews based, he felt, on the fact that he hadn't let the critics see it in advance. In fact, one critic actually told me that's why he panned the movie" (Rebello 1986, 76).

THREE

1. Journalistic reviews of Hitchcock's films released between 1963 and 1976 were drawn from Hitchcock's personal collection (the Hitchcock Collection) as well as from the files of newspaper and magazine clippings of motion picture criticism at the Lincoln Center Library for the Performing Arts, New York City, and the Margaret Herrick Library, the Academy of Motion Picture Arts and Sciences, Beverly Hills. Of the three collections, Hitchcock's was by far the most complete, including most of the reviews of his post-1960 films to appear in major metropolitan newspapers and mass magazines in the United States and Western Europe. Rarely did I find a review of a Hitchcock film in one

of the regional collections that did not also appear among Hitchcock's papers. It should be understood that all assertions of critical consensus and shifts in critical positions made in this chapter are based on assessments of film reviews drawn from these three collections, unless otherwise indicated. Given this chapter's focus, I have concentrated on the New York critics, especially those representing the more highbrow publications. When a review from a major New York newspaper or New York-based periodical was missing from the above-mentioned collections, I attempted to locate the review from some alternative source such as the New York Public Library Newspaper Collection or the Film Study Center of the Museum of Modern Art. Using this procedure, I collected all the reviews of Hitchcock's films released from 1963 to 1976 to appear in the *New York Times, New York Herald Tribune, New York Daily News, New York Post, New York Magazine, Time, Newsweek, Life, New Yorker, Saturday Review, Nation, New Republic,* and *Village Voice.*

2. For an earlier version of this argument, see Kapsis (1989).

3. Rohmer and Chabrol close their book-length study of Hitchcock with the following passage:

> In concluding, let us merely choose from among all the aspects of a multi-faceted genius the one that seems the least indisputable to us. As we have said, Hitchcock is one of the greatest *inventors of form* in the entire history of cinema. Perhaps only Murnau and Eisenstein can sustain comparison with him when it comes to form. Our effort will not have been in vain if we have been able to demonstrate how an entire moral universe has been elaborated on the basis of this form and by its very rigor. In Hitchcock's work form does not embellish content, it creates it. All of Hitchcock can be summed up in this formula. *This is what we wanted to demonstrate.* (1979, 152)

4. This assertion is based on an examination of reviews by U.S. critics of Hitchcock films released between 1950 and 1960 (Collection of Newspaper Clippings. Lincoln Center).

5. From its inception, Allardice scripted the prologues and epilogues to Hitchcock's television series.

6. The original tapes of the Truffaut-Hitchcock interviews verify that Hitchcock expressed these concerns to Truffaut in late August 1962.

7. For a good historical overview of the international art-cinema movement of the fifties and early sixties, see Gomery (1990, 347–87). See also Bordwell (1985) and Neal (1981).

8. For more specifics on the making of *The Birds,* see Kapsis (1987).

9. Hitchcock's point of reference here was an early version of the screenplay. Subsequently, the psychiatrist character was dropped altogether, as was the scene in the movie theater.

10. "I feel sure that the *New Yorker* insists on having a critic who hates

pictures. Well, they write for their readers, you know, and they don't care about the film at all. They have no love of film; they hate films. And, the more they can write about them in a derogatory way and an amusing way, the more they please their readers. You know, it's like the *Time* magazine man will make cracks. I'm waiting for that American expression to come, out—'This picture is only for the birds'" (unpublished portions of the Hitchcock-Truffaut tapes, Hitchcock Collection).

11. It was not *Marnie*'s psychoanalytical framework, per se, that Hitchcock believed would endear highbrow critics to the film. Rather he saw the psychoanalytical angle more as a vehicle for convincing the serious critics of *Marnie*'s plausibility as a character, thereby garnering their endorsement of the film. Another reason why Hitchcock may have believed that the film's psychoanalytic framework would appeal to the more intellectual critics is because of the international art-cinema's preoccupation with mental states. As film historian Douglas Gomery has succinctly put it, the European art-cinema of the fifties and early sixties was "more concerned with the psychological effects of events than with their physical causes. Filmmakers encouraged viewers to become interested in a character's changing mental state through dream sequences, flashbacks of memories, scenes of hallucinations and frequent fantasies. Flashbacks and flash forwards tell the audience what a character is thinking" (Gomery 1990, 349). It is understandable that Hitchcock might think that the highbrow critics who preferred the European art-cinema to the classical Hollywood style would be more approving of a Hitchcock film if they found that it evoked qualities which they had come to associate with the European art film.

12. Absent from the series were *Mr. and Mrs. Smith* (1941) and *Under Capricorn* (1949).

13. Griffith's secretary, James Watters, also disagreed with Bogdanovich's glowing assessment of *The Birds*. After attending the film's press screening, Watters, who would later serve as the entertainment editor of *Life* magazine, had warned Griffith, who had not yet seen the film, that *The Birds* was simply awful:

> This film is a humorless and contrived tale based on a gimmick with a weak, unresolved ending. The audience hissed at the conclusion of the showing. No matter how well-conceived and executed, the special effects are obvious and thus destroy the illusion of reality and negate the terror. Not since the films of the 40's have I seen so much process photography. The actors excepting Jessica Tandy are one-dimensional and unconvincing. Tippi Hedren, Hitchcock's "new personality," is a cold, shallow non-professional who belongs on the cover of *Vogue*. She is so icy the audience last night mistaked [sic] her for a figure of evil—quite the contrary to Hitchcock's concept of the junior sophisticate Miss Hedren plays. She is his worst leading lady since Priscilla Lane. This is minor Hitchcock for

the emphasis is on design details for production value with a complete disregard for developing depth in character and atmosphere and for doing anything with an ineffectual and undeveloped plot line. (28 March 1963, informal memo to Griffith, 1963 Hitchcock Retrospective Exhibition file, MOMA)

14. For an earlier account of the marketing of *The Birds*, see Kapsis (1987).

15. This account of how Hitchcock and his publicity machine attempted to influence the critical reception of *Marnie* is based on information drawn from two sources: *Marnie* publicity files (Hitchcock Collection); and personal interviews (conducted in the spring of 1986) with David Golding, *Marnie*'s director of publicity, Harold Mendelsohn, the film's unit publicist, and Suzanne Gauthier, who between 1962 and 1980 was Hitchcock's private secretary.

16. In describing the backgrounds of individual cast members, the release emphasized their experience in the more prestigious medium of theater rather than in film. For example, *Marnie* allows Sean Connery "a far broader histrionic stage on which to display the skills he meticulously nurtured in British repertory and Shakespearian drama."

17. There were some notable exceptions, however. In May 1963, the film editor of the powerful *Los Angeles Times*, Philip Scheuer, who had been highly critical of Hitchcock's recent films, including *Vertigo, Psycho*, and *The Birds*, was sent a copy of Peter Bogdanovich's monograph, *The Cinema of Alfred Hitchcock* along with a rather lengthy cover letter describing it and the Hitchcock retrospective then under way at the Museum of Modern Art:

> I thought you'd be interested in seeing this monograph . . . of the MOMA Library. . . . The Hitchcock retrospective series is the longest museum series of the work of a single film maker. . . . The monograph is a searching and sometimes startling index to the mind of the imaginative and resourceful director; it is based on an intensive interview with the man who, as Bogdanovich writes in the introduction, "is the only director whose movies are sold on his name alone."
>
> We hope, of course, this might provoke a column comment, but in any case, it should make a good reference piece for your library (Hitchcock Collection).

In Scheuer's subsequent review of Hitchcock's next film, *Marnie*, we find partial evidence that Hitchcock's propaganda campaign had paid off.

> The Old Master is still experimenting. Like *Vertigo, Psycho*, and *The Birds*, Alfred Hitchcock's *Marnie* takes place in a twilight world, one in which even the colors (an unnatural predominance of reds and blues) and the sounds (strangely subdued when Marnie is hearing them) apparently have significance. . . . Nearly all of us, I believe, were sorrowed when the

tongue-in-cheek Hitchcock gave up the chase to enter this new phase—the exploration of the dark recesses of the mind and spirit. But as his astonishing career falls into perspective, he may yet be acclaimed for having taken the step. (Scheuer 1964)

18. Portions of what follows appeared in Kapsis (1988b).

19. Although not mentioning them by name, Kael was responding to the MOMA-sponsored publications that Bogdanovich (1963) and Sarris (1966) had recently prepared on Hitchcock and von Sternberg, respectively.

20. "When film entered the university in the 1970s, the single-author approach was the most popular one, especially in literature departments" (Carringer 1985, ix).

"If one judges by ultimate influence (leaving aside the question of who is right), it appears that Sarris won the battle. The reorganization of film studies at universities, the flood of books on directors, the revival of many obscure American films in directors' retrospectives . . . , the attitudes of young critics and scholars (some of whom have used auteur criticism as a mere convenience), the greater emphasis on directorial personality in the work of the older critics, the portraits of Sarris's auteurs in the popular public television series, "The Men Who Made the Movies"—all of this attests to the progress of the auteur theory in the world outside of film magazines" (Denby 1977, 139).

21. In America, the acceptance of Hitchcock as a great artist preceded the 1972 release of *Frenzy.* That this view of Hitchcock was not yet acknowledged by British critics is evidenced by the largely hostile response the film received in the British press. For many British reviewers, *Frenzy* was too mean-spirited to be of any value. In 1972 British critics were still measuring Hitchcock's worth against the benchmark of his comedy thrillers of the late thirties (Reviews of *Frenzy,* British Film Institute).

22. In his *Boston Phoenix* commentary on Hitchcock's career, a young John Belton, who would become prominent in academic film studies, emphasizes *Frenzy*'s self-conscious reflectiveness:

> Though a film like *Frenzy,* with its unique blend of horror and humor, preserves the traditional image of Hitchcock as an ironic and macabre storyteller, *Frenzy* differs from *Psycho* in its self-conscious reflectiveness. In *Frenzy* Hitchcock carefully calculates his effects and then, as in the potato truck sequence, brilliantly pushes them beyond traditional aesthetic limits. As a result, *Frenzy*'s horror is more grotesque than that in any other Hitchcock film; its humor blacker and more perverse. . . . In contrast to the warm romanticism and rich, major characterizations of Hitchcock's forties, fifties, and early sixties films, the absence of a central romantic relationship in *Frenzy* and the cold precision of its shooting suggest an objective reexamination of the director's earlier, romantic involvement with his material. (*Boston Phoenix,* 29 August 1972)

23. It would be extremely misleading to suggest that during this nine-year period, very many of Hitchcock's foes had become converts to his *mis-en-scène*. As we have seen, there had always been a minority of critics who disliked Hitchcock's approach to the cinema. One of the most outspoken had been *Esquire* magazine critic Dwight Macdonald. In his negative review of *The Birds*, he did more than attack the film for being "a negative print" of Hitchcock's best qualities. He also quite viciously dismissed "the uncritically enthusiastic reviews" of Sarris and Bogdanovich, who he characterized as "two of our *politique des auteurs* hierophants—one can't call them critics" (Macdonald 1963). Pauline Kael of the *New Yorker* and Stanley Kauffmann of the *New Republic*, as reported earlier, were also among those who denounced *The Birds* when it first came out. Like Macdonald, they could not hide their general disdain for the Hollywood Hitchcock—a view from which they would not stray over the next twenty-five years. Kael did not review *Frenzy* but Kauffmann did. While acknowledging that the film was better than Hitchcock's more recent work, Kauffmann still found *Frenzy* and Hitchcock "faintly loathsome" (Kael 1963b; compare Kauffmann 1963a and 1963b with Kauffmann 1972; for a listing of others hostile to Hitchcock's art, see Deutelbaum and Poague 1986, 1–6).

24. According to Schickel, it was precisely Hitchcock's cultivation of his TV persona that had made it so difficult for critics to detect the seriousness of his work. In his book based on the series, Schickel writes:

> the almost entirely fictional persona he has created for himself: the jolly fat man with the macabre, punning sense of humor . . . served to hide from the public the fact that he is a serious artist who has a craving (constantly checked) to be taken seriously. The problem was, I think, that he calculated that this desire (a perfectly reasonable one, after all) might interfere with the popularity of that art; if people saw that he did not create it in an entirely larkish spirit, they might start to probe a little more deeply and thus find themselves discomfited by film they had taught themselves (with a little help from the master) to take lightly. (Schickel 1975)

25. With Hitchcock's recognition as a serious artist seemingly assured among a significant core of reviewers, promotion for *Family Plot* could concentrate on luring the mass audience to the film through repackaging Hitchcock's earlier image as a consummate entertainer with a wonderfully wry sense of humor.

26. Mark Crispin Miller's tribute to Hitchcock was one of the more interesting since it appeared in the *New Republic*, where one of Hitchcock's most persistent detractors, Stanley Kauffmann, was the resident film critic. Unlike Kauffmann's condescending characterization of Hitchcock as a "pop cynic, cinematically ingenious," Miller described him as "the greatest of filmmakers, and among the greatest artists of the century" (Miller 1980). Here was an interesting attempt to persuade Kauffmann's readers to take Hitchcock seriously.

27. There is a general consensus among Hitchcock scholars that the most hackneyed and cliché-ridden thriller that Hitchcock made between *Psycho* (1960) and *Family Plot* (1976) was *Torn Curtain* (1966). Although the initial critical reception to the film was also quite negative, especially among the more highbrow critics, *Torn Curtain* attracted a surprisingly large audience, generating more domestic rental income (approximately $7 million) for its distributor (MCA/Universal) than any of Hitchcock's other films after *Psycho*. See *Variety*, 4 January 1961; 8 January 1964; 6 January 1965; 4 January 1967; 12 May 1971; 3 January 1973; and 5 January 1977).

28. This tribute was prepared for a MOMA film series, "David O. Selznick's Hollywood from the Archives," 2–18 June 1980. The retrospective included two films that Hitchcock made for Selznick—*Spellbound* (1945) and *Notorious* (1946).

29. Hitchcock had also owned *Psycho*. But he then sold the film to Universal.

30. For Grenier, "everything in Hitchcock [is] so arbitrary, so contrived, so false, the dangers so mechanical, the paranoia so copy, that I don't care who killed anyone—or why or how—in any film that Hitchcock ever made" (1980). Following his damaging assessment of Hitchcock's work, Grenier draws on Spoto's documentation of Hitchcock's cruelty to persuade his readership of Hitchcock's unworthiness as an artist.

31. The generally enthusiastic critical response to the reissued films in the United States and abroad also reveals the continuity that was maintained among those championing Hitchcock's work earlier in their careers as critics and filmmakers. That is, those who heralded Hitchcock's work in the late fifties and sixties continued their crusade well into the eighties. Andrew Sarris, Vincent Canby, Richard Schickel, and Robin Wood all wrote glowingly about the reissued films.

FOUR

1. For an earlier version of the *Marnie* section, see Kapsis (1988a).

2. See, for example, Thompson (1964), Hale (1964), and *Cinema Magazine* (1964). Journalistic reviews of *Marnie* were drawn from the files of newspaper and magazine clippings of motion picture criticism at the Lincoln Center Library for the Performing Arts, New York City, and the Margaret Herrick Library, the Academy of Motion Picture Arts and Sciences, Beverly Hills, as well as from the Hitchcock Collection.

3. See, for example, Crist (1964), Coleman (1964), Pacey (1964), Gilliatt (1964), *Time* (1964), and the *New Yorker* (1964).

4. For documentation of a similar assessment of *Citizen Kane* during the sixties, see Bates (1987).

5. See, for example, Archer (1964), Sarris (1964), Winsten (1964), and *Time* (1964).

6. See, for example, Knight (1964), Walker (1964), and *Evening News* (1964).

7. See also Coleman (1964), and *Evening News* (1964).

8. For an early critique of the auteur theory, see Archer (1965).

9. "The cinema," Wood writes, "has its own methods and own scope. We must beware of missing the significance of a shot or a sequence by applying to it assumptions brought from our experience of other arts." (Wood [1965] 1977, 30)

10. "Not only in theme—in style, method, moral attitude, assumptions about the nature of life—Hitchcock's mature films," says Wood, "reveal, on inspection, a consistent development, deepening and clarification."

11. This "nasty taste" phenomenon, says Wood ([1965] 1977, 38), has two causes:

> One is Hitchcock's complex and disconcerting moral sense, in which good and evil are seen to be so interwoven as to be virtually inseparable, and which insists on the existence of evil impulses in all of us. The other is his ability to make us aware, perhaps not quite at the conscious level (it depends on the spectator), of the impurity of our own desires. The two usually operate, of course, in conjunction.

12. Compare with Yacowar's (1977, 265) critique of Johnson (1964). For a less polemical auteurist reading of *Marnie*, see Cameron and Jeffrey (1965).

13. For a different account of why the backdrop and process-shooting in *Marnie* left much to be desired, see Spoto (1983, 500–505).

14. Cameron and Jeffrey (1965) also rationalized Hitchcock's seemingly heavy-handed use of back-projection techniques in the riding sequences involving Marnie and her horse Forio. "After the confinement of offices, hotel rooms, and railway stations, Marnie galloping out on Forio is an image of freedom—but even the image of freedom is illusory in its appearance, for she is riding in front of a studio back-projection machine" (275).

15. Most of the recent auteur assessments of *Marnie* have also been favorable. In his introduction to the third edition of *Hitchcock's Films*, published in 1977, Wood still rates *Marnie* as one of Hitchcock's major achievements (along with *Notorious, Rope, Rear Window, Vertigo, North by Northwest*, and the first half of *Psycho*). And William Rothman in his influential study, *Hitchcock: The Murderous Gaze* (1982), characterizes *Marnie* as Hitchcock's "last great masterpiece." On the other hand, Donald Spoto, an early champion of the film, has recently revised his assessment of it, regarding it now as, at best, a flawed masterpiece. In his 1983 biography of Hitchcock, Spoto revealed that, during the making of *Marnie*, Hitchcock expressed a romantic interest in Tippi Hedren which she forcefully rejected, causing him to lose interest in the *Marnie* project:

> For years, a cadre of Hitchcock's admirers (this author among the most defensive of them) concocted tortuous arguments more admirable for

their ingenuity than consistent with the facts; to account for the sloppy technique of the film, rationalizations were adduced to demonstrate that these aberrations were deliberate on Hitchcock's part, a conscious reversion to an expressionistic style that used artifice to represent a disordered psyche. But the real reason was simpler and sadder, and those reviewers who were critical, it should be admitted, were right: they are simply visually jarring; they mark not a deliberate use of unconventional means, but are simply unpleasant examples of the director's cavalier disinterest in the final product. (Spoto 1983, 505)

Despite his familiarity with these revelations about the making of *Marnie,* Lesley Brill has recently defended all the attention-getting artifice of the film, including the painted sets and the "conspicuous rear projection" as signaling that "the story has reached a moment at which veils are drawn back and actuality revealed" (1988, 244). Apparently, knowledge of production factors continues to lack much relevance in the world of auteur film criticism. Nor was such knowledge important to the short-lived "auteur structuralist" movement. See, for example, Wollen (1982, 34–39) on *Marnie.*

16. In contrast to the auteur critics who glorified directorial authority, the feminist critics "implicitly challenge and decenter directorial authority by considering Hitchcock's work as the expression of cultural attitudes and practices existing to some extent outside the artist's control" (Modleski 1988, 3).

17. For a completely different interpretation of this sequence, see Fletcher (1988, 58–59; cf. Grieg 1987).

18. For a different interpretation of the scene of Marnie's "dismantling and emergence" from her "masquerade," see Fletcher (1988, 59–60).

19. A methodological strategy implied by this cultural power approach is that the various historical or *multiple readings* of a cultural object such as a film should be identified in advance of investigating the *multiple sources* of its "meaning." With respect to *Marnie,* the production files have suggested that Hitchcock's intent to experiment with a looser narrative in order to probe Marnie's personality contributed to the film's capacity to generate multiple interpretations. Hitchcock's preoccupation or obsession throughout the *Marnie* project with the Marnie character may also partly explain the sketchiness and indeterminant quality of Mark. This "flaw" is reflected in the "spaces" or "gaps" in the filmic text that make the film amenable to differing interpretations of Mark's motivation or lack thereof (compare Wood 1977; Bailin 1982; Piso 1986; and Brill 1988, on Mark). An additional source of the film's multivocality is related to the collaborative nature of the *Marnie* project. Contrary to what the auteur theorists would lead one to believe, *Marnie* was not the production of a single author, Hitchcock. As Bailin (1982) has persuasively argued, the film's "female" voice may have had something to do with the fact that the screenplay for *Marnie* was written by Jay Presson Allen, a woman whose work has often reflected femi

nist concerns (Bailin 1982, 34). Moreover, I would maintain that the psychological presence of Winston Graham, the author of the novel upon which the film was based, was a major source of the film's attention and sensitivity to class distinctions and social inequality. Indeed, production information not previously discussed reveals that Hitchcock and Graham negotiated a tie-in agreement which affected not only how both the film and novel would be marketed but also necessitated that much of the spirit of the novel be preserved in the film.

20. While several Hitchcock films have elicited interpretations at least as varied as those represented in the *Marnie* case, including *Notorious, Vertigo, Rear Window,* and *Psycho,* most have not generated such a range of interpretations. Take, for instance, *North by Northwest.* Judging the film from Griswold's criterion that an art work is powerful if it generates a broad range of interpretations, *North by Northwest* is a less powerful work than *Marnie.* While a number of auteur critics (e.g., Wood 1977; Keane 1980; Cavell 1986; Rothman 1983; Brill 1988) have written extensively about the film, their interpretations, with few exceptions, do not diverge significantly from each other. Brill's recent interpretation of the famous Prairie Stop episode is a case in point, differing hardly at all from Wood's earlier account. Both Brill and Wood view the crop-dusting sequence as a critical turning-point in the emotional development of the Roger Thornhill character, from a selfish and cynical person to a more caring and compassionate one. Only a few academic critics have treated *North by Northwest* as a highly reflexive work (see Keane 1980; Rothman 1983; Cavell 1986), while even fewer feminist-oriented film critics (e.g., Bergstrom, under the influence of Bellour) have bothered to examine the film at all. Since art worlds are always in flux, developments in film aesthetics could elevate *North by Northwest*'s standing relative to Hitchcock's other works such as *Vertigo* or *Rear Window,* which, according to academic film studies' current preoccupation with issues of class, gender, and race, are better films.

21. Compare Wood's point about the use of back-projection in *The Birds* to his interpretation of the riding sequence in *Marnie.*

22. The Hitchcock-Truffaut tapes include a number of discussions and references to *The Birds* that are absent in the Truffaut book.

23. Through a systematic analysis of all the bird attacks in the film, Horwitz (1982) has attempted to demonstrate that the bird attacks are linked to the anger expressed by the various female characters in the film, especially, Lyla (Mitch's mother) and Annie (Mitch's ex-girlfriend).

24. Interestingly, both Canby and Chute relied on materials drawn from Truffaut's interview with Hitchcock to add credibility to their more relaxed view of Hitchcock's artistry.

25. Many film scholars have maintained that *Vertigo* is Hitchcock's most fully realized masterpiece. Resisting this view, a minority of journalistic critics, including Janet Maslin (1984) of the *New York Times,* argued that *Vertigo,* while a remarkable film in many respects, had not aged as well as *Rear Window.*

FIVE

1. Portions of this section are adapted from Kapsis (1991). For an earlier account of this short-lived cycle of horror films, see Kapsis (1982).

2. The basic formula of the horror film is that normality is threatened by the Monster. This formula encompasses the entire range of horror films, "being applicable whether the Monster is a vampire, a giant gorilla, an extraterrestrial invader, an amorphous gooey mass . . . a child possessed by the Devil" (Wood 1978, 25–32), or a human psychotic or schizophrenic.

3. There were other commentaries on *Halloween* more consistent in their praise of the film. *New Times* critic Richard Corliss, who would include *Halloween* on his top-ten list for 1978, singled out Carpenter's style. "*Halloween* may be only an exercise in the Hitchcockian style," said Corliss, "but what style. John Carpenter is the most accomplished new director since Martin Scorsese" (1979).

4. Other types of horror films also went into production during this period (e.g., ghost stories, werewolf stories), reflecting the film industry's view that more traditional forms could be revived and rejuvenated by beefing up the violence and through startling special effects. Universal announced plans to make a sequel to *Psycho*. In addition, recent horror-film "cult" classics were reissued such as *Night of the Living Dead, The Texas Chain-Saw Massacre,* and *The Last House on the Left.* Another indication of an environment conducive to horror-film production is that many young filmmakers who were looking for an opportunity to direct their first feature film were handed horror projects, while veteran filmmakers who were still recovering from a string of commercial failures (e.g., John Frankenheimer, Paul Schrader, and Sidney Furie), found work in horror. Directors Wes Craven and Tobe Hooper, who had offended the Hollywood establishment a decade ago with *The Last House on the Left* and *The Texas Chain-Saw Massacre,* respectively, suddenly found themselves employable again. Indeed, by late 1979, a horror-genre boom period had emerged which would last roughly until early 1981.

5. Statistics also tell part of the story. Between 1979 and 1981, horror performed strongly in both domestic and foreign markets. In 1978 only nine horror films earned at least $1 million in domestic rentals. That rate doubled and tripled over the next two years. Seventeen horror films in 1979 and twenty-six in 1980 topped the million-dollar mark. (The rate of change in the profitability of horror is only slightly reduced after controlling for ticket-price inflation.) Over the same period foreign production of horror films dramatically increased— from only twenty-three new films starting production in 1978 to thirty-three in 1979 and fifty-five in 1980. Another indication that a bullish market for horror had arrived is that roughly one-fourth of all movies screened and pitched at the international sales events at Cannes, Milan, and Los Angeles were horror films (*Variety,* 1982, 1984).

6. Pressure groups have been an important influence on film cycles, affecting both their duration and content. Since the inception of motion pictures at the turn of the century, groups of concerned citizens have attacked the popular medium, perceiving it as a potential threat to the established order. Fearing government censorship, the film industry imposed its own controls on film content. The National Review Board, the Hays Office, the Production Code Administration, and the Classification and Rating Administration were all manifestations of the film industry's attempt, during different periods, to regulate film content on its own without government interference. A number of historical studies have documented how pressure groups have caused popular genres to either disappear or change their basic formulas. Pressure from the Catholic Legion of Decency, for example, triggered the strict enforcement of the production code during the mid-1930s, resulting in the sudden disappearance of the then popular gangster genre (see, e.g., Parker 1986).

7. The auteur theory also contributed to the growing sense among both audiences and critics of "the American Cinema's dense intertextuality." According to Ray, auteurism "inescapably implied that the movies, far from being 'real,' were artifacts, the products of particular individuals working in particular eras" (Ray 1986, 266). The new directors who made films in Hollywood during the 1960s and 1970s also encouraged self-consciousness. Many specialized in films that were ironic, parodic, or camp versions of traditional genres. Carpenter, De Palma, and other horror directors of this period were products of this development.

8. *Newsweek* critic David Ansen had praised John Carpenter's *Halloween* as "a superb exercise in the art of suspense. . . . From a movie's dazzling prologue in 1963 to its chilling conclusion in 1978, we are being pummeled by a master manipulator" (Ansen 1978).

9. For evidence of this acceptance of horror among academic critics during the late 1970s and early 1980s see Waller (1987), especially chapters 7–9 and the annotated bibliography.

10. According to *Variety*, "With the glut of product on the market, and the reluctance of both indies and major distribs to hold press screenings for violence (and gore) films, most national and New York publications have stopped reviewing low-budget horror pictures" (1983a, 7).

11. Richard D. Heffner, the chairman of CARA, admitted to me that the version of the film CARA first saw was not as violent as some of the earlier films in the "slasher" series that had received an R. But, he stressed, this had nothing to do with punishing the sequel because the original had spawned the slasher cycle, as the film's producers had alleged, but because CARA's standards had stiffened over the last few years. CARA's harder line, Heffner was quick to point out, reflected what the board perceived as changing parental attitudes toward violence. According to Heffner, CARA is not a moral agent imposing its posi-

tion on the film industry but rather a "barometer" of the country's changing moral climate (Personal interview, 1981).

12. For a detailed account of the making of *Halloween II,* see Kapsis (1986b).

13. While working in 1975 on what proved to be his last film, *Family Plot,* Hitchcock received a letter on behalf of several graduate students enrolled in the American Film Institute's filmmaking program, who wanted to make a documentary about the making of Hitchcock's latest film. According to the students, the project would function both as a tribute to his talent "for combining all the elements of the medium" and as an "opportunity to share the benefit of [Hitchcock's] experience with other young filmmakers." "Every young creative person," wrote the students, "needs to serve some form of apprenticeship and we feel your work most appropriately illustrates the basics of cinematic techniques." In another letter from the same period, an educator wrote Hitchcock, "I find your films excellent for education because one can study them at many levels: the plots are tidy and have no loose ends; they keep moving and employ a variety of camera angles . . . and their suspense prevents any students going to sleep" (Hitchcock Collection). By the 1980s, many journalistic film critics had adopted similar views about Hitchcock.

14. The commercial success of slasher horror films also affected the marketing of more Hitchcock-type thrillers. With *Road Games,* another film released during this period, director Richard Franklin had set out to make a "*Rear Window*-type thriller." While the press kit for *Road Games* did emphasize the film's Hitchcockian spirit, the ad campaign suggested a slasher film with its imagery of a sexy woman in jeopardy.

15. Newspaper clipping file, the Margaret Herrick Library, the Academy of Motion Picture Arts and Sciences, Beverly Hills.

16. My focus on Hitchcock and the backlash against horror might leave the impression that the crusade successfully snuffed out the horror cycle. Let me suggest a somewhat different explanation to account for why horror films as a whole performed so poorly at the box office in 1983.

Contrary to the reflection thesis that films mirror the wider society, the sudden collapse of a genre may result from shrinking or expanding markets having little to do with actual shifts in audience taste preferences. That is, one factor that might affect the duration of a film cycle is the perception of how markets (audiences) might respond to the genre. According to many movie industry observers, for a genre boom period to emerge and persist, there must be strong indications that the genre will thrive in at least two of the three major theatrical markets—domestic, foreign, and ancillary (such as sales to network and cable television and video-tape playback). That the domestic market for a particular genre may be good is no guarantee that film studios will back future projects in that genre. Thus, if a type of genre film remains popular with American audiences but fails overseas, Hollywood will schedule fewer such films for production in the future, especially if the ancillary market for such films is limited.

The sudden bust of horror films in 1983 is largely explained by the perceived failure of the genre overseas two years earlier and Hollywood's subsequent decision to start pulling out of horror. This decision is reflected in the relatively few American-made horror films that went into production in 1982—less than half the figure for 1981 (see Kapsis 1991). Data from *Variety* (1984) also show that the decline in the production of foreign-made horror films started in 1981—one year before the decline of American-made horror films. Indeed, the 1981 decline of horror in foreign territories was interpreted by a number of industry observers as a signal to pull out of horror. "It was the overseas market that sent the signal," explained Leonard Shapiro, president of Shapiro Entertainment, who during the early 1980s was vice-president of film acquisitions and marketing services at Avco Embassy. "That market dried up six months before the U.S. market did. So the writing was definitely on the wall that the making of horror film deals was in for a slow-down period" (Personal interview, October 1981).

Yet horror remained popular with American audiences in 1982. As we recall, horror-film rentals were higher that year than for any other year. A record thirty-one horror films earned at least $1 million dollars in domestic rentals in 1982 compared to twenty-two in 1981 and twenty-six in 1980 at the height of the horror craze. But because of Hollywood's decision before 1982 to start cutting back drastically in the production of horror, 1983 found relatively few new horror films available to American audiences. Indeed, *Variety* (1984) reported that of the fifty-one new horror films released during 1983, "over half (some 27 titles) were shelved pictures actually filmed in 1981 or earlier and dumped on the market at this time." One might speculate that if audiences in 1983 had been offered a fresher product, the horror genre would have survived longer than it did. Moreover, the dismal performance of horror in 1983 suggests that genre films need to be produced in sufficient numbers in order to create a sense that they are the hallmark of a group (generational or subcultural) consciousness.

The media backlash against horror may also have influenced Hollywood's decision to cut back on horror. However, its influence was probably small compared to the market constraints described above. Filmmakers working in horror are willing to risk a hostile press. "I make films for audiences, not critics," said Debra Hill, line producer for the *Halloween* series. "It is a business. I'm not dumb." And for distributors of horror, media ads or spots are more important than reviews as a means of selling their films. Thus, the reluctance of certain newspapers and magazines during the height of the backlash to publish movie ads depicting explicit violence may have discouraged some film companies from competing in the horror sweepstakes (Kapsis 1991).

17. In 1986 the film's director, Richard Franklin, told me that he had total freedom on the project, with everything going exactly the way he wanted it.

18. In fact, Aljean Harmetz (1988) maintained that it was *Jagged Edge* that convinced Hollywood professionals that Hollywood's audience was getting older and pickier. According to Harmetz, a survey taken for the Motion Picture Association of America by the Opinion Research Corporation of New Jersey showed that "men and women over the age of 40 bought 71 million more movie tickets in 1987 than they did in 1986. Over the last three years, the gap between teen-agers and more mature moviegoers has narrowed dramatically. Teen-agers have dropped from 32 percent of the audience in 1984 to 25 percent in 1987; ticket buyers 40 and older accounted for 15 percent of all admissions in 1984 and 20 percent in 1987."

19. Other critics saw their review of *The Bedroom Window* as an opportunity to comment on the importance of casting in Hitchcock's films. *Wall Street Journal* critic Julie Salamon wrote, "Alfred Hitchcock knew what he was doing when he cast Cary Grant and James Stewart as his leading men" (Salamon, 1987a). In a similar vein, a critic for *L.A. Weekly* wrote, "In order for us to sympathize in films like this, it's essential that the hero be a true innocent and not an idiot. (Cary Grant never made any blunders; he simply and suavely stumbled into misadventures.) But *The Bedroom Window* misses the mark because Lambert is an idiot, though Guttenberg is less irritating than he's ever been" (Dare 1987). See also Denby (1987a) who in *New York Magazine* wrote, "Part of Hitchcock's charm, of course, came out in his choice of players. I don't know if Hanson selected his leading man or if Steve Guttenberg was forced on him by the film's backers but *someone* has a lousy taste in men."

20. Kehr (1987a) also admired a sequence in which Hanson implements other Hitchcockian touches such as point-of-view camera work and the use of "hushed sound levels" to create a powerful atmosphere, which Kehr claimed was far superior to that of the *Vertigo* sequences in Brian De Palma's *Dressed to Kill*.

21. See also Canby's (1987a) commentary on thriller films (*Morning After, The Bedroom Window,* and *Scene of the Crime*); see also his earlier review of *The Bedroom Window,* where he writes, "Mr. Hanson runs out of invention almost immediately. To push this story to the point where Terry, the innocent and good Samaritan finds himself in serious jeopardy, Mr. Hanson is forced to impose on him several totally absurd decisions that forever cut the audience loose from its commitment to both character and situation. It's something that Alfred Hitchcock—though he loathed what he called "the plausibles"—would never have allowed to happen. Either Hitchcock wouldn't have given the audience time to question plausibility, or he would have found some way of making the irrational appear, at least for the moment, utterly rational. This is beyond Mr. Hanson" (Canby 1987b).

22. Critics were more likely to relate *Black Widow* to the tradition of film noir than to Hitchcock's work (see, for example, Ansen 1987). Regardless of the film tradition involved, critics tended to view the film as falling short of that tradition.

23. Like the Hitchcock tradition, the tradition of film noir had also influenced several generations of Hollywood filmmakers. As *Newsweek* critic David Ansen put it, "Like a *femme fatale* who lures innocent men into deep and dangerous waters, the '40s film noir has cast a spell over every succeeding generation of Hollywood filmmakers. How to recapture that dark magic in terms that make sense for a new era?" By adding modern, feminist touches. That, according to Ansen, is what director Bob Rafelson set out to accomplish with *Black Widow.* How? Through exploring the significance of the bond between the two women. Unfortunately, says Ansen, "there's less here than meets the eye." "*Black Widow* is an honorable attempt to rewire a favorite formula, but it doesn't go far enough. If you're going to play 'Persona' games with the film noir, you've got to risk a dive off the deep end" (Ansen 1987).

24. "This is postmodernist film noir," says Kael, in part because the behavior of the characters is unmotivated (1987a).

25. No doubt such an assessment of *Marnie* would have delighted Hitchcock. Many of the so-called serious critics of the pre-auteurist generation had attacked Hitchcock's films for lacking psychological realism. Hitchcock became especially sensitive to this issue during the early sixties, when he decided to do something about it. With both *The Birds* and *Marnie,* as we have seen, Hitchcock took great care to present psychologically believable characters.

26. For a number of academic film critics, Hitchcock's "greatest films" were precisely those which seemed to offer a critique of patriarchal society. For example, Robin Wood's reason for not rating the 1956 version of *The Man Who Knew Too Much* as quite among Hitchcock's best was that "the material does not permit the radical critique of patriarchal structures that Hitchcock undertook (whether he knew it or not) in, for example, *Notorious, Rear Window,* and *Vertigo,* which is what gives those films their profundity, their sense of being at once both profoundly disturbed and profoundly disturbing" (Wood 1989, 359). And that, stated Wood, was also what was wrong with the much heralded 1986 thriller *Blue Velvet* (1989, 43–49).

27. For a good source of pre-1970 thrillers, see Derry (1988). For reviews of pre-1970 thrillers, I relied primarily on the review files of the Academy Library.

28. For more on the distinction between "traditional" and "nontraditional" genre films, see Gehring (1988).

SIX

1. Kubler argues that the life of an artist should not be the major unit of study in the history of art, for that would be like "discussing the railroads of a country in terms of the experiences of a single traveler on several of them" (1962, 6). Instead, an artist's output should be viewed as part of a series "extending beyond him in either or both directions, depending upon his position in the track he occupies." The focus, that is, should be on the position that the artist occupies within an artistic tradition or genre.

2. "The mechanics of fame are such," says Kubler, "that their predecessors' talent is magnified, and their own is diminished, when talent itself is only a relatively common predisposition for visual order, without a wide range of differentiation. Times and opportunities differ more than the degree of talent" (1962, 7–8).

3. Shot on a budget of $40,000, *Greetings* (1968) grossed over a million dollars. Interestingly, this happened one year before the enormous financial success of *Easy Rider*.

4. Concluding his commentary, Sarris speculated that critics who liked *Obsession* must not be very familiar with *Vertigo*. After all, Sarris informs his reader, *Vertigo* had not been accessible for over a decade. "What I would like to see once the first run of *Obsession* is completed," says Sarris, "is a double bill of both films. Then my readers could judge for themselves whether I'm correct in my judgment that *Vertigo* is one of Hitchcock's most heartrendingly personal works, whereas *Obsession* is merely a mannered cerebral exercise without any emotional underpinning or unconscious feeling of its own" (Sarris 1976a).

5. A few prominent critics actually raved about *Obsession,* including *New York Post* critic Frank Rich, who would become head drama critic for the *New York Times*. He devoted two columns to the film, noting that it "is a complex and idiosyncratic piece of work. . . . Comparing *Vertigo* and *Obsession* is a prime example of your basic apples-and-oranges syndrome. It's only at the plot level that the two movies resemble each other, and in *Obsession,* as in many good movies, the plot is simply a catalyst that sets off the emotional and visual cataclysms that are the film's true rewards. . . . *Obsession* mixes suspense storytelling, sick comedy and heartwrenching romance until they merge into a unique vision that can't be classified according to the conventions of existing movie genres. It's a peculiar mix indeed—and one that is achieved by sophisticated and often risky, stylistic means" (Rich 1976c).

6. Was *Carrie* that superior to *Obsession?* It may have seemed so back in 1976 but it has become less self-evident over the years. For an impassioned defense of *Obsession* against earlier detractors, see Laemmle (1981).

7. Several critics and commentators had attacked *Obsession* for its solemnity and total lack of humor, for being a mere exercise in pure cinema, lacking the satiric vision so evident in many of De Palma's earlier films. A film commentator for the *New York Times,* for example, had written:

> To say that *Obsession* is wanting in wit is more courtesy than criticism. This movie takes itself so seriously that just when one ought to be gasping with surprise at the climactic turns on screen, one finds oneself chuckling at the exertions of the moviemakers—fuzzy pictures, wavy pictures, slow motion pictures, and inevitably, the up-to-the-minute stop-action picture, all put to the service of a preposterous denoument. Whatever shred of credibility the movie retains is dispersed by the final, dead-serious directorial hocus-pocus. (Goodman, 1976)

Critics wanted to know what had happened to De Palma. After having seen *Carrie,* Kael (1976) offered an explanation—Paul Schrader. "If the De Palma spirit was barely in evidence in *Obsession,*" writes Kael, "that was because the romantic conception operated on only one level; it lacked humor—this is where Paul Schrader, its scenarist, is weak."

8. Another criticism frequently lodged against De Palma's earlier films was that they lacked a cohesive narrative. Several critics attributed the success of *Carrie* to the fact that it was De Palma's first movie adapted from a novel. "King's novel," says Farber, "gives him the simple, cohesive narrative that he needs, though he transcends the novel, just as Francis Ford Coppola transcended Mario Puzo's novel of *The Godfather*" (Farber 1976).

9. Also in the thriller mode, *The Fury* (1978) received generally favorable reviews although not so overwhelmingly as did *Carrie.* A few reviewers, such as Kevin Thomas (1978), a critic for the *Los Angeles Times* and an early champion of De Palma's work, judged it to be even better than *Carrie.* Another long-time De Palma advocate, Pauline Kael (1978), wrote so ecstatically about the film that her entire review was used in an ad for the film that circulated in a number of metropolitan newspapers including the *Los Angeles Times* and *Washington Post.*

10. During this period, the Motion Picture Association of America's (MPAA) rating board began assigning X ratings to films which two years earlier would have received an R rating. When first rated, *Dressed to Kill* received an X—the designation for hard-core pornography and extreme violence, which angered De Palma. After making certain strategic cuts, he resubmitted the film to the ratings board. This time it received an R rating. Understandably upset with the rating board, De Palma used the media to vent his frustration. Labeling the activity of the MPAA's rating board as "repression" and "censorship," De Palma told a *New York Times* reporter that he sensed "a repressive era beginning in the country again. I always gauge these things," said De Palma, "by who's headed for the White House" (Wood 1980).

11. After completing *The Fury* in 1978, De Palma returned to Sarah Lawrence College, where he had earned a master's degree, to teach a course in filmmaking. Making *Home Movies* became the major project for the course. While De Palma directed the low-budget film, students performed many of the other key creative and administrative roles. De Palma got into a dispute with the film's distributor, United Classics, over how to best release it. De Palma wanted *Home Movies* to open first in New York City where he anticipated (correctly as it turned out) good reviews which could then be used to sell the picture to the rest of the nation. (After all, two of his most faithful supporters over the years were Vincent Canby and Pauline Kael. As we have seen, De Palma had reproduced Pauline Kael's rave review of *The Fury* in ads to promote the film.) United Classics reluctantly went along with De Palma's request but granted him only ten thousand dollars for advertising in New York City. He was furious, venting

his anger with United Classics in interviews conducted at around the time *Home Movies* was scheduled to open in New York.

12. For earlier evidence of Denby's attraction to Kael's style of criticism see Denby (1977).

13. Sarris interpreted the first encounter between Michael Caine and Angie Dickinson as "the equivalent of the first encounter between Tony Perkins and Janet Leigh in *Psycho*." He was also horrified that De Palma had unashamedly lifted whole sequences from other Hitchcock classics such as *Vertigo*. For instance, Sarris found the silent sequence at the Metropolitan Museum of Art to be roughly analogous to the gallery scene in *Vertigo*.

14. While Sarris (1980b) had found much of the film's dialogue simply awful, Kael (1980) had hardly anything to say about it. "There's very little dialogue altogether in *Dressed to Kill*," she said. "[W]hat talk there is," she added, is "casual, funny, and often good-naturedly off-color."

15. De Palma also reiterated his displeasure with the MPAA movie-ratings board for originally assigning *Dressed to Kill* an X, thereby forcing him to make a number of cuts before the film could receive an R. In his view, the ratings board had penalized his film for being effective.

16. After *Dressed to Kill*, De Palma had wanted to make a nonthriller, *Prince of the City*, based on a true story about an undercover police officer in New York City, but negotiations broke down.

17. Following *Scarface*, De Palma openly expressed his desire to get out of directing horror thrillers. One project he wanted to direct centered on a rock-and-roll singer whose career was on the skids. After that project failed to materialize, he fell back on *Body Double*, a project which originally he had no interest in directing.

18. In fact, *Scarface* made a weak showing at the box office, just breaking even.

19. In the same interview, De Palma expressed the view that changing attitudes towards women had not only reduced the number of suspense films with women in jeopardy but also accounted for why so few erotic movies were being made or "suspense movies with a sexual relationship. . . . I shudder to have you count on your fingers how many there've been. If you get past two, it's a miracle. I think it's an aspect of cinema that's been driven out by the sociology" (Darling 1987).

20. De Palma was frequently criticized for lacking a good ear for dialogue. Accordingly, a number of critics had advised him to work from somebody else's material rather than his own. With *The Untouchables*, it seemed that De Palma was finally following their advice.

SEVEN

1. From their perspective, Hitchcock and other American genre directors such as Howard Hawks and John Ford were not so unlike Shakespeare, whose plays had amused and entertained the general public (see, e.g., Wood 1968).

2. Foreshadowing Peter Wollen's (1969) argument in his later and more influential study of Hawks, Wood (1968) attempts to demonstrate that although Hawks, unlike Hitchcock, worked in a variety of genres a consistent vision or personal philosophy about the human condition underlies all his films.

3. In 1945 Capra had just returned to Hollywood from his World War II service in the Office of War Information. *It's a Wonderful Life* was his first postwar film project, succeeding his madcap comedy, *Arsenic and Old Lace,* which was made in 1941 but not released until 1944.

4. Truffaut and Lang corresponded briefly in the mid-fifties until Lang withdrew. Truffaut speculated that Lang had been put off because Truffaut had spoken "too highly of *The Blue Gardenia,*" a Lang film which Lang himself disowned (Truffaut 1956).

5. For a discussion of the distinction between recognition and renown, see Lang and Lang (1988, 84–86).

6. A noticeable difference between Eastwood in 1985 and Hitchcock in 1963 was Eastwood's openness with the general press regarding his wish to be taken seriously as a director. His forthrightness, I believe, helped nourish the debate over his stature as a filmmaker.

7. Horowitz's tenure at RCA was characterized by long lulls in his recording activity. To convey the impression that he was an active recording artist, RCA issued a number of recordings which appeared to be new but consisted of selections taken from previously issued recordings.

8. Horowitz's first Columbia recording received a Grammy Award for best classical recording of 1962, precipitating his brief return to the concert stage. But his infrequent recitals received mixed reviews, and he again retired in 1969. In 1974 he resumed concertizing with a vengeance, determined to become a media celebrity. His appearance on CBS's popular prime-time series, "Sixty Minutes," on 26 December 1977 exemplified his shift in image maintenance. In addition to exhibiting silly and childlike behavior, Horowitz performed a dazzling section from his transcription of "The Stars and Stripes Forever." Horowitz as showman had returned. During this period he expressed an indifference toward critics. Although many of his concerts and recordings during the seventies were not well received, a discernible shift in the aesthetics of musical performance toward a greater tolerance of a performer's "interpretative" skills made critics more receptive to Horowitz's idiosyncratic approach to musical performance than had been the case in earlier decades.

9. During the 1980s (and 1990s) journalistic music critics increasingly accepted the performer as a re-creative artist and were less in awe of the composer as the bastion of truth in art, a reaction, no doubt, to the early-music movement and its orthodoxy of textual fidelity.

10. Horowitz's career also illustrates this basic truth about managing reputations, namely, that one must not minimize the contributions of others in shaping an artist's work and reputation. For example, Horowitz's record producer, Thomas Frost, was a key influence in reshaping the pianist's art in the twilight of

his career. Horowitz made some of his finest recordings during the sixties and early seventies for Columbia Masterworks, with Frost as his producer. The piano sound on these recordings was noticeably less percussive and more mellow and the pace less frantic and more relaxed than in many of Horowitz's earlier recordings for RCA. Reviewers believed that his Columbia Masterwork recordings reflected a growing maturity in his artistry. But there is a problem with such an interpretation. Horowitz's live performances during this period were not as well received as were his recent recordings. I suggest that, apart from nerves, a major reason for the qualitative differences between his recordings and live performances was that Frost was himself more attuned to the introspective than to the flamboyant qualities of Horowitz's playing. (Like Robert Schumann's piano compositions, which he favored, Horowitz's playing always harbored elements of both the Apollonian and the Dionysian.) And Frost saw to it that on those recordings under his supervision the more meditative Horowitz would reign.

In the mid-seventies, when Horowitz resumed recording for RCA, the qualities of his playing, as reflected on these new recordings, seemed a throwback to his earlier RCA recordings—impulsive, percussive, and flashy. Clearly he was getting different advice from key collaborators at RCA.

Ten years later, Horowitz was recording for Deutsche Gramophone and later Sony, producing recordings reminiscent of those he had made during his glory days at Columbia during the sixties. A new maturity? Horowitz asked Frost to produce these new recordings, as he had in the sixties. Frost and probably other of Horowitz's close associates advised him to move away from bravura show pieces and to concentrate instead on more introspective miniatures that would showcase his melodic lyricism, rich sonorities, and broad dynamic range—qualities which had always been present in his playing alongside the more bravura ones. Under the skilled management of Frost, Horowitz's art was subtly reshaped and packaged along these lines.

11. However, in writing this book, one of my major concerns was to show how an "art world" or "production of culture" orientation could be fruitfully applied to the study of reputation, reception, and genre. For example, many of the results underscore the importance of the interorganizational links between film production companies, marketing firms, and cultural gatekeepers, such as critics and museum curators, in the creation and maintenance of a film director's reputation. Recall, for example, the coordinated collective action that produced the 1963 Hitchcock retrospective at the Museum of Modern Art. Also, the implementation of this approach in chapter 5 ("Hitchcock's Posthumous Reputation and the Contemporary Thriller") suggests that a similar chronicling of the production, dissemination, and reception of future cycles of thriller films would provide a rich context for determining what riches future filmmakers, movie executives, media gatekeepers, and audiences might claim or fabricate from the Hitchcock legacy.

BIBLIOGRAPHY

Academy Library (Margaret Herrick Library), The Academy of Motion Picture Arts and Sciences, Beverly Hills.

Allen, Jeanne Thomas. 1985. "The Representation of Violence to Women: Hitchcock's *Frenzy*." *Film Quarterly* 38, no. 3 (Spring): 30–38.

Allen, Robert C. 1987. "Reader-Oriented Criticism and Television." In Robert C. Allen, ed., *Channels of Discourse*. Chapel Hill: University of North Carolina Press, 74–112.

Allen, Robert C., and Douglas Gomery. 1985. *Film History: Theory and Practice*. New York: Alfred A. Knopf, esp. pp. 65–108.

Allen, Tom. 1978. Review of *Halloween*. *Village Voice*, 6 November.

Alpert, Hollis. 1956. Review of *The Man Who Knew Too Much*. *Saturday Review*, 26 May.

———. 1959. Review of *North by Northwest*. *Saturday Review*, 18 July.

———. 1962a. *The Dreams and the Dreamers*. New York: Macmillan.

———. 1962b. "This Year At Cannes." *Saturday Review*, 16 June.

———. 1963. "So Deeply Obscure, So Widely Discussed." *New York Times*, 21 April.

———. 1966. Review of *Torn Curtain*. *Saturday Review*, 13 August.

———. 1969. Review of *Topaz*. *Saturday Review*, 27 December.

Andrews, Nigel. 1984. Review of *The Man Who Knew Too Much* (1956). *Financial Times*, 15 June.

Ansen, David. 1975. Review of *The Eiger Sanction*. *Real Paper*, May.

———. 1978. "Trick or Treat." *Newsweek*, 4 December.

———. 1985. "Clint: An American Icon." *Newsweek*, 22 July.

———. 1987. Review of *Black Widow*. *Newsweek*, 16 February.

Archer, Eugene. 1964. Review of *Marnie*. *New York Times*, 23 July.

———. 1965. "Cahiers An In Word That Means Far Out." *New York Times*, 23 May.

Arnold, Gary. 1980. "The Enduring Image of Alfred Hitchcock." *Washington Post*, 4 May.

Asselle, Giovanna, and Behroze Gandhy. 1982. "A Discussion." *Screen* 23, nos. 3–4 (September–October): 137–43.

Austin, Bruce A. 1989. *Immediate Seating: A Look At Movie Audiences*. Belmont, Calif.: Wadsworth.

Bailin, Rebecca. 1982. "Feminist Readership, Violence, and *Marnie.*" *Film Reader* 5: 24–35.

Barry, Iris. 1941. "Film Library." *The Bulletin of The Museum of Modern Art* 8, no. 5.

Barthes, Roland. 1977. *Image/Music/Text.* Trans. Stephen Heath. New York: Hill and Wang.

Basinger Jeanine. 1986. *The It's A Wonderful Life Book.* New York: Alfred A. Knopf.

Bates, Robin. 1987. "Fiery Speech in a World of Shadows: Rosebud's Impact on Early Audiences." *Cinema Journal* 26, no. 2 (Winter): 3–26.

Bayer, William. 1968. "Was That Any Way To Greet 'Greetings'?" Letter to the Editor. *New York Times,* Sunday, 12 January.

Beaver, Frank Eugene. 1974. *Bosley Crowther: Social Critic of the Film. 1940–1967.* New York: Arno Press.

Becker, Howard S. 1974. "Art as Collective Action." *American Sociological Review* 39 (December): 767–76.

———. 1982. *Art Worlds.* Berkeley: University of California Press.

Belfrage, Cedric. 1926. "Alfred the Great, World's Youngest Filmmaker." *Picturegoer,* March.

Bellour, Raymond. 1969. "Les Oiseaux: Analyse d'une Séquence." *Cahiers du Cinéma* 216: 24–38.

———. 1975. "Le Blocage Symbolique." *Communications* 23: 235–350.

———. 1977. "Hitchcock, the Enunciator." *Camera Obscura* 2: 69–94.

———. 1979. "Psychosis, Neurosis, Perversion." *Camera Obscura* 3–4: 104–32.

Belton, John. 1969. "Mechanics of Perception." *Cambridge Phoenix,* 16 October. From the Hitchcock Collection.

———. 1970. Review of *Topaz. Boston After Dark,* 4 February.

———. 1972. Review of *Frenzy. Boston Phoenix,* 29 August.

Bender, Harold. 1958. "Profile of a TV Murderer." *Pictorial TVview.* Sunday, 6 April.

Bennett, Tony. 1982. "Text and Social Process: The Case of James Bond." *Screen Education* 41 (Winter/Spring): 9–14.

Bennett, Tony, and Janet Woollacott. 1987. *Bond and Beyond: The Political Career of a Popular Hero.* New York: Methuen.

Bergman, Andrew. 1971. *We're in the Money.* New York: New York University Press.

Bergson, Philip. 1984. Review of *The Man Who Knew Too Much* (1956). *What's On,* 14 June.

Bergstrom, Janet. 1979. "Enunciation and Sexual Difference (Part I)." *Camera Obscura,* nos. 3–4: 32–69.

Bioscope. 1926. Review of *The Lodger.* 16 September.

Blowen, Michael. 1984. Review of *The Man Who Knew Too Much* (1956). *Boston Globe,* 20 April.

Bogdanovich, Peter. 1963. *The Cinema of Alfred Hitchcock*. New York: Museum of Modern Art (Doubleday).

⸺. 1968. *Fritz Lang in America*. London: Studio Vista.

Borde, Raymond, and Etienne Chaumeton. 1955. *Panorama du Film Noir Américain*. Paris: Les Editions de Minuit, reprinted as part of "Sources of Film Noir," *Film Reader* 3, 1978.

Bordwell, David. 1981. *The Films of Carl Dreyer*. Berkeley: University of California Press.

⸺. 1985. *Narration in the Fiction Film*. Madison: University of Wisconsin Press.

⸺. 1989. *Making Meaning: Inference and Rhetoric in the Interpretation of Cinema*. Cambridge: Harvard University Press.

Bordwell, David, Janet Staiger, and Kristin Thompson. 1985. *The Classical Hollywood Cinema: Film Style & Mode of Production to 1960*. New York: Columbia University Press.

Bordwell, David, and Kristin Thompson. 1986. *Film Art: An Introduction*. Second Edition. New York: Alfred A. Knopf.

Boston Globe. 1956. Review of *The Man Who Knew Too Much*. 30 June.

Bourdieu, Pierre. 1984. *Distinction: A Social Critique of the Judgment of Taste*. Trans. Richard Nice. Cambridge: Harvard University Press.

Boyer, Peter J. 1981. "Film Clips." *Los Angeles Times*, 2 September.

Boyle, Robert. 1986. Personal interview, 16 April.

Brien, Alan. 1956. Review of *The Man Who Knew Too Much*. *Evening Standard*, 21 June.

Brill, Lesley. 1988. *The Hitchcock Romance: Love and Irony in Hitchcock's Films*. Princeton: Princeton University Press.

Brown, Gene. ed. 1984. *The New York Times Encyclopedia of Film*. New York: Times Books.

Brown, Royal S. 1982. "Hermann, Hitchcock, and the Music of the Irrational." *Cinema Journal* 21, no. 2 (Spring): 14–49.

Budd, Michael. 1981. "*The Cabinet of Dr. Caligari*. Conditions of Reception." *Cine-Tracts* 12 (Winter): 41–49.

⸺. 1986. "The National Board of Review and the Early Art Cinema in New York: *The Cabinet of Dr. Caligari* as Affirmative Culture." *Cinema Journal* 26, no. 1 (Fall): 3–18.

Cahiers du Cinéma. 1970. "Young Mr. Lincoln de John Ford." August: 29–47.

Cahill, Tim. 1985. "Clint Eastwood: The Rolling Stone Interview." *Rolling Stone*, 4 July.

Cameron, Ian. 1962a. "The Mechanics of Suspense." *Movie* 3, October: 5–7.

⸺. 1962b. "Review of *The Man Who Knew Too Much* (1956)." *Spectator*, 10 December.

⸺. 1963. "Suspense and Meaning." *Movie* 6.

⸺. 1976. "Review of *Family Plot*." *Spectator*, 4 September.

Cameron, Ian, and Richard Jeffery. 1965. "The Universal Hitchcock." *Movie* 12: 21–24.

Canby, Vincent. 1969a. "Who Made the Unkindest Cuts?" *New York Times,* 22 June.

———. 1969b. Review of *Topaz. New York Times,* 20 December.

———. 1972. Review of *Frenzy. New York Times,* 22 June.

———. 1973. Review of *Sisters. New York Times,* 27 September.

———. 1976a. Review of *Obsession. New York Times,* 2 August.

———. 1976b. "The Unscariest Horror Film." *New York Times.* Sunday, 5 December.

———. 1979. "Chilling Truths about Scaring." *New York Times.* Sunday, 21 January.

———. 1980a. "Alfred Hitchcock Was the Poet of Civilized Suspense." *New York Times.* Sunday, 11 May.

———. 1980b. Review of *Dressed to Kill. New York Times,* 23 July.

———. 1983. Review of *Rear Window. New York Times.* Sunday, 9 October.

———. 1984. "Three New Movies Enrich Their Genres." *New York Times.* Sunday, 23 September.

———. 1985. Review of *Pale Rider. New York Times,* 28 June.

———. 1987a. "In the Dark, It's Reality That Woos the Audience." *New York Times.* Sunday, 8 February.

———. 1987b. Review of *The Bedroom Window. New York Times,* 16 January.

Cantor, Muriel G. 1971. *The Hollywood TV Producer: His Work and His Audience.* New York: Basic Books.

———. 1980. *Prime-Time Television: Content and Control.* Beverly Hills: Sage.

Capra, Frank. 1936. "Mr. Capra (Humanist) Shares A Bow." *New York Times,* 19 April.

———. 1971. *The Name Above the Title: An Autobiography.* New York: Macmillan, 1971, especially 296–97.

Carney, Raymond. 1986. *American Vision: The Films of Frank Capra.* Cambridge: Cambridge University Press.

Carringer, Robert L. 1985. *The Making of Citizen Kane,* Berkeley: University of California Press.

Carroll, Kathleen. 1987. Review of *The Bedroom Window. New York Daily News,* 16 January.

Carroll, Noel. 1979. "Film History and Film Theory: An Outline for an Institutional Theory of Film." *Film Reader* 4: 81–96.

Castell, David. 1984. Review of *The Man Who Knew Too Much* (1956). *Sunday Telegraph,* 17 June.

Cavell, Stanley. 1986. "*North by Northwest.*" In Marshall Deutelbaum and

Leland Poague, eds., *A Hitchcock Reader.* Iowa: Iowa State University Press, 249–64.

Cawelti, John. 1970. *The Six-Gun Mystique.* Bowling Green: Bowling Green Popular Press.

Champlin, Charles. 1972. "A Return of Hitchcock Magic." *Los Angeles Times,* 14 July.

———. 1976. Review of *Family Plot. Los Angeles Times,* 9 April.

Christian Science Monitor. 1966. Review of *Torn Curtain.* 15 July.

Chute, David. 1980. "The De Palma Touch: *Dressed to Kill* and Its Delights." *Boston Phoenix,* 29 July.

———. 1983. Review of *Rear Window. Los Angeles Herald-Examiner,* 6 October.

Cinema Magazine. 1964. Review of *Marnie.* August.

Coleman, John. 1964. Review of *Marnie. New Statesman,* 10 July.

Connolly, Mike. 1954. "Losing 56 Pounds was *Fun.*" *Sunday Mirror Magazine,* 11 November.

Cook, Pam. ed. 1986. *The Cinema Book.* New York: Pantheon.

Corliss, Richard. 1976. Review of *Family Plot. New Times,* 16 April.

———. 1979. Review of *Halloween. New Times,* 18 January.

———. 1980. "Hitchcock Without Screams." *Soho News,* 7 May.

———. 1987. "The Ghost of Alfred Hitchcock." *Time,* 16 February.

———. 1990. "All Thumbs." *Film Comment* 26, no. 2 (March–April): 14–18.

Creelman, Eileen. 1939. "Alfred Hitchcock, English Director, to Take a Look at Hollywood." *New York Sun,* 15 June.

Crist, Judith. 1964. Review of *Marnie. New York Herald Tribune,* 23 July.

———. 1972. Review of *Frenzy. New York Magazine,* 26 June.

Crowther, Bosley. 1941. Review of *Suspicion. New York Times,* 21 November.

———. 1942. Review of *Saboteur. New York Times,* 8 May.

———. 1943. Review of *Shadow of a Doubt. New York Times,* 13 January.

———. 1944. Review of *Lifeboat. New York Times,* 13 January.

———. 1945. Review of *Scarlet Street. New York Times,* 15 February.

———. 1948. Review of *Rope. New York Times,* 29 August.

———. 1951. Review of *Strangers on a Train. New York Times,* 8 July.

———. 1954a. Review of *Rear Window. New York Times,* 5 August.

———. 1954b. A Point of View. *New York Times.* Sunday, 15 August.

———. 1955. Review of *The Wages of Fear. New York Times,* 20 February.

———. 1956. Review of *The Man Who Knew Too Much. New York Times,* 17 May.

———. 1958a. Review of *Vertigo. New York Times,* 29 May.

———. 1958b. "Thrills and Such." *New York Times.* Sunday, 1 June.

———. 1960a. Review of *Psycho. New York Times,* 17 June.

———. 1960b. "The Year's Best Films." *New York Times,* 25 December.

———. 1963. Review of *The Birds*. *New York Times,* 29 March.

———. 1966. Review of *Torn Curtain*. *New York Times,* 28 July.

———. 1967. *The Great Films: Fifty Golden Years of Motion Pictures*. New York: G. P. Putnam.

Culler, Jonathan. 1981. *The Pursuit of Signs: Semiotics, Literature, and Deconstruction*. London: Routledge and Kegan Paul.

Daily Express. 1926. Review of *The Lodger*. 15 September.

Daily Variety. 1972. Review of *Frenzy*. 26 May.

Danto, Arthur C. 1964. "The Art World." *Journal of Philosophy* 61: 571–84.

Dare, Michael. 1987. Review of *The Bedroom Window*. *L.A. Weekly,* 23 January.

Darling, Cary. 1987. "Brian De Palma at Bat." *BAM,* 31 July.

Delaplane, Stan. 1960. "I'm Just Wild About . . . " *Los Angeles Examiner,* 12 August.

Demonsablon, Philippe. 1959. "The Imperious Dialectic of Fritz Lang." In Stephen Jenkins, ed, *Fritz Lang: The Image and the Look*. London: British Film Institute, 18–25. Originally appeared in *Cahiers du Cinéma,* no. 99 (September).

De Palma, Brian. 1974. "De Palma Discusses *Phantom of the Paradise* at Arthur Knight's Film Class." University of Southern California. Reel to reel tape. 19 December.

———. 1978. "Seminar with Brian De Palma." Center for Advanced Film Studies, American Film Institute, Beverly Hills, Calif. 4 April 1973.

Denby, David. 1980. Review of *Dressed to Kill*. *New York Magazine,* 28 July.

———. 1983. Review of *Psycho II*. *New York Magazine,* 20 June.

———. 1984a. Review of *The Man Who Knew Too Much* (1956). *New York Magazine,* 30 April.

———. 1984b. Review of *Tightrope*. *New York Magazine,* 27 August.

———. 1987a. Review of *The Bedroom Window*. *New York Magazine,* 2 February.

———. 1987b. Review of *Black Widow*. *New York Magazine,* 16 February.

Denby, David. ed. 1977. *Awake in the Dark. An Anthology of American Film Criticism 1915 to the Present*. New York: Vintage Books.

Denzin, Norman K. 1990. "Reading Cultural Texts: Comment on Griswold." *American Journal of Sociology* 95, no. 6 (May): 1577–80.

Derry, Charles. 1988. *The Suspense Thriller: Films in the Shadow of Alfred Hitchcock*. Jefferson, N.C.: McFarland.

Deutelbaum, Marshall, and Leland Poague, eds. 1986. *A Hitchcock Reader*. Ames: Iowa State University Press.

DeVault, Marjorie L. 1990. "Novel Readings: The Social Organization of Interpretation." *American Journal of Sociology* 95, no. 4 (January): 887–921.

Dickie, George. 1975. *Art and the Aesthetic: An Institutional Analysis*. Ithaca: Cornell University Press.

Dickstein, Morris. 1980. "The Aesthetics of Fright." *American Film* (September): 32–37 + [9pp].

DiMaggio, Paul. 1982. "Cultural Entrepreneurship in Nineteenth-Century Boston: The Creation of an Organizational Base for High Culture in America." *Media, Culture & Society* 4 (January): 33–50.

Doane, Mary Ann. 1987. *The Desire to Desire: The Woman's Film of the 1940s*. Bloomington: Indiana University Press.

Douchet, Jean. 1960. "Hitch et son Public." *Cahiers du Cinéma* 19, no. 3: 7–15.

Dubal, David. 1984. *Reflections from the Keyboard. The World of the Concert Pianist*. New York: Summit Books.

Dunning, Jennifer. 1978. "Brian De Palma: I Operate On The Principal of Escalating Terror." *New York Times*. Sunday, 23 April.

Dyer, Richard. 1979. *Stars*. London: British Film Institute.

Eco, Umberto. 1977. *The Role of the Reader*. Bloomington: Indiana University Press.

Ebert, Roger. 1990. "All Stars." *Film Comment* 26, no. 3 (May–June): 45–51.

Edelstein, David. 1987. Review of *The Stepfather*. *Village Voice,* 3 March.

Edwards, Gregory J. 1985. *The International Film Posters: The Role of the Poster in Cinema Art, Advertising and History*. Salem, N.H.: Salem House.

Esterow, Milton. 1956. "All Around the Town with *The Wrong Man*." *New York Times,* 29 April.

Evening News. 1926. Review of *The Lodger*. 20 September.

———. 1964. Review of *Marnie*. 9 July.

Farber, Stephen. 1976. Review of *Carrie*. *New West*. 26 December.

———. 1981. "Why Do Critics Love Trashy Movies?" *American Film* (April): 65–66 + [3pp].

Faulkner, Robert R. 1983. *Music On Demand: Composers and Careers in the Hollywood Film Industry*. New Brunswick: Transaction Books.

Ferrara, Patricia. 1987. "The Discontented Bourgeois: Bourgeois Morality and the Interplay of Light and Dark Strains in Hitchcock's Films." *New Orleans Review* 14, no. 4: 79.

Film and Filming. 1970. Review of *Topaz*. January.

Film Daily. 1958. Review of *Vertigo*. 14 May.

Fish, Stanley. 1980. *Is There a Text in This Class?* Cambridge: Harvard University Press.

Fletcher, John. 1988. "Versions of Masquerade." *Screen* 29, no. 3 (Summer): 43–70.

Flitterman, Sandy. 1978. "Woman, Desire, and the Look: Feminism and the Enunciative Apparatus in Cinema." *Ciné-Tracts* 2 (Fall): 63–68.

French Film Office. 1960. "Cannes, 1960." *Letter from France,* March–April–May.

French, Philip. 1984. Review of *The Man Who Knew Too Much* (1956). *London Observer,* 17 June.

Gans, Herbert J. 1974. *Popular Culture and High Culture: An Analysis and Evaluation of Taste.* New York: Basic Books.

Gardner, Paul. 1969. "The French They Are a Movie Race." *New York Times,* 18 May.

Gehring, Wes D., ed. 1988. *Handbook of American Film Genres.* New York: Greenwood Press.

Gelmis, Joseph. 1970. "Brian De Palma." In *The Film Director As Superstar.* Garden City: Doubleday, 21–32.

Geng, Veronica. 1981. Review of *Blow Out. Soho Weekly News,* 22 July.

Gilliatt, Penelope. 1964. Review of *Marnie. Observer,* 12 July.

———. 1976a. Review of *Family Plot. New Yorker,* 19 April.

———. 1976b. Review of *Obsession. New Yorker,* 2 August.

Gitlin, Todd. 1983. *Inside Prime Time.* New York: Pantheon.

Glatzer, Richard, and John Raeburn, eds. 1975. *Frank Capra: The Man and His Films.* Ann Arbor: University of Michigan Press.

Gleiberman, Owen. 1983. Review of *Vertigo. Boston Phoenix,* 27 December.

Godard, Jean-Luc. 1956. Review of *The Man Who Knew Too Much. Cahiers du Cinéma* 64 (November).

Goldstein, Patrick. 1987. Review of *The Stepfather. Los Angeles Times,* 23 January.

Gomery, Douglas. 1991. *Movie History: A Survey.* Belmont, Calif.: Wadsworth.

Goodman, Walter. 1976. "The Man Who Would Be Hitchcock." *New York Times.* Sunday, 8 August.

Graham, Sheila. 1960. "Hollywood Today." *Courier Journal,* 24 July.

Grant, Barry Keith. 1986. "Experience and Meaning in Genre Films." In Barry Keith Grant, ed., *Film Genre Reader.* Austin: University of Texas Press, 114–28.

Grant, Barry Keith, ed. 1986. *Film Genre Reader.* Austin: University of Texas Press.

Grant, Lee. 1978. "*Halloween* in South Pasadena." *Los Angeles Times,* 27 May.

Greenberg, Abe. 1964. Review of *Marnie. Citizen-News,* 6 August.

Greenspun, Roger. 1970. Review of *Hi, Mom! New York Times,* 28 April.

Greig, Donald. 1987. "The Sexual Differentiation of the Hitchcock Text." *Screen* 28, no. 1 (Winter): 28–46.

Grenier, Richard. 1983. Review of *The Dark Side of Genius: The Life of Alfred Hitchcock,* by Donald Spoto. *New York Times Book Review,* 6 March.

Griffith, Richard. 1950. "Wyler, Wellman, and Huston." *Films in Review* 1, no. 1 (February): 1–5, 48.

———. 1951. "Part Three: The Film Since Then." In Paul Rotha. *The Film Till*

Now: A Survey of World Cinema. Revised Edition. New York: Funk and Wagnalls, 413–620.

————. 1958a. *Fred Zinnemann*. New York: The Museum of Modern Art Film Library.

————. 1958b. "*Vertigo* Pleases New York." *Los Angeles Times,* 17 June.

Griffith, Richard and Arthur Mayer. 1970. *The Movies*. Revised Edition. New York: Simon and Schuster.

Griswold, Wendy. 1986. *Renaissance Revivals: City Comedy and Revenge Tragedy in the London Theater, 1576–1980*. Chicago: University of Chicago Press.

————. 1987. "The Fabrication of Meaning: Literary Interpretation in the United States, Great Britain, and the West Indies." *American Journal of Sociology* 92, no. 5 (March): 1077–1117.

Grove, Martin A. 1987. "Hollywood Report." *Hollywood Reporter,* 9 January.

Guback, Thomas. 1969. *The International Film-Industry*. Bloomington: Indiana University Press.

Guernsey, Otis L. 1954a. Review of *Rear Window. New York Herald Tribune,* 5 August.

————. 1954b. Commentary on *Rear Window. New York Herald Tribune.* Sunday, 15 August.

Hale, Wanda. 1964. Review of *Marnie. New York Daily News,* 23 July.

Handel, Leo A. 1950. *Hollywood Looks at Its Audience.* Urbana: University of Illinois Press.

Hark, Ina Rae. 1990. "Keeping Your Amateur Standing: Audience Participation and Good Citizenship in Hitchcock's Political Films." *Cinema Journal* 29, no. 2 (Winter): 8–22.

Harmetz, Aljean. 1980. "Quick End of Low-Budget Horror Film." *New York Times,* 2 October.

————. 1988. "The Figures Don't Lie: Hollywood's Audience is Older and Pickier." *New York Times,* 7 March.

Hatch, Robert. 1958. Review of *Vertigo. Nation,* 14 June.

Henahan, Donal. 1987. "Talent Can Certainly Help, But a High E.Q. Is Essential." *New York Times,* Sunday, 15 February.

————. 1990. "Creator vs. Re-creator: Who Wins?" *New York Times.* Sunday, 5 August.

Hillier, Jim, ed. 1985. *Cahiers du Cinéma: The 1950s. Neo-Realism, Hollywood, New Wave*. Cambridge: Harvard University Press.

Hinson, Hal. 1981. Interview with Brian De Palma. Newspaper clipping, anonymous source, ca. July, Academy Library.

Hirsch, Paul M. 1972. "Processing Fads and Fashions: An Organization-Set Analysis of Cultural Industry Systems." *American Journal of Sociology* 77: 639–59.

Hirschberg, Lynn. 1984. "Brian De Palma's Deathwish." *Esquire*, January.
Hitchcock, Alfred. 1943. "Alfred Hitchcock Reduces as Plant Expands." *Life*, 27 December: 12–14.
———. 1950. "Core of the Movie—The Chase." Interview. *New York Times Magazine*, 29 October.
———. 1957a. "Alfred Hitchcock Presents: The Great Hitchcock Murder Mystery." *This Week Magazine*, 4 August.
———. 1957b. "Why You Need Chills and Thrills." *This Week Magazine*, 22 September.
———. 1959. "Master of Suspense Explains His Art." *Life*, 13 July.
Hitchcock Collection (Alfred Hitchcock Collection), Margaret Herrick Library, Academy of Motion Picture Arts and Sciences, Beverly Hills.
Hoberman, J. 1980. Review of *Dressed to Kill*. *Village Voice*, 23–29 July.
———. 1984. Review of *Tightrope*. *Village Voice*, 28 August.
———. 1988. Review of *Bird*. *Village Voice*, 4 October.
Hollywood Citizen-News. Review of *Psycho*. 11 August.
Hollywood Reporter. 1958. Review of *Vertigo*. 12 May 1958.
———. 1972. Review of *Frenzy*. 26 May.
Horkheimer, M., and T. W. Adorno. 1972. *Dialectic of Enlightenment*. New York: Herder and Herder.
Horowitz, Joseph. 1987. *Understanding Toscanini. How He Became an American Culture-God and Helped Create a New Audience for Old Music*. Minneapolis: University of Minnesota Press.
Horowitz, Vladimir. 1989. "Program Notes." *Horowitz at Home*. Deutsche Grammophon.
Horwitz, Margaret M. 1982. "*The Birds:* A Mother's Love." *Wide Angle 5*, no. 1: 42–48.
Houston, Penelope. 1956. Review of *The Man Who Knew Too Much*. *Sight and Sound* 26, no. 1 (Summer): 31.
———. 1963. "The Figure in the Carpet." *Sight and Sound* 34, no. 4: 159–64.
———. 1980. "Alfred Hitchcock." In Richard Roud, ed., *Cinema: A Critical Dictionary. The Major Film-Makers*. New York: Viking, 487–501.
Huss, Roy, and Norman Silverstein. 1968. *The Film Experience*. New York: Harper and Row.
Huyssen, Andreas. 1986. *After the Great Divide: Modernism, Mass Culture, Postmodernism*. Bloomington and Indianapolis: Indiana University Press.
Iser, Wolfgang. 1978. *The Act of Reading*. Baltimore: Johns Hopkins University Press.
Jauss, Hans Robert. 1982. *Toward an Aesthetic of Reception*. Trans. Timothy Bahti. Minneapolis: University of Minnesota Press.
Jenkins, Stephen, ed. 1981. *Fritz Lang: The Image and the Look*. London: British Film Institute Publication.

Jensen, Paul M. 1969. *The Cinema of Fritz Lang.* New York: A. S. Barnes.

Johnson, Erskine. 1946. "In Hollywood." *New York World Telegram,* 19 February.

Johnson, William. 1964. Review of *Marnie. Film Quarterly* 18 (Fall): 38–42.

Kael, Pauline. 1963a. "Circles and Squares." *Film Quarterly* 16, no. 3 (Spring): 12–26.

———. 1963b. "Films of the Quarter." *Film Quarterly* 16, no. 4 (Summer): 35.

———. 1969. Review of *Topaz. New Yorker,* 27 December.

———. [1968] 1970. "Trash, Art, and the Movies." In *Going Steady.* Boston: Little, Brown, 85–129. Originally appeared in *Harper's* in 1968.

———. 1971. *The "Citizen Kane" Book.* Boston: Little, Brown.

———. 1972. Review of *Dirty Harry. New Yorker,* 15 January.

———. 1974. Review of *Phantom of the Paradise. New Yorker,* 11 November.

———. 1976. Review of *Carrie. New Yorker,* 22 December.

———. 1978. Review of *The Fury. New Yorker,* 20 March.

———. 1980. Review of *Dressed to Kill. New Yorker,* 4 August.

———. 1981. Review of *Blow Out. New Yorker,* 27 July.

———. 1987a. Review of *Black Widow. New Yorker,* 23 February.

———. 1987b. Review of *The Stepfather. New Yorker,* 9 February.

———. 1987c. Review of *The Untouchables. New Yorker,* 29 June.

Kaplan, George [Robin Wood]. 1972. "Alfred Hitchcock: Lost in the Wood." *Film Comment* 8, no. 4: 46–53.

Kapsis, Robert E. 1982. "Dressed to Kill." *American Film* (March): 52–56.

———. 1986a. "Hitchcock: Auteur or Hack—How the Filmmaker Reshaped His Reputation Among the Critics." *Cineaste* 14: 30–35.

———. 1986b. "Hollywood Filmmaking and Audience Image." In Sandra Ball-Rokeach and Muriel Cantor, eds., *Media, Audience, and Social Structure.* Beverly Hills: Sage, 161–73.

———. 1987. "Hollywood Filmmaking and Reputation Building: Hitchcock's *The Birds.*" *Journal of Popular Film and Television* 15 (Spring): 5–15.

———. 1988a. "The Historical Reception of Hitchcock's *Marnie.*" *Journal of Film and Video* 40, no. 3 (Summer): 46–63.

———. 1988b. "Hitchcock in the James Bond Era." *Studies in Popular Culture* 11 (1): 64–79.

———. 1989. "Reputation Building and the Film Art World: The Case of Alfred Hitchcock." *Sociological Quarterly* 30, no. 1: 15–35.

———. 1991. "Hollywood Genres and the Production of Culture Perspective." In Bruce Austin, ed., *Current Research in Film,* vol. 5, Norwood, N.J.: Ablex Publishing, 68–85.

Kauffmann, Stanley. 1963a. Review of *The Birds. New Republic,* 13 April.

———. 1963b. "Films of the Quarter." *Film Quarterly* 16, no. 4 (Summer): 35.

————. 1972. Review of *Frenzy. New Republic,* 8 July.

————. 1976. Review of *Obsession. New Republic,* 18 September.

————. 1980. Review of *Dressed to Kill. New Republic,* 23 August.

————. 1981. Review of *Blow Out. New Republic,* 22 August.

Keane, Marian. 1980. "The Designs of Authorship: An Essay on *North by Northwest.*" *Wide Angle* 4, no. 1: 44–52.

————. 1986. "A Closer Look at Scopophilia." In Marshall Deutelbaum and Leland Poague, eds., *A Hitchcock Reader.* Ames: Iowa State University Press, 231–48.

Kehr, Dave. 1983. Review of *Vertigo. Chicago Reader,* 16 December, 32–33.

————. 1984. "Hitch's Riddle." *Film Comment* 20, no. 3 (May–June): 9–18.

————. 1987a. Review of *The Bedroom Window. Chicago Tribune,* 21 January.

————. 1987b. Review of *The Stepfather. Chicago Tribune,* 27 February.

————. 1990. "Cannes-do spirit. Eastwood once again is the festival's class act." *Chicago Tribune,* Sunday, 20 May.

Kenas, Alex. 1983. Review of *Psycho II. Newsday,* 3 June.

Kinematograph. 1926. Review of *The Lodger.* 23 September.

Kine Weekly. 1926. Review of *The Lodger.* 7 October.

King, Norman. 1984. *Abel Gance: A Politics of Spectacle.* London: British Film Institute.

Klinger, Barbara. 1989. "Digressions at the Cinema: Reception and Mass Culture." *Cinema Journal* 28, no. 4 (Summer): 3–19.

Knight, Arthur. 1954. Review of *Rear Window. Saturday Review,* 21 August.

————. 1957. *The Liveliest Art.* New York: New American Library.

————. 1958. Review of *Vertigo. Saturday Review,* 7 June.

————. 1963a. Review of *The Birds. Saturday Review,* 6 April.

————. 1963b. "The Auteur Theory." *Saturday Review,* 4 May.

————. 1964. Review of *Marnie. Saturday Review,* 5 September.

————. 1972. Review of *Frenzy. Saturday Review,* 24 June.

————. 1976a. Review of *Family Plot. Hollywood Reporter,* 18 March.

————. 1976b. Review of *Carrie. Hollywood Reporter,* 1 November.

————. 1978. "I Remember MOMA." *Hollywood Reporter,* 21 April.

————. 1988. "Teacher/Critic Looks Back on 40 Years in the Movies." *Los Angeles Times,* 13 March.

Kroll, Jack. 1983. Review of *Psycho II. Newsweek,* 13 June.

Kubler, George. 1962. *The Shape of Time.* New Haven: Yale University Press.

Laemmle, Ann. 1981. "Program Notes for *Obsession.*" *Cinema Texas* 21, no. 2 (19 November).

Lang, Fritz. 1974. "Fritz Lang Seminar." *Dialogue on Film* 3, no. 5 (April), 2–13.

Lang Collection (Fritz Lang Collection), Department of Special Collections, Doheny Library, University of Southern California.

Lang, Gladys Engel, and Kurt Lang. 1988. "Recognition and Renown: The Survival of Artistic Reputation." *American Journal of Sociology* 94, no. 1 (July): 79–109.

LaValley, Albert J., ed. 1972. *Focus on Hitchcock*. Englewood Cliffs, N.J.: Prentice-Hall.

Leff, Leonard. 1987. *Hitchcock and Selznick*. New York: Weidenfeld & Nicolson.

Lejeune, C. A. 1934. Review of *The Man Who Knew Too Much*. London Observer. Sunday, 29 December.

———. 1956. Review of *The Man Who Knew Too Much*. London Observer, 24 June.

———. 1958. Review of *Vertigo*. London Observer, 10 August.

———. 1960. Review of *Psycho*. London Observer, 7 August.

Levine, Lawrence W. 1988. *Highbrow/Lowbrow: The Emergence of Cultural Hierarchy in America*. Cambridge: Harvard University Press.

Lincoln Center, Billy Rose Theatre Collection, Library for the Performing Arts, New York.

Lloyd, Norman. 1977. "Seminar with Norman Lloyd." Center for Advanced Film Studies, American Film Institute, Beverly Hills, Calif., 9 October 1973.

Loder, Kurt. 1987. "Brian De Palma." *Rolling Stone*, 17 December.

Look. 1957. "Hitchcock's World." 26 November.

———. 1964. "Sean Connery: The Reluctant James Bond." 8 September.

Los Angeles Examiner. 1958. Review of *Vertigo*, 29 May.

Los Angeles Magazine. 1987. Review of *The Stepfather*. February.

Los Angeles Mirror. 1960. Review of *Psycho*. 11 August.

Los Angeles Mirror-News. 1956. Review of *The Man Who Knew Too Much*. 23 May.

Los Angeles Times. 1954. Review of *Rear Window*. 12 August.

———. 1955. "Hitchcock, Master of Suspense, Turns to TV." 11 September.

———. 1957. Review of *The Wrong Man*. 24 January.

———. 1958. Review of *Vertigo*. 29 May.

———. 1980. "Devil and Mr. LaLoggia." Calendar Section, 9 November.

Lounsbury, Myron O. 1973. *The Origins of American Film Criticism, 1909–1939*. New York: Arno Press.

Lovell, Glenn. 1972. Review of *Sisters*. Hollywood Reporter, 29 November.

Low, Rachel. 1971. *The History of the British Film, 1918–1929*. London: Allen and Unwin.

Lurie, Susan. 1981–82. "The Construction of the Castrated Woman in Psychoanalysis and Cinema." *Discourse* 4 (Winter): 52–74.

Macdonald, Dwight. 1963. Review of *The Birds*. Esquire, October.

———. 1969. *Dwight Macdonald On Movies*. Englewood Cliffs, N.J.: Prentice-Hall.

Mackinnon, Kenneth. 1990. *Misogyny in the Movies: The De Palma Question*. Newark: University of Delaware Press.

Mailer, Norman. 1983. "All the Pirates and People." *Parade Magazine,* 23 October, 4–7.

Maland, Charles J. 1989. *Chaplin and American Culture: The Evolution of a Star Image*. Princeton: Princeton University Press.

Malcolm, Derek. 1984. Review of *The Man Who Knew Too Much* (1956). *Guardian,* 14 June.

Martin, Pete. 1957. "I Call on Alfred Hitchcock." *Saturday Evening Post,* 27 July.

Maslin, Janet. 1972. Review of *Frenzy. Boston After Dark.* 20 June.

———. 1976. Review of *Carrie. Newsweek,* 9 August.

———. 1980. "Hitchcock: The Master Puts On Immortality." *New York Times.* Sunday, 4 May.

———. 1984. Review of *Vertigo. New York Times,* 15 January.

Mast, Gerald. 1982. *Howard Hawks, Storyteller*. New York: Oxford University Press.

Masters, Dorothy. 1960. "Spine-Chiller Alfie Really Tension-Easer." *New York Daily News,* 19 June.

Mayerson, Donald J. 1969. Review of *Greetings. The Villager,* 13 February.

Mayne, Judith. 1985. "Feminist Film Theory and Criticism." *Signs* 11 (Autumn): 81–100.

Mazzocco, Robert. 1970. "It's Only a Movie." *New York Review of Books,* 26 February.

McArthur, Colin. 1972. *Underworld U.S.A.* New York: Viking Press.

———. 1985. "British Film Reviewing: A Complaint." *Screen* 26, no. 1 (January–February): 79–84.

McBride, Joseph. 1969–70. Review of *Topaz. Film Heritage* 5, no. 2 (Winter): 17–23.

McBride, Joseph, ed. 1972. *Focus on Howard Hawks*. Englewood Cliffs, N.J.: Prentice-Hall.

McCarten, John. 1955a. Review of *The Wages of Fear. New Yorker,* 26 February.

———. 1955b. Review of *Diabolique. New Yorker,* 26 November.

———. 1958. Review of *Vertigo. New Yorker,* 7 June.

Merton, Robert K. 1968. "The Matthew Effect in Science." *Science* 199: 55–63.

Miller, Mark Crispin. 1980. "In Memoriam—A. H. (1899–1980)." *New Republic,* 26 July, 27–31.

Mishkin, Leo. 1968. Review of *Greetings, New York Morning Telegraph,* 16 December.

Mizell, Mary. 1980. "Cashing in on *Halloween.*" *Premiere* 11, no. 3.

Modleski, Tania. 1982. "Never to Be Thirty-Six Years Old . . . Rebecca as Female Oedipal Drama." *Wide Angle* 5: 34–41.

———. 1988. *The Women Who Knew Too Much: Hitchcock and Feminist Theory.* New York: Methuen.

MOMA, Department of Film, Exhibition, Study Center, and Office files, Museum of Modern Art, New York.

Montagu, Ivor. 1972. "Interview with Ivor Montagu." *Screen* 13, no. 3: 71–113.

———. 1980. "Working with Hitchcock." *Sight and Sound* 49, no. 3 (Summer): 189–93.

Motion Picture Exhibitor. 1969. Review of *Topaz.* 17 December.

Mourlet, Michel. 1959. "Fritz Lang's Trajectory." In Stephen Jenkins, ed., *Fritz Lang: The Image and the Look.* London: British Film Institute, 12–17. Originally appeared in *Cahiers du Cinéma,* no. 99 (September).

Mulkay, Michael, and Elizabeth Chaplin. 1982. "Aesthetics and the Artistic Career: A Study of Anomie in Fine-Art Painting." *Sociological Quarterly* 23 (Winter): 117–38.

Mulvey, Laura. 1975. "Visual Pleasure and Narrative Cinema." *Screen* 16 (Autumn): 6–18.

Murray, Edward. 1975. *Nine American Film Critics: A Study of Theory and Practice.* New York: Frederick Ungar.

Museum of Modern Art. 1964. "The Museum of Modern Art Film Library Presents The Films of Billy Wilder, December 13, 1964–February 6, 1965" (published as a press kit for publicity in connection with the exhibition). New York: Museum of Modern Art.

Naremore, James. 1973. *Filmguide to Psycho.* Bloomington: Indiana University Press.

———. 1990. "Authorship and the Cultural Politics of Film Criticism." *Film Quarterly* 44, no. 1 (Fall): 14–22.

Natale, Richard. 1987. "Movie Talk." *Los Angeles Herald Examiner,* 3 April.

Nation. 1956. Review of *The Man Who Knew Too Much.* 9 June.

———. 1957. Review of *The Wrong Man.* 5 January.

———. 1970. Review of *Topaz.* 12 January.

Neal, Steve. 1981. "Art Cinema as Institution." *Screen* 22, no. 1: 11–39.

Newsweek. 1956. "Alfred Hitchcock—Director: On TV or at the Movies, Suspense Is Golden." 11 June.

———. 1957. Review of *The Wrong Man.* 7 January.

———. 1958. Review of *Vertigo.* 2 June.

———. 1966. Review of *Torn Curtain.* 8 August.

———. 1972. Review of *Frenzy.* 26 June.

New York Daily News. 1956. Review of *The Wrong Man.* 24 December.

———. 1958. Review of *Vertigo.* 29 May.

———. 1964. Review of *Marnie.* 23 July.

New York Herald Tribune. 1956. Review of *The Man Who Knew Too Much.* 17 May.

———. 1958. Review of *Vertigo.* 29 May.

———. 1959. Review of *North by Northwest*. 7 August.

New York Journal American. 1964. Review of *Marnie*. 23 July.

New York Post. 1959. Review of *North by Northwest*. 7 August.

New York Times. 1956. Review of *The Wrong Man*. 24 December.

———. 1959. Review of *North by Northwest*. 7 August.

———. 1960. Letter to the Editor on the Subject of *Psycho*. 11 September.

———. 1964. Review of *Marnie*. 23 July.

New Yorker. 1953. Review of *The Wages of Fear*. 16 May.

———. 1954. Review of *Rear Window*. 7 August.

———. 1956. Review of *The Man Who Knew Too Much*. 26 May.

———. 1957. Review of *The Wrong Man*. 5 January.

———. 1958. Review of *Vertigo*. 7 June.

———. 1959. Review of *North by Northwest*. 15 August.

———. 1960. Review of *Psycho*. 25 July.

———. 1964. Review of *Marnie*. 1 August.

Nugent, Frank S. 1936. Review of *Fury*. *New York Times*, 6 June.

———. 1946. "Mr. Hitchcock Discovers Love." *New York Times Magazine*, 3 November.

Olddie, Allan. 1980. "Making *The Fog*: An Interview with Director John Carpenter." *Film and Video Monthly Filmmakers* 13, no. 5 (March), 17–21.

Oster, Jerry. 1973. Review of *Sisters*. *New York Daily News*, 27 September.

Ott, Frederick W. 1979. *The Films of Fritz Lang*. Secaucus, N.J.: The Citadel Press.

Pacey, Ann. 1964. Review of *Marnie*. *Daily Herald* (London), 10 July.

Palmer, Jerry. 1979. *Thrillers: Genesis and Structure of a Popular Genre*. New York: St. Martin's Press.

Palmer, R. Barton. 1986. "The Metafictional Hitchcock: The Experience of Viewing and the Viewing of Experience in *Rear Window* and *Psycho*." *Cinema Journal* 25, no. 2 (Winter): 4–19.

Parker, James J. 1986. "Organizational Environment of the Motion Picture Sector." In Sandra Ball-Rokeach and Muriel Cantor, eds., *Media, Audience, and Social Structure*. Beverly Hills: Sage, 143–60.

Paul, William. 1972. Review of *Frenzy*. *Rolling Stone*, 20 July.

Pearson, Kenneth. 1956. Review of *The Man Who Knew Too Much*. *London Times*. Sunday, 24 June.

Perry, Simon. 1981. "Cannes, Festivals and the Movie Business." *Sight and Sound* 50, no. 4 (Autumn): 226–32.

Peterson, Richard A. 1982. "Five Constraints on the Production of Culture: Law, Technology, Market, Organizational Structure and Occupational Careers." *Journal of Popular Culture* 16: 143–53.

Piso, Michele. 1986. "Mark's Marnie." In Marshall Deutelbaum and Leland Poague, eds., *A Hitchcock Reader*. Ames: Iowa State University Press, 288–303.

Place, J. A., and L. S. Peterson. 1974. "Some Visual Motifs of Film Noir." *Film Comment* 10 (January–February): 30–32.

Plaskin, Glenn. 1983. *Horowitz*. New York: William Morrow.

Poague, Leland A. 1975. *The Cinema of Frank Capra: An Approach to Film Comedy*. South Brunswick and New York: A. S. Barnes.

————. 1982. *Howard Hawks*. Boston: Twayne.

Pollock, Dale. 1982. "Carpenter: Doing His 'Thing' Despite Critics." *Los Angeles Times*, Calendar Section, 9 July.

Posner, Richard A. 1990. *Cardozo: A Study in Reputation*. Chicago: University of Chicago Press.

Prouty, Howard. 1984. "The Alfred Hitchcock Teleguide." Unpublished reference draft. West Hollywood, Calif.

Rafferty, Terrence. 1987. Review of *The Stepfather*. *Nation*, 30 May.

Rainer, Peter. 1984. Review of *Body Double*. *Los Angeles Herald Examiner*, 26 October.

Ray, Robert B. 1985. *A Certain Tendency of the Hollywood Cinema, 1930–1980*. Princeton, N.J.: Princeton University Press.

Read, Herbert. 1937. *Art and Society*. New York: Macmillan.

Rebello, Stephen. 1986. "Psycho: The Making of Alfred Hitchcock's Masterpiece . . . " *Cinefantastique* 16, nos. 4–5 (October): 48–63 + [28 pp].

————. 1990. *Alfred Hitchcock and the Making of Psycho*. New York: Dembner Books.

Reed, Rex. 1976. Review of *Obsession*. *New York Daily News*, 30 July.

————. 1980. "'Dressed to Kill' Tops in Bad Taste." *New York Daily News*, 25 July.

Rich, Frank. 1976a. Review of *Family Plot*. *New York Post*, 17 April.

————. 1976b. Review of *Obsession*. *New York Post*, 2 August.

————. 1976c. "Obsession, Obsession, Obsession." *New York Post*, 7 August.

Rodden, John. 1989. *The Politics of Literary Reputation: The Making and Claiming of 'St. George' Orwell*. New York: Oxford University Press.

Rohmer, Eric, and Claude Chabrol. 1957. *Hitchcock*. Paris: Editions Universitaires.

————. 1979. *Hitchcock: The First Forty-Four Films*. Trans. Stanley Hochman. New York: Frederick Ungar.

Root, Jane. 1986. "Film Noir." In *The Cinema Book*, ed. Pam Cook. New York: Pantheon, 93–98.

Rose, Jacqueline. 1976–77. "Paranoia and the Film System." *Screen* 17, no. 4 (Winter): 85–104.

Ross, Don. 1960. "Psycho Took Skill to Placate Censor." *New York Herald Tribune*, Sunday, 26 June.

Rotha, Paul. 1951. *The Film Till Now: A Survey of World Cinema*. Revised Edition. New York: Funk and Wagnalls.

Rothman, William. 1982. *Hitchcock: The Murderous Gaze*. Cambridge: Harvard University Press.

―――. 1983. "*North by Northwest.*" *North Dakota Quarterly* 51, no. 3 (Summer): 11–24.

Ryall, Tom. 1986. *Alfred Hitchcock and the British Cinema*. Urbana and Chicago: University of Illinois Press.

Ryan, Desmond. 1984. Review of *The Man Who Knew Too Much*. *Philadelphia Inquirer*, 25 June.

Sage Collection (George Byron Sage Collection), Louis B. Mayer Library, American Film Institute, Los Angeles.

Salamon, Julie. 1987a. Review of *The Bedroom Window*. *Wall Street Journal*, 22 January.

―――. 1987b. Review of *Black Widow*. *Wall Street Journal*, 5 February.

―――. 1987c. Review of *The Untouchables*. *Wall Street Journal*, 4 June.

Sarris, Andrew. 1955. "The Trouble With Hitchcock." *Film Culture* 1, nos. 5–6 (Winter): 31.

―――. 1960. Review of *Psycho*. *Village Voice*, 11 August.

―――. 1961. "The Director's Game." *Film Culture*, nos. 22–23 (Summer): 68–81.

―――. 1962a. "Notes on the *Auteur* Theory in 1962." *Film Culture* 27 (Winter): 1–8.

―――. 1962b. "The World of Howard Hawks." Parts 1, 2. *Films and Filming* 8, no. 10 (July): 20–23+; no. 11 (August): 44–48.

―――. 1963. Review of *The Birds*. *Village Voice*, 4 April.

―――. 1964. Review of *Marnie*. *Village Voice*, 9 July.

―――. 1966. *The Films of Joseph von Sternberg*. New York: The Museum of Modern Art.

―――. 1968a. *The American Cinema*. New York: Dutton.

―――. 1968b. "Directors, How Personal Can You Get?" *New York Times*, 12 May.

―――. 1968c. "Jules and Jim Meets Psycho: A Review of *Hitchcock*, by François Truffaut." *Book World, Washington Post*, 14 January.

―――. 1969. Review of *Topaz*. *Village Voice*, 25 December.

―――. 1976a. Review of *Obsession*. *Village Voice*, 30 August.

―――. 1976b. Review of *Carrie*. *Village Voice*, 29 November.

―――. 1978. "Howard Hawks: The Perplexing Auteur." *Village Voice*, 16 January.

―――. 1979. "MOMA & The Movies." *Art News* (October 1979): 109–13.

―――. 1980a. Review of *Dressed to Kill*. *Village Voice*, 23–29 July.

―――. 1980b. "Dreck to Kill." *Village Voice*, 17 September.

―――. 1981. Review of *Blow Out*. *Village Voice*, 29 July–4 August.

―――. 1982. "The Last Word on Cannes." *American Film*, May.

―――. 1983a. "The Critical Anatomy of Alfred Hitchcock." *Village Voice*, 18 October.

———. 1983b. Review of *Psycho II*. *Village Voice*, 14 June.

———. 1984a. "Films in Focus." *Village Voice*, clipping with no date, British Film Institute (Spring 1984).

———. 1984b. "Hitchcock's Les Parents Terribles." *Village Voice*, 12 June.

———. 1985. *The American Cinema: Directors and Directions, 1929–1968*. With a New Foreword. Chicago: University of Chicago Press.

———. 1987. Review of *The Untouchables*. Village Voice, 28 July.

Saturday Review. 1954. Review of *Rear Window*. 21 August.

———. 1956. Review of *The Man Who Knew Too Much*. 26 May.

———. 1957. Review of *The Wrong Man*. 19 January.

———. 1958. Review of *Vertigo*. 7 June.

———. 1959. Review of *North by Northwest*. 18 July.

Schaefer, Stephen. 1980. "A 'Master' of Schlock But Hardly a Hitchcock." *US Magazine*, 2 September.

Schapiro, Steve, and David Chierichetti. 1979. *The Movie Poster Book*. New York: E. P. Dutton.

Schatz, Thomas. 1981. *Hollywood Genres: Formulas, Filmmaking, and the Studio System*. Philadelphia: Temple University Press.

———. 1988. *The Genius of the System: Hollywood Filmmaking in the Studio Era*. New York: Pantheon.

Scheuer, Philip K. 1960. Review of *Psycho*. *Los Angeles Times*, 11 August.

——— . 1963. Review of *The Birds*. *Los Angeles Times*, 29 March.

———. 1964. Review of *Marnie*. *Los Angeles Times*, 6 August.

Schickel, Richard. 1964. *Movies: The History of an Art and an Institution*. New York: Basic Books.

———. 1969. "Don't Go to the Movies to Escape—The Movies Are Now High Art." *New York Times*, 5 January.

———. 1970. Review of *Hi, Mom! Life*, 5 June.

———. 1972a. Review of *Frenzy*. *Life*, 2 June.

———. 1972b. "We're Living in a Hitchcock World, All Right." *New York Times Magazine*, 29 October.

———. 1973a. Review of *High Plains Drifter*. *Time*, 23 April.

———. 1973b. Review of *Sisters*. *Time*, 30 April.

———. 1975. *The Men Who Made The Movies*. New York: Atheneum.

———. 1976. Review of *Carrie*. *Time*, 8 November.

———. 1980. "Master of Existential Suspense. Alfred Hitchcock: 1899–1980." *Time*, 12 May.

———. 1983. Review of *Psycho II*. *Time*, 20 June.

———. 1984. *D. W. Griffith: An American Life*. New York: Simon and Schuster.

———. 1985. "The Final Mystery." *On Cable*, June.

Schrader, Paul. 1972. "Notes on Film Noir." *Film Comment* 8 (Spring): 8–13.

Sharff, Stefan. 1982. *The Elements of Cinema: Toward a Theory of Cinesthetic Impact*. New York: Columbia University Press.

———. 1991. *Alfred Hitchcock's High Vernacular: Theory and Practice*. New York: Columbia University Press.

Sheed, Wilfred. 1969. Review of *Greetings*. *Esquire,* April.

Sheehan, Henry. 1984. Review of *The Man Who Knew Too Much* [1956]. *Boston Phoenix,* 8 May.

Sight and Sound. 1992. "Top 10 Films." Vol. 2, no. 8 (December): 18–30.

Silverman, Kaja. 1983. *The Subject of Semiotics*. New York: Oxford University Press.

Silverman, Stephen M. 1984. "People Yearn for Hitchcock Movies, Says His Daughter." *New York Post,* 5 March.

Simon, John. 1976. Review of *Carrie*. *New York Magazine,* 6 December.

Sklar, Robert. 1975. "The Imagination of Stability: The Depression Films of Frank Capra." In Richard Glatzer and John Raeburn, eds., *Frank Capra: The Man and His Films*. Ann Arbor: University of Michigan Press, 121–48.

Skolsky, Sidney. 1948. "Hollywood Is My Beat." *New York Post,* 19 September.

Slesar, Henry. 1985. Introduction. In Francis M. Nevins, Jr., and Martin Harry Greenberg, eds., *Hitchcock in Prime Time*. New York: Avon Books, 1–7.

Smelser, Neil J. 1976. *Comparative Methods in the Social Sciences*. Englewood Cliffs, N.J.: Prentice-Hall.

Sontag, Susan. [1966] 1982. "One Culture and the New Sensibility." In Sontag, *Against Interpretation and Other Essays*. New York: Farrar, Straus and Giroux.

Spoto, Donald. 1976. *The Art of Alfred Hitchcock. Fifty Years of His Motion Pictures*. New York: Hopkinson and Blake.

———. 1983. *The Dark Side of Genius: The Life of Alfred Hitchcock*. New York: Balantine.

Stack, Peter. 1983. Review of *Psycho II*. *San Francisco Chronicle,* 4 June.

Staiger, Janet. 1983. "Individualism Versus Collectivism." *Screen* 23, nos. 4–5 (July/October): 68–79.

———. 1985. "The Politics of Film Canons." *Cinema Journal* 24 (Spring): 4–23.

———. 1986. "The Handmaiden of Villainy. Methods and Problems in Studying Historical Reception of a Film." *Wide Angle* 8, no. 1: 19–27.

———. 1990. "Announcing Wares, Winning Patrons, Voicing Ideals: Thinking about the History and Theory of Film Advertising." *Cinema Journal* 29, no. 3 (Spring): 3–31.

Stam, Robert, and Roberta Pearson. 1983. "Hitchcock's *Rear Window:* Reflexivity and the Critique of Voyeurism." *Enclitic* 7 (Spring): 136–45.

Sterritt, David. 1983. Review of *Psycho II*. *Christian Science Monitor,* 23 June.

———. 1984. Review of *Body Double*. *Christian Science Monitor,* 13 November.

Stevenson, James. 1980. "Profiles" (John Carpenter). *New Yorker*, 28 January, 41–42.

Suleiman, Susan R., and Inge Crosman, eds. 1980. *The Reader in the Text*. Princeton: Princeton University Press.

Summers, Jimmy. 1984. Review of *Body Double*. *Box Office*. December.

Swidler, Ann, Melissa Rapp, and Yasemin Soyal. 1986. "Format and Formula in Prime-Time TV." In Sandra J. Ball-Rokeach and Muriel G. Cantor, eds., *Media, Audience, and Social Structure*. Newbury Park, Calif.: Sage, 324–37.

Swingewood, Alan. 1987. *Sociological Poetics and Aesthetic Theory*. New York: St. Martin's Press.

Taylor, Clarke. 1976. "Brian De Palma Boxed in by Shadows." *Los Angeles Times*. Sunday, Calendar Section, 19 September.

Taylor, Gary. 1989. *Reinventing Shakespeare: A Cultural History From the Restoration to the Present*. New York: Oxford University Press.

Taylor, John Russell. 1978. *Hitch: The Life and Times of Alfred Hitchcock*. New York: Pantheon.

Thomas, Kevin. 1970a. Review of *Hi, Mom! Los Angeles Times*, 25 June.

———. 1970b. "Filmmaker at the Gut Level." *Los Angeles Times*, 7 July.

———. 1973. Review of *Sisters*. *Los Angeles Times*, 18 April.

———. 1978. Review of *The Fury*. *Los Angeles Times*, 15 March.

Thompson, Anne. 1987. "Return of the Thriller." *L.A. Weekly*, 20–26 February.

Thompson, Jack. 1964. Review of *Marnie*. *New York Journal American*, 23 July.

Time. 1954. Review of *Rear Window*. 2 August.

———. 1957. Review of *The Wrong Man*. 14 January.

———. 1958. Review of *Vertigo*. 16 June.

———. 1960. Review of *Psycho*. 27 June.

———. 1963. Review of *The Birds*. 5 April.

———. 1964. Review of *Marnie*. 31 July.

Tomaševskij, Boris. 1978. "Literature and Biography." In Ladislav Matejka and Krystyna Pomorska, eds., *Readings in Russian Poetics: Formalist and Structuralist Views*. Ann Arbor: Michigan Slavic Publications, 47–55.

Tompkins, Jane. 1985. *Sensational Designs: The Cultural Work of American Fiction 1790–1860*. New York: Oxford University Press (esp. chap. 1, on Hawthorne's literary reputation).

Tompkins, Jane, ed. 1980. *Reader-Response Criticism: From Formalism to Post-Structuralism*. Baltimore: Johns Hopkins University Press.

Truffaut, François. [1954] 1964. "Skeleton Keys." *Film Culture* 32 (Spring): 63–67. Originally appeared in *Cahiers du Cinéma*.

———. 1956. Letter to Luc Moullet. In François Truffaut. *Correspondence: 1945–1984*. New York: Farrar, Straus and Giroux, 1989, 93.

———. 1967. *Hitchcock*. Revised edition, 1984. New York: Simon and Schuster.

Tuchman, Gaye. 1984. "Consciousness Industries and the Production of Culture." *Journal of Communication* 33: 330–41.

———. 1989. *Edging Women Out: Victorian Novelists, Publishers, and Social Change*. New Haven: Yale University Press.

TV Guide. 1957. "No Problem for Mr. Hitchcock; the old master contends he enjoys more freedom in TV than the movies ever offered." 30 November.

Variety. 1958. Review of *Vertigo*. 14 May.

———. 1963. Review of *The Birds*. 27 March.

———. 1982. "Fear 'Stalk & Slash' Horror." 26 May.

———. 1983a. "Incredible Shrinking Horror Market." 16 February.

———. 1983b. Review of *Psycho II*. 1 June.

———. 1984. "Horrid Year for Horror." 25 January.

———. 1987. Review of *The Bedroom Window*. 5 January.

Vinocur, John. "Clint Eastwood, Seriously." *New York Times Magazine*, 24 February.

Walker, Alexander. 1964. Review of *Marnie*. *Evening Standard* (London), 9 July.

Waller, Gregory A., ed. 1987. *American Horrors: Essays on the Modern American Horror Film*. Urbana: University of Illinois Press.

Warner Bros. Archives, Department of Special Collections, Doheny Library, University of Southern California.

Warner, Laurie. 1980. "Horrors! It's Getting to Be No Joke!" *Los Angeles Times*. Sunday, 24 August.

Weinberg, Joel. 1987. Review of *Black Widow*. *New York Native*, 23 February.

Weis, Elisabeth. 1982. *The Silent Scream: Alfred Hitchcock's Sound Track*. Rutherford: Fairleigh Dickinson University Press.

Wexman, Virginia Wright. 1986. "The Critic as Consumer: Film Study in the University, *Vertigo*, and the Film Canon." *Film Quarterly* 39, no. 3 (Spring): 32–41.

Willis, Ellen. 1987. "Sins of the Fathers." *Village Voice*, 15 December, 85–86.

Wilmington, Michael. 1983. Review of *Vertigo*. *L.A. Weekly*, 25 November–1 December.

———. 1987. Review of *The Bedroom Window*. *Los Angeles Times*, 16 January.

Winnington, Richard. 1953. Review of *The Man Who Knew Too Much* (1934). *News Chronicle* (London), 25 April.

Winsten, Archer. 1963. Review of *The Birds*. *New York Post*, 29 March.

———. 1964. Review of *Marnie*. *New York Post*, 23 July.

———. 1968. Review of *Greetings*. *New York Post*, 16 December.

———. 1980. Review of *Dressed to Kill*. *New York Post*, 25 July.

Wolf, William. 1980. "The Thrill is Gone." *New York Magazine*, 26 May.

Wolfe, Charles, ed. 1989. *Meet John Doe*. New Brunswick, N.J.: Rutgers University Press.

Wolff, Janet. 1983. *Aesthetics and the Sociology of Art*. London: George Allen and Unwin.

Wollen, Peter. 1969. *Signs and Meaning in the Cinema*. Bloomington: Indiana University Press.

———. 1982. *Readings and Writings: Semiotic Counter-Strategies*. London: Verso.

Wood, Peter. 1980. "*Dressed to Kill*.—How a Film Changes From 'X' to 'R'." *New York Times*. Sunday, 20 July.

Wood, Robin. 1968. *Howard Hawks*. Garden City: Doubleday.

———. [1965] 1977. *Hitchcock's Films*. 3d ed. South Brunswick and New York: A. S. Barnes.

———. 1978. "Return of the Repressed." *Film Comment*, 25–32 July.

———. 1983. "Fear of Spying." *American Film* 7, no. 1: 28–35.

———. 1989. *Hitchcock's Films Revisited*. New York: Columbia University Press.

Wright, Will. 1975. *Sixguns and Society: A Structural Study of the Western*. Berkeley: University of California Press.

Yacowar, Maurice. 1977. *Hitchcock's British Films*. Hamden: Shoestring Press.

Zilsel, Edgar. 1926. *Die Entstehung des Geniebegriffs*. Tubingen: J. C. B. Mohr (Siebeck).

Zolberg, Vera L. 1990. *Constructing a Sociology of the Arts*. New York: Cambridge University Press.

INDEX

Controlled comparison, 216
Corliss, Richard, 117, 180, 268 n. 3
Crist, Judith, 112, 123
Criticism: in Britain and America,
    156–57; on genre films, 186–87;
    and Hitchcock's reputation, 1;
    Hitchcock's response to, 81;
    New Criticism, 102–3; and real-
    ism, 12, 100, 107, 218; on
    thrillers, 1–2, 13, 15, 185–86.
    See also Auteur theory; Feminist
    film theory
Cronyn, Hume, 77
Crowther, Bosley, 27–28; on
    Hitchcock, 245 nn. 13, 14, 256
    n. 26; on Hollywood films, 101;
    on *The Man Who Knew Too
    Much*, 44; on *Psycho*, 63; and so-
    cial problem films, 1; on *Torn
    Curtain*, 98; on *Vertigo*, 53; on
    The Wages of Fear, 185
Cundey, Dean, 168, 169

Dali, Salvador, 25
Day, Doris, 43, 45, 153, 179
Dead and Buried, 171
Denby, David: on *The Bedroom
    Window*, 178–79; on *Black
    Widow*, 181; on *Dressed to Kill*,
    203, 204, 205; on *Psycho II*,
    175; Sarris on, 207; on *Tight-
    rope*, 233
De Palma, Brian, 188–215; as
    American Godard, 190–95; as
    artist, 196, 209; as brilliant
    "sicko," 208–12; ceasing to
    make thrillers, 187, 213, 215;
    critical responses to, 15, 275 n. 8;
    early reputation of, 11–12, 190–
    93; and Hitchcock, 165, 251 n.
    7; Kael on, 189–90, 191, 204–5,
    209, 275 n. 7; as new master of
    suspense, 196–208; response to
    critics, 208, 211; as respectable

director, 212–15; on suspense,
    201; youth-market appeal of,
    196
De Sica, Vittorio, 28
Diabolique, 53, 54, 57
Dial M for Murder, 26, 248
Dickinson, Angie, 206
Directors: auteurist pantheon of,
    216–17; in film publicity,
    16–17; Hitchcock on, 20;
    Hitchcock's reputation as, 23;
    as major source of meaning, 228;
    studio directors, 217. *See also*
    Auteur theory
Dirty Harry, 229
Downes, Olin, 241
Downhill, 247
Dressed to Kill: and *Blow Out*, 209;
    boycott of, 202; critical response
    to, 201–8, 276 nn. 13, 14; and
    De Palma's early reputation, 12;
    rating of, 275 n. 10, 276 n. 15
Dr. No, 96
Dyer, Peter John, 151
Dyer, Richard, 34

Eastwood, Clint, 213, 228–34, 277
    n. 6
Easy Virtue, 247
Ebert, Roger, 157, 165
Eiger Sanction, The, 229
Ellison, Harlan, 210
European art film, 49, 65, 78, 79,
    256 n. 30
Exorcist, The, 159, 167

Family Plot: critical response to,
    116–17, 155–56, 243; De Palma
    on, 198; publicity for, 115, 263
    n. 25; studio and date, 248
Farber, Stephen, 166, 171, 200,
    207–8, 275 n. 8
Farmer's Wife, The, 247
Fatal Attraction, 212–13

Harmetz, Aljean, 272 n. 18
Harrison, Joan, 30–31, 39, 40
Haskell, Molly, 231
Hatch, Robert, 45
Hawks, Howard, 218–22; critical
    views on, 217, 277 n. 2; Museum
    of Modern Art retrospective, 87,
    88; works as art, 163
Hedren, Tippi: alleged rejection of
    Hitchcock, 120, 265 n. 15;
    Hitchcock's refusal to discuss,
    143; in *Marnie*, 81, 129, 131,
    138, 145; Watters on, 260 n. 13
Heffner, Richard D., 269 n. 11
Herrmann, Bernard, 196
High Plains Drifter, 229
Hill, Debra, 160, 167, 171–72, 271
    n. 16
Hi Mom!, 190, 203
Hirsch, Paul M., 6
Hitchcock, Alfred: academic interest
    in, 101, 103; as artist, 1, 74, 106,
    108, 110–14, 116, 117, 118,
    120, 122, 139, 155, 216, 262 n.
    21; artistic reputation, 14, 17–
    18, 23, 67, 69–70, 82, 94, 114,
    217–18, 243, 244–46; art-world
    perspective on reputation of, 7–
    8; audience and critical reaction
    to films of the late fifties, 42–64;
    as auteur, 13, 69, 110, 131, 154;
    auteurists on, 217; Belfrage on,
    17–18; biographical legend of,
    11; British and American views
    on, 150–57; cameo in *Marnie*,
    133; Capra compared to, 222–
    25; commercial control over five
    films, 119; communication with
    audience, 35–38; critical views
    on, 1–2, 7, 12–13, 256 n. 26; on
    criticism of his films, 81; and
    Dali, 25; dark side of, 120–21;
    and De Palma, 188–215; early

genre films, 21–22; Eastwood
    compared to, 230; feminist view
    of, 14, 122, 132–39, 144–46; in
    the fifties, 25–42; films of, 247–
    48; films made for reviewers not
    public, 21; first cameo appear-
    ance, 20, 21; first films, 18–20;
    and genre films, 232; Griffith on,
    86; Hawks compared to, 218–
    19, 221–22; Hedren's alleged re-
    jection of, 120, 265 n. 15;
    Hitchcock touch, 43; honorary
    doctorate, 110; Horowitz com-
    pared to, 235, 238, 240; Kael on,
    108–9, 204–5; Lang compared
    to, 225–28; later films, 95–113;
    as master of suspense, 117–18,
    182, 216, 218; and "The Men
    Who Made the Movies," 113–
    14, 115; Museum of Modern Art
    show, 72, 85, 86–89, 261 n. 17;
    mystery magazine, 30; obesity of,
    22–23, 253 n. 8; *Obsession* as
    homage to, 196–97; persona of,
    34–35, 51, 263 n. 24; and plau-
    sibility, 179, 181; posthumous
    reputation and influence, 158–
    87; profile, 20; promotional ac-
    tivities of the thirties, 22–25;
    publicity use, 15, 20–21; the
    quintessential Hitchcock film,
    55; as real star of his films, 83;
    relations with audience, 64–68;
    reputation in sixties and seven-
    ties, 14; Rohmer and Chabrol on,
    259 n. 3; Schikel on, 112, 114–
    15, 121; Selznick contract, 24;
    Shakespeare compared to, 125;
    shifting assessment of, 122–57;
    sponsorship of, 71–72; as stan-
    dard for thrillers, 12, 14–15,
    159; on suspense, 23–24, 36, 55,
    156, 182; Thalberg and Griffith

Lang, Gladys, 119
Lang, Kurt, 119
La Valley, Albert J., 124
Le Bret, Robert Favre, 89
Leff, Leonard, 25
Lehman, Ernest, 116
Leigh, Janet, 58, 59
Lejeune, C. A., 63, 150, 151, 156
Lifeboat, 248
Lloyd, Norman, 30, 31, 39, 40, 41, 42
Lodger, The: compared to German expressionism, 18–19, 226; critical response to, 18–20, 21; Hitchcock's first cameo appearance, 20; studio and date, 247
Lurie, Susan, 144

McCarten, John, 54
Macdonald, Dwight, 263 n. 23
MacPhail, Angus, 46
Madden, David, 167, 177
Mailer, Norman, 231
Maland, Charles J., 9–10, 102
Mankiewicz, Herman J., 207
Man Who Knew Too Much, The: box office success of, 39; critical response to, 43–45, 150–54, 273 n. 26; Crowther on, 44; happy ending of, 38; Hitchcock's commercial control of, 119; Hitchcock's thrillers of the thirties, 22; made for press rather than public, 21; promotional strategies for, 42–43; studio and date, 247, 248
Manxman, The, 247
Mark, Laurence, 177
Marnie: auteur theorists on, 124, 129, 131; 265 n. 15; *The Birds* compared to, 144, 145–46; *Black Widow* compared to, 181; box office failure of, 67; as

character study, 80–81; critical response to, 11, 14, 93–95, 122–24, 126–31, 139–40, 261 n. 17; feminist analysis of, 131–39; as forgotten masterpiece, 122; Hedren's rebuff of Hitchcock, 120, 265 n. 15; Hitchcock cameo, 133; in Hitchcock's campaign to reshape his reputation, 74; multiple interpretations of, 266 n. 19; press kit, 93; psychoanalytic framework of, 82, 123, 260 n. 11; publicity for, 84; studio and date, 248
Maslin, Janet, 117, 267 n. 25
Mass media, 5–6, 7–8
Mast, Gerald, 219
Matthew effect, 116, 117
Mayne, Judith, 132
Meaning, 8–9, 139, 245
Meet John Doe, 224
Mekas, Jonas, 192
"Men Who Made the Movies, The," 113–14, 115
MGM, 26
Miles, Vera, 173
Miller, Mark Crispin, 263 n. 26
Modleski, Tania, 134
Monsieur Verdoux, 9–10
Montagu, Ivor: on British Film Society, 17; on Hitchcock, 21; and Hitchcock's thrillers of the thirties, 22; work on *The Lodger*, 18
Moore, Brian, 95, 100
Motion-picture industry: film cycles, 158; exploitation of Hitchcock's stature, 115; mass-media influence on, 6; self-censorship of, 269 n. 6; studio system, 4, 29, 217. *See also* Film
Mountain Eagle, The, 18, 247
Mozart, 220
Mr. and Mrs. Smith, 247